THE MEMOIRS OF
ANNE, LADY HALKETT
AND ANN, LADY FANSHAWE

THE MEMOIRS OF

Anne, Lady Halkett

AND

Ann, Lady Fanshawe

Edited with an introduction by

JOHN LOFTIS

CLARENDON PRESS · OXFORD

1979

Oxford University Press, Walton Street, Oxford OX2 6DP

OXFORD LONDON GLASGOW
NEW YORK TORONTO MELBOURNE WELLINGTON
IBADAN NAIROBI DAR ES SALAAM LUSAKA CAPE TOWN
KUALA LUMPUR SINGAPORE JAKARTA HONG KONG TOKYO
DELHI BOMBAY CALCUTTA MADRAS KARACHI

British Library Cataloguing in Publication Data

The memoirs of Anne, Lady Halkett and Ann, Lady Fanshawe.

1. Fanshawe, Ann, *Lady* 2. Halkett, Anne, *Lady* 3. Great Britain—History—Charles II, 1660–1685 I. Halkett, Anne, *Lady*. Memoirs of Anne, *Lady* Halkett II. Nichols, J G III. Fanshawe, Anne, *Lady*. Memoirs of Lady Ann Fanshawe IV. Nicolas, *Sir* H N V. Loftis, John
942.06′092′2 DA447.F2 78–40238

ISBN 0–19–812087–7

Printed in Great Britain by
The University Press
Aberdeen

PREFACE

THE TWO Memoirs that comprise this volume, written in the later seventeenth century by the widows of Royalists who had been prominent in the Civil Wars, provide first-hand accounts of important events and persons of their era. The Memoirs record honestly the lives of strong-minded and adventurous women. Both Memoirs have been out of print for generations. Yet authoritative manuscripts of them are in the British Library, that of Lady Halkett in her own hand and that of Lady Fanshawe in the hand of a copyist whose work she corrected—somewhat capriciously—herself. The latter work is likely to be familiar to students of English literature or history with an interest in the seventeenth century; the former is unlikely to be familiar except to historians of the Civil Wars. This is in part owing to the inaccessibility of the Halkett Memoirs, which have been printed only once previously, in 1875 by the Camden Society in an edition prepared by John Gough Nichols, with additional work on it, after Nichols's death before it was published, by the eminent historian Samuel Rawson Gardiner.

Lady Fanshawe's Memoirs were widely read in manuscript copies even before they were first published in 1829, in an edition prepared by Sir Harris Nicolas. Sir Harris published another edition, without significant textual changes, in 1830. In his preface of 1829 he remarked that it was curious the work had not "long since been given to the world; more particularly, as it has not only been frequently cited, but copiously quoted, in various popular works . . .". Nicolas's name does not appear as the editor, but he is identified as such by H. C. Fanshawe (who again did not put his name on his title-page), the editor of a monumental edition published in 1907, which is based on the manuscript now in the British Library.

In annotating the two Memoirs, I have been confronted with opposite problems: in the case of Lady Fanshawe with an over-abundance of detailed information provided by H. C. Fanshawe, who in his edition of 1907 included massive annotation, more than four times as extensive as the text itself. Fanshawe's annotation is of great value. But in referring to it I have often been reminded of what a distinguished modern biographer of Defoe, James Sutherland, wrote about one of his nineteenth-century predecessors: that to make use of the earlier biography was in itself a minor form of research. By contrast, there is little published information specifically about Lady Halkett that is not derived from her Memoirs. The only other important source of information about her life is an anonymous biography published in 1701, two years after her death, as a preface to an edition of a selection from her devotional works. This biography was based in part on the manuscript of her Memoirs, as well as on other of her unpublished writings. It was written by someone who knew her and provides information about her later years not available in the Memoirs. The biographical preface to the edition published by the Camden Society in 1875 and the account of her life in the *Dictionary of National Biography* are based primarily on the Memoirs and the biography of 1701.

Although in presenting the texts of the manuscripts of the two Memoirs I have followed editorial principles that differ in minor details, my objective in both is the same: to reproduce the texts of the manuscripts as faithfully as possible without carrying over into the printed text barriers to ready intelligibility.

I gratefully acknowledge obligations incurred in editing the two Memoirs in this volume: to Professor James Kinsley, whose encouragement led me to undertake the task; to Mrs. Pauline B. Tooker, whose editorial and stenographic skill provided a typescript used in subsequent collations; to Dr. Roger Harm for aid in collation; to Dr. Elizabeth Harris and Dr. Helen Pellegrin for research assistance in preparing explanatory notes; to Dr. Carl Maves for perceptive editorial criticism. My greatest obligation, in all phases of my work, is to Mrs. Carol B. Pearson, who in addition to much else prepared the biographical index. Although this book is primarily the literary property of two Ladies who lived three hundred years ago, I have an editor's minority share in it. I dedicate this share to Mrs. Pearson.

JOHN LOFTIS
Stanford, California
November 1976

CONTENTS

Abbreviations viii

Introduction ix

Select Bibliography xix

THE MEMOIRS OF ANNE, LADY HALKETT

A Note on the Text 3

A Chronology of Anne, Lady Halkett 5

The Memoirs of Anne, Lady Halkett 9

THE MEMOIRS OF ANN, LADY FANSHAWE

A Note on the Text 91

A Chronology of Sir Richard Fanshawe and Ann, Lady Fanshawe 95

The Memoirs of Ann, Lady Fanshawe 101

Lady Halkett, *Memoirs*, Explanatory Notes 193

Lady Fanshawe, *Memoirs*, Explanatory Notes 208

Lady Halkett, *Memoirs*, Textual Notes 222

Lady Fanshawe, *Memoirs*, Textual Notes 224

Biographical Index 229

ABBREVIATIONS

Apologie *Colonel Joseph Bamfeild's Apologie*, 'Written by himselfe and printed at his desire' ([London?], 1685).

Clarendon *The History of the Rebellion and Civil Wars in England . . . by Edward, Earl of Clarendon*, ed. W. Dunn Macray, 6 vols. (Oxford, 1888). Reference is made to book and paragraph.

Clarendon, *State Papers* *Calendar of the Clarendon State Papers Preserved in the Bodleian Library*, ed. O. Ogle, W. H. Bliss, H. O. Coxe, W. Dunn Macray, F. J. Routledge, 5 vols. (Oxford, 1872–1970).

Clarke, *James II* J. S. Clarke, *The Life of James the Second* 'Collected out of Memoirs Writ of His Own Hand', 2 vols. (London, 1816).

Complete Baronetage *Complete Baronetage*, ed. G. E. C.[okayne], 5 vols. (Exeter, 1900–6).

Complete Peerage *The Complete Peerage of England, Scotland, Ireland, Great Britain, and the United Kingdom*, ed. G. E. C.[okayne], rev. edn., 12 vols. (London, 1910–59).

DNB *Dictionary of National Biography.*

HCF *The Memoirs of Ann Lady Fanshawe*, ed. H. C. Fanshawe (London, 1907).

Heathcote Manuscripts Historical Manuscripts Commission, *Report on the Manuscripts of J. M. Heathcote, Esq.* (Norwich, 1899).

JGN *The Autobiography of Anne Lady Halkett*, ed. John Gough Nichols (London, 1875).

Keeler Mary F. Keeler, *The Long Parliament 1640–41* (Philadelphia, 1954).

Life S. C., *The Life of the Lady Halket* (Edinburgh, 1701).

M *Memoirs of Lady Fanshawe*, ed. Beatrice Marshall (London, 1905).

MS Manuscript of Lady Halkett's Memoirs (B.L. Add. MS. 32376) *or* Manuscript of Lady Fanshawe's Memoirs (B.L. Add. MS. 41161), as context reveals.

N *Memoirs of Lady Fanshawe*, ed. Sir N. Harris Nicolas (London, 1829; reprinted 1830).

OED *Oxford English Dictionary.*

Scots Peerage *The Scots Peerage Founded on Wood's Edition of Sir Robert Douglas's Peerage of Scotland*, ed. Sir James Balfour Paul, 9 vols. (Edinburgh, 1904).

Thurloe, *State Papers* *A Collection of the State Papers of John Thurloe Esq.*, ed. Thomas Birch, 7 vols. (London, 1742).

INTRODUCTION

THE MEMOIRS of Lady Halkett and Lady Fanshawe, both written in the latter half of the 1670s by widows separated by only two years in age, are appropriate companion pieces in a single volume. They record, from a perspective of pious middle age, their authors' youthful adventures as Royalists during the Civil Wars and their personal associations with the Royal family. Although different temperamentally, these two Ladies wrote with similar political and religious assumptions. Yet they wrote Memoirs that are fundamentally unlike: Lady Halkett's introspective and personal, about her emotional responses to the events of her life; Lady Fanshawe's commemorative of her late husband and the families into which she and her husband were born.

Ann Harrison married Richard Fanshawe at nineteen, and most of her Memoirs are devoted to the years after her marriage. Anne Murray married Sir James Halkett at thirty-three and in her Memoirs, if not in her experience of life, the marriage is anticlimactic even though it brought her—in 1656, the year in which the surviving portion of her Memoirs breaks off—to the security of a settled position. Hers is a relation of a young woman caught up in the turmoil of the Civil Wars; and it is, even more movingly, an account of two love affairs that for her ended in frustration. She wrote about them retrospectively, twenty and more years afterwards, and she wrote with intense piety and with a troubled conscience. We are compelled to draw inferences from what she says to understand what happened—or may have happened—particularly in her narrative of her prolonged association with Colonel Joseph Bampfield. If she leaves much unsaid, at least in the manuscript as it has survived, it is surprising that she wrote so much on the subject, which even in her widowhood could not have been free of embarrassment for her. She apparently wrote for herself alone, as she wrote many of her religious meditations, employing her literary talent in an effort to sort out the pattern of her life, above all in its spiritual dimension.

A better literary stylist than Lady Fanshawe (who occasionally writes as though she is transcribing household records), Lady Halkett writes in fluent prose, the expression of a high intelligence fully engaged in what she is saying. Her long sentences, even when they make severe demands on our powers of concentration, are firmly under control; and they can convey emotional nuances and conflicts that we are more accustomed to encounter in prose fiction than in seventeenth-century biographical writing; and indeed the experiences she describes, the adventurous ones such as her assistance in the escape of the young Duke of York from St. James's Palace, and the romantic ones, would serve a novelist well. Unlike Lady Fanshawe, she wrote copiously, though little of what she wrote was published.[1]

Lady Fanshawe lived at a higher social level than Lady Halkett, and her Memoirs gain in importance from the eminent people she knew or knew at one remove through her husband. Although she describes no episode so momentous as Lady Halkett's account of the rescue of the Duke of York, she writes about persons who had principal roles in mid-seventeenth-century affairs, among whom she lived from her marriage in 1644 until her husband's death in 1666. Hers was a different kind of life from Lady Halkett's, and her Memoirs are important for different reasons.

Lady Halkett's intelligence and sensitivity, her attractiveness to men, her position as a gentlewoman with family relationships to the nobility: all these advantages joined with such meagre financial resources that she could not marry appropriately in early youth, put us in mind of characters in Jane Austen's novels. In her family situation as in her personality she is not unlike Elizabeth Bennet—though no kindly providence ensured her ultimate happiness. Her account of her love affair with Thomas Howard, eldest son and heir to Lord Howard of Escrick, resembles, in the strategems she and the young man employed to communicate and to meet despite parental opposition, an episode in one of the novels. So too the bitter dénouement, when she learns that Howard, his protestations of love notwithstanding, has married the daughter of an earl.

This was a painful discovery for her. Even more painful discoveries were ahead, when her affections were captured by Colonel Bampfield. The tone of Richardson's *Clarissa* replaces that of *Pride and Prejudice*.[2]

Lady Halkett's Memoirs are above all a study in personal relationships: with the two men she loved but could not marry, Howard and Bampfield, with the man she in fact married, Sir James Halkett, and with many other persons. Occasionally she writes about events of the great world—meeting Charles II in Scotland during 1650 and meeting wounded soldiers after the Battle of Dunbar in September of that year—but she writes mainly about her own affairs, and she rarely encountered the small number of persons whose decisions determined the course of events.

1. A descriptive bibliography of manuscript 'Books written by the Lady Halket' is appended to the early biography of her written by 'S. C.': *The Life of the Lady Halket* (Edinburgh, 1701). Most of them were on devotional subjects.

2. James Sutherland has aptly remarked that Lady Halkett's autobiography 'might have provided Samuel Richardson with all the material he could possibly need for another novel . . .': *English Literature of the Late Seventeenth Century* (Oxford, 1969), p. 263.

Her Memoirs provide a poignant account of humiliation and suffering that resulted from a poverty which, because she was a gentlewoman, she could do little to overcome. Often she was dependent on the hospitality of others, and the hospitality could become strained, as during her visit of 1649 and 1650 to Sir Charles Howard and his wife at Naworth Castle, with embarrassing results for her. It is not the least of her accomplishments in the Memoirs that she conveys, unobtrusively and unselfconsciously, the difficulties inherent in her position.

Lady Halkett's account of her prolonged relationship with Bampfield dominates the surviving portion of her Memoirs, though not necessarily the complete Memoirs as she wrote them. The tension she experienced between passionate affection and, in opposition to it, a habitual moral rectitude reinforced by religious conviction is nowhere more apparent than in her understated—at times enigmatic—account of her involvement with Bampfield, who deceived her. She met him in late 1647 or early 1648, when he was acting as a secret agent for the King. Her devotion to the King in those difficult times for the Royalists led her into a close association with Bampfield. The association brought the great adventure of her life: her assistance to Bampfield in April 1648 when, on orders from the King, he rescued the young Duke of York from St. James's Palace and conveyed him to the Continent. Her biographer of 1701 attributes her subsequent relationship with Bampfield to her loyalty. The success of the rescue of the Duke of York, the biographer writes,

> did both encourage and engage her, in other Designs for the King's Interest; which were committed to the managment of the same Gentleman who had convoyed the Duke to *France*. . . .
>
> The earnest desire she had to serve His Majesty, made her omit no opportunity, wherein she could be useful; Her Zeal kept her from considering the Inconveniencies she exposed herself too; Her Intentions, being just and innocent, she reflected not upon the disadvantagious constructions might be made upon the frequent privat Visites, she was obliged to make to that Gentleman, who since his return, durst not appear in publick. . . .

However, the biographer adds, she soon became aware of 'the Calumnies and Prejudices, which this her converse brought upon her . . .'.[3] Her Memoirs tell of secret visits to Bampfield in his own quarters, and it is worth noting, as an indication of the informality of their relationship, that on one visit she found him 'lying upon his bed' (p. 27). She insists, however, that 'loyalty' to the King was 'the principle that first led mee to a freedome of converse with him' and led her to continue seeing him (p. 27).

But more than 'loyalty' soon entered into the relationship, which brought her prolonged uncertainty, emotional turmoil, and finally

3. *Life of . . . Lady Halket*, p. 16.

frustration. She was a vulnerable young woman when she met Bampfield, of marriageable age but without a dowry or even a dependable source of income. This is not to say that her interest in Bampfield as a possible husband had origin in a prudential desire for security. She quite simply fell in love with him. For several years he lied to her or kept her in uncertainty about his marital status and his intentions towards her.

Her Memoirs convey the impression, though only by implication, that in his relations with her he was an unconscionable opportunist.[4] Anne Murray, as she was before her marriage in 1656, was an attractive and resourceful young woman: the responses she evoked from men, Thomas Howard and Sir James Halkett as well as Bampfield, testify to her beauty as convincingly as her Memoirs to her intelligence. Bampfield desired to retain a close relationship with her. A man of his resourcefulness in the King's service would have had means to determine whether or not his wife was alive, no matter where in England she resided. Yet at some time following the Duke of York's escape in April 1648, probably in the autumn of that year, he told Anne Murray that his wife was dead and proposed marriage to her. She agreed to marry him as soon as they could take precautions to preserve their property. She continued to see him in the intervals of their travels and to regard herself as betrothed to him despite repeated warnings of his faithlessness, including forceful ones from her brother and sister.

Augmenting his guilt in deceiving her, Bampfield tried to prevent, and succeeded in delaying, her marriage to Sir James Halkett, an honourable man and a suitable husband for a woman approaching middle age who needed the security of marriage. We feel resentment at him, despite the three intervening centuries, when we read that in 1652 Bampfield wished to respond appropriately to Sir James Halkett's generous treatment of him

> and did regrett the misfortune of nott having itt in his power to obleige him, for hee knew noe thing could doe itt more then his resigning his interest in mee; and that was nott posible for him to doe, though hee would often tell mee if any thing should arive to deprive him of mee, hee thought in gratitude I was obleiged to marry Sir J.[ames] H.[alkett].

Lady Halkett adds that 'nothing butt the death of C.[olonel] B.[ampfield] could make mee ever thinke of another' (pp. 68–9), not then believing the reports, soon to be confirmed past doubt, that Bampfield's wife had not died.

Was Anne Murray the mistress of Colonel Bampfield? The question is difficult to answer because our major source of information is a narrative written years later by a pious woman then in widowhood, and further-

4. As we would expect, he does not mention her in his own *Apologie*, published in 1685, though in fairness it should be added that he wrote about public affairs, with a defensive political purpose.

more a narrative in which two leaves of the manuscript, at crucial places, have been removed. The earlier leaf told of her introduction to Bampfield; the latter, of her emotional upheaval upon receiving definitive news that his wife was alive. But what else did the leaves record? Lady Halkett was still deeply troubled in conscience about her relationship with Bampfield at the time she wrote her Memoirs late in 1677 and early in 1678.[5] Her narrative begins in mid-sentence just after the second of the relevant missing leaves:

> unworthy, and in what apeared so, none living could condemne mee more then I did my selfe. Butt I had some circumstances to plead for mee withoutt which I had beene unpardonable, and that was the concealing my intended mariage meerely because hee durst not withoutt hazard of his life avowedly apeare, and therfore itt had beene imprudence to puplish what might have beene (in those times) ruine to us both. (p. 72)

This sounds as though her guilt arose merely from her secret engagement to a man who, unknown to her, was married.

Stronger evidence that her association with Bampfield had not, at least by 1649, proceeded to sexual relations appears in her account of an illness she suffered while a guest at Naworth Castle:

> Aprehending the aproach of death, I desired my Lady H.[oward] to vindicate mee to my brother and sister, for as I was ignorant and inocentt of the guilt they taxed mee with, and so I beleeved C.[olonel] B.[ampfield] was. (p. 33)

Again the charge from which she desired defence in case of death was that of continuing an association with Bampfield, in whose good faith she believed despite the warnings of her brother and sister. Her statement made on what she thought was her death-bed carries force, and she could scarcely have made it if she had had illicit relations with Bampfield, whether or not he was married.

Yet the intensity and duration of her sense of guilt—and the missing leaves—give us cause to wonder. She hesitated long before marrying Halkett, believing that her earlier relationship with Bampfield made her unworthy of him, and knowing that her reputation had been damaged. In an effort to overcome her misgivings, Sir James, who seems to have acted with exemplary clarity of mind as well as devotion to her, suggested that she consult a Mr. David Dickson, a clergyman for whom Sir James knew she had a high regard.

She agreed, and Mr. Dickson came to see her 'usually . . . once in a weeke', and to him under a pledge of secrecy she unburdened her troubled conscience. He heard her out with compassion and replied with strong good sense,

5. A marginal notation specifies the time at which she was writing as 8 January 1677/8 (see Textual Notes, 82:25).

that since what I did was suposing C.[olonel] B.[ampfield] a free person, hee nott proving so, though I had beene puplickely maried to him and avowedly lived with him as his wife, yett the ground of itt failing, I was as free as if I had never seene him; and this, hee assured mee, I might rely upon, that I might withoutt offence either to the laws of God or man marry any other person when ever I found itt convenientt . . . (p. 76).

This sounds as though her relationship with Bampfield had been more intimate than usual between two persons under a mutual promise to be married. The Memoirs reveal that Anne Murray and Bampfield had often been alone in situations that would have permitted intimacy. Had there been some kind of secret marriage ceremony? We cannot know.

Good sense in the persons of Mr. Dickson and Sir James Halkett prevailed; and if her conscience was never totally clear, she escaped the destructive self-torture of Richardson's Clarissa Harlowe. She married Sir James in 1656, and when she wrote the Memoirs, after his death in 1670, she reported that the marriage had been a happy one (p. 84).

Sir James appears to good advantage as a kind and wise man, devoted to the woman who became his second wife, too sensible to be deterred from his courtship by gossip about her. Yet their marriage was no youthful love match. Lady Halkett writes affectionately about him, but not with the adulation Lady Fanshawe reveals for her own late husband. Lady Halkett was thirty-three when she married; Sir James was older, probably considerably older. At the time of their marriage, he was a widower with two sons and two daughters,[6] the older of the daughters being 'neere a woman'. The fact that Lady Halkett does not mention the sons would suggest—though not prove—that they were older and no longer residents of their father's household. The marriage brought her to a measure of comfort and security, though after her husband's death she found it necessary to supplement her income by teaching.[7] Her marriage to Sir James may seem to us an anticlimax in the life of the remarkable woman she was. But she lived in the historical world of the seventeenth century and not in the fictional worlds created by Samuel Richardson and Jane Austen in the eighteenth century.

Lady Fanshawe's is in a specialized sense a family memoir: a record of her own and her husband's families, of her husband's career, and of their married life. She addressed the Memoirs to her only surviving son, Sir Richard Fanshawe (1665–94), as an instructive memorial of the prominence and achievements of his forebears and particularly of his father, who had died when the son was less than a year old. The nature of the Memoirs is conditioned by Lady Fanshawe's intention in writing

6. *Life of . . . Lady Halket*, p. 30.
7. Ibid., p. 45.

them, an intention in which publication had no part. Those passages which may to us seem boastful should be read with an awareness that she envisaged, not an audience at large, but a family audience who would read the Memoirs in manuscript. She intended to provide her descendants with a record of their lineage.

The passages devoted to family history are often tedious. Yet Lady Fanshawe's concern to preserve a comprehensive record of the family in its many branches provides insight into the structure of that level of English society made up of the richer gentry and the lesser nobility. Her concern to describe the family's sufferings, in life and in property, in the Royalist cause reveals in convincing detail the depth of the social upheaval among persons of her rank. If, as has been suggested, the Civil Wars had no great consequences for the English citizenry at large, they had devastating consequences for the social class to which Lady Fanshawe (and Lady Halkett) belonged. Lady Fanshawe's Memoirs provide a human dimension to generalized interpretations of the Wars' impact on the gentry and aristocracy.

Referring to her son's first cousins and their families, on Sir Richard's side, she writes (p. 108) that she could assert 'without vanity none exceeded them in their loyalty, which cost them dear, for there was as many [of them], . . . and those that matched to them, ingaged and sequestred for the Crown in the time of the late rebellion, as their revenue made near eighty thousand pounds a year . . .'. She writes about her father, with an introductory clause implying some doubt (p. 110), that 'He made it appeare with great truth that during the time of the war he lost by the rebells above an hundred and thirty thousand pounds . . .'. She explains the circumstances leading to a part of her father's loss (p. 111):[8] in November 1640 her brother, then a member of the House of Commons (but only until the King set up his standard), persuaded their father to lend the Crown £50,000 'to pay the Scots, who had then entered England, and as it seems was to be both payd and prayd to goe home'. These are immense sums in seventeenth-century currency, so large we might reasonably assume that Lady Fanshawe, writing in the mid-1670s and in reduced circumstances, exaggerated them. But there can be little doubt that the family's losses were large.

Lady Fanshawe's reliability as a reporter of the events she recounts is not uniform throughout the Memoirs. We may accept the impression she conveys of huge Royalist losses without regarding the sums of money she mentions as accurate; and we may more confidently accept her reports of the deaths in battle of friends and relations, some of whom she names. But she is frequently in error about dates, particularly when writing about her husband's life before they were married in 1644, when

8. See also Mary F. Keeler, *The Long Parliament, 1640–1641* (Philadelphia, Pa., 1954), pp. 205–6.

he was nearly thirty-six years old. Yet in the latter portions of the Memoirs devoted to her husband's embassies to Portugal and Spain, she is so precise, so meticulous in specifying dates and sums of money, that we may assume she wrote with personal records before her. Several passages have indeed the discontinuity that would result from the transcription of a diary she had written earlier. The discontinuity of sentences within a single paragraph is occasionally such as to suggest she dictated them to an amanuensis (cf. pp. 151–2, 162).

Despite the momentous events she witnessed, Lady Fanshawe writes as a woman preoccupied with practical affairs, largely ignoring the ideological conflicts inherent in the Civil Wars. Her closest approach to an expression of the emotional and intellectual convictions held by many of the Royalists appears in her reverence for Charles I. She tells of visiting him in the autumn of 1647, when he was held captive at Hampton Court (p. 120):

> I went 3 times to pay my duty to him, both as I was the daughter of his servant and wife to his servant. The last time I ever saw him, when I took my leave, I could not refraine weeping. When he had saluted me, I prayd to God to preserve His Majesty with long life and happy years. He stroked me on my cheek and sayd, 'Child, if God pleaseth, it shall be so, but both you and I must submitt to God's will, and you know in what hands I am in.'

The King then turned to her husband, addressing him as 'Dick', and gave him oral instructions to be conveyed to the Prince of Wales and letters to the Queen, both of whom were then in France.

Lady Fanshawe's reverence for Charles II, as the Prince became in January 1649, is conveyed rather by silence about his failings—except for a single reference to his indulging his pleasures (p. 142)—than by anything she writes. Her silence did not extend to his Ministers. She omits gossip about licentiousness, but her Memoirs are not charitable in their judgement of Englishmen in high office—the Royal family always excepted. She is consistently severe in references to Sir Edward Hyde, the Earl of Clarendon as he became at the Restoration, her animus apparently arising from a conviction that Clarendon was responsible for Charles II's failure to keep a promise to make Sir Richard one of his Secretaries of State. She regards Clarendon 'and his party' (pp. 178–9) as responsible for the English objections to the terms of a peace settlement with Spain negotiated by Sir Richard, and for his recall as ambassador to Spain. She writes acidly about the Earl of Sandwich, who succeeded Sir Richard in Madrid. After alluding to his alleged cowardice, she writes that 'He neither understood the customes of the [Spanish] court, nor the language, nor indeed anything but a vitious life, and thus was he shuffled into your father's imployment to reap the benefit of his five years' negotiation of the peace of England, Spaine, and Portugall . . .'

(p. 179). This is less than a comprehensive account of a complicated subject.[9]

Lady Fanshawe appears to best advantage in her loving portrait of her husband. The bitterness of her comments on Lord Clarendon, Lord Sandwich, and Lord Shaftesbury arose in part from her partisanship on his behalf. She believed that he—and after his death she—had been treated ungenerously and even unjustly, and in the privacy of her Memoirs she expressed resentment at those she considered responsible. She had no reluctance to tell an anecdote to her own disadvantage if it illustrated the good judgement of her husband, as in the episode, not long after their marriage, when at the instigation of a woman of rank she tried to persuade him to tell her confidential information about the Royal family (pp. 115–16). Her detailed account of her husband's kind but firm response to her indiscretion, a response that in its restraint had a fatherly quality about it, can remind us that he was almost seventeen years older than she.

A man, heterosexual as Sir Richard obviously was, who married for the first time at thirty-five, is likely to have had a cool temperament. On the evidence of his wife, he had a loving and compassionate even if reserved nature, different from that of the 'hoyting' girl (as Lady Fanshawe describes herself when very young) he married. He experienced more than one man's share of the vicissitudes of fortune, and he seems to have accepted them with equanimity. The positions of responsibility he held from young manhood to death except during the years of Cromwell's ascendancy testify to his abilities. When after the Battle of Worcester he was captured and imprisoned, and—after his wife's intercession with Cromwell—released on bail and compelled to live in quiet retirement, he characteristically made profitable use of his time, indulging his aptitude for poetry. During his period of adversity he produced his most successful literary work, a translation of the Portuguese epic, Camoens's *Os Lusiadas*.

The decision to translate the epic, 'in so *uncourted* a *language* as *that* of PORTUGALL'[10] (as he puts it in his dedicatory epistle), testifies to his lifelong interest in the countries of the Iberian Peninsula as well as to his intellectual audacity. The final years of his life, before his death at fifty-eight, brought the culmination of his public career in his appointments as ambassador to Portugal and then to Spain. The embassy to Spain, even though he failed to accomplish the English diplomatic objectives and was recalled, has a fitness about it as the closing period in the life of a man in whose career knowledge of the country and the language had

9. H. C. Fanshawe includes an appendix on 'Sir Richard Fanshawe's Treaty with Spain, December, 1665': *Memoirs* (1907), pp. 234–51.

10. Luis de Camoens, *The Lusiads*, trans. Fanshawe, ed. Geoffrey Bullough (London, 1963), p. 33.

been formative. A Hispanophile from his youth, Sir Richard had resided in Madrid before the Civil Wars, as traveller and diplomat, for nearly five years. With his wife he travelled in Spain during the Royal exile. With her he spent the final two years of his life in Spain. Through his translations he made Spanish poetry, as well as the great Portuguese epic, better known to his countrymen. He saw performances of Spanish plays during the later years of the Golden Age, when Calderón de la Barca was still alive, and so did the gentlemen in his retinue, who no doubt reported what they saw when they returned to England. Lady Fanshawe's Memoirs indeed suggest the possibility—I think probability—that one of the Englishmen attending Sir Richard was William Wycherley, whose first two plays include borrowings from Calderón.[11]

Lady Fanshawe's Memoirs are important for the record they provide of persons, events, and places. Hers is a utilitarian prose, rarely ambiguous but stylistically uneven and undistinguished. In her literary skills, she is not at all like Lady Halkett, to whom writing was a habitual mode of self-expression. She cannot approximate Lady Halkett's stylistic fluency and subtlety in the analysis of emotion. Lady Halkett had her reticences, leaving much unsaid. Yet unlike Lady Fanshawe she does not keep the reader at a distance, and sometimes she permits glimpses of her innermost life.

11. See below, p. 153. In his *An Evening's Love, or The Mock Astrologer* (1668), John Dryden with a curious precision specifies a time and place of dramatic action: 'The Scene *Madrid*, in the Year 1665. The Time, the last Evening of the Carnival.' Two of the principal characters belong to the retinue of the English ambassador, who in historical reality would have been Sir Richard Fanshawe. I would guess that Dryden had some personal references in mind that are not known to us.

SELECT BIBLIOGRAPHY

THE ONLY previous edition of Lady Halkett's Memoirs (or 'Autobiography' as it is there called) is that prepared by John Gough Nichols and published by the Camden Society in 1875. A prefatory biography is included in the volume, and there is a short account of Lady Halkett in the *Dictionary of National Biography*. The early biography by 'S. C.', published in 1701, two years after Lady Halkett's death, and the Memoirs themselves are the only important published sources of information about her life. However, the selections from her devotional writings—published in 1701 and again in 1778—provide insight into her most private thoughts. The edition of the 'Autobiography' of 1875 includes an appendix made up of a miscellaneous group of her 'Meditations' that reveal, among other things, the religious basis for her political convictions.

The Memoirs have received less attention than their quality merits. Even so, they have been the subject of perceptive comment. A literary assessment of them, as well as an accurate narrative biography of Lady Halkett, was written by L. M. Cumming: 'Anne, Lady Halkett', *Blackwood's Magazine*, ccxvi (Nov. 1924), 654–76. Although Cumming's study obviously embodies extended research, its value is limited by the absence of citation of sources for the information provided. A comprehensive account of the Memoirs appears in Margaret Bottrall, *Every Man a Phoenix: Studies in Seventeenth-Century Autobiography* (London, 1958).

Glimpses of the enigmatic figure of Colonel Joseph Bampfield, so prominent in the Memoirs, are provided in the volumes of the *Calendar of the Clarendon State Papers Preserved in the Bodleian Library* (Oxford, 1872–1970), in the indices of which Bampfield's name frequently appears. Clarendon mentions him several times in *The History of the Rebellion*. A number of his letters are printed in the volumes of *A Collection of the State Papers of John Thurloe Esq.* (London, 1742). In 1685 he published *Colonel Joseph Bamfeild's Apologie*, primarily a defensive political tract, though it includes autobiographical material, including information about the rescue of the Duke of York from St. James's Palace in which Anne Murray (Lady Halkett) assisted. However, Bampfield makes no reference to her assistance, nor does he elsewhere in the *Apologie* allude to her.

For detailed study of the lives of Sir Richard and Lady Fanshawe and their families, the edition of the Memoirs by Mr. H. C. Fanshawe, published in 1907, is indispensable. The extensive annotation and the appendices Mr. Fanshawe provided, presenting, along with much else, information derived from family records not now available, will be permanently valuable. He wrote, and acknowledged that he did so, with a concern to preserve a record of the illustrious family to which he belonged; and one can detect a bias in his commentary. But his family piety led to no major distortion of historical fact: rather, to an excessive elaboration of detail which occasionally obscures essential information the reader needs. Mr. Fanshawe's text of the Memoirs is in modern spelling. It is complete, including, as had no previous edition, the passages that Lady Fanshawe cancelled. In the main Mr. Fanshawe is faithful to the manuscript, though occasionally he takes minor liberties with awkward phrases which, if consistent with Edwardian editorial principles, are not consistent with those of the later twentieth century. Twenty years after the publication of his edition of the Memoirs, his *History of the Fanshawe Family* (Newcastle upon Tyne, 1927) was 'printed privately', as stated in the preface, to present information relevant to the Memoirs collected after 1907 and also to provide a consecutive history of several branches of the family, extending into the twentieth century.

The three editions of the Memoirs published prior to 1907—those of 1829 and 1830 prepared by Sir Harris Nicolas and that of 1905 by Beatrice Marshall—are not reliable textually. Yet all three include as appendices valuable selections from the correspondence of Sir Richard Fanshawe. Because of Sir Richard's prominence in political affairs as well as his accomplishments as poet and translator, many of his letters and official dispatches survive, either in published or manuscript form. A volume published by the Historical Manuscripts Commission in 1899, *Report on the Manuscripts of J. M. Heathcote, Esq., of Conington Castle*, includes a comprehensive account of and numerous quotations from Sir Richard's public and private letters. An early collection, *Original Letters of his Excellency Sir Richard Fanshaw* . . . (London, 1702), prints letters and papers pertaining to the earlier part of his embassy to Spain, January 1663/4 to January 1664/5. An unpublished continuation of this volume, containing letters and papers deriving from the latter part of his embassy to Spain, extending to his death in Madrid in June 1666, is preserved in the British Library: Harleian MS. 7010. Gerard Langbaine provides in *An Account of the English Dramatick Poets* (Oxford, 1691) a seventeenth-century assessment of Fanshawe's literary achievement. Sir Keith Feiling provides a modern account, authoritative though severely critical, of Fanshawe's embassies to Portugal and Spain in *British Foreign Policy, 1660–1672* (London, 1930). Geoffrey Bullough has edited Sir Richard's translation of Camoens's *The Lusiads* (London, 1963), including in the introduction a succinct account of Fanshawe's adventurous life.

The Memoirs of both Lady Halkett and Lady Fanshawe are briefly examined in Donald A. Stauffer, *English Biography before 1700* (Cambridge,

Mass., 1930); Wayne Shumaker, *English Autobiography: Its Emergence, Materials, and Form* (Berkeley, Calif., 1954); Paul Delany, *British Autobiography in the Seventeenth Century* (London, 1969); and James Sutherland, *English Literature of the Late Seventeenth Century* (Oxford, 1969).

THE MEMOIRS OF
Anne, Lady Halkett

A NOTE ON THE TEXT

THE TEXT is based on a manuscript in the author's hand now in the British Library. This manuscript (B.L. Add. MS. 32376), sixty-one leaves in small folio pasted on to stubs, of a later date, in a bound volume, was given to the British Museum in 1884 by William Johnston Stuart. It is defective: an unknown number of leaves are missing after the Memoirs break off abruptly in an account of events of 1656, the year of Lady Halkett's marriage; the first leaf, on which there was but one page of text, is also missing; the second leaf (the first surviving) is mutilated; and two other leaves—or four pages of text—are missing in separate parts of the manuscript. We can be confident that, apart from the first leaf and an unknown number of missing ones at the close of the Memoirs, only the two leaves are lost. An original pagination, extending to number 126, is visible. In this pagination number 58 is through error repeated; hence, the total number of pages was 127, on sixty-four leaves, of which only one page was filled on the first and two pages on each of the other two missing leaves.

The contexts in which the later missing leaves would have appeared suggest that they were purposely removed by Lady Halkett or some member of her family, for reasons of privacy. In both instances (in the original pagination, pp. 24–5 and 101–2, and in my pagination, pp. 23 and 72) Lady Halkett wrote about her relationship with Colonel Joseph Bampfield.

In the introduction to his edition of 1875, John Gough Nichols noted 'the obscurity in which Lady Halkett studiously wrote' (p. i). He referred not to an ambiguity of prose style but to Lady Halkett's frequent use of initials rather than names when referring to persons of her acquaintance. The identification of some of those persons has eluded me; that of others is apparent from the context in which she wrote; that of still others can be learned from the index to the edition of 1875. Because Nichols died before his edition was published, Samuel Rawson Gardiner, with his unparalleled knowledge of the history of mid-seventeenth-century England, saw the volume through the press. Although there is little evidence that Gardiner spent much time on the task, presumably he at least supervised preparation of the index; and, more than anyone else of his century, he was qualified to supply the names signified by the initials used by Lady Halkett. Drawing on his index, on the context of the Memoirs, as well as on other sources, I have when possible identified persons referred to by initials in the explanatory notes or in the biographical index.

I have followed the spelling of the manuscript as closely as possible without sacrificing intelligibility, noting any necessary changes in or additions to the original spelling in my textual notes. I have frequently found it necessary to depart from the manuscript in punctuation, paragraphing, and capitalization. I have in fact been compelled to capitalize according to modern principles because in many if not most instances Lady Halkett's capitals cannot be differentiated from her usual script. The corrections in the manuscript, often in the form of interlineations over cancelled words, reveal Lady Halkett's concern for precision and grace of prose style. Accordingly, I have described her corrections, as fully as the legibility of the manuscript permits, in the textual notes. I have silently expanded unambiguous abbreviations in the manuscript except in instances of initials referring to persons, and I have silently followed the conventional methods of indicating the possessive case of nouns, or initials representing nouns, in the instances in which Lady Halkett neglected to do so.

A CHRONOLOGY OF ANNE, LADY HALKETT

		Age
1623*	Born, London, 4 January, younger daughter of Thomas Murray, Provost of Eton College, formerly tutor to Charles I; and of Jane Drummond Murray, subsequently governess to the Duke of Gloucester and the Princess Elizabeth	
1623	Death of her father (April)	
c. 1627–*c.* 1639	Educated by tutors employed by her mother	6–18
1644	From her youth studies medical science. Frequently visits the estate of her brother-in-law, Sir Henry Newton, at Charlton, in Kent. Affections engaged by Thomas Howard, eldest son of Edward, Lord Howard of Escrick. She is forbidden by her mother to marry him, but promises to marry no one else before he marries	21
1646	Howard marries Lady Elizabeth Mordaunt	23
1647	Death of her mother (August). Resides with her oldest brother Henry and his wife for about a year afterwards. Assists Colonel Joseph Bampfield, a secret agent employed by Charles I, beginning late in 1647 or early in the following year	24 or 25
1648	Helps Colonel Bampfield contrive the escape of the Duke of York from St. James's Palace by procuring women's clothes for the duke and dressing him in them (April). Bampfield tells her that his wife is dead. She promises to marry him when they have taken precautions against the sequestration of their property	25
1649	Her brother Will, banished from attendance on Charles II, becomes ill and dies at Gravesend. She attends his death-bed. Departs (September) on a visit to Anne, wife of Sir Charles Howard of Naworth Castle. While there hears that Bampfield has been	

* See Note at end of this Chronology.

	arrested by the Parliamentarians and that his wife is alive. Becomes seriously ill. Hears of Bampfield's escape. She still believes in his good faith	26
1650	Arrives at Edinburgh (June) to attempt recovery of part of her inheritance from her mother. Is welcomed by leaders of the Royalist party and in Dunfermline is introduced to Charles II, from whom she receives thanks for her assistance in the Duke of York's escape. Leaves for the north (September); remains two days at Kinross attending soldiers wounded in the Battle of Dunbar. Receives thanks from the King and a gift of fifty pieces for her service. Visited by Bampfield, in whose innocence she still believes	27
1650–2	Resides with the Countess of Dunfermline at Fyvie, Aberdeenshire, where she employs her skill as a physician	27–29
1652	Returns to Edinburgh (June) where she initiates a lawsuit for the recovery of part of her inheritance. Introduced to Sir James Halkett, a widower with two sons and two daughters. Bampfield arrives in Edinburgh, active in the Royalist cause	29
1653	Shortly after Bampfield's departure for the north (February), she learns that his wife is undoubtedly alive and residing in London. Warns the Earl of Balcarres (May) of his imminent arrest, making possible his escape. Assumes charge of Sir James Halkett's daughters. Agrees to marry him, on condition she can first settle her debts	30
1654	Goes to London in an attempt to settle her debts. Receives a surprise visit from Colonel Bampfield; tells him she is already married to Sir James Halkett	31
1656	Marries Sir James Halkett (2 March) at her sister's house at Charlton. Returns with him to his estate at Pitfirrane in Scotland. Her daughter Elizabeth born	33
1658	Her son Henry born	35
1661	Her son Robert born, the only one of her children to survive infancy. Applies for compensation for the loss of her property in the King's service, but receives only five hundred pounds from the	

	Exchequer and fifty pounds from the Duke of York as a gift to her infant child. Her daughter Jean born	38
1670	Death of Sir James Halkett (September). Lady Halkett takes up residence in Dunfermline	47
1671	Sir James Halkett's elder son by his first marriage, Charles, created a baronet	48
1677–8	Writes her Memoirs	54–55
1683	Supplements her income by caring for and teaching children	60
1684	Her son Robert commissioned a captain	61
1685	Receives a pension of one hundred pounds a year from James II as a reward for her service to him when he was Duke of York	62
c. 1690	Robert Halkett serves under James II in Ireland. Robert Halkett captured; imprisoned in London until 1692	67
1692	Death of Robert Halkett	69
1697	Death of Sir Charles Halkett	74
1699	Dies, 22 April	76

Note on birthdate of Lady Halkett:

Although all previous accounts of Lady Halkett have stated that she was born 4 January 1622, I have concluded that in accordance with the modern practice of following the Old Style Calendar but considering a year as beginning on 1 January rather than 25 March, she was born 4 January 1623. The only known records pertaining to the date of her birth are her statement in the Memoirs (p. 10) that her father, soon after becoming Provost of Eton College, 'died when I was but three months old'; and the statement in the biography of her by 'S.C.' published in 1701 (p. 3) that she was born 'the *4th* of *January* 1622'. Because the biography was published before the reformation of the calendar, the writer could have referred to January 1623, New Style. He uses a double date once, in referring to the trial of King Charles I in *January* 4^{8}_{9} (p. 18). The only evidence that he considered a year as beginning on 1 January is inconclusive: the dates given (p. 30) for the births of the younger two of Lady Halkett's children, only eight months apart if 25 March marked a new year. But as the youngest child, a girl, died young, she may well have been born prematurely.

Lady Halkett's statement that she was three months old when her father died is consistent with a birthdate of January 1622/3. It is beyond reasonable doubt that her father, whose date of death is recorded on a monument in the Chapel of Eton College, died 9 April 1623.

THE MEMOIRS OF ANNE, LADY HALKETT

[The first leaf of the manuscript, on which only one page of text was written, is missing; the second—and first surviving—leaf is mutilated, and a portion of it cannot be read consecutively or completely. However, enough of the leaf survives to reveal the topics Lady Halkett wrote about and to convey important information. The introductory section of the Memoirs was devotional in nature. The following is the surviving portion of it:]

his word. And since wee have an advocate with the Father of Christ the righteous, hee will plead for mee wherin I am inocentt and pardon wherin I have beene guiltty; for God sentt nott his Son into the world to condemne the world, butt that the world through him might bee saved, in whom we have boldnese and adrese with confidence by the faith of him. And that is the reason why I faint nott under tribulation, for there is noe sin that ever I have been guilty of in my whole life butt I repent with as much sincearity as I seeke pardon. And I suplicate for grace and live uprightly here with the same fervor that I seeke for heaven here affter. And if the Lord sees fitt to continue mee still in the furnace of affliction, his blesed will bee done so that I may bee one of his chosen.

[This is followed by an extra space before the next paragraph. In this space the following statement, in an early hand but not Lady Halkett's, is written:]

'This Manuscript'

written by Anne, Daughter of Mr. Thomas Murray, Provost of Eton and Preceptor of Charles 1st. She was Lady of the Bedchamber to Queen Henrietta Maria, and married Sir James Halkett, Knight of Pitfirren

[The four succeeding paragraphs, again in Lady Halkett's hand, represent the beginning of her autobiographical narrative. Owing to a tear in the leaf, portions of some lines are missing. The following is a transcription of the surviving portion of the text, with the missing parts of lines represented by the irregularities of the margins:]

For my parentts I need nott say much, since they were
And I need nott bee ashamed to owne them
was mentioned as my reproach that I was of
ion, whereas hee that now succeds to that fa

was once which was as good a gentleman as any ter, I shall ever bee sattisfied with what can the advantage of that familly, but some that to, both by father and mother would take itt ill nott thought gentlemen; for my father claimed of beeing derived from the Earle of Tillibardin's familly and my mother from the Earle of Perth's.

Hee was thought a wise King who made choice of my f[ather] to bee tuter to the late King of blessed memory; and what the excellentt Prince learnt in his youth kept him stedfast in his relligion though under all the temptations of Spaine, temperate in all the exceses that attend a court, vertuous and constant to the only lawfull imbraces of the Queene, and [unmove]able and undisturbed under all his unparaleld sufferings. For all recompence to my father's care in discharging his duty, hee was made Provost of Eaton Colledge, where hee [li]ved nott long butt died when I was butt three months old; yett itt seemes the short time hee lived amongst those prebends, they were so well sattisfied both with him and my mother that affter my father's death they pettitioned to have his place continued to my mother a yeare, which was never before granted to any woman. And during her time they all renued there leases as a testimony of there respect and desire to give her that advantage.

As this may evidence what my father's partts were, so my mother may bee best knowne by beeing thought fitt both by the late King and Queene's Majesty to bee intrusted twice with the charge and honor of beeing governese to the Duke of Glocester and the Princese Elizabeth, first during the time that the Countese of Roxbery (who owned my mother for her cousin) wentt and continued in Holland with the Princese Royall, and then againe when my Lady Roxbery died. The first was only by a verball order, butt the last was under the signett dated [ ] which I have by mee to produce if itt were nesesary.

By this short accountt I have given of my pa[rents] seene what trust the greatest thought them cap erfore they could nott butt performe a duty to tt that care was wholy left (next to God's pro my mother (my father dying when we were all very who spared noe expence in educating all her ch[ildren] the most suitable way to improve them; and if I made [no]tt the advantage I might have done, itt was my owne fault and nott my mother's, who paid masters for teaching my sister and mee to writte, speake French, play [on the] lute and virginalls, and dance, and kept a gentlewoman to teach us all kinds of needleworke, which shows I was nott brought up in an idle life. Butt my mother's greatest care, and for which I shall ever owne to her memory the highest gratitude, was the great care shee tooke that even from our infancy wee were instructed never to neglect to begin and end the day with prayer, and orderly every morning to read the Bible, and ever to keepe the church as offten as there was occation to meett there either for prayers or preaching. So that for many yeares together I was seldome or never absentt from devine service att five a clocke in the morning in the summer and sixe a clocke in the winter till the usurped power putt a restraintt to that puplicke worship so long owned and continued in the Church of England; where I blese God I had my education and the example of a good mother, who kept constantt to her owne parish church and had allways a great respect for the ministers under whose charge shee was.

What my childish actions were I thinke I need nott give accountt of here, for I hope none will thinke they could bee either vicious or scandalous. And from that time till the yeare 1644 I may truly say all my converse was so inocentt that my owne hart cannott challenge mee with any imodesty, either in thought or behavier, or an act of disobedience to my mother, to whom I was so observantt that as long as shee lived I doe nott remember that I made a visitt to the neerest neibour or went any where withoutt her liberty. And so scrupulous I was of giving any occation to speake of mee, as I know they did of others, that though I loved well to see plays and to walke in the Spring Garden sometimes (before itt grew something scandalous by the abuse of some), yett I cannott remember 3 times that ever I wentt with any man besides my brothers; and if I did, my sisters or others better then my selfe was with mee. And I was the first that proposed and practised itt, for 3 or 4 of us going together withoutt any man, and every one paying for themselves by giving the mony to the footman who waited on us, and hee gave itt in the play howse. And this I did first upon hearing some gentlemen telling what ladys they had waited on to plays and how much itt had cost them, upon which I resolved none should say the same of mee.

In the yeare 1644 I confese I was guilty of an act of disobedience, for I gave way to the adrese of a person whom my mother, att the first time that ever hee had occation to bie conversantt with mee, had absolutely discharged mee ever to allow of: and though before ever I saw him severalls did tell mee that there would bee something more then ordinary betwixt him and mee (which I beleeve they fudged from the great friendship betwixt his sister and mee, for wee were seldome assunder att London, and shee and I were bedfellows when shee came to my sister's howse att Charleton, where for the most part shee staed while wee continued in the country), yett hee was halfe a yeare in my company before I discovered any thing of a particular inclination for mee more then another, and as I was civill to him both for his owne meritt and his sister's sake, so any particular civility I receaved from him I looked upon itt as flowing from the affection hee had to his sister and her kindness to mee.

After that time itt seemes hee was nott so much master of himselfe as to conceale itt any longer. And having never any opertunity of beeing alone with mee to speake himself, hee imployed a young gentleman (whose confidentt hee was in an amour betwixt him and my Lady Anne, his cousin german) to tell mee how much hee had indeavored all this time to smother his passion which hee said began the first time that ever hee saw mee, and now was come to that height that if I did nott give him some hopes of faver hee was resolved to goe backe againe into France (from whence hee had come when I first saw him) and turne Capucin.

Though this discourse disturbed mee, yett I was a weeke or ten days before I would bee perswaded so much as to heare him speake of this subject, and desired his friend to representt severall disadvantages that itt would bee to him to pursue such a designe. And knowing that his father had sentt for him outt of France with an intention to marry him to sum rich match that might improve his fortune, itt would bee high ingratitude in mee to doe any thing to hinder such a designe, since his father had beene so obleeging to my mother and sister as to use his Lordship's interest with the Parliamentt to preventt the ruine of my brother's howse and k[in]. Butt when all I could say to him by his friend could nott prevaile, butt that hee grew so ill and discontented that all the howse tooke notice, I did yield so farre to comply with his desire as to give him liberty one day when I was walking in the gallery to come there and speake to mee. What hee said was handsome and short, butt much disordered, for hee looked pale as death, and his hand trembled when hee tooke mine to lead mee, and with a great sigh said, 'If I loved you lese I could say more.'

I told him I could nott butt thinke my selfe much obleeged to him for his good opinion of mee, butt itt would bee a higher obligation to confirme his esteeme of mee by following my advise, which I should now give him my selfe, since hee would nott receave it by his friend. I used many arguements to diswade him from pursuing what hee proposed, and in conclusion told him I was 2 or 3 yeare older then hee, and were there no other objection, yett that was of such weight with mee as would never lett mee allow his further adrese.

'Madam', said hee, 'what I love in you may well increase, butt I am sure itt can never decay.'

I left arguing and told him I would advise him to consult with his owne reason and that would lett him see I had more respect to him in denying then in granting what with so much passion hee desired.

After that, hee sought, and I shunned, all opertunittys of private discourse with him; butt one day in the garden his friend tooke his sister by the hand and lead her into another walke and left him and I together. And hee with very much seriousnese began to tell mee that hee had observed ever since hee had discovered his affection to mee that I was more reserved and avoided all converse with him, and therefore, since hee had noe hopes of my faver, hee was resolved to leave England, since hee could nott bee hapy in itt. And that what ever became of him that might make him displease either his father or his friends, I was the occation of it, for if I would not give him hopes of marying him, hee was resolved to putt himselfe outt of a capacity of marying any other and goe imediately into a conventt, and that hee had taken order to have post horses ready against the next day.

I confese this discourse disturbed mee, for though I had had noe respect for him, his sister, or his familly, yett relligion was a tye upon mee to indeaver the prevention of the hazard of his soule. I looked on this as a violent passion which would nott last long and perhaps might grow the more by beeing resisted, when as a seeming complaisance might lessen itt. I told him I was sory to have him intertaine such thoughts as could nott butt bee a ruine to him and a great affliction to all his relations, which I would willingly preventt if itt were in my power.

Hee said itt was absolutely in my power, for if I would promise to marry him hee should esteeme himselfe the most hapy man living, and hee would waite what ever time I thought most convenientt for itt. I replied I though itt was unreasonable to urge mee to promise that which ere long hee might repentt the asking, butt this I would promise to sattisfy him, that I would nott marry till I saw him first maried. Hee kist my hand upon that with as much joy as if I had confirmed to him his greatest hapinese and said hee could desire noe more, for hee was secure I should never see nor heare of that till itt was to my selfe. Upon this wee parted, both well pleased, for hee thought hee had gained much in what I promised, and I looked upon my promise as a cure to him, butt noe inconvenience to myselfe, since I had noe inclination to marry any. And though I had, a delay in itt was the least returne I could make to so deserving a person.

But I deceaved my selfe by thinking this was the way to moderate his passion, for now hee gave way to itt withoutt any restraintt and thought himselfe so secure of mee as if there had beene nothing to opose itt, though hee managed itt with that discretion that itt was scarce visible to any within the howse; nott so much as either his sister or mine had the least suspittion of itt, for I had injoyned him not to lett them or any other know what his designes were because I would not have them accessory, what ever fault might bee in the prosecution of itt.

Thus itt continued till towards winter that his sister was to goe home to her father againe, and then, knowing hee would want much of the opertunity hee had to converse with mee, hee was then very importunate to have mee consent to marry him privately, which itt seemes hee pleased himselfe so with the hopes of prevailing with mee that hee had provided a wedding ring and a minister to marry us. I was much unsattisfied with his going that lengh, and in short, told him hee need never expect I would marry him withoutt his father's and my mother's consentt. If that could bee obtained, I should willingly give him the sattisfaction hee desired, butt withoutt that I could nott expect God's blesing neither upon him nor mee, and I would doe nothing that was so certaine a way to bring ruine upon us both. Hee used many argumentts from the examples of others who had practised the same and was hapy both in there parentts' faver and in one another, butt finding mee fixt beyond any perswasion, hee resolved to aquaintt my sister with itt and to imploy her to speake of itt to his father and my mother.

Shee very unwillingly undertooke it, because shee knew itt would bee a surprise to them and very unwellcome. But his impertunity prevailed, and shee first aquainted my mother with itt, who was so pasionately offended with the proposall that, whereas his father might have beene brought to have given his consentt (having ever had a good opinion of mee and very civill), shee did so exasperate him against it that nothing could sattisfy her, but presently to putt itt to Mr. H.'s choice either presenttly to marry a rich cittisen's daughter that his father had designed for him, or els to leave England. The reason I beleeve that made my mother the more incensed was, first, that itt was what in the beginning of our aquaintance shee had absolutely discharged my having a thought of allowing such an adrese; and though in some respect his quality was above mine and therfor better then any shee could expect for mee, yett my Lord H.'s fortune was such as had need of a more considerable portion then my mother could give mee, or els it must ruine his younger chilldren. And therfore my mother would nott consentt to itt, though my Lord H. did offer to doe the uttmost his condition would allow him if shee would lett mee take my hazard with his son. But my mother would nott bee perswaded to itt upon noe consideration, lest any should have though itt was began with her allowance; and to take away the suspittion of that, did, I beleeve, make her the more violent in opposing itt and the more seavere to mee.

My sister made choice of Sunday to speake of itt; first, because shee thought that day might put them both in a calmer frame to heare her, and confine there passion, since itt would bee the next day before they would determine anything. Butt finding both by my mother and my Lord H. that they intended nothing butt to part us so as never to meett againe, except itt was as strangers, Mr. H. was very importunate to have an opertunity to speake with mee that night, which I gave. My sister beeing only with mee, wee came downe together to the roome apointed to meett with him. I confese I never saw those two pasions of love and regrett more truly represented, nor could any person exprese greater affection and resolution of constancy, which with many solemne oaths hee sealed of never loving or marying any butt my selfe. I was not sattisfied with his swearing to future performances, since I said both hee and I might find itt most convenient to retract, butt this I did assure him, as long as hee was constantt hee should never find a change in mee, for though duty did oblieege mee nott to marry any withoutt my mother's consent, yet itt would nott tye mee to marry without my owne.

My sister att this rises and said, 'I did nott thinke you would have ingaged mee to bee a wittnese of both your resolutions to continue what I expected you would rather have laid aside, and therfore I will leave you.'

'Oh, madam,' said hee, 'can you imagine I love att that rate as to have itt shaken with any storme? Noe, were I secure your sister would nott suffer in my absence by her mother's sevearity, I would nott care what misery I were exposed to, butt to thinke I should bee the occation of trouble to the person in the earth that I love most is unsuportable.'

And with that hee fell downe in a chaire that was behind him, butt as one withoutt all sense, which I must confese did so much move mee that, laing aside all former distance I had kept him att, I satt downe upon his knee, and laying my head neere his I suffred him to kisse mee, which was a liberty I never gave before; nor had nott then had I nott seene him so overcome with greefe, which I indeavered to suprese with all the incouragementt I could, butt still presing him to bee obedientt to his father, either in goeing abroad or staying att home as hee thought most convenient.

'Noe,' says hee, 'since they will nott allow mee to converse with you, France will bee more agreeable to mee then England, nor will I goe there except I have liberty to come here againe and take my leave of you.' To that I could nott disagree if they thought fitt to allow itt, and so my sister and I left him, butt shee durst nott owne to my mother where shee had beene.

The next morning early my Lord H. went away, and tooke with him his son and daughter, and left mee to the seaveritys of my offended mother, who nothing could pacify. Affter shee had called for mee and said as many bitter things as passion could dictate upon such a subject, she discharged mee to see him and did solemly vow that if she should heare I did see Mr. H. shee would turne mee outt of her doores and never owne mee againe. All I said to that part was that itt should bee against my will if ever shee heard of itt.

Upon Tuesday my Lord H. writt to my mother that hee had determined to send his son to France, and that upon Thursday after hee was to begin his journey, butt all hee desired before hee wentt was to have liberty to see mee; which hee thought was a sattisfaction could nott bee denyed him, and therfore desired my mother's consentt to it, which shee gave upon the condittion that hee should only come in and take his leave of mee, butt nott to have any converse butt what shee should bee a wittnese of her selfe. This would nott att all please Mr. H., and therfore seemed to lay the desire of itt aside. In the meanetime my chamber and liberty of lying alone was taken from mee, and my sister's woman was to bee my guardian, who watched sufficiently so that I had nott the least opertunity either day or night to bee without her. Upon Thursday morning early my mother sentt a man of my sister's (whose name I must mention with the rest that att that [time] was in the familly, for there was Moses, Aron, and Miriam all att one time in itt, and none either related or aquainted together till they met there)—this Moses was sentt to my Lord H. with a letter to inquire if his son were gone.

I must here relate a little odd incounter which agravated my misfortune. There came noe returne till night, and, having gott liberty to walke in the hall, my mother sentt a child of my sister's and bid him walke with mee and keepe mee company. I had nott beene there a quarter of an hower butt my maid Miriam came to mee and told mee shee was walking att the backe gate and Mr. H. came to her and sentt her to desire mee to come there and speake butt two or three words with him, for hee had sworne nott to goe away withoutt seeing mee; nor would hee come in to see my mother, for he had left London that morning very early and had rod up and downe that part of the country only till itt was the gloome of the evening to have the more privacy in comming to see mee. I bid her goe back and tell him I durst nott see him because of my mother's oath and her discharge. While shee was presing mee to run to the gate and I was neere to take the start, the child cried outt, 'O, my aunt is going', which stoped mee, and I sent her [Miriam] away to tell the reason why I could not come.

I still staid walking in the hall till shee returned, wondering shee staid so long. When shee came shee was hardly able to speake and with great disorder said, 'I beleeve you are the most unfortunate person living, for I thinke Mr. H. is killed.'

Any one that hath ever knowne what gratitude was may imagine how these words disordered mee, butt impatientt to know how (I was resolved to hazard my mother's displeasure rather then nott see him), shee told mee that while shee was telling him my answeare, there came a fellow with a great club behind him and strucke him downe dead, and others had seazed upon Mr. T. (who formerly had beene his governer and was now intrusted to see him safe on shipboord) and his man. The reason of this was from what there was too many sad examples of att that time, when the devission was betwixt the King and Parliamentt, for to betray a master or a friend was looked upon as doing God good service.

My brother-in-law Sir Henry Newton had beene long from home in attendance on the King, for whose service hee had raised a troope of horse upon his owne expence and had upon all occations testified his loyalty; for which all his estate was sequestred, and with much dificulty my sister gott liberty to live in her owne house and had the fifth part to live upon, which was obtained with impertunity. There was one of my brother's tenants called Musgrove, who was a very great rogue, who farmed my brother's land of the Parliamentt and was imployed by them as a spye to discover any of the Cavaliers that should come within his knowledge. Hee, observing 3 gentlemen upon good horse scouting aboutt all day and keeping att a distance from the high way, aprehends itt was my brother who had come privately home to see my sister, and resolves to watch when hee came neere the house, and had followed so close as to come behind and give Mr. H. that stroake, thinking itt had beene my brother Newton, and seased upon his governer and servantt (the post boy beeing left att some distance with the horses).

In the midst of this disorder Moses came there, and Miriam having told what the occation of itt was, he told Musgrove itt was my Lord H.'s son hee had used so, upon which hee and his complices wentt imediately away, and Moses and Mr. H.'s man caried him into an alehouse hard by and laid him on a bed, where hee lay some time before hee came to himselfe. So, hearing all was quiett againe and that hee had noe hurt, only stonished with the blow, I wentt into the roome where I had left my mother and sister, which beeing att a good distance from the backe gate they had heard nothing of the tumult that had beene there.

A litle after, Moses came in and delivered a letter from my Lord H., which after my mother had read, shee asked what news att London. Hee answeared, the greatest hee could tell was that Mr. H. went away that morning early post to Deepe and was going to France, butt hee could nott learne the reason of itt. My mother and sister seemed to wonder att itt, for none in the familly except my maid knew any thing that had fallen outt, or had any suspition that I was concerned in itt, butt my mother and sister.

After Moses wentt outt my mother asked mee if I was nott ashamed to thinke that itt would bee said my Lord H. was forced to send away his son to secure him from mee.

I said I could nott butt regrett what ever had occationed her displeasure or his punishmentt, butt I was guilty of noe unhandsome action to make mee ashamed; and therfore, what ever were my presentt misfortune, I was confident to evidence before I died that noe child shee had had greater love and respect to her, or more obedience.

To which shee replied, 'Itt seemes you have a good opinion of your selfe.'

My mother now beleeving Mr. H. gone, I was nott as former nights sentt to my bed, and the guard upon mee that was usuall, butt I staid in my mother's chamber till shee and my sister (who lay together) was abed. In the meanetime Mr. H. had sentt for Moses and told him what ever misfortune hee might suffer by his stay there, hee was fully determined nott to goe away without seeing mee, and desired I would come to the banketting howse in the garden and he would come to the window and speake to mee; which hee told mee, and with all that Mr. T. (who was a very serious good man) did earnestly intreat mee to condescend to his desire to preventt what might bee more inconvenient to us both. I sentt him word when my mother was abed I would contrive some way to sattisfy him, butt nott where hee proposed, because itt was within the view of my mother's chamber window.

Affter I had left my mother and sister in there bed, I went alone in the darke through my brother's closett to the chamber where I lay, and as I entred the roome I laid my hand upon my eyes and with a sad sigh said, 'Was ever creature so unfortunate and putt to such a sad dificulty, either to make Mr. H. forsworne if hee see mee nott, or if I doe see him, my mother will bee forsworne if shee doth nott expose mee to the uttmost rigour her anger can inventt.' In the midst of this dispute with my selfe what I should doe, my hand beeing still upon my eyes, itt presently came in my mind that if I blindfolded my eyes that would secure mee from seeing him, and so I did not transgrese against my mother. And hee might that way sattisfy himselfe by speaking with mee. I had as much joy in finding outt this meanes to yeeld to him withoutt disquiett to my selfe as if itt had beene of more considerable consequence. Imediately I sentt Moses to tell him upon what condittions I would speake with him: first, that hee must allow mee to have my eyes covered, and that hee should bring Mr. T. with him, and if thus hee were sattisfied I ordered him to bring them in the backe way into the cellar where I with Miriam would meett them the other way; which they did.

As soone as Mr. H. saw mee hee much impertuned the taking away the covert from my eyes; which I nott suffering, hee left disputing that, to imploy the litle time hee had in regretting my nott yielding to his impertunity to marry him before his affection was discovered to his father and my mother. For had itt beene once past there power to undoe, they would [have] beene sooner sattisfied, and wee might have beene hapy together and nott indured this sad separation.

I told him I was sory for beeing the occation of his discontentt, butt I could nott repentt the doing my duty what ever ill succese itt had, for I ever looked upon marying withoutt consentt of parentts as the highest act of ingratitude and disobedience that chilldren could committ, and I resolved never to bee guilty of itt. I found his greatest trouble was the feare hee had that my mother in his absence would force mee to marry M. L. (who was a gentleman of a good fortune who some people thought had a respect for mee). To this I gave him as much assurance as I could that neither hee nor any other person living should lessen his interest till hee gave mee reason for itt himselfe. Itt is unnesesary to repeatt the solemne oaths hee made never to love nor marry any other, for as I did not aprove of itt then, so I will nott now agravate his crime by mentioning them. Butt there was nothing hee left unsaid that could exprese a sinceare, virtuous, true affection.

Mr. T. (who with Moses and Miriam had all this time beene so civill to us both as to retire att such a distance as nott to heare what we said) came and interupted him and desired him to take his leave lest longer stay might bee prejudiciall to us all. I called for a bottle of wine and, giving Mr. T. thankes for his civility and care, drunk to him, wishing a good and hapy journey to Mr. H. So taking a farewell of them both, I wentt up the way I came and left them to Moses' care to conduct them outt quiettly as hee led them in. (This was upon Thursday night, the 10th of October, 1644.)

This was nott so secrettly done butt some of the howse observed more noise then ordinarily used to bee att that time of night and, by sattisfying there curiosity in looking outt, discovered the occation of itt; butt they were all so just as none of them ever aquainted my mother with itt, though I did nott conceale itt from my sister the first opertunity I had to bee alone with her.

I was in hopes, affter some time that Mr. H. was gone, my mother would have receaved mee into her faver againe, butt the longer time shee had to consider of my fault the more shee did agravate itt. And though my Lord H. (who returned shortly after with his daughter) and my sister did use all the argumentts imaginable to perswade her to bee reconciled to mee, yett nothing would prevaile except I would solemly promise never to thinke more of Mr. H. and that I would marry another whom shee thought fitt to propose. To which I beged her pardon, for till Mr. H. was first maried I was fully determined to marry noe person living. Shee asked mee if I was such a foole as to beleeve hee would bee constantt. I said I did, butt if hee were nott, itt should bee his fault, nott mine, for I resolved nott to make him guilty by example.

Many were imployed to speake to mee. Some used good words, some ill; butt one that was most seavere, after I had heard her with much patience raile a long time, when shee could say noe more, I gave a true accountt how inocentt I was from having any designe upon Mr. H. and related what I have allready mentioned of the progrese of his affection; which when shee heard, shee sadly wept and beged my pardon and promised to doe mee all the service shee could. And I beleeve shee did, for shee had much influence upon my Lord H. (having beene with his lady from a child), and did give so good a caracter of mee and my proceedings in that affaire with his son, that hee againe made an offer to my mother to send for his son if shee would consentt to the mariage. Butt shee would nott heare itt spoken of, butt said shee rather I were buried then bring so much ruine to the familly shee honored.

My mother's anger against mee increased to that height that for fourteene months shee never gave mee her blesing, nor never spoke to mee butt when itt was to reproach mee, and one day said with much bitternese shee did hate to see mee. That word I confese strucke deepely to my hart and putt mee to my thoughts what way to dispose of my selfe to free my mother from such an object. Affter many debates with my selfe and inquirys what life I could take to that was most inocentt, I resolved and writt to Sir Patrick Drumond, a cousin of my mother's, who was Conservator in Holland, to doe mee the favor to informe mee if itt was true that I had heard that there was a nunery in Holland for those of the Protestant relligion; and that hee would inquire upon what condittions they admitted any to there society, because if they were consistent with my relligion, I did resolve upon his advertisement imediately to goe over, and desired him to hasten an answeare and nott devulge to any what I had writt to him.

Aboutt a fortnight after, my mother sentt for mee one morning into her chamber and examined mee what I had writt to Sir Patrick Drumond. I ingeniously gave her an accountt, and the reason of itt, for since I found nothing would please her that I could doe, I was resolved to goe where I could most please my selfe, which was in a solitary retired life, and so free her from the sight shee hated; and since itt was upon that consideration I did nott doupt the obtaining her consentt. Itt seemes Sir Patrick Drumond, who was a wise and honest gentleman, aprehending discontentt had made mee take that resolution which I had writt to him about, instead of answearing my letter, writtes to my mother a very handsome, serious letter aquainting her with my intention; and concluded itt could proceed from nothing but her seaverity, perhaps upon unjust grounds, and therfore used many arguments to perswade her to returne to that wonted kindnese which shee had ever shewed to all her chilldren, and what hee was sure I would deserve, what ever opinion shee had lately intertained to the contrary. This hee presed with so much of reason and earnestnese that itt prevailed more with my mother then what ever had beene said before, and from that time shee receaved mee againe to her faver, and ever affter used mee more like a friend then a child.

In the meane time all care was used that might preventt Mr. H.'s corespondence and mine. But hee found an excuse for sending home his man, beleeving him honest and faithfull to him, and with him hee writt and sent mee a presentt, butt instead of delivering them to mee gave them to his father, who otherways disposed of them. Yet in requitall I sent backe with him a ring with five rubys, and gave him something for his paines, when hee came to mee and indeavered to vindicate himselfe by protesting that unexpectedly hee was searched as soone as ever hee entred his lord's howse, and all was taken from him; but I found affterwards hee was nott so honest as I beleeved, for he never delivered my ring to his master, nor any thing I intrusted him with.

Att this time my Lord H. had a sister in France who gloried much of her witt and contrivance and used to say shee never designed any thing butt she accomplished itt. My Lord H. thought shee was the fittest person to devert his son from his amour, and to her hee writtes and recomends itt to her managementt, who was not negligent of what shee was intrusted with, as apeared in the conclusion; though her cariage was a great disapointment to Mr. H., for hee expected by her mediation to have obtained what hee desired, and that made him the more willing to comply with her, who designed her owne advantage by this to obliege her brother, who might bee the more useful to her in a projected mariage shee had for her owne son.

Upon Thursday the 13 of February, 1645/6, word was brought to my mother that the Countese of B. was come outt of France and Mr. H. with her, which was a great surprise to her and all his relations. My mother examined mee if I had sentt for him or knew anything of his comming, which I assured her I had nott, and shee said nott much more. Butt I was as much disturbed as any, sometimes thinking hee was come with an assurance from his auntt that shee would accomplish what hee had so passionatly desired, or els that hee had laid all thoughts of mee aside and was come with a resolution to comply with his father's desires. The last opinion I was a litle confirmed in, having never receaved any word or letter from him in ten days after his returne; and meeting him accidentally where I was walking, hee crosed the way, and another time was in the roome where I came in to visitt some young ladys, and neither of these times tooke any notice of mee more then of one I had never seene. I confese I was a litle disordered at itt, butt made noe conclusions till I saw what time would produce.

Upon Tuesday the 4 of March, my Lady Anne W. his cousin came to my mother's, and having staid a convenient time for a visit with my mother (for then itt was not usuall for mothers and daughters to be visited apart), I waited on her downe, and taking mee aside shee told mee shee was desired by her cousin T. H. to presentt his most faithfull service to mee and to desire mee nott to take itt ill that hee did nott speake to mee when hee met mee. For finding his aunt nott his friend as hee expected, hee seemed to comply with her desire only to have the opertunity of comming home with her, and had resolved for a time to forbeare all converse with mee and to make love to all that came in his way; butt assured mee itt was only to make his friends thinke hee had forgot mee, and then hee might with the lese suspition prosecute his designe, which was never to love or marry any butt mee. And this, shee said, hee confirmed with all the solemne oaths imaginable.

In pursuance of this hee visitted all the young ladys aboutt the towne.

Butt an earle's daughter gave him the most particular wellcome, whose mother nott allowing him to come as a pretender, shee made apointment with him and mett him att her cousin's howse frequently, which I knew and hee made sport of. The summer beeing now advancing, my mother and her familly wentt with my sister to her howse in the country, which beeing nott farre from London wee heard often how afaires wentt there, and amongst other discourse that it was reported Mr. H. was in love with my Lady E. M. and shee with him; att which some smiled and said it might bee her witt had taken him, butt certainly nott her beauty (for shee had as litle of that as my selfe).

Though these reports putt mee upon my guard, yett I confese I did not beleeve hee was reall in his adrese there; neither did his sister, who was sometimes a wittnese of there converse and gave mee accountt of itt. Butt I aproved nott of his way, for I thought it could nott butt reflect upon himselfe and injure either that lady or mee. But shee tooke a way to secure her selfe; for upon the last Tuesday in July, 1646, a litle before super, I receaved a letter from Mrs. H., a particular friend of mine, who writt mee word that upon the Tuesday before Mr. H. was privately maried to my Lady E. M., and the relations of both sides was unsattisfied.

I was alone in my sister's chamber when I read the letter, and flinging my selfe downe upon her bed, I said, 'Is this the man for whom I have sufred so much? Since hee hath made himselfe unworthy my love, hee is unworthy my anger or concerne.' And rising, imediately I wentt outt into the next roome to my super as unconcernedly as if I had never had an interest in him, nor had never lost itt.

A litle after, my mother came to the knowledge of itt from my Lord H., who was much discontented att his son's mariage and offten wished hee had had his former choice. Nothing troubled mee more then my mother's laughing att mee, and perhaps soe did others, butt all I said was I thought hee had injured himselfe more then mee and I much rather hee had done itt then I. And once, I confesse, in passion, beeing provoked by something I had heard, I said with too much seriousnese, 'I pray God hee may never dye in peace till hee confese his fault and aske mee forgivenese.' Butt I acknowledge this as a fault and have a hundred times beged the Lord's pardon for itt. For though in some respects itt might bee justified as wishing him repentance, yett many circumstances might make itt imposible for mee to bee a wittnese of itt. And God forbid that any should wantt peace for my passion.

When Miriam first heard hee was maried, shee lifted up her hands and said, 'Give her, O Lord, dry breasts and a miscarying wombe', which I reproved her for. Butt itt seemes the Lord thought fitt to grantt her request, for that lady miscaried of severall chilldren before shee brought one to the full time, and that one died presently after it was borne; which may bee a lesson to teach people to governe there wishes and there toung that neither may act to the prejudice of any, lest it bee placed on there accounts att the day of reckoning. Not only was this couple unfortunate in the chilldren, butt in one another, for itt was too well knowne how short a time continued the sattisfaction they had in one another. Nor did his aunt, the Countese of B., who first putt him upon . . .

[*one leaf* (*two pages*) *missing*]

. . . time, and nott the worse that hee proffesed to have a great friendship for my brother Will!

This gentleman came to see mee sometimes in the company of ladys who had beene my mother's neibours in St. Martin's Lane, and sometimes alone. Butt when ever hee came, his discourse was serious, handsome, and tending to imprese the advantages of piety, loyalty, and vertue; and these subjects were so agreeable to my owne inclination that I could nott butt give them a good reception, especially from one that seemed to bee so much an owner of them himselfe. Affter I had beene used to freedome of discourse with him, I told him I aproved of his advise to others, butt I thought his owne practise contradicted much of his proffession, for one of his aquaintance had told mee hee had nott seene his wife in a twelvemonth; and itt was imposible, in my opinion, for a good man to bee an ill husband, and therefore hee must defend himselfe from one before I could beleeve the other of him. Hee said itt was nott nesesary to give everyone that might condemne him the reason of his beeing so long from her, yett to satisfy mee hee would tell mee the truth, which was that, hee beeing ingaged in the King's service, hee was oblieged to bee att London, where itt was nott convenient for her to bee with him, his stay in any place beeing uncertaine. Besides, she lived amongst her friends, who though they were kind to her yett were nott so to him, for most of that country had declared for the Parleament and were enemys to all that had, or did, serve the King; and therfore his wife, hee was sure, would not condemne him for what hee did by her owne consentt. This seeming reasonable, I did insist noe more upon that subject.

Att this time hee had frequent letters from the King, who imployed him in severall affaires, butt that of the greatest concerne which hee was imployed in was to contrive the Duke of Yorke's escape outt of St. James' (where His Highnese and the Duke of Glocester and the Princese Elizabeth lived under the care of the Earle of Northumberland and his lady). The dificultys of itt was representted by Collonel B., butt His Majestie still pressed itt, and I remember this expresion was in one of the letters: *I beleeve itt will bee dificult, and if hee miscary in the attempt itt will bee the greatest afliction that can arive to mee, butt I looke upon James' escape as Charles's preservation, and nothing can content mee more. Therfore bee carefull what you doe.*

This letter amongst others hee shewed mee, and where the King aproved of his choice of mee to intrust with itt, for to gett the Duke's cloaths made and to drese him in his disguise. So now all C.B.'s busynese and care was how to manage this busynese of so important concerne which could not bee performed withoutt severall persons' concurrence in itt. For hee beeing generally knowne as one whose stay att London was in order to serve the King, few of those who were intrusted by the Parliamentt in puplicke concernes durst owne convearse or hardly civilitty to him, lest they should have beene suspect by there party, which made itt deficult for him to gett accese to the Duke. Butt (to bee short) having comunicated the designe to a gentleman attending His Highnese, who was full of honor and fidelity, by his meanes hee had private accese to the Duke, to whom hee presented the King's letter and order to His Highnese for consenting to act what C.B. should contrive for his escape; which was so cheerefully intertained and so readily obayed, that beeing once designed there was nothing more to doe then to prepare all things for the execution.

I had desired him to take a ribban with him and bring mee the bignese of the Duke's wast and his lengh to have cloaths made fitt for him. In the meanetime C.B. was to provide mony for all nesesary expence, which was furnished by an honest cittisen. When I gave the measure to my tailor to inquire how much mohaire would serve to make a petticoate and wast-coate to a young gentlewoman of that bignese and stature, hee considered it a long time and said hee had made many gownes and suites, butt hee had never made any to such a person in his life. I thought hee was in the right; butt his meaning was, hee had never seene any women of so low a stature have so big a wast. However, hee made itt as exactly fitt as if hee had taken the measure himselfe. It was a mixt mohaire of a light haire couler and blacke, and the under petticoate was scarlett.

All things beeing now ready, upon the 20 of Aprill, 1648, in the evening was the time resolved on for the Duke's escape. And in order to that, itt was designed for a weeke before every night as soone as the Duke had suped, hee and those servants that attended His Highnese (till the Earle of Northumberland and the rest of the howse had suped) wentt to a play called hide and seeke, and sometimes hee would hide himselfe so well that in halfe an hower's time they could not find him. His Highnese had so used them to this that when he wentt really away they thought hee was butt att the usuall sport. A litle before the Duke wentt to super that night, hee called for the gardiner (who only had a treble key, besides that which the Duke had) and bid him give him that key till his owne was mended, which hee did. And after His Highnese had suped, hee imeadiately called to goe to the play, and went downe the privy staires into the garden and opened the gate that goes into the parke, treble locking all the doores behind him. And att the garden gate C.B. waited for His Highnese, and putting on a cloake and perewig, huried him away to the parke gate where a coach waited that caried them to the watter side. And taking the boate that was apointed for that service, they rowed to the staires next the bridge, where I and Miriam waited in a private howse hard by that C.B. had prepared for dresing His Highnese, where all things were in a readinese.

Butt I had many feares, for C.B. had desired mee, if they came nott there prescisly by ten a clocke, to shift for my selfe, for then I might conclude they were discovered, and so my stay there could doe noe good, butt prejudice my selfe. Yett this did nott make mee leave the howse though ten a clocke did strike, and hee that was intrusted, [who] offten wentt to the landing-place and saw noe boate comming, was much discouraged, and asked mee what I would doe. I told him I came there with a resolution to serve His Highnese and I was fully determined nott to leave that place till I was outt of hopes of doing what I came there for, and would take my hazard. Hee left mee to goe againe to the watter side, and while I was fortifying my selfe against what might arive to mee, I heard a great noise of many as I thought comming up staires, which I expected to bee soldiers to take mee; butt itt was a pleasing disapointmentt, for the first that came in was the Duke, who with much joy I tooke in my armes and gave God thankes for his safe arivall. His Highnese called, 'Quickely, quickely, drese mee', and putting off his cloaths I dresed him in the wemen's habitt that was prepared, which fitted His Highnese very well and was very pretty in itt. Affter hee had eaten some thing I made ready while I was idle, lest His Highnese should bee hungry, and having sentt for a Woodstreet cake (which I knew hee loved) to take in the barge, with as much hast as could bee His Highnese wentt crose the bridge to the staires where the barge lay, C.B. leading him, and imediately the boatmen plied the oare so well that they were soone outt of sight, having both wind and tide with them. Butt I affterwards heard the wind changed and was so contrary that C.B. told mee hee was terribly afraid they should have beene blowne backe againe. And the Duke said, 'Doe any thing with mee rather then lett mee goe backe againe', which putt C.B. to seeke helpe where itt was only to bee had, and affter hee had most fervently suplicated assistance from God, presently the wind blew faire and they came safely to there intended landing place. Butt I heard there was some deficulty before they gott to the ship att Graves-End, which had like to have discovered them had nott Collonell Washington's lady assisted them.

Affter the Duke's barge was outt of sight of the bridge, I and Miriam wentt where I apointed the coach to stay for mee and made drive as fast as the coachman could to my brother's howse, where I staid. I met none in the way that gave mee any aprehension that the designe was discovered, nor was itt noised abroad till the next day. For (as I related before) the Duke having used to play att hide and seeke, and to conceale himselfe a long time when they mist him att the same play, thought hee would have discovered himselfe as formerly when they had given over seeking him. Butt a much longer time beeing past then usually was spentt in thatt deverttisementt, some began to aprehend that His Highnese was gone in earnest past there finding, which made the Earle of Northumberland (to whose care hee was committed), affter strict scearch made in the howse of St. James and all theraboutts to noe purpose, to send and aquaint the Speaker of the Howse of Commons that the Duke was gone, butt how or by what meanes hee knew nott; butt desired that there might bee orders sent to the Cinque Ports for stoping all ships going outt till the passengers were examined and scearch made in all suspected places where His Highnese might bee concealed.

Though this was gone aboutt with all the vigillancy immaginable, yett itt pleased God to disapoint them of there intention by so infatuating those severall persons who were imployed for writting orders that none of them were able to writt one right, butt ten or twelve of them were cast by before one was according to there mind. This accountt I had from Mr. N., who was mace bearer to the Speaker att that time and a wittnese of it. This disorder of the clarkes contributed much to the Duke's safety, for hee was att sea before any of the orders came to the ports and so was free from what was designed if they had taken His Highnese. Though severalls were suspected for beeing accesory to the escape, yett they could not charge any with itt butt the person who wentt away, and hee beeing outt of there reach, they tooke noe notice as either to examine or imprison others.

Affter C.B. had beene so succesfull in serving the Duke, the Prince imployed him and commanded him backe againe to London with severall instructions that might have beene serviceable to the King had nott God Allmighty thought fitt to blast all indeavers that might have conduced to His Majesty's safety. As soone as C.B. landed beyond the Tower, hee writt to desire I would doe him the faver as to come to him, as beeing the only person who att that time hee could trust; and when hee should aquaint mee with the occation of his comming, hee doupted nott butt I would forgive him for the liberty hee had taken. I knowing hee could come upon noe accountt butt in order to serve the King, I imediately sentt for an honest hackney coachman who I knew might bee trusted, and, taking Miriam with mee, I wentt where hee was, who giving mee a short information of what hee was imployed aboutt and how much secresy was to bee used both as to the King's interest and his owne security, itt is nott to bee doupted butt I contributed what I could to both, and, taking him backe in the coach with mee, left him att a private lodging nott very farre from my brother's howse, that a servantt of his had prepared for him.

The earnest desire I had to serve the King made mee omitt noe opertunity wherin I could bee usefull, and the zeale I had for His Majesty made mee not see what inconveniencys I exposed my selfe to; for my intentions beeing just and inocentt made mee nott reflect what conclusions might bee made for the private visitts which I could nott butt nesesarily make to C.B. in order to the King's service. For what ever might relate to itt that came within my knowledge I gave him accountt of, and hee made such use of itt as might most advance his designe. As long as there was any posibility of conveying letters secrettly to the King, hee frequently writt and receaved very kind letters from His Majesty with severall instructions and letters to persons of honour and loyalty; butt when all access was debarred by the strict guard placed aboutt the King, all hee could then doe was to keepe warme those affections in such as hee had influence in till a seasonable opertunity to evidence there love and duty to His Majesty. Though C.B. discovered himselfe to none butt such as were of knowne integrity, yett many comming to that place where hee lay made him thinke itt convenient for his owne safety to goe sometime into the country and att his returne to bee more private.

One evening when I wentt to see him I found him lying upon his bed, and asking if hee were nott well, hee told mee hee was well enough butt had receaved a visitt in the morning from a person that hee wondred much how hee found him outt. Hee was a solicittor that was imployed by all the gentlemen in the county where hee lived, which was hard by, where his wife dwelt, and hee had brought him word shee was dead and named the day and place where shee was buried. I confese I saw him nott in much greefe and therfore I used nott many words of consolation, but left him after I had given him accountt of the busynese I wentt for. I neither made my visitts lese nor more to him for this news, for loyalty beeing the principle that first led mee to a freedome of converse with him, so still I continued itt as offten as there was occation to serve that interest. Hee putt on mourning and told the reason of itt to such as hee conversed with, butt had desired the gentleman who had first aquainted him with itt nott to make itt puplicke, lest the fortune hee had by his wife and shee injoyed while shee lived should bee sequestred.

To bee short, affter a litle time hee, on a day when I was alone with him, began to tell mee that now hee was a free man hee would say that to mee which I should have never knowne while hee lived if itt had beene otherways; which was that hee had had a great respect and honour for mee since the first time hee knew mee, butt had resolved itt should die with him if hee had nott beene in a condittion to declare itt withoutt doing mee prejudice. For hee hoped if hee could gaine an interest in my affection itt would nott apeare so unreasonable to marry him as others might representt itt, for if it pleased God to restore the King of which hee was nott yett outt of hopes, he had a promise of beeing one of His Majesty's bedchamber; and though that should faile, yett what hee and I had together would bee aboutt eight hundred pound sterling a yeare, which with the Lord's blesing might bee a competency to any contentmentt minds.

Hee so offten insisted on this when I had occation to bee with him that att last hee prevailed with mee, and I did consentt to his proposall and resolved to marry him as soone as itt apeared convenientt; but wee delayed itt till wee saw how itt pleased God to determine of the King's afaires. I know I may bee condemned as one that was too easily prevailed with, butt this I must desire to bee considered: hee was one who I had beene conversantt with for severall yeares before; one that proffesed a great friendship to my beloved brother Will; hee was unquestionably loyall, handsome, a good skollar, which gave him the advantages of writting and speaking well, and the cheefest ornamentt hee had was a devoutt life and conversation. Att least hee made itt apeare such to mee, and what ever misfortune hee brought upon mee I will doe him that right as to acknowledge I learnt from him many excellentt lessons of piety and vertue and to abhorre and detest all kind of vice. This beeing his constantt dialect made mee thinke my selfe as secure from ill in his company as in a sanctuary. From the prejudice which that opinion brought upon mee I shall advise all never to thinke a good intention can justify what may bee scandalous, for though one's actions bee never so inocentt, yett they cannott blame them who suspect them guilty when there is apearance of there deserved reproach. And I confese I did justly suffer the scourge of the toung for exposing my selfe upon any consideration to what might make mee liable to itt, for which I condemne my selfe as much as my sevearest enemey.

The King's misfortune dayly increasing and his enemy's rage and malice, both were att last determined in that execrable murder, never to bee mentioned withoutt horror and detestation. This putt such a dampe upon all designes of the Royall Party that they were for a time like those that dreamed, butt they quickely roused up themselves and resolved to leave noe meanes unesayed that might evidence there loyalty. Many excellentt designes were laid, butt the Lord thought fitt to disapoint them all, that his owne power might bee the more magnified by bringing home the King in peace when all hostile attempts failed.

In the meanetime C.B. was not idle, though unsuccesfull, and still continued in or aboutt London where hee could bee most secure. One day when I wentt to see him, I found him extreordinary melancholy, and having taken mee by the hand and lead mee to a seate, wentt from mee to the other side of the roome, which I wondred att because hee usually satte by mee when I was with him. With a deepe sigh he said, 'You must nott wonder att this distance, for I have had news since I saw you that, if itt bee true, my distance from you must bee greater and I must conclude my selfe the most unfortunate of men.'

I was much troubled att the discourse, butt itt was increased when hee told mee the reason of itt, for hee said one had informed him that his wife was living. What a surprise that was to mee none can imagine, because I beleeve none ever mett with such a tryall. Hee seeing mee in great disorder said, 'Pray, bee nott discomposed till the truth bee knowne, for upon the first intimation of itt I sentt away my man Ned B., who served mee long and knows the country and persons where shee lived, who will returne within a fortnight. If itt bee falce, I hope you will have noe reason to change your thoughts and intentions. If itt should bee true, God is my wittnese, I am nott guilty of the contrivance of the report of her beeing dead, nor had noe designe butt what I thought justifiable.'

I could nott contridict what hee said, and charity led mee to beleeve him. I left him in great disturbance, butt could conclude nothing till the returne of his servantt, who brought word that his wife died att the same time that hee first gott knowledge of itt, and that hee was att her grave where shee was buried, which I beleeving, continued former resolutions and intended to marry as soone as wee could putt our affaires in such order as to preventt sequestration.

Aboutt this time my brother Will came home much discontented, as hee had great reason, for some persons who made itt there busynese to sow the seed of jelousye betwixt the King and Duke of Yorke, in pursuite of that accused my brother that hee kept a corespondence with C.B., who staid att London to hold intteligence in Scotland, and ther designe was to have the Duke of Yorke come there to bee crowned King. Though the King did not beleave itt, as hee told my brother when hee sentt for him, yett such was his presentt condittion that hee must either banish him or els disobleige those persons whose service was most usefull to him. This His Majesty expresed with some trouble, 'Butt, Will (sayed hee), to shew you I give noe creditt to this accusation, when ever you heare I am in Scottland (where I hope shortly to bee), come to me and you shall have noe doupt of my kindnese.'

My brother humbly intreated His Majesty to lett him know his accusers and put him to a tryall, and if they could make good what they charged him with hee would willingly die.

'Noe,' says the King, 'I will not tell you who they are, and if you have any suspittion of the persons, I charge you upon your allegeance, and as you expect my faver heraffter, nott to challenge them upon itt.'

Thus with great injustice and sevearity was my brother banished the three courts, the King's, Queene Mother's, and the Princese Royall's. When hee came outt from the King, a gentleman tooke him in his armes who expreseed great kindnese and much trouble for his ill usage, who hee knew undouptedly to bee one of his greatest enemys. All he said to him was, 'You know the King hath tied mee up, and therfore I will say noe more.' Had not duty and former obligations beene a tye to all hee was capable to performe, itt was but an ill requittall for many years faithfull service and much hardship with hazard of his life, for none could brand him with disloyalty or cowardise. Nor did hee know how to refuse any imployment that was serviceable to the King, though never so dangerous to undertake.

Butt this injury contributed through the mercy of God to his etternall good, for hee tooke ship imediatly and landed neere Cobham, where by the faver of the Duke and Duchese of Richmond hee was well intertained; butt nothing could free him of the great melancholy hee tooke, for as a person of worth told mee who was a wittnese of itt, hee would steale from the company and going into the wood and lye many houres together upon the ground, where perhaps hee catched cold; and that, mixing with discontented humours, turned to a feaver wheroff hee died.

Butt I blese God I had the sattisfaction to see him dye as a good Christian. For as soone as [he] found himselfe distempered, hee writt to mee to gett him a private lodging neere the watter side, which I did, and hee comming there imediately wentt to bed and never rise outt of itt. Affter hee had given mee accountt of what I have now related, hee told mee hee had heard Doctor Wild preach att Cobham, and that hee was extreamely well pleased with his sermon, and desired mee to inquire for him and intreat him to come to him, which hee did willingly and frequently, and they had both much sattisfaction in one another. My brother beeing desirous to receave the comunion, the Doctor apointed the next morning for the celebration, butt before wee were to comunicate, my brother said, 'I am now going to pertake of that most holy sacramentt and shortely affter to give an accountt to God Allmighty for all my actions in this life. And I hope, sir (said hee to Doctor W.), you will beleeve I durst nott speake an untruth to you now, and therfore I take this time to assure you that I am not guilty of what they have accused mee of to the King, and I desire you to vindicate mee.'

I asked him if hee thought C.B. had any hand in such a designe. Hee said hee thought hee might say as much for him as for himselfe. So, having sometime composed himselfe after saying this, the usuall prayers of the church beeing ended, my brother, weake as hee was, putt himselfe upon his knees in the bed and so receaved the blesed sacrementt, and wee that were with him. Hee had before expresed great charity in forgiving his enemys, and though hee had told mee who (upon good grounds hee had reason to beleeve) they were, yett hee injoyned mee as I loved him to forgive them; for they had proved his best friends, for by there meanes hee came to see the vanity of the world and to seeke after the blesednese of that life which is unchangeable.

While hee lay sicke C.B. came once to see him, and but once, because there was scearch made for him. The constant attendance I gave my brother kept mee from seeing C.B. or sending often to him, butt early one morning one of his sarvants came and told mee that, beeing sentt early outt, as they returned they saw an officer with some soldiers marching that way where hee privately lay, and that hee feared his master was betraid. I then tooke my sister into the next roome and told her I must now comunicate something to her that I had concealed as knowing shee would nott aprove of my inttention; butt all considerations beeing now laid aside I must owne the concerne I had for C.B., and with teares beged of her, by all the kindnese shee had for mee or if ever shee desired to contribute anything to my contentmentt, that shee would make inquiry what was become of C.B. and asist him to escape if itt was posible. The trouble shee saw mee in prevailed so with her that itt made her say litle as to what I might expect of sevearity. And [she] tooke a coach and wentt imediately where shee thought itt most likely to doe him service; and itt proving butt a false alaruum served only to make him the more circumspect, and did affterwards something justify mee that I att that time owned to my sister my resolution of marrying him.

My brother's feaver increasing and his strengh decaying, a few days putt an end to his conflict; for as death was wellcome to him, so hee came peaceably as a friend and nott an enemy, for I beleeve never any died more composedly of a feaver in the strengh of there youth. Hee seldome or never raved nor expresed much of dissattisfaction att the usage hee had mett with; only once hee said, 'Were I to live a thousand yeares, I would never sett my foott within a court againe, for there is nothing in itt butt flattery and falshood.'

Affter my brother was buried in the Savoy Church neere my father and mother, within a few days I wentt againe to my brother Murray's, where I staid till the impertunity of my Lady H. prevailed with mee to goe home with her to the North. My brother and sister aproved of itt and C.B. most willingly consentted to itt, resolving sodainly to follow mee and then puplickly to avow what wee intended and to live with a gentleman, a friend of his that was a great Royallist, where hee expected to bee wellcome till such time as wee found itt convenient for us to returne where wee had more interest. This beeing determined, I left all that concerned mee in such hands as hee advised, with hopes of preventing sequestration, butt itt fell outt unhapily, as many things els did, and occationed greater inconvenience.

One of the great motives that invited mee to goe north was that it began to bee discoursed of amongst many Parliamentt men that I had beene instrumentall in the Duke's escape, and knowing that severall weemen were secured upon lese ground, I thought itt best to retire for a time outt of the noise of itt. It was nott withoutt trouble that I left my brother and sister, butt finding itt nesesary made itt the more easy. Wee began our journy September 10th, 1649, and had nothing all the way to disturbe us till wee came to H., beyond Yorke, to a howse of Sir C. H. where his sisters lived. There in one night both Sir C. and his lady fell so extreamely ill, with vomitting and purging in so great violence [that] nothing butt death was expected to them both, and some were so ill natured as to say they were poisoned, butt it pleased God they recovered. And then there son tooke the small poxe, who was aboutt 3 years old, his feaver great and apearance of beeing extreordinary full; and by the advise of Sir Thomas Gore (who studied phisicke more for devertisement then gaine), hee tooke a purge which carried away a great part of the humour so that nature, as hee said, would bee able to master the rest, and itt had so good succese that hee recovered perfectly well withoutt the least prejudice. I cannott butt mention this from the extreordinarynese of the cure.

As soone as his health would allow of travaile, wee tooke journy and came to Naworth Castle, where I was so obleigingly intertained by Sir Ch. and his lady, and with so much respect from the whole familly, that I could nott butt thinke my selfe very hapy in so good a societty; for they had an excellentt governed familly, having great affection for one another, all there servantts civill and orderly, had an excellentt preacher for there chaplaine who preached twice every Sunday in the chapell, and dayly prayers morning and evening. Hee was a man of a good life, good conversation, and had in such veneration by all as if hee had beene there tutelar angell.

Thus wee lived sometime together with so much peace and harmony as I thought nothing could have given an interuption to itt. But itt was too great to last long, for the post (going by weekely) one day brought mee sad letters, one from C.B. giving mee accountt that just the night before hee intended to come north, having prepared all things for accomplishing what we had designed, hee was taken and secured in the gatehowse att Westminster and could expect nothing butt death. With much dificulty hee had gott that conveyed outt to mee to lett mee know what condittion hee was in, and that hee expected my prayers, since nothing els I could doe could be avealable; for hee had some reason to aprehend those I was concerned in and might have influence upon was his enemys, and therfore I might expect litle assistance from them. Presenttly affter I receaved a letter from my brother M. and another from my sister N., his very seveare, hers more compasionate, butt both representing C.B. under the caracter of the most unworthy person living, that hee had abused mee in pretending his wife was dead, for shee was alive, and that her unckle Sir Ralph S. had assured them both of itt; which made nott only them but all that ever had kindnese for mee so abhorre him thatt, though hee were now likely to dye, yett none pittyed him.

Had the news of either of these come singly, itt had beene enough to have tryed the strengh of all the relligion and vertue I had, butt so to bee surrounded with misfortunes conquered what ever could resist them, and I fell so extreamely sicke that none expected life for mee. The care and concerne of Sir Ch. and his lady was very great, who sentt post to Newcastle for a phisitian; butt hee beeing sicke could nott come, but sentt things which proved ineffectuall. My distemper increased, and I grew so weake that I could hardly speake. Aprehending the aproach of death, I desired my Lady H. to vindicate mee to my brother and sister, for as I was ignorant and inocentt of the guilt they taxed mee with, and so I beleeved C.B. was; and therfore I earnestly intreated her to writte to her father to bee his friend, and that malice might nott bee his ruine, which shee promised. And having taken my last leave (as I thought) of them all, I desired Mr. N. (the chaplaine) to recomend mee to the hands of my Redeemer, and I lay waiting till my change should come; and all was weeping aboutt mee for that I expected as the greatest good. Butt it seemes the mercy of God would nott then condemne mee into hell, nor his justice suffer mee to goe to heaven, and therfore continued mee longer upone earth that I might know the infinitenese of his power that could suport mee under that load of calamitys.

Having laine some houres speechlese (how I imployed that time may herafter bee knowne if the Lord thinke fitt to make itt usefull unto any), I began to gape many times one after another, and I found sencibly like a returne of my spirit; which Mrs. Cullcheth seeing, came to mee and told mee if I saw another in that condittion I could prescribe what was fitt for them, and therfore itt were a neglect of duty if I did nott use what meanes I thought might conduce to my recovery. Her discourse made mee recollect what I had by mee that was proper for mee. I called to Crew (who served mee) for itt, and with the use of some cordialls I siencibly grew better, to the sattisfaction of all that was aboutt mee. I confese death att that time had beene extreamely wellcome, butt having intirely resigned my selfe up to the disposall of my gracious God, I could repine att nothing hee thought fitt to doe with mee, for I knew hee could make either life or death for my advantage.

Though that was great disturbance to mee which my brother and sister had written to mee concerning C.B.'s wife's beeing alive, yett I gave nott the least creditt to itt because I thought there information might come from such as might report itt outt of malice or designe; for none of her relations loved him because hee was nott of there principles. And a considerable part of her portion beeing still in there hands, I judged itt might bee still to keepe that they raised that story; which had litle influence upon mee, because I gave itt noe beleefe, only looked upon itt as a just punishmentt to have that thought true now which I once mentioned when I thought itt nott true, only to conceale my intentions. For my Lord H. and my sister Murray (having observed C.B. come sometimes when hee durst steale abroad to see mee) said to mee one night, 'I lay a wager you will marry C.B.' I smiled and said, 'Sure, you would nott have mee marry another woman's husband.' They replied they knew nott hee had beene maried, upon which I told them whose niece shee was (whom they both knew) that was his wife. Butt I did nott say shee was dead, though att that time I beleeved itt, and therfore now looked on this as inflicted for my disimulation; for God requireth truth in the inward parts, and I have a thousand times beged his pardon for that failing.

Upon these grounds itt was that I gave so litle intertainmentt to that story. And all my trouble and feares was after I began to recover for C.B., lest the Parliamentt should condemne [him] to dye as they had many gallant gentlemen before; butt I was much suported one day by reading what fell outt to be part of my morning devotion, Psalm 102, verses 19, 20, '*For hee hath looked downe from the height of his sanctuary; from heaven did the Lord behold the earth; to heare the groaning of the prisoner; to loose those that are apointed to death.*' I cannott omitt to mention this because itt was so seasonable a promise, and I was so asisted by faith to rely upon itt that in a manner itt overcame all my feares. To confirme itt is nott in vaine to beleeve and expect promised mercys, within few days there came severall letters both to Sir C. H., his lady, and my selfe that C.B. had made his escape outt of the gatehowse just the night before hee was to have beene brought to his tryall.

None then could give accountt how or by what meanes hee had gott outt, butt affterwards I was informed by the person hee imployed that, having with much dexterity conveyed into him a glase of aqua fortis, hee with that and much paines cutt the iron bars of the window asunder, butt lett itt stand by a litle hold till the time was fitt to make use of itt. And then, having found meanes to apointt such as hee relyed upon to bee under the window att such a time as the guards were past that tour, hee tooke the ropes of the bed and fastnened them to some part by the window and so wentt downe by them, butt his weight made them faile and hee fell downe not withoutt hurt. Butt the next dificulty was a pailing that was aboutt the verge of the window, butt his asistants by standing upon one another's shoulders reached over to him and gott him over the pailing, and so escaped the fury of his enemys; which many was glad of and more had joyned with them if they had nott beene posesed with a prejudice against him for the injury they suposed hee had done mee in persuading mee his wife was dead when shee was alive.

Butt hee nott beeing now in a capacity to vindicate himselfe, itt was easy to lay upon him what guilt they pleased; butt all that his enemys could alleadge never prevailed with mee to lessen one graine of my concerne for him, because all they could say was the report that shee was living, butt they never named the person that could testify itt from there owne knowledge except such as might bee biased by what I have mentioned allready. I cannot butt acknowledge I had great sattisfaction in the news of his escape, and though I was sometimes disturbed because I heard nott from him where hee was or how, yett I pleased my selfe with the hopes hee was well and secure; and so the better dispenced with my wantt of letters, since I knew hee could nott convey them withoutt hazard of beeing discovered.

Itt is nott to bee imagined by any pious, vertuous person (whose charity leads them to judge of others by themselves) butt that I looked upon itt as an unparaleld misfortune (how inocentt so ever I was) to have such an odium cast upon mee as that I designed to marry a man that had a wife, and I am sure none could detest mee so much as I abhored the thought of such a crime. I confese I looked upon itt as the greatest of afflictions, butt that I might nott sett limitts to my selfe, the Lord thought fitt to shew hee could make mee suffer greater and yett suport mee under them.

The first Sunday that my health and strengh would permitt mee to goe outt of my chamber, I went to the chapell in the morning (with the rest of the familly) to offer up thanksgiving to my God who had raised mee from the gates of death, and after dinner retiring into my chamber as I usually did, the doore beeing locked and I alone, I was reading a sermon with which I was very well pleased; butt on a sodaine I was so disordered and in so great an agony that I thought it nott fitt to bee alone, and all the servants beeing att dinner and none within my call, I wentt imediately to Mr. N.'s chamber, who was much surprised seeing mee come in so much disordered. I freely told him every circumstance, imagining hee was a person fitt to intrust with any disorder of my soule, and desired his prayers, which the Lord blest with so good succese that I imediately left trembling and found a great serenity both of mind and body. Having given him thankes for the great concerne hee shewed for mee and had his promise to conceale what I had comunicated to him, I left him to goe and make my selfe ready for attending my Lady H. to the chapell, thinking my selfe as secure of what I had said to him as if itt had beene within my owne breast; where itt should have beene still if I had then beene aquainted, as I have been offten since, with the effects of melancholy vapours, butt having never knowne them before in others or my selfe made them apeare the more dreadfull. But those who have experience of them will I hope have the more charity for mee when they consider what effects they have had upon themselves.

I am sory I cannott relate my owne misfortunes withoutt reflecting upon those who was the occation of them, especially beeing one of that profesion that I have ever looked upon with great respect. I have allready given a caracter of Mr. N.'s parts and practise and how much hee was valued by all the familly and such as conversed with him. One day he having preached att Carlile att the meeting for the sise, when hee came home hee came to my chamber and told mee hee had left Sir Charles and came home with Mr. Culc. who had intertained him by the way with many variety of discourse. 'Butt amongst the rest (said hee), hee tells mee that my Lady H. is jelouse of Sir Ch. and you.'

I was strangely surprised to heare that, and said, 'Sure hee was drunke, for as I am sure I never gave her the least occation, so I am confidentt shee knows her owne interest so great in Sir Ch. that shee need nott feare beeing suplanted by any. And besides, shee knows all the concerne I can have for any is allready fixed and that may secure her were there nothing els; butt I am very farre from intertaining the least thought that shee can have any such suspittion.'

'If I had itt (said hee), from any other hand I would thinke so too, butt noe doupt hee hath had itt from his wife, who you know was governese to her before shee was maried and is still intrusted with all her concernes.' Hee insisted much on this discourse and used many argumentts to confirme hee had reason to beleeve itt true, and withall that hee had observed of late shee was nott so kind to mee as formerly and that hee thought itt a strange thing that shee should use one so ill who had left all relations and friends to come to a remote place outt of kindnese to her.

I assured him I found nothing of allteration in her and that I was resolved to tell her what I heard (though nott the auther), and expected from the long friendship betwixt us that ingenuity as freely to owne if shee were guilty of the imperfection of jelousy; and that shee might dispose of mee how shee pleased in order to her owne sattisfaction.

'Can you imagine', said hee, 'that shee will owne to you shee is jelouse? Noe, shee hath too much pride for that.'

'What will you then advise mee to doe?' I replied.

'The truth is shee is of so odd a humour', said hee, 'that itt is hard in such a case what to advise. I hartily pitty Sir Ch. who I looke upon as one of the finest gentlemen in the nation; and had hee had the good fortune to have had you to have beene his wife, hee had beene the hapiest man alive.'

All I concluded att that time was that hee should bee free in telling mee what ever hee saw in my cariage that looked like giving ground for such a suspittion. With many serious protestations hee freed mee for giving any occation, butt dayly gave mee accountt of the increase of itt. To bee as short as the circumstances will allow, hee was never with mee butt hee magnified Sir Ch. up to the skys, spoke much to his lady's disadvantage, butt what hee said of mee was so greatly allied to flattery that I should have obhored itt from any other that had nott apeared as hee did.

Att last I began to observe my Lady H. grow more reserved then usuall and the whole familly abate much of there respect; only Sir Ch. continued as formerly to mee. I used dayly to bee till five a clocke with my

Lady H. working, or any other devertisementt that shee imployed her selfe in, and then retired to my chamber for halfe an hower. Then Sir Charles and his lady came and staid with mee (till the time wee wentt to the chapell), either playing on the gitarre or with the chilldren that lay neere mee or discoursing, and this was for a long time our constant practice. Butt on a sodaine I found an allteration, for my Lady H. would come to the doore with Sir C., butt when hee came in shee wentt into the chilldren's chamber; which I observing followed her and left Sir C. in my chamber.

One night as I was thus going outt to follow his lady, hee pulled mee backe and would nott lett mee goe, and the more presing hee was to have mee stay, the more earnest I was to goe; but seeing hee was resolute, I staid. Hee told mee hee had observed of late that I was growne very strange to him and that when ever hee came in I wentt outt of my chamber. I said it was only to waite upon his lady, and therfore hee could nott take itt ill. Hee saw mee in great disorder and was very urgentt to know what the reason of itt was. I confese the teares were in my eyes, which hee seeing vowed hee would nott goe outt of the roome till I resolved him. I told him I would upon the condition hee would promise nott to speake of itt to any person and that hee would doe what I should desire. Hee said hee would if itt were in his power, and bid mee bee free with him.

I said, 'Sir, I confese I have receaved much civility from you ever since I came into your familly, and as I know you shewed itt as a testimony of your affection to your lady because I had an interest in her faver, so I valued itt upon that accountt and nott as I beleeved I deserved itt. But now I must desire you, as you respect your selfe, as you love your lady, or have any regard to mee, retrench your civility in to more narow bounds, els you may prejudice your selfe in the opinion of those who thinke mee unworthy your converse.'

Hee grew angry and said hee must know who those persons were. I said hee must pardon mee, for that itt was enough I had told him how hee might preventt an inconvenience, and if hee either devulged what I had said or did nott performe the condittion in doing what I desired, I would goe outt of his howse upon the first discovery.

I left him after I said this and wentt to his lady, who sometimes would bee free enough, another time so reserved as shee would hardly speake to mee, either att table or any other time, which made mee then give the more creditt to what Mr. N. had told mee of her. Butt againe I was att a stand when beeing alone with her one day shee told mee shee knew nott what to thinke of Mr. N., butt shee bid mee bee upon my guard when I conversed with him, for shee assured mee hee was nott my friend so much as I beleeved. I thanked her for her advise, butt knew nott what to conclude, because hee had posesed mee with an opinion that shee was lesened in her respect to him because hee was so civill to mee. Butt this I concealed from her, knowing itt was upon another ground, which may nott bee amisse to insertt here.

There was two young ladys in the howse who had beene bred up Papists and by Sir Ch.'s example and care was turned Protestants. These two Sir C. recomended to Mr. N.'s care to instruct them in the principles of our relligion, and they dayly wentt to his chamber, sometimes together, sometimes alone, as there conveniency led them. They, beeing very young and hugely vertuous and inocentt, and having Sir C.'s order for going frequently to his chamber, thought the oftener they wentt the better, and sometimes affter super would goe and stay there an hower or two. They had a discreet woman attended them who I had recomended. Shee came to mee one morning and told mee shee could nott butt aquaint mee with something that shee would seeke my advise in. I said I should give itt freely.

Says shee, 'You know I am intrusted with the care of these young ladys and that Sir Ch. orders them to goe frequently to Mr. N.'s chamber. Butt I have observed the eldest of them stay much longer then the other and to goe affter super and sometimes stay there till 12 a clocke, and though I have gone severall times to call her, yett shee would nott come with mee.'

I said I was sory to heare that, for though I did beleeve shee might as inocently converse with him as with her brother, yett itt might give occation of reflection upon them both, which I wished might bee prevented, butt withoutt saying anything to Sir Ch. or his lady.

This fell outt to bee aboutt the begining of my Lady H.'s growing a litle reserved to mee; butt when ever I had any opertunity of converse with her, I still brought in some discourse of love and friendship and jelousy, and that sometimes itt might bee where there was greatest intimacy, butt if I could have a suspition of any person that I thought worth my friendship, shee should bee the first person her selfe that I would declare itt to. For if shee were vertuous, there is nothing I could desire her to doe that she would omitt for my sattisfaction, and if I beleeved her vicious, shee were nott worthy my converse. I uttered this with more then an ordinary sence, which I thought made some impresion of her; and I thought I was fully confirmed, when early one morning shee came into my chamber before I was outt of my bed, and lying downe by mee, shee said, 'I have so much confidence of your friendship and discretion that I am come to seeke your advise and assistance how to manage what I have of late discovered, that if nott prevented will make great disorder amongst us.'

I tooke her in my armes with great joy and told her shee might as freely comunicate any thing to mee as to her owne hart, for I should bee fast in concealing and active doing what ever shee pleased to instrust mee with, beeing fully perswaded if shee were guilty of that imperfection of jelousy, shee was now come to aquaint mee with itt and to advise aboutt a remedy. Butt I was in a mistake; for shee told mee shee had of late made some litle observation that Mrs. F., who was the eldest of the two sisters, was looked upon more kindly by Mr. N. then was usuall with his gravity; which gave her the curiosity the day before when shee wentt outt of the dining roome affter dinner, all the company beeing gone, and remembring shee had left them two together, shee turned backe, and looking through the crany of the doore shee saw Mr. N. pull her to him and with much kindnese lay her head in his bosome.

I said that might bee very inocently done, though I confesed itt had beene better undone. 'For sure hee can have noe ill designe, beeing I beleeve a very good man, and shee is too much a child to thinke of marying her, though there were nothing els to object.'

Shee said shee was nott so much a child as her stature made her apeare, and therfore had great aprehensions that the respect Sir Charles had for him might incourage him to hope if hee could gaine her consentt to obtaine his. 'Butt if hee should have the least ground to suspect what I feare, hee would never suffer him in his sight. And if wee wanted him, you know', says my Lady, 'that in these times wee should find it deficult to gett one in his place who could so well discharge his duty to our sattisfaction, and yet so discreet as nott to give offence to those of a contrary judgementt such as most are hereaboutt.'

I accknowledged itt was true that her Ladyship said, and in my opinion itt would bee best for mee to speake (since her Ladyship would intrust none els with itt) to him aboutt itt. And I thought hee was so ingenious a person, and had offten profesed to have so great an opinion of mee, that I thought hee would nott conceale his intention from mee, and I should freely give her Ladyship an accountt of his answeare. I made use of this opertunity to insist much upon the sattisfaction I had in her long continued friendship, and that I hoped what ever my presentt misfortune was, yett that shee would make noe conclusions to my prejudice withoutt giving mee leave to vindicate my selfe; which shee promised and left mee, having ingaged mee to lett none know what had passed betwixt us.

The first conveniency I had I told Mr. N. that I was going to aske him a question and that I desired and expected hee would bee ingenious in resolving mee, because itt was nott to sattisfy my owne curiosity but outt of an intent to serve him, which I could nott doe if hee were reserved in his answeare. Hee seemed to bee surprised with this discourse, butt assured mee hee would bee very ingenious. I asked him then if hee had any inclination for Mrs. F. or any designe to marry her. Hee protested with much seriousnese hee had nott. I said I was very glad to heare itt, for now with the more confidence I could suprese the suspittion which some had of itt.

'But,' said he, 'what would you have done if I had confesed I had loved her?'

'Truly (I replied), I would have representted to you the prejudice you would have brought upon your selfe, for undouptedly Sir Ch., who is now your great friend, would turne your proffesed enemy and make all others so that hee had influence upon.' Therfore as his intentions was free from such a designe, so I desired his converse might bee suitable, and I would then indeavour to convince them of there error who aprehended what I had told him.

I gave my Lady H. an account of what discourse Mr. N. and I had, which shee was satisfied with; butt this was the ground upon which I knew my Lady H. had nott so good an opinion of Mr. N. as formerly, and therfore I could nott well know what to thinke when my Lady told mee, as I have allready mentioned, that hee was nott my friend so much as I beleeved, nor so good a secretary. I had the same information from her woman too (a discreet person who till that time loved mee well). I thought I would take a triall of him. And the first time hee came into my chamber, hee falling upon his usuall discourse, regretting to see my Lady H. so unkind to mee, I said I confesed I could nott butt looke upon itt as my greatest misfortune and such as swallowed up my former trouble; because to any one that should beleeve mee guilty of such unworthynese as occationed her unkindnese, itt could nott butt bee a confirmation of the crime laid to my charge with C.B. and the more unpardonable because ignerance in this could bee noe excuse. I said I would comunicate a secrett to him if hee would solemely promise nott to discover itt to any person living, which hee ingaged with all the protestations that was fitt for one of his proffesion. I told him I was maried, and if hee beleeved I understood what either love or duty tied mee to, that was enough to secure my Lady H. from her aprehensions, though I had never had a value for her friendship. (I confese I only told him this out of designe to try if hee would speake of itt againe and was indifferent whether itt was beleeved true or falce, since I hoped a litle time would make the discovery.) Hee seemed to bee highly sencible of the injury shee did mee, and at my request undertooke to tell her that hee had observed her unkindnese and, as much as was fitt for him, to prese for the reason of itt; which if shee gave, then to asert my inocence and the wrong shee did bothe to her husband and her selfe, and in this I thought hee would obleige both them as well as mee. This hee promised, butt how hee performed itt shall bee affter manifest.

I saw dayly my Lady H. grow now to that height of strangenese that when I spoke to her shee would give mee noe answeare, or if shee did, itt was with that slightnese that I could nott butt bee very sencible of itt. And that which angred mee most was that when ever Sir Ch. came where I was, hee was ten times more free in his converse then hee had beene before I had spoken to him. These two extreames with my owne presentt condittion was deplorable, having spentt all the mony I brought with mee, being in a strange place where I had neither friendship nor aquaintance with any. To London I durst nott goe for feare of beeing secured upon the accountt of the Duke's escape, and besides, I knew I need not expect anything butt unkindnese from my brother and sister; and how to send to C.B. to advise with him I knew nott. To stay where I was, I had noe manner of sattisfaction. And if I had knowne whither to goe, to leave that familly with such an odium as was laid upon mee could nott butt make mee unwellcome any where.

Thus when I reflected upon my disconsolate condittion, I could find content in nothing butt in resorting to the Hearer of prayer, who never leaves nor forsakes those that trust in him. To the God of mercy I poured forth my complaint in the bitternese of my soule, and with abundant teares presented my suplication to him that judgeth righteously and did know my inocence; and therfore I interceded for the meritts of my Redeemer that hee would deliver mee outt of the trouble that incompased mee round and direct mee how to dispose of my selfe in that sad exegentt that I was in. And having resigned my selfe wholy to the disposall of his will, I did with confidence expect a deliverance because I knew him whom I trusted.

By the way I cannott omitt to mention what was remarkeable the time I was in that familly. One night, beeing fast asleepe, I was sodainly wakened with the shaking of the bed, somewhat violentt butt of short continuance. In the morning I told Sir Ch. and my Lady that I had heard of earthquake butt I was confidentt I had felt one that night and related how itt was. They laughed att mee and said I had only dreamt of itt. I could nott convince them nor they mee, butt a litle before dinner came in some gentlemen that lived within 3 or 4 mile, and Sir Charles asked them what news. They replied the greatest they knew was that there had beene an earthquake that night and that severall howses were shaken downe with itt. Then they beleeved what I had told them.

Another day my Lady H. and I was sitting together alone in my chamber, aboutt an ell or more distant from on-another, and sodainly the roome did shake so that both our heads knockt together. Shee looked pale like death and I beleeve I did the same, and wee were hardly well recovered from our feares when Sir C. came in to see how wee were, and told us he was walking in the gallery with Mr. N. and that they were so shaken they could skarce hold there feett and was forced to hold themselves on the sides of the howse. These both hapened in the yeare 1649.

Butt to returne where I left, my Lady H.'s strangenese did nott make mee neglect any thing that I usually did before. And one Sunday morning I wentt to her chamber to waite upon her as formerly when shee wentt to the chapell. I found the doore shutt, butt heard her talke to her weemen, so I knockt. One of them came to the doore and asked who was there. When they knew itt was I, they said they could nott open the doore for there lady was busy. I thought this was a great allteration; however, I said nothing, butt wentt up to walke in the gallery, which was the usuall pasage to the chapell, till shee was ready to goe. I had not walked a turne or two butt Sir Ch. came to mee. I was in disorder, which hee seeing, asked what ailed mee. I told him I found hee had beene unjust to mee, and I should bee so just to my selfe in keeping my promise as that I resolved the next day to leave his howse, for I could nott suffer to live in any place where I had nott the faver of the owners.

'I know', says hee, 'that you take itt ill to see my wife so strange to you, and shee doth itt a purpose that you may inquire the reason of itt from her selfe, and then shee will resolve you.'

I said that should nott bee long in doing, nor had itt beene so long undone, butt that shee had avoided all occations that might give mee opertunitty of speaking to her. (Another reason which I did nott mention was that Mr. N. had used many argumentts to diswade mee from taking notice of itt to her, some of them nott much to her advantage.)

Wee went all to the chapell together, and affter sermon the post came with letters while wee were at dinner, some to them and some to mee. I made use of this when wee rose from the table to tell my Lady H. that I had receaved letters from London and that there was something of concerne I had to say to her Ladyship, and asked where I might have her alone. Shee told mee shee would come within a litle while to my chamber, where I wentt, and within a litle while shee came there, and I, taking her in my arms, kist her and wellcomed her to my chamber as a great stranger. So locking the doore, wee satte downe.

'Madam,' said I, 'though I made a letter the pretence for seeking this faver to speake with you, yett there is nothing in that worth your Ladyship's knowledge; and the only thing I have to say is to beg of you by all the friendship and kindnese you ever had for mee to bee free with mee and lett mee know what I have done to make you of late so unkind.'

'Truly,' said shee, 'I wondred you were so long inquiring, and resolved till you asked the question I would never tell you. Butt now you have begun, lett mee aske you how you could have the vanity to beleeve Sir Ch. was in love with you and I was jealous of you, and have the confidence to speake of itt to Mr. N. and speake so unworthily of mee as you have done to him this long time, as if I were the most contemptable creature living and that you pittied Sir Ch. for having such a wife? Was this done like a friend? Oh,' said shee, 'if I had nott had itt from Mr. N., who is so good a man that I cannott butt beleeve him, I should never have given faith to itt from any other person.'

I was, I confese, astonished to heare him given as the athour of that accusation, beeing all his owne words which hee had often used to mee as his opinion; butt itt seemes hee had represented them as mine. 'Madam (said I), I cannott wonder att that strangenese if you beleeved this true, butt rather how you could suffer such a one within your familly.'

'Had I followed Mr. Nicolls's advise,' shee replied, 'I had sentt you away long since. For hee prest itt often, and when hee could nott prevaile with mee, hee writt to my father from whom I receaved a very seveare letter for letting you stay so long with mee. This I now tell you plainely to confirme what I once told you before, that Mr. N. was nott your friend so much as you beleeved, nor I so unworthy as the caracter you gave of mee.'

'Madam (said I), I must accknowledge I did beleeve him my friend, and so excellentt a man that I thought, as all in your family did, that itt was a blesing to have him in the howse. Butt now so much the greater is my misfortune to have him for my accuser, who is so much respected by all and whose very proffesion would inforce beleefe. I love nott retaliation and to returne ill for ill, butt since I have noe other way to asert my owne inocency, I must freely declare hee was himselfe the only person that tooke paines to perswade mee you were jelouse of mee. And when I resolved to vindicate my selfe from what ever might seeme to give occation for itt, hee diswaded mee and said you had too much pride to owne itt and that you would butt laugh att mee and t'would expose mee to your scorne; and what hee related as my words were his owne which, when att any time I contredicted, hee would say itt was my partiality made mee defend you and nott my reason. This, madam, is so great a truth that I will owne itt before him when ever you find itt convenient. Butt pray, madam (said I), when hee told you all these things to my disadvantage, did itt nott lesen your beleefe of itt, comming from a person who profesed to have so great respect for mee and yett performing acts so contrary to itt? Did not this plead for mee in your thoughts, that hee who could disemble might be unjust and I inocentt?'

'I confese', said my Lady, 'itt did prevaile much on your side, and one day when hee was railing against you I said to him, "How comes you are so civill to her and profese so great an esteeme of her if you have so ill an opinion of her?" "I, an esteeme of her? (replied hee). I could nott butt bee civill to her because I saw Sir Ch. and your Ladyship respect her, butt, God is my wittnese, I never looked upon her butt as one of the ayreiest things that ever I saw and admired what itt was your Ladyship and Sir Ch. saw in her to bee so kind to her." '

I smiled and said, 'I wish I could as easily confirme hee was the auther of what hee related of mee as I can, under his owne hand, that hee had better thoughts of mee then "so ayry a thing" as hee then represented mee.'

She was desirous to see the letter, which I shewed her with the copy of my owne to which his was an answeare; and was the first letter that ever I copied of my owne, and fell outt well that I had itt, els his would nott have beene well understood. (The occation of itt was att the first notice I had of C.B.'s wife's beeing alive, before itt came to bee publickly knowne. Itt is nott to bee imagined butt itt putt mee in great disorder, and, having none I would comunicate itt to, I writt a serious letter to him representing something of [the] disorder I was in and earnestly desired his prayers, to which his letter answered; and were itt nott too tedious I should insert them both here.)

As soone as my Lady H. read the letter, she said, 'I am afraid this man hath deceaved us all and will prove a villaine.'

While wee were att this discourse Sir Ch. knoct att the doore. Wee let him in, and hee smiling said, 'I hope you understand one another.' Wee gave him some short accountt of what had beene betwixt us, which he said did confirme what hee had beene of opinion of a pritty while. 'But,' sayed hee, 'I will injoyne you both, what ever paseth betwixt you when you are alone, lett noe person know butt that you are still att the same distance you were before, till my returne; for I am imediately informed of some mose troopers that are plundering in the country, and I and all my men are going to try if wee can take them. Therfore you must pray for mee, since I cannott goe with you now to the chapell.'

Wee both promised to follow his injunctions and parted. Though I did what I could to conceale any thing of sattisfaction, yett the joy I had to see some glimps of light apeare for my vindication putt a visible change upon mee. And my Lady H. found itt dificult to restraine her former kindnese from apearing affter shee began to find shee had beene injured as well as I.

When Sir Ch. returned hee was a wittnese of many debates betwixt us. When shee considered what a person Mr. N. was, shee then condemned mee guilty of all hee accused mee of, butt when I urged the many yeares' experience shee had had of my converse and whether shee had ever knowne mee doe any unworthy act, then, when shee reflected upon that, shee condemned him. Butt, to bee short, shee concluded that itt was fitt to have her cleared from the aspersion of jelousy and the consequences of itt, which one of us had taxed her with, and none had more reason to prese that then I who suffred most by itt. Att last wee resolved as the fairest way, for mee to goe to Mr. N. and tell him that I was resolved to vindicate my selfe, and therfore to desire him nott to take itt ill if I brought him for a wittnese of my inocency, who was the first and only person that told mee of my Lady's beeing jelouse, and who had often assured mee hee saw nothing in my cariage that could give the least ground for itt. Sir C. had left us to our contrivance. And when wee were determined, I left my Lady H., and apointing the garden to bee our meeting place where I was to bring Mr. N., I wentt to his chamber, butt found him nott there.

I imediately wentt alone to the garden to the walke where my Lady H. and I had designed to meett, and in the way to itt I saw Sir C. and Mr. N. very serious together in a close walke. I tooke noe notice I saw them, butt wentt on to the place apointed, and while I was walking there I began to consider that itt fell outt well I had nott mett with Mr. N. alone; for hee, that had allready injured mee so much, might posibly alleadge that I had prevailed with him to take that upon him hee had never said, only to conceale my guilt, and so I might still bee thought what hee first represented mee. Therfore, I resolved to propose itt to my Lady H., when shee came, to goe together where Sir Ch. and hee was walking and there speake of itt to him before them. Shee aproved of my reason and resolution, and said itt was very likely hee might make such a use of itt. And that this way would bee more sattisfaction to her then the other.

So wee wentt together to the close walke where Sir Ch. and hee was walking together. (By the disorder I saw him in, I knew Sir Ch. had given him some hint of what was amongst us, and the reason hee gave his lady and I afterwards was because hee had nott a mind to have him too much surprised and knew that that meeting would nott bee for his advantage.)

'Mr. N. (said I), you could nott butt have observed a great strangenese from my Lady H. to mee a good while, and beeing noe longer able to suffer itt, I have presed to know the reason and, beeing informed of itt, I know itt is in your power to make the reconcilalition, and therfore I expect itt from you.'

'Truly, Mrs. M.,' replied hee, 'I shall bee very glad to bee an instrumentt in so good a worke.'

'Then,' said I, 'Mr. N., doe you nott remember that day you came from Carlile you told mee of a person that informed you my Lady was jealous of mee?'

'Noe indeed,' said hee, 'I remember noe such thing.'

'Itt is imposible', I replied, 'your memory can bee so ill, butt to make itt better I will beg leave of Sir Ch. and my Lady to whisper the person in your eare that you named, because I desire nott to disobleige him with this contest.'

They both gave leave and I whispered softly, 'Did nott you tell mee Mr. C. told you, and you were shure hee had itt from his wife, and so you could nott doupt the truth of itt?'

'I remember indeed', said hee, 'that I told you your cariage was such that if you did nott mind itt you would give my Lady occation to bee jelouse.'

I lifted up my eyes and hands to heaven and said, 'Good God, hath this man the confidence to say this?' I turned to Sir Ch. and my Lady and then repeated severall things allready mentioned wherin hee had condemned my Lady and magnified mee to a high degree of flattery. And I said, 'I confese itt is a great disadvantage I have to contest with such a person whom there is much more reason should bee beleeved then I. But, Sir, you are a Justice of Peace and therfore may lawfully take my oath, and I will most solemely give itt upon the Bible that hee did say these things to mee and insisted offten on them, and diswaded mee often when I was resolved to have justified my selfe to your Lordship.'

'And I (replied hee), will take my oath upon the same Bible that itt is nott true shee says.'

My admiration was such to heare him speake att that rate that I was allmost strucke dumbe, and all I said more was, very calmely, 'Mr. N., you have made more use of the Bible then I have done, and therfore perhaps thinke you may bee bolder with itt, butt I would nott sweare your oath to have Sir C.'s estate.'

Hee would have insisted, butt Sir Ch. and his lady interupted him and desired there might bee noe more of itt. I said I could say noe more then what I had offred, and I left my part to bee made evidentt by the great and holy God, who knew how I was wronged, and to Him I did referre my selfe, who I knew would doe mee right.

My Lady and I then wentt in, and Sir Ch. followed us. And when wee were together, every one freely gave accountt what caracter hee had given of us. My Lady and I hee had most equally balanced together; for what ever ill hee had said of mee to her, hee had said as much of her Ladyship to mee. And as hee indeavored to posess mee with the opinion of her beeing jelouse, so hee perswaded her that shee had reason for itt by my beeing desperately in love with Sir Ch. Sir Ch. laughed att this discourse and said, 'Hee hath beene so wise as nott to have [said] much of this to mee. Only once hee said that hee was sure you were in love with mee, and I could nott butt perceave itt, and I told him, as I was an honest man, I had never seene any thing like itt.'

'Well,' said I, 'then itt seemes in this hee had something of justice, that hee had a mind I should thinke as well of you in gratitude as hee would have your thoughts beene of mee; for hee gave you high comendations, and one of your excellentt qualitys was that you had a great value for mee, which I did then and shall still accknowledge I have receaved much more civilitys from you then I deserved, yett noe more then I might expect from any civill person in there owne howse who loved there lady and for her sake would obleege those shee loved. Itt was, Sir (continued I), upon this accountt that I both receaved and returned what you gave and I paid. And now, before your lady, I conjure you by all the hopes you have of hapiness here or heraffter, and as you would avoid all the curses threatned to disemblers, freely declare what I have ever done or said since I came within your familly that might confirme you of Mr. N.'s opinion of mee.'

Hee most solemely declared hee never saw noe ground for itt, and that that was the first thing which made him aprehend Mr. N. nott beeing what hee should bee, by the contradiction hee saw in that.

There was nothing more contributed to vindicate mee then the disorder which from that day apeared in Mr. N.; for itt was visible to the meanest in the howse, though few knew the reason of itt, because Sir Ch. had a respect for him and desired all should respect him, and therfore did as much as could bee to conceale what had beene amongst us. Some time affter this the sacrementt was to bee celebrated in the chapell, and I had many debates with my selfe what to doe. Att last beeing resolved, I sentt for Mr. N. to my chamber and told him itt was nott withoutt great disputes in my thoughts of the good and ill of partaking or leaving that holy mistery that had made mee send for him; and though hee had injured mee beyond a posibility of beeing forgiven by any as a woman, yett as a Christian I forgave him, and though hee had wronged mee, yett I would nott wrong my selfe by wanting the benefitt which I hoped for and did expect in that blesed participation. 'This (said I) I thought fitt to tell you that you may nott thinke I goe for coustume or formality, butt with a sence of both my duty and advantage; and lett nott my charity make you thinke litle of that fault, for withoutt great repentance, great will bee your judgement.'

Hee aproved much of my charity and would have said something to vindicate himselfe, butt I interupted him and desired him to consider what hee was goeing aboutt, and that itt would agravate his guilt to thinke to justify himselfe, since noe excuse could bee made. I instanced that particular that was an undenyable fault, which was his going imediately from mee to tell my Lady Howard that I had as a secrett told him I was maried. 'How can I butt suspect (said I) the truth of all you speake outt of the pulpitt, when you devulged that affter such solemne engagementts of secresy, which I only said for a triall of your fidelity?'

'O,' replyed hee, 'if you knew what temptation I had to make that discovery, you would forgive mee.'

'Itt was only to tell you that (said I) that I sentt for you. And againe I repeat itt, that I doe forgive you and pray God to make you penitentt for your sin that so you may obtaine mercy, and that your taking the holy sacrementt may nott bee for your greater condemnation. And this is all I have to say to you.' So hee left mee.

Affter the solemne tone of our devotion was over, I began seriously to thinke what way to dispose of my selfe, for though Sir Charles and his lady were returned to there former kindnese, yett I thought itt nott fitt to stay where I had beene so injuriously traduced. Therfore, to leave that familly I was fully resolved; butt where to goe I could nott determine.

In all this time I had never heard nothing of C.B., nor from him, which had beene trouble enough to mee, had itt nott beene overcome by the presentt trouble I was in, which made mee unsencible of what was att a greater distance. Butt noe sooner was I delivered from the sadnese and discontentts occationed by what I have now related, then a new misfortune arives. When I was hardly well composed affter one storme, another rises, which by the danger of others involved mee by sympathy and gratitude in great disturbance.

My sister writtes mee a long letter full of passion and discontentt, informing mee that a cosen of her husband's, an heire to whom hee was to succeed, was stollen away, and that affter much inquiry hee heard that the gentleman who had stollen her away had caried her to Flanders, and that shee had fled to a monestary to secure her selfe till my brother could come there to releeve her. And unhapily, in the same ship that hee wentt over in, C.B. was a passenger. And though hee was disguised, yett my brother knew him, and as soone as they landed, hee challenges him. They chose there seconds, fight, and my brother was wounded in the hand so dangerously that to loose the use of itt was the least that was expected. How sadly this surprised mee is nott to bee imagined, for I should have beene conserned in his misfortune though a stranger had occationed itt. Butt to thinke itt was upon my accountt and done by one I was interested in, these considerations did highly agravate my trouble and made mee conclude the same that my sister did in her letter, that I was the most unhapy person living. For I had nott only made my selfe so, butt brought misfortune upon all that related to mee. Yett in the midst of all these disconsolations, I cannott butt accknowledge I had a sattisfaction to know so worthy a person as my brother N. owned a concerne for mee, which hee would never have done (I was assured) if hee had beleeved mee vicious.

Within a litle while affter, C.B. sent an exprese to mee, who was one of the persons who had assisted him in his escape and could therfore give mee a true accountt of itt, and where hee was concealed till that unhapy time of the incounter betwixt my brother N. and him. C.B. knew very well I could nott butt heare of itt and that itt would very much afflict mee, and therfore hee writt a long letter in his owne vindication; and lest I should have a doupt of what hee said, hee referred the confirmation of itt to an inclosed letter, directed to mee, written by the two seconds and subscribed by them both, who had beene two collonells in the King's army. My brother's second I cannott for the presentt remember his name, butt C.B.'s second was Collonel Loe (who affterwards came into Scottland with the King).

The account they gave was this. When they were all foure in the place apointed, and there doubletts off, C.B. with his sword in his hand came to my brother N. and told him hee was never ingaged in any imployment more contrary to his inclination then to make use of his sword against him who drew his in the deffence of the person hee loved beyond any living. That hee knew nott butt what hee was going now to say might bee the last that ever hee should speake, and therfore as such hee desired to bee beleeved. Hee said hee did beleeve there was nott a more vertuous person in the world then I, nor did hee know his wife was living, and as this was true, so hee desired the Lord to blese him in what hee was going aboutt. So they fight, and had severall passes withoutt advantage to either, butt my brother receaving a wound in his hand and bleeding fast, the seconds ran in and parted them, C.B. extreamly regretting what hee had done and my brother seeming to bee sattisfied that hee had nott gott itt unhandsomely. This in short was the substance of there relation, which they concluded with a great complementt to mee. Though I never aproved of duells, yett if my prayers were heard for my brother's recovery, I thought this would nott bee to my disadvantage.

Butt that which pleased mee most was that C.B. had mett with my Lord Dunfermeline in Flanders (who with other Commissioners were sentt from Scottland to invite His Majesty home), and aquainting his Lordship with what had beene betwixt him and mee and justified himselfe as to what reports had beene made to his disadvantage, to obleige both him and mee, the Earle of Dunfermeline writt very earnestly to desire mee to come into Scottland, where the King intended to bee shortly; and therfore hee thought that would bee the most convenient time for mee to come, when I would have many friends to asist mee for the recovery of my portion which was in Scotch hands. C.B. seconded this, with many arguments to perswade mee to hasten my journy all that was posible while the road was cleare, for there was reason to aprehend that Cromwell would soone march thither with the army when hee heard the King was landed.

I shewed my Lady H. my letters and my resolution of obaying them, butt my dificulty was how to undertake the journy or live in a strange place, having litle or noe mony. Butt as to that, my Lady H. very generously said I need nott trouble my selfe, for I should nott wantt what mony I desired, nor horses and men to attend mee to Edenborough. I was nott then long determining of the day for my departure. And Sir Charles apointed an old gentleman, a kinsman of his owne, with others to bee ready to conduct mee (and shee that served mee) att the time prefixed.

The night before I was to come away I sentt for Mr. N. and told him hee should now have his desire in seeing mee outt of the howse, which was what hee had used many unhandsome ways to bring aboutt. And had itt nott beene for him, itt is posible I had left that howse with more regrett. Now I was likely to bee att a great distance from him, and therfore might expect hee would bee the more liberall in his discourse of mee, when I could nott vindicate my selfe. 'But,' said I, 'remember when ever you speake anything to my disadvantage you are heard by the Allmighty God, who will plead for mee, and your owne conscience (if you have one) will condemne you, for you know I am inocentt of those unworthy things you charged mee with.'

'I confese (replied hee) there hath some unhapy circumstances fallen outt that may seeme to give you reason for what you say. Butt I must suffer rather then vindicate my selfe to the prejudice of those under whose roofe I dwell; butt if ever I am so hapy as to see you outt of this familly, I shall then lett you see how much you have beene mistaken of mee, and to evidence what my thoughts are of you, I will give itt yuo under my hand that I doe beleeve you as vertuous a person as lives.'

I smiled att that, and with a disdainefull looke told him my vertue would have butt a weake suport if I had nothing to uphold itt butt a testimony from him. 'Noe (said I), I have a better hand to rely upon to defend mee, and such a one as will make you ashamed for what you have done, except you repentt. The respect I have to your calling and the benefitt I have had by your preaching and prayer shall keepe mee from devulging your faults, butt as you expect the Lord's blesing upon your ministeriall office and would avoid the beeing a scandall to itt, leave off the course you have begun with mee, lest if you practise itt on any other, itt may bring to remembrance the injury you have done mee and so agravate your future crime.' Affter I said this I left him and gave my Lady H. accountt of what I had said to him.

The next day I tooke my leave of my Lady and all the familly, and Sir Ch. with a good attendance wentt part of the way; and none in the familly butt gave some evidence of there concerne in parting with mee except Mr. N., who hardly wentt to the gate with mee, and for that was much censured by all, especially my Lady H., who had great expresions of kindnese to mee and said if that journy proved unhapy to mee, itt would bee a trouble to her as long as shee lived because shee was sure I had never undertaking itt so willingly if I had nott beene disobleeged where I was. I could nott contredict so great a truth, nor bee unsencible of her very great friendship, which was the more to bee valued because it had mett with so strong a tryall and yett continued firme.

The second night (Thursday, 6 June 1650) affter I left Naworth Castle I came to Edenborough and lodged at Sainders Peeres att the foott of the Canongate. I had discharged all that were with mee to tell my name to anyone till I could find outt some that I had formerly knowne in England. That night att super, the old gentleman beeing with mee and the Mrs. of the howse, and siting fast against mee, I could nott butt looke earnestly upon her, and I said, 'Mrs., I cannott butt have a kindnese for you because you have a very great resemblance of my mother.'

Att that shee clapt her hands and said, 'Nay, then I will never inquire any more who you are, for I am sure you are Will Murray's sister, for hee offten told mee the same.' Shee then informed mee of a kinsman of my mother's (who shee made her executor) that had beene att her howse that day, and shee knew hee would be glad to see me. And I was well pleased to heare of him and sentt for him to advise whether I should continue where I was or take a more private lodging. Butt hee told mee itt was a very civill howse and the best quality lay there that had not howses of there owne. When the gentleman and those that came with mee had rested some time and seene the towne, they returned backe againe with all the accknowledgements I was capable to make to Sir Ch. and his lady for there great civility and kindnese.

When I had beene two or three days in the towne I receaved a visitt from the Earle of Argile, who invited mee to his howse and the next day sentt his coach for mee, which I maid use of to waite upon his lady. When I came up staires I was mett in the outtward roome by my Lady Anne Campbell, a sight that I must confese did so much surprise mee that I could hardly beleeve I was in Scottland. For shee was very handsome, extreamely obleiging, and her behavier and drese was equall to any that I had seene in the court of England. This gave mee so good impresions of Scottland that I began to see it had beene much injured by those who represented itt under another caracter then what I found itt. When I was brought in to my Lady Argile, I saw then where her daughter had derived her beauty and civility; one was under some decay, butt the other was so evident and so well proportioned that while shee gave to others shee reserved what was due to her selfe.

Affter I had staid a convenient time I returned home to my lodging where, amongst severall persons that visitted mee, Sir James Dowglas came and earnestly invited mee to Aberdour to stay some time with his lady. Itt was too obleeging an offer to refuse, and upon the 15 of June I wentt with him and crosed att Leith to Brun Island. As soone as I landed, Sir James Dowglas had mee by one hand and the Laird of Maines by the other, and they bid mee wellcome to Fife; and imediately I fell flat downe upon the ground and said, 'I thinke I am going to take posesion of itt.' They blamed one another for having had so litle care of mee, butt what I thought then accidentall I have since looked upon as a presage of the future blesings I injoyed in Fife, for which I shall for ever blese my God, and the memory of that prostration shall raise in mee praise to the Lord of bounty and mercy while I live.

When I came to Aberdour I was led in through the garden, which was so fragrant and delightfull that I thought I was still in England. I intended to have stad there butt 2 or 3 nights, butt they would nott part with mee till the 22 of June, and then I returned to Edinburgh butt with a promise to bee back againe, which I made good the 27 day.

Aboutt this time the news came that the King was landed in the North and was comming south. I began to reflect upon my owne misfortune in the unhapy report that was of C.B.'s wife's beeing alive, and it was knowne to severalls aboutt the courtt what my concerne in him was. This, with the unhandsome and unjust caracter given both to him and my brother Will, made mee aprehend mightt make mee nott bee so well looked upon by the King as otherways I might expect. And therfore, to informe my selfe what reception I should gett, I sentt an exprese to Mr. Seamor, who was one of the Groomes of the Bed Chamber and who had beene fellow servantt with my brother Charles; and to him I writt representing the disadvantages I lay under and that I expected his friendship in advising mee whether I should goe to kisse the King's hands or forbeare, for I had much rather wantt the honor then receave it with a frowne. To which this was his answeare, dated from Faulkland the 17 of July 1650: 'I shal have only time to tell you that His Majesty saith that you shall bee very wellcome to him when-soever you will give your selfe that trouble, and that the world is too full of falce rumours easily to ingage his beleefe in any thing that shall bee to your prejudice; and I am very confidentt when you have spoken with him you will rest as assured of the esteeme that hee hath of you, as that I am upon all occations, your very humble servantt, H. Seymour.'

I was much sattisfied with this letter, and now my greatest concerne was to find outt a convenient time and place where to performe my duty. Butt I was soone putt outt of that dispute by the Counttese of Dunfermeline, who came to Aberdour to see her brother and his lady, and then told mee shee had receaved a letter from her lord aquainting her what day the King had determined to bee att Dunfermeline (where his Lordship had invited His Majesty) and injoyned her to give mee an invitation to bee there that day, as knowing noe place in Scottland I had more interest in, nor fitter for mee then there to attend the King. My Lady was pleased to second her lord's desire with soe many obleiging expresions that I could nott in civility have denied to obay her commands, though itt had beene contrary to my inclination. Butt knowing itt both my honour and advantage to bee presentted to the King in that noble familly, I accknowledged the offer for a very great favor and promised to waite upon her Ladyship the day apointed; which I made good by the assistance of Sir James D., who wentt along with mee, and wee came to Dunfermeline some three houres before the King's arivall.

Affter His Majesty had beene some time in the bedchamber reposing affter the journy, I waited upon my Lady Dunfermeline and my Lady Anne Areskine to kisse the King's hand, beeing introduced by my Lord Argile and other persons of honour, and the first person I saw in the bedchamber was one of them who my brother Will had told mee was his enemy. I cannott butt accknowledge I was att first disordered when I saw him, and the more that hee putt a question to mee to answeare which

I was obleiged either to dissemble or say what was very unfitt for the King to heare; butt I avoided both with that reason, because I was so neere, for the King heard my answeare and smiled. When I recollected the promise I had made my brother to forgive that person and never to quarrell with him for the injury hee had done him, I so farre made itt good that I had an opertunity that with much ease and unknowne I could have had him putt from the court att that time when many were dismissed that had come home with the King; for a person who had great influence upon those who then governed inquired of mee particularly concerning him, of whom I gave so faverable a caracter that hee was continued to attend His Majesty.

During the time the King continued at Dunfermeline, which was 8 or ten days, beeing royally intertained by the Earle of Dunfermeline and all those who attended His Majesty, every day I waited upon my Lady and her neece when they wentt to attend the King either att dinner or super. And though att those times hee was pleased to looke faverably upon mee, yett itt was noe more then what hee did to strangers. This did much trouble mee, and therfore, the day before the King was to goe from Dunfermeline, I sentt for Mr. Harding in the morning to my chamber and told him though my aquaintance with him was butt of a short date, yett for the friendship I heard hee had for my brother Charles, who was his fellow-servant, I made choice of him whose age and experience might make more sencible (of what I could nott butt regrett) then those whose youth made them unconcerned in any trouble that was nott there owne. I then vindicated my brother Will from the aspersion hee lay under, and which I am confidentt occationed his death, and representted my owne misfortune, which posibly I might have avoided if I had not ingaged in serving His Highnese, the Duke of Yorke, in his escape, many circumstances attending that having contributed to my present suffering both as to my fame and fortune. For beeing nesesitate to leave London for my owne security, itt was easy for the malicious to deprive mee of both when I was nott in a capacity to speake in my owne defence. 'And affter all this (said I), itt is an agravation of my trouble to see the King never take notice of mee, which may bee a great discouragementt to those persons of honor who have beene very civill to mee to continue so, when they see mee so litle regarded by His Majesty.' I could nott utter this withoutt teares, in which the good old gentleman did keepe mee company, expresing a very great respect for mee, and promised to speake to the King and give an accountt of what I had said.

The next day presenttly affter the King had dined, when His Majesty had taken leave of my Lady Dunfermeline and given her a complementt and my Lady Anne Areskine (her lord's neece), hee came to mee and said, 'Mrs. Murray, I am ashamed I have beene so long a'speaking to you, butt itt was because I could nott say enough to you for the service you did my brother. Butt if ever I can command what I have right to as my owne, there shall bee nothing in my power I will nott doe for you.' And with that the King laid his hand upon both mine as they lay upon my breastt. I humbly bowed downe and kist His Majesty's hand, and said I had done nothing butt my duty, and had recompence enough if His Majesty accepted of itt as a service and allowed mee his favor. Affter some other discourse which I have forgott, the King honored mee with the farwell hee had given the ladys and imediately wentt to horse.

As soone as the King parted from mee, there came two gentlemen to mee; one tooke mee by one hand, the other by the other, to lead mee outt (to the court where all the ladys wentt to see the King take horse), with so many flattering expresions that I could nott butt with a litle disdaine tell them I thought they acted that part very well in *The Humourous Lieutenant*, whene a stranger comming to see a solemnity was hardly admitted to looke on by those who affterwards troubled her with there civility when they saw the King take notice of her. This answeare putt them both a litle outt and made them know I understood there humour.

To allay the joy that all the Loyall Party had for the King's returne, there was two great occations for disturbance, the one beeing strenghened by the other: Cromwell comming in with an army when there was so great devissions both in Church and State, and such unsuitable things proposed for accomodation as I wish were buried in perpetuall silence. After the King had been invited to severall places and intertained suitably to what could bee expected, His Majesty returned againe to Dunfermeline, having ordered the forces to march; and one morning came letters from the army lying att Dunbar thatt they had so surrounded the enemy that there was noe posibility for them to escape, which news gave great joy and much security. Butt the sad effects made us see how litle confidence should bee placed in anything butt God, who in his justice thought fitt to punish this kingdome and bring itt under subjection to an usurper because they paid nott that subjection that was due to there lawfull King.

The unexpected defeat which the King's army had att Dunbar putt every one to new thoughts how to dispose of themselves, and none was more perplexed then I where to goe or what to doe. Againe my Lady Dunfermeline invited mee to goe north with her Ladyship, assuring mee of much wellcome and that I should fare as shee did, though shee could nott promise anything butt disorder from so sodaine a removall to a howse that had nott of a long time had an inhabitantt. I had much reason to accept of this offer with more then an ordinary sence of God's goodnese; for there could nott have beene a more seasonable act of generosity then this to a stranger that was destitute of all meanes that should asist mee in a retreat. I sentt my woman over to Edinburgh and writt to a lady who I had knowne from my infancy att London and another letter to the gentleman who was my mother's executor and from both I desired to borow what mony they could conveniently spare. I named the sum I desired from the lady, which shee very freindly sentt upon the note of my hand; butt my cousin excused himselfe because hee had it nott of his owne, butt said hee had spoken to Sir G. S., who had promised to lend mee 25£ sterling upon my note, which hee made good; and then I was the better sattisfied to waite upon my Lady Dunfermeline to the North when I was provided so with mony as thatt I should bee the lese troublesome to her Ladyship.

Upon Satturday, the 7 of September, wee left Dunfermeline and came that night to Kinrose, where wee staid till Monday. I cannot omitt to insert here the opertunitty I had of serving many poore wounded soldiers; for as wee were riding to Kinrose I saw two that looked desperately ill, who were so weake they were hardly able to goe along the high way; and inquiring what ailed them, they told mee they had beene soldiers att Dunbar and were going towards Kinrose, if there wounds would suffer them. I bid them when they came there inquire for the Countese of D.'s lodging and there would bee one there would drese them. Itt was late, itt seemes, before they came, and so till the next morning I saw them nott, but then they came, attended with twenty more. And betwixt that time and Monday that wee left that place, I beleeve threescore was the least that was dresed by mee and my woman and Ar. Ro., who I imployed to such as was unfitt for me to drese; and besides the plaisters or balsom I aplied, I gave every one of them as much with them as might drese them 3 or 4 times, for I had provided my selfe very well of things nesesary for that imploymentt, expecting they might bee usefull.

Amongst the many variety of wounds amongst them, two was extreordinary. One was a man whose head was cutt so that the [ ] was very visibly seene and the watter came bubling up, which when Ar. R. saw hee cried outt, 'Lord have mercy upon thee, for thou art butt a dead man.' I seeing the man who had courage enough before begin to bee much dishartened, I told him hee need nott bee discouraged with what hee that had noe skill said, for if itt pleased God to blese what I should give him hee might doe well enough; and this I said more to harten him up then otherways, for I saw itt a very dangerous wound. And yett itt pleased God hee recovered, as I heard affterwards, and wentt frankly from dresing, [I] having given him something to refresh his spiritts. The other was a youth aboutt 16 that had beene run through the body with a tuke. Itt wentt in under his right shoulder and came outt under his left breast, and yett [he] had litle inconvenience by itt, butt his greatest prejudice was from so infinitt a swarme of creatures that itt is incredible for any that were nott eye wittneses of itt. I made a contribution and bought him other cloaths to putt on him and made the fire consume what els had beene unposible to distroy.

Of all these poore soldiers there was few of them had ever beene drest from the time they receaved there wounds till they came to Kinrose, and then itt may bee imagined they were very noisome; butt one particularly was in that degree who was shott through the arme that none was able to stay in the roome, butt all left mee. Accidentally a gentleman came in, who seeing mee (nott withoutt reluctancy) cutting off the man's sleeve of his doublet, which was hardly fitt to bee toutched, hee was so charitable as to take a knife and cutt itt off and fling [it] in the fire.

When I had dresed all that came, my Lady D. was by this time ready to goe away, and came to St. Johnston that night where the King and court was. My Lady A. A. and I waited upon my Lady into her sister the Countese of Kinowle, and there my Lord Lorne came to mee and told mee that my name was offten before the Councell that day. I was much surprised, which his Lordship seeing kept mee the longer in suspence. Att last hee smiling told mee there was a gentleman (which itt seemes was hee that had cutt off the man's sleeve) that had given the King and Councell an accountt of what hee had seene and heard I had done to the poore soldiers; and representing the sad condittion they had beene in withoutt that releefe, there was presenttly an order made to apointt a place in severall townes and chirugions to have allowance for taking care of such wounded soldiers as should come to them. And the King was pleased to give mee thankes for my charity. I have made this relation because itt was the occation of bringing mee much of the devertissements I had in a remotter place.

Upon Thursday night, the 19 of September, my Lady Dunfermeline kist the King's hands and tooke leave of all her relations in St. Johnston to goe on her journy to Fivye. The first night wee lay att Glames, the next two nights att Brighon, upon Monday night att Donotter, the next night att Aberdeene, where we staid till Friday the 27, and that night came to Fivye, where I was intertained with so much respect and civility both by my Lady Dunfirmeline and my Lady Anne Areskene and the whole familly that I shall ever accknowledge itt with all the gratitude imaginable.

Affter I had beene there some time the King came to Aberdeene, and my Lord D. came home for a weeke to see his lady and told mee that Sir G. S. had desired his Lordship to lett mee know that some friends of his was to presentt the King with a purse with gold, and if I would imploy any that I had interest in to speake to the King for mee, hee doupted nott butt His Majesty would give mee part of the presentt. When my Lord returned, I writt of itt to Mr. Seamor, and att the first proposall the King was pleased to give order for sending fivety pieces to mee. Halfe of itt I paid to the gentleman that had formerly lentt itt mee, who had found this way to secure himselfe and obleige mee. And so I was free of that dept to my very greatt sattisfaction.

I had nott beene long injoying the tranquility of that retired condittion I was in, when I receaved a letter from C.B. that hee was att Aberdeene and desired to know if hee might have liberty to come and see mee at Fivye. I was alltogether averse to itt and used many argumentts to diswade him from itt, beeing positively determined nott to see him till hee could free himselfe of what hee was taxed with; for though I did not beleeve itt, [and though] hee had so fully sattisfied my Lord Dun. in Holland that his Lordship (as hee offten told mee) had nott the least doupt, yett I thought the safest way was to keepe att a distance till itt was past dispute. Hee so offten impertuned mee that at last hee prevailed, and having aquainted my Lady Dunfermeline with his desire and obtained her Ladyship's liberty, I gave my consentt; butt while the question was in debate the King returned towards Sterling; and hee attending (as the rest did) His Majesty, itt tooke up a considerable time before my answeare could come to him and hee come to Fivye.

Butt affter I had dispatched his footboy I began to have great debates with my selfe, and the conflict betwixt love and honor was so great and prevalent that neither would yield to other, and betwixt both I was brought into so great a distemper that I expected now an end to all my misfortunes; butt itt seemes the Lord had some further use for mee in the world and therfore thought fitt then againe to spare mee. What the trialls were thatt I mett with under that sickenese are knowne to some yett living, and the submission under them was, I hope, acceptable to Him that gave itt.

Before I recovered so much strength as to bee able to sitt up, C.B. came, whose sattisfaction in seeing mee was much abated to find mee so weake, and for seeming so douptfull of the reports concerning him. And since what hee had said to my brother N. (when hee thought itt might have beene the last moment of his life) did nott sattisfy mee, hee offred to take the most holy sacrementt upon itt that hee was inocentt if it should bee true that his wife was living, and gave so many reasons why itt should nott bee true that I could nott butt accknowledge pleaded much for him. I alltogether disallowed of making use of that sacred institution for the end hee proposed, since I did nott thinke itt warrantable; nor could itt convince mee of the untruth of the report, though itt might confirme hee was inocent of itt, and that charity inclined mee to beleeve. For hee could expect noe advantage with mee to countervaile the contrivance of so ill a designe, and I thought noe person could bee so ill as doe what's sinfull meerely because itt is a sin, and therfore I concluded either the report falce or hee miserably abused as well as I. Affter hee had staid two nights hee tooke his leave of mee, [I] having assured him ever to keepe a due distance with him till the truth were evidentt beyond any one's contradiction; and if I found hee had beene injured, hee might bee confidentt noe other misfortune under heaven should seperate mee from him when ever I found I might lawfully and conveniently make good what I had designed.

Itt would bee too tedious to relate here how I spentt the time I was att

Fyvie, which was neere two yeares, butt itt was so agreeably that in all my life I never was so long together so truly contented. For the noble familly I was in dayly increased my obligation to them, and the Lord was pleased to blese what I gave to the helpe of the sicke and wounded persons came to mee, part of them from Kinrose; and some English soldiers came to try my charity, which I did nott deny to them, though they had itt nott withoutt exhorting them to repent there sin of rebellion and become loyall.

The variety of distempered persons that came to mee was not only a deverttismentt butt a helpe to instruct mee how to submit under my owne croses by seeing how patientt they were under thers, and yett some of them intollerable by wanting a sence of faith which is the greatest suport under afflictions. There was three most remarkeable of any that came to mee: one, Isbell Stevenson, who had beene three yeare under a discomposed spiritt; the other was a young woman who had beene very beautyfull and her face became loathsomely deformed with a cancerous humour that had overspread itt, which deprived her of her nose and one of her eyes and had eaten much of her forhead and cheecke away; the third was a man that had a horne on the left side of the hinder part of his head betwixt 4 and 5 inches aboutt and two inches long, and his wife told mee shee had cutt the lengh of her finger off (as shee usually did) when, two or three days before, he came to mee because the weight of itt was troublesome. A further accountt of these may bee had herafter if itt bee nesesary.

The misfortune in the King's affaires gave his enemys the greater advantage, and was a discouragementt to the Loyall Party to see how succesfull Cromwell's army was, who now marched where they pleased and gave laws to the whole kingdome. The Earle of D., beeing left behind the King (when His Majesty marched into England) with others of the Councell to order what was fitt to bee done in His Majesty's absence, they were soone putt from actting any thing and was forced to suffer what they could nott preventt. Butt as long as they had any retreat, they still retired to bee outt of there enemy's hands; and my Lord D. came to Fyvie, and when the army came to Aberdeene, hee wentt to Muray, till hee could make some capitulation for himselfe; for when noe resistance could bee made, the next remedy was to make as good condittions as every one could for themselves.

The army comming now towards Fyvie, some scattering soldiers came in there who had noe officer butt one they made amongst themselves and called him Major. When they came into the howse they were very rude, beating all the men came in there way and frighting the weemen and threatening to pistoll who ever did nott give what they called for. My Lady Dunfermline, beeing then great with child, was much disordered with feare of there insolence, and with teares in her eyes desired mee to goe and speake to them to see if I could prevaile with them as beeing there countrywoman. 'Butt,' says shee, 'I know nott well how to desire itt, because I heare they say they are informed there is an English woman in the howse, and if they get her, they will bee worse to her then any.' 'Madam,' said I, 'if my going to them can doe your Ladyship service, I will take my hazard, and had gone to them before, butt that I thought itt nott fitt for mee in your Ladyship's howse to take upon mee to say any thing to them till I had your Ladyship's command for itt.'

Then calling my woman I wentt downe where they were, and beeing instructed which was the Major (as they called him), who ordered the rest as hee pleased (and I beleeve gott that authority by humouring them in all they desired), I made my adrese first to him, beleeving if I prevailed with him, the rest were soone gained. As soone as I came amongst them, the first question they asked mee was if I were the English whore that came to meett the King, and all sett there pistolls just against mee. (I had armed my selfe before by seaking assistance from Him who only could protect mee from there fury, and I did so much rely upon itt that I had nott the least feare, tho naturally I am the greatest coward living.) I told them I owned my selfe to bee an English woman and to honor the King, butt for the name they give mee, I abhorred itt; butt my comming to them was nott to dispute for my selfe, butt to tell them I was sorry to heare that any of the English nation, who was generally esteemed the most civill people in the world, should give so much occation to bee thought barbarously rude as they had done since there comming into the howse, where they found none to resist them, butt by the contrary, what ever they called for, either to themselves or horses, was ordered by my Lady to bee given them.

'What advantage', said I, 'can you propose to your selves to fright a person of honor who is great with child, and few butt chilldren and weemen in the howse? And if by your disorder any misfortune hapen to my Lady or any belonging to the familly, you may expect to bee called to an accountt for itt, because I am very confidentt you have noe allowance from your officers to bee uncivill to any. And I am sure itt is more your interest to obliege all you can then to disobliege them, for the one will make you loved, the other hated, and judge which will bee most for your advantage.'

They heard mee with much patience, and att last, flinging down there pistolls upon the table, the Major gave mee his promise that neither hee nor any with him should give the least disturbance to the meanest in the familly, only desired meatt and drinke and what was nesesary that they called for. And they did so keepe there word that my Lord Dunfermeline was by there staying in the howse secured from many insolencys that were practised in other places.

A litle affter there came to Fyvie three regimentts with there officers, beeing commanded by Collonel Lilburne, Collonel Fitts, and Collonel Overton. My Lady D. inquired of mee, when shee heard they was comming, if I knew any of those, because shee would desire mee if I did to gett a pase for my Lord D. to have liberty to returne home. I said I had only seene Collonel Fitts when I was att Naworth Castle butt had never spoken to him, and if hee owned the knowledge of mee I would then indeaver to serve her Ladyship, butt if nott I would speake to those I had never seene rather then him. When they all came up to the dining roome and saluted my Lady D. and my Lady A. Arisken, when Colonel Fitts came to salute mee, hee lifted up his hands as beeing astonished to see mee there and came to mee with the greatest joy hee could exprese; and taking mee by the hand said to my Lady Dun., 'Madam, I must beg liberty to speake with Mrs. M. and give her accountt of her friends in England.'

So hee and I sat downe together att some distance from the rest, and hee gave mee a relation of all that had hapened in Naworth Castle affter my comming away; some things that I was sory for, even for Mr. N., who itt seemes had nott followed my advice, butt traducing a person (who came there presently affter I wentt away) who could nott suffer itt as I had done, but tooke a revenge suitable enough to the fault, though unsuitable to one of his function. And I cannott omitt to remarke that itt was performed in the garden nott farre from the place where hee so confidently denyed a truth, which I hope beeing punished there made him reflect upon his sin and made him penitentt for itt; and I have reason nott only to forgive him butt to thanke him for the injury hee did mee, since the Lord turned itt to my advantage.

When I found Collonel Fitts thus free and civill, offring mee any service in his power, I told him how much hee would obleige my Lady D., who was now neere her time, if hee would give a pase for my Lord to returne, which hee promised and made good when hee came to Elgin where my Lord was; for hee wentt to him and prevented his Lordship seeking any thing by making offer of all hee could desire.

That day the oficers wentt away, Collonel Overton sitting by mee att dinner said to mee that God had wonderfully evidenced his power in the great things hee had done. I replied, noe doupt butt God would evidence his power still in the great things hee designed to doe. I spoke this with more then ordinary earnestnese, which made him say, 'You speake my words, but nott I thinke to my sence.'

'When I know that sence (said I then), I will tell you whether itt bee mine or noe.'

'I speake', said hee, 'of the wonderfull workes that God hath done by his servantts in the late times that are beyond what any could have brought aboutt withoutt the imediate assistance of God and his derection.'

'Sir,' said I, 'if you had nott begun this discourse, I had said nothing to you; butt since you have desired my opinion (which hee did) of the times, I shall very freely give itt upon the condittion that what ever I say, you may nott make use of itt to the prejudice of the noble familly I live in, for I can hold my toung butt I cannott speake any thing contrary to what I thinke. I cannott butt confese you have had great succese in all your undertakings, butt that's noe good rule to justify ill actions. You pretend to great zeale in relligion and obedience to God's words. If you can shew mee in all the Holy Scripture a warrant for murdering your lawfull King and banishing his posterity, I will then say all you have done is well and will bee of your opinion. Butt as I am sure that cannott be done, so I must condemne that horrid act and what ever is done in prosecution of itts vindication.'

He replied that those who had writt upon the prophesy of Daniell shewed that hee foretold the distruction of monarky many yeares since, and that itt was a tiranicall governmentt and therfore fitt to bee destroyed.

'How comes (said I) you have taken the power from the Parliamentt and those succesive interests that have governed since you wanted the King?'

'Because,' said hee, 'wee found after a litle time they began to bee as bad as hee, and therfore wee changed.'

'And,' said I, 'so you will ever find reason to change what ever governmentt you try till you come to beg of the King to come home and governe you againe, and this I am as confident of as I am speaking to you.'

'If I thought that would bee true (replied hee), I would repentt all that I have done.'

'It will come to that, I dare assure you,' said I, 'and the greatest hinderance will bee that you thinke your crimes have beene such as is imposible hee should forgive you. Butt to incourage you I can assure you there was never any prince more inclined to pardon nor more easy to bee intreated to forgive.'

'Well,' says hee, 'if this should come to pase, I will say you are a prophetese.' Here we broke off because wee saw the rest of the table take notice of our seriousnese. I found affterwards hee was nott unsattisfied with my discourse, for hee came severall times to see mee when I came to Edinburgh and remembred many things I had said to him which I have now forgott.

When the whole kingdome was now brought under the bondage of the Usurper, and finding noe remedy butt to submitt till the Lord thought fitt to give them deliverance, every one thought now of returning where there interest led them. And my Lord Dunfermeline having beene att Fyvie some time and staid till his lady was delivered of her daughter, my Lady Henrietta, and mending againe, his Lordship resolved to goe to Edinburgh aboutt his affaires, and I thought itt would bee a convenientt time for mee to returne then with his Lordship. Butt hee having first some occation to goe to Elgin, my curiosity to see that country made mee prevaile with my Lady Anne Areskine to goe with her unckle and lett mee waite upon her to Murray. Wee wentt from Fyvie, Wednesday, the 2d of June, 1652, and crosed the river Spey att the Boge; upon Friday came backe againe to Garmuth and crosed there the next day, and came home by Fordice to Fyvie.

Though I was resolved of my journy to Edinburgh, yett I was much troubled how to performe itt, for my mony was neere spentt, and having beene so long a trouble to my Lady D. I had nott the confidence to seeke to borrow any for carying mee south. Many deficultys in the way represented themselves to mee, and what I might meett with att Edinburgh, and my woman was weeping by mee as beeing much discouraged with the inconveniences shee aprehended I might bee exposed to. I smilled upon her and bid her have a good hart, for though my presentt condittion seemed very darke and cloudy, yett I was confident I should see a sun-shyny day. For though I was now incompased round with misfortunes, yett I was very sure I should bee as hapy as I could desire, though I could nott tell which way itt would come to pase; and for my presentt suplys I would rely upon God, who had never yett left mee in my greatest deficultys, and to his direction I resigned my selfe, beeing confidently asured hee would provide some unexpected meanes to free mee of my presentt trouble. And with that conclusion I wentt to bed with as quiett repose as if I had had nothing to disturbe mee.

The next morning early the midwife (who had come from Dalkeith to my Lady) came into my chamber with her riding cloaths on to take her leave of mee and said shee had a request to mee before shee wentt, which was (hearing that I intended to bee att Edinburgh shortly) that I would doe her the favor to take the mony shee had gott from my Lady and others att the christening and bring itt south with mee, because shee durst take noe more with her then her expences by the way, because shee aprehended beeing plundered by the soldiers. I told her if shee thought itt secure with mee, I should doe her that courtisy and deliver itt where shee would apointt att Edinburgh. So I receaved itt from her and gave her a note of my hand for itt, beeing about ten pound sterling, and shee wentt away very well pleased; butt litle knew how much more reason shee had given mee to bee so, for I looked nott on itt only as a presentt advantage, butt as a recompence for the reliance I had upon my most gracious God and an incouragementt still to doe so.

Itt was noe wonder if I had trouble to part with the noble familly att Fyvie, where I had beene neere two yeare treated with all the kindnese imaginable and where my sattisfaction was so great that I could contentedly have spentt the remainder of my life there if itt had beene as convenientt as itt was pleasing. Butt now itt was time to free my Lady of the trouble I had given her so long, and nesesary for mee to goe to

Edinburgh to looke affter what was my concerne and to begin a law suite for recovering the most considerable part of my portion. So having taken my leave of my Lady and my Lady A. Areskin and all the familly, not with dry eyes on either side (butt the teares that moved mee most was from that good old man Mr. George Sharpe, minister of Fyvie, and his wife, to and from whom I gave and receaved much respect), upon Thursday the 24 of June, 1652, my Lord Dunfermeline, with his nephew the late Lord Lyon and severall other gentlemen, wentt from Fyvie, allowing mee and my woman the honour of there company, and lay that night att my Lord Frazer's att Mohall; the next night att Northwatter Brig; and Saturday night att Belcarese, where we staid till Tuesday; that night came to Brunt Island, and Wednesday, the 30, to Edinburgh, where I wentt to my former lodging att Sainders Speers and staid there some time, till Sir Robert Moray and his lady came to towne, who lying att the Neither Bow perswaded mee to take a chamber neere them; which was an advantage nott to bee refused, having allso the conveniency of beeing neerer the place where all my busynese cheefely lay. The lodging they chused for mee was up the staires by John Meene's shop, belonging to a discreet old gentlewoman who had a backe way up to the roomes she used her selfe.

I had not beene there two or three nights when, my Lord Dunfermeline and my Lord Belcarese having supt with mee and gone away aboutt 9 a clocke, I sate up later then ordinary to write letters to Fyvie with one going there the next morning, and before I had quite done there came soldiers to the chamber doore and knockt very rudely. Att first I made them noe answeare, butt they knockt with that violence that I thought they would have broke up the doore, and then I inquired who they were and what they would have. They told mee they would come in and see who was with mee or what I was doing. I told them I knew noe warrantt they had for that inquiry, yett to sattisfy them I assured them there was none there butt my selfe and my woman. They told mee I lyed and that if I would nott open the doore they would breake itt open. I knew nott what to say or doe, butt I bid Crew (which was my woman's name) goe and desire the Mrs. of the howse to come downe. They, hearing the backe doore open, cried outt, 'Shee hath now lett them outt att the backe doore; goe and stope them', and with that they forced up the doore and run through the roome and some wentt up staires and some downe the staires, butt finding noe body they came in in a great chafe.

I asked them if they had found those they wentt to seeke. They said noe, for I had lett them outt. 'Gentlemen,' said I, 'you may assure yourselves I will complaine of you to your officers, for if I may nott have liberty in my owne lodging to sitt up and burne a candle as long as I please withoutt having such a disturbance, and upon such unworthy grounds as you would inferre, I thinke few will heare of itt that will nott condemne your uncivill actions.'

They seemed to justify themselves by an order they said they had to breake up any doores where they saw lights affter ten a clocke, and that they had beene civill and expected I would give them something to drinke. I told them when they deserved itt they should have itt, but sure they could nott expect itt from mee, having done as much as they could to bring a scandall upon mee that was a stranger newly come there, and therfore might bee the greater prejudice. They saw mee very angry, and that they could nott prevaile to get any thing, and therfore left mee in disorder enough to thinke what the neibours aboutt might thinke of mee to heare what they said and did att my chamber doore.

The next morning I sentt for W. Muray of Hermiston, who was very great with the English officers, and desired him to goe to there captaine and complaine, which hee did, and there captaine sent downe to refferre to mee there punishmentt, for they had noe allowance for what they did. I soone remitted there punishmentt, condittionally that they did nott practice the like againe. The noise of this came to as many persons' eares as I was aquainted with, and the disorder I was in by aprehending itt might bee usuall to have such alarums as long as I lay there, having a great window to the streett and none in the howse butt weemen, this made mee thinke of changing my lodging. Butt where to fixe I was undetermined when my Lord Twedale and my Lady very obleigingly offred mee the use of some roomes in his Lordship's howse, they beeing then to goe outt of towne and left only one roome furnished and a porter to take care of the howse. I accepted of the offer with very great sence of the faver, butt my next deficulty was where to borow or hire furniture for my chamber and my women's. That wantt was withoutt my seeking suplied by my Lady Belcarese, who very civilly lent mee all nesesary accomodations. So I removed my lodging into my Lord Tweedale's howse, which I had never had the offer of if the insolency of the soldiers had nott given occation for itt, and so I had an advantage by the prejudice they intended mee.

Affter I had beene some time setled I inquired for Mr. W. H., who was the lawier who (in my mother's life time had upon her asignation to mee of the bond of 2000£ sterling with interest from [16]47) began the suite in my name against Ar. Hay, who was caution for that sum with the Earle of Kinowle. A. Hay beeing now dead, I was to proceed against his executors. What the trouble and expence of that procese was is too tedious to relate here, butt in gratitude I shall ever accknowledge the obligation I had to my Lord Newbeth and his father, who I could never perswade to take one peny of mee, and yett they were as ready to asist mee with there advice and attendance to solicitte the judges as they who tooke most from mee. The great disadvantage I had was that my antagonist was very favorably looked upon by the English judges as beeing inclined to there principles, and they looked upon mee as a

Malignantt, and therfore they gave him all the advantage hee could desire against mee; which was by delays while hee secured himselfe by fraudulentt conveyencys of all the mony in good hands, and then they gave mee a decreet for recovering the rest. What I have now related in few words cost mee some yeares' attendance. Butt I shall leave what relates to that to mention some other particulars more to my sattisfaction.

Affter I had beene some time att my Lord Tweedale's howse, one Thursday my Lord Dunfermeline came to see mee and brought a gentleman with him who I had never seene before and told mee they had beene both dining with my Lady Morton, who was going to Sir John Gilmour's lady's buriall and had promised to call [for] them, and they had only so much time as to come in and aske how I liked my new lodging. I had scarce given an answeare when one came in to tell mee Mr. D. Dickson was withoutt. I wentt to the doore to bring him in, butt cheefely to aske one of my Lord D.'s servantts what gentlemen that was with his lord, who told mee itt was Sir James Halkett. I said, 'If hee had nott come with your Lord, I would nott have beene so civill as I am to him, because hee hath a sword aboutt him'; for all the nobility and gentry had that marke of slavery upon them that none had liberty to weare a sword, only such as served there interest and disowned the King, which made mee hate to see a Scotch man with a sword.

Mr. Seaton, who I was speaking to, smiled and said I was mistaken, for itt was only a sticke hee held in his hand under his coate that stucke outt like a sword, for hee was too honest a gentleman to weare one now. Going in again and seeing my error made mee change my thoughts of him. Presently affter, word came that my Lady Morton staid in her coach for them at the doore, and they wentt away. This was the first time I saw Sir Ja. Halkett, butt before Satturday night I had five visitts from him, every time making a severall pretence, either inquiring for Sir Robert Moray or my Lord D., or bringing some commission to mee from my Lady Morton. Hee was cousin german with Sir R. M., and much respected and very intimate with the other, and therfore I could nott butt bee very civill to him upon that accountt; and I saw noe reason butt that hee might challenge itt upon his owne.

After I had beene some time att Edinburgh I had a visit from one who had frequently beene att my mother's and was much obleiged to a neere relation of mine, and to him I told the deficulty I had to get any mony outt of England and the few I had interest in to borow of in Edinburgh, and hee very civilly lentt mee what paid the mony which the midwife trusted to my care and for other nesesary occations.

Beeing now setled and putt my affaires in such hands as would bee carefull of them in my absence, I resolved to goe into England and see my Lady H., having the conveniency of horses lentt mee by my Lord Dunfermeline's mother, who was extreamly obleiging to mee, and the more because shee knew I was a faithfull servantt to all that owned the King's interest, for shee was an extreordinary Royallist. Beeing provided with all things for my journy, and intending to goe first to the Fleurs, where I was invited by the Countese of Roxbery, to hasten my journy I receaved a letter from C.B. writt in cipher, giving mee accountt that after many hazards and deficultys hee was come to the North of England, where hee staid privately till hee could inquire where I was, and that I could advise him where hee might speake with Sir R. Moray. I gave him an answeare by the same way I receaved his and aquainted him with my intention of going to Naworth Castle, and apointed a day that I intended to bee att Anwicke, where if hee durst venture to come, I should then lett him know Sir R. Moray's opinion of the fittest place for to meett with him, for I had told Sir R. my designe and had his aprobation.

When I was come to the Fleurs and staid there two or three days, I wentt on my intended journy towards Naworth Castle, butt when I came to Anwicke, C.B. diswaded mee from going there because there was some there that I was nott desirous to see; and so I returned backe againe the next day and came to the Fleurs, where I staid till Crew came backe, who I sentt to Naworth Castle to bring my trunkes and what I had left there for wantt of conveniency to bring them with my selfe (when I came from thence). The intertainmentt I had att the Fleurs was so agreeable that I had noe reason to bee weary the time I was there, nor was I unsattisfied to returne to Edinburgh because C.B. was uncertaine how to dispose of himselfe till hee heard againe from mee. I gave Sir R. M. and my Lord D. an accountt of his designes, which was to waite all opertunitys wherein hee might serve the King, and if there were any probability of doing itt in Scottland, hee would then come there and hazard his life as farre as any could propose itt to bee rattionall. The advice they gave was to conceale himselfe where hee was for some-time, till they saw a fitt opertunity to invite him to Edinburgh, where they beleeved hee might bee secure enough since hee was knowne to very few there butt such as was his friends. While hee continued in the North of England I heard frequently from him and still gave him account of what hopes or feares there was of acting anything for the King, which I had the more opertunity to doe because my chamber was the place where Sir Robert M. most commonly mett with such persons as were designing to serve the King. Amongst the rest Sir James H. seldome missed to bee one.

Sir R. M.'s lady, beeing great with child and having noe convenient lodging where shee used to lye, desired some roomes in my Lord Tweedall's howse, which his Lordship readily granted to my very great sattisfaction, for I could nott desire the converse of any person more for my advantage; for shee was devoutly good withoutt shew or affectation, extreamly pleasing in discourse, civill to all, and of a constant cheerefull humour. Wee allways eate together, and seldome asunder any other part of the day except for convenient retirements, and though that howse was the rendevous of the best and most loyall when they came to towne, yett none was so constantly there as Sir James H. And though his relation to Sir Robert was ground enough for his frequentt beeing there, yett any that saw him in my company could nott butt take notice that hee had a more then ordinary respect for mee, which though I thought my selfe obleiged to him for, yett itt was a great trouble to mee, since I was nott in a capacity to give him such a returne as hee might expect or deserve.

And to preventt his declaring to mee what was visible enough, I resolved to give him an opertunity of beeing in my chamber alone with mee (which before I had much avoided) that I might putt an end to his beeing further concerned in mee. When hee came in and was sett downe, affter some generall discourse I told him I had beene very much obleiged to his civility ever since I knew him, and I looked upon him as so worthy a person that I could nott conceale from him the greatest concerne I had and my greatest misfortune, which was that when I had ingaged my selfe to a person who I was fully determined to marry, my brother and sister to diswade mee from itt found noe motive so strong as to indeaver to perswade mee that I was abused in beleeving his wife was dead, for shee was alive. And because I did rather beleeve him then they, this occationed there unkindnese.

'You may beleeve', said I, 'such a report could nott butt make mee thinke my selfe extreamely unhapy. Butt those whose judgementts I rely upon more then my owne, as Sir R. M. and my Lord Dun., who hath spoke with him, are so fully convinced that hee is injured that they chide mee when I seeme to have the least doupt of itt. Now, Sir,' said I, 'this relation may confirme I have a great confidence of your friendship, when I trust you with this and doe intend when hee comes here, which I shortly expect, to presentt him to you as one that I hope you will nott beleeve unworthy your knowledge.'

This discourse did strangely surprise him. Butt hee indeavored to hide his disorder as well as hee could, and said hee was sory for my brother's unkindnese and if hee were neere him hee would indeavor to reconcile him againe (for hee was well aquainted with him when hee was in Scottland); and for C.B., when ever hee came to towne hee would serve him to the uttmost of his power, for hee could nott butt beleeve hee was deserving since hee had my esteeme. Presently affter this hee left mee and I expected hee would have laid aside all concerne for mee, butt I soone found my mistake and that I was in an error when I beleeved hee loved mee att an ordinary rate, for itt was never more visible then when hee had least hopes of a recompence, and changed that affection to a vertuous freindship from which att first hee might have expected a lawfull injoyment.

Some time after this I was advised to writte to C.B. to come to Edinburgh, which hee did as soone as was posible affter the receit of my letter and had a lodging provided for him and his man in a private howse neere my Lord Tweedale's howse, where hee might come withoutt beeing seene upon the street. Every night in the close of the evening hee came in, and that was the time apointed where those persons mett with him who were contriving some meanes to asert there loyalty and free there country from continuing inslaved. Those who most frequently mett was Earle Dunfermeline, Lord Belcarese, Sir James H., and Sir G. Mackery of Tarbott, who Sir Ro. Moray had a great opinion of (though hee was then very young) and brought him into there caball as one whose interest and parts might make him very usefull to there designes. Affter they had formed itt in the most probable way to bee succesfull, they found itt nesesary to bee armed with the King's authority for what they did, and therfore sentt to aquaint His Majesty with what they intended and to desire commission for severall persons nominate and some blancke for such as might afterwards bee found fitt for the imploymentt.

A few days affter these letters were sentt (the materiall part whereof was writt in white inck and what was writt in ordinary incke was only to convey the other withoutt suspittion), Sir G. Mack. came in to dinner to Sir R. M. and told him hee had beene in a stationer's shop and, taking up a booke accidentally, the first thing hee saw in itt was derection to writt withoutt beeing discovered, and there found the same way which they had beene making use of in there adrese to the King; which putt them in some disorder, butt Sir R. M. said the only hopes hee had was that if that booke came into the English hands they would nott beleeve any thing so common as to bee in print would bee made use of in any busynese of consequence. Butt nott long affter they receaved an account of there letters comming safe to His Majesty's hands and a full complying with there desire in sending the commissions with a safe hand to the North of Scottland where those persons were to attend there arivall.

In the meanetime Sir G. M. was preparing for his journy north and C.B. was to goe with him under another name, for hee needed no other disguise, beeing knowne to none in the kingdome butt those persons I have mentioned who was too much his freinds and mine to have done him any prejudice. Amonst all his aquaintance none proffest more freindship to him then Sir James H. and made itt good in all circumstances wherein hee could make itt apeare, giving him severall presentts usefull for the imploymentt hee was going aboutt and a fine horse durable for service. C.B. understood very well upon what accountt itt was that hee receaved these testimonys of kindnese and did regrett the misfortune of nott having itt in his power to obleige him, for hee knew noe thing could doe itt more then his resigning his interest in mee; and that was nott posible for him to doe, though hee would often tell mee if any thing should arive to deprive him of mee, hee thought in gratitude I was obleiged to marry Sir J. H. I could nott butt owne a very great sence of his civilitys, butt nothing could bee more disagreeable to mee then speaking either in jest or earnest of my marrying him, for nothing butt the death of C.B. could make mee ever thinke of another (for what after fell outt I had noe beleefe of and therfore could not aprehend itt as a reason for my change). The day beeing come apointed for Sir G.M.'s and C.B.'s departure, some interuption interveened, and therfore itt was delayed for a time.

Upon Christmas day an English woman who had beene a servantt to my Lady Belcarese, (Sir R. M.'s lady's mother), according to the English coustome had prepared (in her owne howse where shee kept a change) better fare then ordinary, and amongst the rest a dish of minced pies of which, when wee were att dinner, shee brought over two and said one shee intended for Sir Ro. and his lady and the other for Sir J. H. (who was then there) and mee. All the table smiled att what shee said, butt I looked very gravely upon itt, and rather wished itt with him that had more interest in mee. All the company beeing in a better humour then ordinary, wee were all extreamely mery. A woman beeing in the howse called Jane Hambleton, who they say had the second sight, observing all very well pleased, said to my Lady M.'s woman and mine, 'There is a great deale of mirth in this howse to day, butt before this day eight days there will bee as much sadnese'; which too truely fell outt.

For within 3 or 4 days my Lady Moray tooke her paines, butt they all strucke up to her hart, and all meanes beeing unsuccesfull shee died with as much regrett as any person could have. Though her patience was as great as was imaginable for any to have upon the racke, and her love to her husband greatt as her other qualiffications were, yett shee earnestly desired death many houres before itt came; and Sir R. sate constantly upon her bed side, feeling her pulce, and exhorting her cheerefully to indure those momentts of paine which would soone bee changed to everlasting pleasure. And though noe doupt her death was the greatest misfortune could arive to him, yett hee did speake so excellently to her as did exceed by farre what the best ministers said who frequently came to her, and was so composed both att and after her death that neither action nor word could discover in him the least passion. Hee imediately tooke care for transporting her body to Belcarese to bee bueried there with her child which shee caried with her to her grave, beeing never seperated.

This was a sad lose to mee, for besides the advantage I had in her obleiging converse, I had the assistance of Sir R.'s advise in any deficulty in my busynese, and hee wentt offttimes to consultations with mee and imployed his interest as farre as itt could bee usefull to mee. And when hee wentt away, hee very earnestly recomended mee and my concernes to his cousin Sir J. Halkett, who was not ill pleased with the imploymentt. This for some time putt a stop to Sir G. M. going north, because Sir R. had some thoughts of going with him, which hee either did or followed soone affter.

Upon Monday, 7 of February, 1652/3, Sir G. M. and C. B. began there journy from Edinburgh. The night before, the Earle of Dunfermeline supt with him and mee att my chamber and then ordered the way of keeping corespondence, and what advise hee thought fitt for the action hee was going aboutt. Itt is nott to bee imagined butt my trouble was great to part with him considering the hazards hee was exposing himselfe to, butt I must confese itt was increased by reflecting upon what Jane Hambleton had severall times said to Crew: that shee had observed a gentleman come privately to my chamber and sayd shee knew that I and severalls looked upon him as one I intended to marry, butt hee should never bee my husband. And remembring how truly butt sadly fell outt what shee had foretold before, made mee the more aprehencive of this separation, though I was one that never allowed my selfe to inquire or beleeve those that pretended to know future eventts.

I had of late beene so used to good company that I was the more sencible now of the wantt of itt, and finding itt would bee more for my advantage to bee in some private howse where my meatt might bee dresed then to have itt from the cooke's or keepe one for that use, therfore I resolved to take another lodging; and having returned the furniture I borowed with my humble thankes for there use and the use of the howse, I tooke two roomes in Mr. Hew Walace's howse in the foot of Blackefryar Wind.

Butt one remarkeable passage I mett with before I left the Earle of Tweedale's howse which I cannott butt mention. One evening towards the close of daylight there came a tall proper man into the roome where I was and desired hee might speake to mee. I went towards him, and hee told mee hee was one who had not beene used to seeke butt was now reduced to that nesesity that hee was forced to aske my charity to keepe him from starving. His lookes were so suitable to his words that I could nott butt compasionate his condittion and regrett my owne, for all I had was butt one poore shilling nor knew I where to borrow two pence. I thought to give him all I had might apeare vanity if any one should know itt, and to give him lese could nott suply his wantt, and therfore I resolved to give itt him all and refferred my selfe to His hands for whom I did itt (concluding that perhaps some would lend mee that would nott give him). And I doupted nott butt God would provide for mee. So I gave him the shilling, which raised so great a joy in him that I could nott butt bee highly pleased to bee the instrumentt of that which brought such praises to the God of Mercy, who left mee nott withoutt a recompence; for the next morning before I was ready, the Earle of Roxborough came to my chamber, who was newly come from London, and brought mee a very kind letter from my sister and twenty pound sterling for a testimony of her affection, which I receaved as a reward for my last night's charity.

To make good the promise Sir J. H. made to Sir R. M., hee never came to towne butt I was the first person hee visitted and was very solicitous in any of my concernes and wentt with mee when I had occation to attend the judges. I found frequency of converse increased what I was sory to find, and to devert itt from my selfe I offten perswaded him to marry, and used severall arguments from what hee had aqainted mee with in his owne condition that made mee, by way of freindship to him and for preventing some inconveniences to his familly, very seriously advise him to marry; and I confese I proposed itt as a great sattisfaction to my selfe to have his condittion such as might make itt utterly imposible for him to have any thoughts of mee butt what might bee allowable to him in a maried state. I att last prevailed so farre with him that hee accknowledged hee was convinced itt would bee for his advantage to have a good discreet wife, and hee had had severall in his thoughts, since I was so urgentt with him, and now was determined upon one, butt was resolved I should bee the first proposer of itt. I was very well pleased to undertake the imployment, and the way hee designed was by my recomending him by a letter to my Lord Belcarese, who had an interest in a handsome young widow, and to desire his Lordship's assistance to obtaine his designe. This hee did only to complementt mee, for his owne interest with my Lord B. was much more then any I could pretend to; for hee had a great esteeme for Sir J., and I remember once when I was att Belcarese (where I wentt frequently) my Lord was speaking something of Sir James, and I said, 'Pray, my Lord, give mee leave to aske what the ground was that some people takes to speake with some reflection upon him?'

'Truly (my Lord replied), I beleeve never person was more injured nor worse requited for a gallantt action. And hee could nott have desired a better wittnese to vindicate him then the King, for hee was a wittnese all the time, standing upon the leads of my Lord Belmerinoth's howse att Leith and saw the whole proceedure; for if itt had nott beene for Sir James and those hee commanded, all the King's forces att that time att Muslebrough had beene cutt off, and hee stood in the face of the enemy while the rest retreated and came handsomely off with very litle disadvantage. And as I am a Christian (said my Lord) this is true, and I have heard the King speake severall time of itt with greatt aplause to Sir James and anger att those who traduced him in what was so eminently falce.'

And upon that occation hee heard the King say, 'Lord, keepe mee from there malice, for I see they will spare none they have a prejudice against.'

To confirm that this humour did then very much reigne, I cannott butt mention what I was a wittnese of my selfe. One day Sir James came to see mee and brought a gentleman with him who hee beleeved much his freind, and affter severall discourses of puplicke affairs, the gentleman satte sillent a litle while and then smiling said, 'Sir James, now that I am convinced you are an honest man and love the King and his interest, I will make a confesion to you. You were so great with my Lord Argile that I thought itt imposible you could bee honest, and therfore I have laine in my bed in a morning inventing some ill story of you and reported itt when I wentt abroad, and itt was joy to mee to have itt beleeved; and, now I see my error, I aske your pardon'; which Sir James soone gave and past itt over as a jest.

Butt to returne where I left. After Sir James was resolved to make adrese to that lady, hee intended to goe upon Monday, the 21 of March, 1652/3, to Belcarese and desired to have my letter ready, and in the morning hee would call for itt. I was nott long in writting, and did recomend the designe to my Lord Belcarese with as much earnestnese as the greatest concerne I could have, and had the letter ready against hee came for it, which was punctually the time hee apointed.

When hee came into my chamber I saw something of joy in his face that I had nott observed in a long time, and I said I was glad to see him looke so well pleased, for had hee sooner resolved to goe a wooing, I had sooner seene a change in him. Though I saw him well pleased, yett I saw him in disorder with itt, and hee stood still a pritty while withoutt speaking a word. Att last hee said, 'I have heard news this morning, and though I know itt will trouble you, yett I thinke itt is fitt you should bee aquainted with itt. Just as I was turning downe Blacke-fryar Wind (said hee) to come here, Collonel Hay called to mee and told mee the post that came in yesterday morning had brought letters from London that undouptedly C.B.'s wife was living and was now att London, where shee came cheefely to undeceave those who beleeved her dead.'

'Oh,' said I, with a sad sigh, 'is my misfortune so soone devulged? . . .

[*one leaf* (*two pages*) *missing*]

. . . unworthy, and in what apeared so, none living could condemne mee more then I did my selfe. Butt I had some circumstances to plead for mee withoutt which I had beene unpardonable, and that was the concealing my intended mariage meerely because hee durst not withoutt hazard of his life avowedly apeare, and therfore itt had beene imprudence to puplish what might have beene (in those times) ruine to us both.

As soone as I could get my selfe composed so as to goe abroad, I wentt where duty led mee more then inclination, for I aprehended every one that saw mee censured mee, and that was noe litle trouble to mee when I reflected on my misfortune that gave them butt too just grounds. Butt that I was with patience to suffer, and what ever els my Lord God thought fitt to inflict, to whom I did intirely submitt and could make nothing unwellcome from His hand who had so wonderfully suported mee in so unparaleld a triall.

In May 1653 the Earle of Dunfermeline came to my chamber and told mee hee had got certaine information that there was a party of horse to bee sentt the next day to Belcarese and take my Lord and bring him prisoner to Edinburgh, which hee durst nott writt nor communicate to any butt mee, and desired I would goe and lett him know what was designed, that hee might escape, which I undertooke, and wentt early the next morning, taking only a man with mee (for I was nesesitate to leave my woman to looke affter some busynese then fell outt), and the tide falling to bee betwixt 3 and 4 in the morning and a very great wind so as few butt the boatman and my selfe ventured to goe over, which contributed well, for I landed safe and was att Belcarese before ten a clocke. And my Lord and Lady wentt away imediately and had desired mee to stay in the howse with the chilldren and take downe all the bookes and convey them away to severall places in trunkes to secure them (for my Lord had a very fine library, butt they intrusted were nott so just as they should have beene, for many of them I heard afterwards were lost). I was very desirous to serve them faithfully in what I was intrusted, and as soon as my Lord and Lady were gone, I made locke up the gates and with the helpe of [ ] Logan, who served my Lord, and one of the women, both beeing very trusty, I tooke downe all the bookes and, putting them in trunkes and chests, sentt them all outt of the howse in the night to the places apointed by my Lord, taking a short way of inventory to know what sort of bookes was sentt to every person; and with the toile and wantt of sleepe (for I wentt nott to bed that night and had butt litle sleepe the night before) that I tooke the sodainest and the most violentt bloudy fluxe that ever I beleeve any had in so short a time, which brought mee so weake in ten days time that none saw mee that expected life for mee.

But I forgott to tell that the things had nott beene two houres outt of the howse when the troope of horse came and asked for my Lord. There officer came up to mee, and I told him my Lord had beene long sicke, which was true enough, and finding itt inconvenientt to bee so farre from the phisitians was gone to Edinburgh for his health. They searched all the howse, and seeing nothing in itt butt bare walls and weemen and chilldren, they wentt away. I gave accountt by an exprese what I said according to there order, and affter some few days staying concealed att Edinburgh, my Lord and Lady wentt to the North and from thence wentt abroad.

I had sentt for my woman, who came the next day affter I fell sicke and prest much my sending for a phisitian; butt I knew none butt Dr. Cuningham, and I could nott send for him because I knew hee was with my Lord Bel., and those phisitians who lived neere Belcarese was nott att home. So I concluded that the Lord had determined now to putt an end to all my troubles, and death was very wellcome to mee, only I beged some releefe from the violentt paine I had, which was in that extreamitty that I never felt any thing exceed itt. Butt itt seemes itt was only sentt for a triall and to lett mee find the experience of the renued testimony of God's favor in raising mee from the gates of death.

During my sicknese I was much obleiged to the frequentt visitts of most of the ladys theraboutts, butt particularly the Lady Ardrose. And Mr. D. Forett and Mr. H. Rimer seldome missed a day of beeing with mee. They were both pious, good men, and there conversation was very agreeable to mee. As soone as I was able to goe outt and had beene att the church, the Lady Ardrose's impertunity prevailed with mee to stay with her a weeke before I wentt to Edinburgh, which I did, and then having taken my leave of all those whose civility to mee made itt nesesary, I returned to Edinburgh; where I had nott beene long before Sir J. Halkett came to see mee (who had sentt offten to inquire affter mee when I was att Belcarese) and excused nott comming himselfe, which hee did refraine lest itt should occation discourse of that which hee knew would displease mee. I seemed nott to understand what hee mentt, neither was I curious to bee resolved, only thanked him for what hee had done and what hee left undone, for itt was nott reasonable for mee to expect a visitt from him att that distance.

From the first day of my aquaintance with him I discovered a particular respect hee had for mee, and I have allready related what way I tooke to preventt the increase of that which could have noe hope of a suitable returne, and yett how obleiging hee was to that person who cheefely interupted itt. Now thatt beeing, as hee thought, removed, I found by many circumstances and indirect words that hee pleased himselfe with what I never had a thought of, though I had beene highly ingrate if I had nott had more then an ordinary value for him. Butt lest hee should speake derectly to mee of what I knew too well (and did regrett), hee seldome was with mee that I did nott mention my resolution never to marry and that nothing kept mee from vowing itt butt that I questioned if such vows were lawfull. The more hee used argumentts to diswade mee from that resolution, I urged the greater reasons I had to confirme mee in itt, and att this rate wee conversed severalls months, hee seeking and I avoiding all occations of his discovering his affection to mee.

Att last one day, when hee had beene some time with mee speaking of many variety of subjects, when I least expected itt hee told mee hee could noe longer conceale the affection hee had for mee since the first visitt hee ever made mee, and had resolved never to mention itt had my condittion beene the same itt was; butt now, looking upon mee as free from all obligation to another, hee hoped hee might now pretend to the more favor, having formerly prefferred my sattisfaction above his owne. I was much troubled att this discourse, which hee could nott butt observe, for the teares came in my eyes. I told him I was sencible that the civillity I had receaved from him were nott of an ordinary way of freindship and that there was nothing in my power that I would nott doe to exprese my gratitude. Butt if hee knew what disturbance any discourse like that gave mee, hee would never mention itt againe, 'For as I never propose any thing of hapinese to my selfe in this world, so I will never make another unhapy, and in this denyall I intend to evidence my respect to you much more then if I intertained your proposall. And therfore I intreatt you, if you love either your selfe or mee, lett mee never heare more of itt.'

'Butt,' said hee, 'I hope you will nott debarre my conversing with you.'

'Noc (replied I), I will nott bee so much my owne enemy, and upon the condittion you will forbeare ever to speake againe of what you now mentioned, noe person shall bee wellcomer to mee, nor any will I bee willinger to serve when ever I have opertunity.'

Hee said itt should bee against his will to doe anything to displease mee, butt hee would make no promises.

A litle after, hee desired mee to lett his two daughters stay with mee, for hee designed to bring them to Edinburgh to learne what was to bee taught there, and if I would lett them stay with mee, hee would thinke himselfe obleiged to mee. I told him I had formerly promised him any service that lay in my power and hee need not doupt my performance; and if hee or they could dispence with what intertainementt I could give them hee needed nott doupt of there beeing wellcome, and itt would bee an advantage to mee to have so good company. His youngest daughter was butt a child, butt his eldest was neere a woman, and even then by more then ordinary discretion gave expectation of what since shee hath made good. The lodging I was then in nott beeing convenientt for more then my selfe, I removed up to Mrs. Glover's att the head of Blacke-friar Wind, where they and there woman came and staid with mee; and wee lived with very much quiett and content in our converse, Sir James comming offten to see them and bringing many times there unckle and cousin, Sir R. Montgomery and Haslehead, who were both extreamely civil to mee and frequentt in there visitts.

Itt is so usuall where single persons are often together to have people conclude a designe for mariage, that it was noe wonder if many made the same upon Sir James and mee, and the more that his daughters were with mee. Butt I had noe thoughts of what others concluded as done, for I thought I was obleiged to doe all I could to sattisfy him, since I could nott doe what hee cheefely desired. I often desired him to dine and sup with his daughters, which had been a neglect if I had omitted, considering hee was often sending provision from his owne howse to them. For hee knew I was nott of a humour to take boord, nor did hee offer itt, butt made it that way equivalent; nott withoutt trouble to mee, for my inclination was ever more to give then receave.

Towards the winter hee staid most constantly att Edinburgh and then grew so impertunate with mee, nott only to allow his adrese butt to give him hopes that itt should bee succesfull, that to putt him past all further pursuit I told him I looked upon itt as an addition of my misfortune to have the affection of so worthy a person and could nott give him the returne hee deserved; for hee knew I had that tye upon mee to another that I could nott dispose of my selfe to any other if I expected a blesing, and I had too much respect to him to comply with his desire in what might make him unhapy and my selfe by doing what would bee a perpetuall disquiett to mee. Hee urged many things to convince mee that I was in an error, and therfore that made itt void; butt when hee saw nothing could prevaile, hee desired mee for his sattisfaction that I would propose itt to Mr. David Dickson (who was one hee knew I had a great esteeme of his judgmentt) and rely upon his determination. This I was contentt to doe, nott doupting butt hee would resolve the question on my side.

The first time Mr. Dickson came to mee (which hee usually did once in a weeke), beeing alone, I told him I was going to comunicate something to him which hitherto I had concealed butt now would intrust him with itt under promise of secresy, and beeing impartially ingenious in giving mee his opinion in what I was to aquaint him with; which hee promising, I told him I did not doupt butt hee and his wife and many others in Edinburgh did beleeve Sir Ja. Halkett's frequentt visits to mee was upon designe of mariage. And I would avow to him that itt was what hee had offt with great importunity proposed, and had a long time evidenced so reall an affection for mee that I could nott butt accknowledge if any man alive could prevaile with mee itt would bee hee, butt I had beene so farre ingaged to another that I could nott thinke itt lawfull for mee to marry another; and so told him all the story of my beeing unhapily deceaved and what lengh I had gone, and rather more then lese. Hee heard mee very attentively and was much moved att the relation, which I could nott make withoutt teares. Hee replied hee could nott butt say itt was an unusuall tryall I had mett with and what hee praid the Lord to make usefull to mee. Butt withall, hee added, that since what I did was suposing C.B. a free person, hee nott proving so, though I had beene puplickely maried to him and avowedly lived with him as his wife, yett the ground of itt failing, I was as free as if I had never seene him; and this, hee assured mee, I might rely upon, that I might withoutt offence either to the laws of God or man marry any other person when ever I found itt conveniantt, and that hee thought I might bee guilty of a fault if I did nott when I had so good an offer. Hee used many argumentts to confirme his opinion, which though I reverenced comming from him, yett I was not fully convinced butt that itt might bee a sin in mee to marry. Butt I was sure there was noe sin in mee to live unmarried.

I was very just to Sir James in giving him accountt what Mr. Dickson had said, though nott till he urged to know itt. And beeing determined on what hee had offten pleaded, for hee hoped now I would have nothing more to object, I told him though hee had made itt apeare lawfull to mee, yett I could nott thinke itt convenient, nor could I consentt to his desire of marying withoutt doing him so great prejudice as would make mee apeare the most ungrate person to him in the world. I accknowledged his respect had beene such to mee that, were I owner of what I had just right to, and had never had the least blemish in my reputation (which I could nott butt suffer in considering my late misfortune), I thought hee deserved mee with all the advantages was posible for mee to bring him. Butt itt would bee an ill requitall of his civilitys nott only to bring him nothing, butt many inconveniences by my beeing greatly in dept; which could nott butt bee expected, having (except a hundred pound) never receaved a peny of what my mother left mee, and had beene long att law both in England and Scottland, which was very expencive. And I gave him a particular accountt what I was owing. Yett all this did nott in the least discourage him, for hee would have beene content att that time to have maried mee with all the disadvantages I lay under, for hee said hee looked upon mee as a vertuous person, and in that proposed more hapinese to himselfe by injoying mee then in all the riches of the world.

Certainly none can thinke butt I had reason to have more then an ordinary esteeme of such a person, whose eyes were so perceptable as to see and love injured vertue under so darke a cloud as incompassed mee aboutt. When I found hee made use of all the argumentts I used to lessen his affection as motives to raise itt higher, I told him, since hee had left caring for himselfe, I was obleiged to have the more care of him, which I could evidence in nothing more then in hindring him from ruining himselfe; and therfore told him I would bee ingenious with him and tell him my resolution was never to marry any person till I could first putt my affaires in such a posture as that if I brought no advantage where I maried, att least I would bring noe trouble. And when ever I could doe that, if ever I did change my condittion, I thought hee was the only person that deserved an interest in mee.

And this I was so fixt in that nothing could perswade mee to allter, which gave him both trouble and sattisfaction by delay and hopes. Many proposalls hee made wherin hee designed to remove my objections, butt though they were great expresions of his affection, yett I would nott admitt of them; butt they had this effect as to make mee the sooner project the putting my selfe in a capacity to comply with his desires, since

I found they were unchangeable. And I did resolve as soone as the winter session was done, which I expected would putt a close to my law suite here, I would goe to London and vindicate my selfe from the suposed guilt I was charged with, and then try what I could perswade my brother to doe in order to the paying what I owed. I aquainted Sir James with my intention, which hee aproved of, since hee could nott perswade mee to nothing els.

Presently affter this Sir James came and shewed mee a letter hee had receaved from London from the Countese of Morton, who very earnestly desired him to come to her, for shee had instrusted him with the oversight of her jointure, and itt related to the setling of that and other things of concerne that made her importunate for his comming to her. Hee told mee my Lady M. was a person who had ever showne much respect to him and that hee would willingly serve her Ladyship, butt the cheefe thing that would make him now obay her commands was in hopes his beeing att London might bee serviceable to mee if I would imploy him. I said if his owne conveniency would allow of his journy and that hee did incline to itt, I would writte with him to my sister, who I would obleige to bee civill to him upon my accountt, though hee deserved itt for his owne. Within two days hee wentt, and I gave my sister such a caracter of him as made his reception liker a brother then a stranger. I refferred much to him to say which was not convenientt to writte, and desired her to speake to my brother and give mee accountt what I might expect of his kindnese in the proposall I have lately mentioned, of which I expected noe answeare till Sir James returned.

Aboutt a weeke affter hee was gone, I fell into a feaverish distemper which continued some time, so that I found itt nesesary to send for Doctor Cunningham, which gave occation to some people to say that I fell sicke with hartbreake because Sir James H. was gone to London to marry my Lady Morton, which report wentt currantt amongst some, though nott beleeved by any that was well aquainted with any of the three; butt this aquainted mee with the humour of some people that use to make conclusions of there owne rather then seeme ignorantt of any thing. By the speedy returne Sir James made, hee convinced them of there folly who raised the report, and brought much sattisfaction to mee by the assurance I had from my sister of beeing very wellcome to her when ever itt was convenient for mee to come, and till then shee thought itt best to delay speaking of any partticular to my brother. Butt for her husband, I might bee secure of his kindnese to bee ever the same I had found itt. Att the same time I allso receaved severall letters from them who had formerly had much freindship for mee, by which I found itt had noe abatementt by the late tryall I had mett with, which did much incourage mee to kepe my resolution of going to London when ever the season of the yeare would admitt of itt.

In the meane time I indeavered the setling of my busynese so as itt might receave noe prejudice by my absence, butt gott so many delays, yett dayly hopes of beeing putt to a close, that itt was the begining of September '54 before I could take journy; which I was much asisted to performe by the kindnese and favor of the old Countese of Dunfermeline, who invited mee to goe with her to Pincky the Satturday before I was to goe for London, and beeing very inquisitive how I was provided for my journy, by my ingenuity her Ladyship found I was nott very certaine of what was convenientt. And upon the Monday when I was comming away my Lady brought mee ten pound, and said if shee had been better provided shee would have lentt mee more, butt shee had borowed itt of her lord. I gave her Ladyship many thankes, who unasked had so civilly asisted mee, and desired to know whether I should make the note of my hand (which I should send the next day) in my Lord's name or her Ladyship's; and shee desired itt might bee in my Lord's name, which accordingly I did, and paid since I was a widow.

The great civilitys I receaved from all Sir James H.'s relations made mee withoutt scruple goe to his sister to the Cavers the first night, where hee wentt with mee and his eldest daugher, who staid there till my returne. The youngest hee left att skoole in Edinburgh. Sir James wentt another day's journy with mee and would have gone further, butt I would nott give him any further trouble, butt urged his returne; and wentt on my journy to Yorke, where I expected to meett the post coach, butt was disapointed and forced to ride another day's journy.

Sir James had an excellentt footman who hee had promised my sister and sentt him along with mee, who I gave mony to pay for his diett and lodging affter wee came to the coach, because I thought itt nott reasonable to expect hee could keepe up with itt. Affter wee had gone halfe the first day's journy and the coachman driving att a great rate, I heard the coachman and postillion saying, 'Itt cannott bee a man; itt is a devill, for hee letts us come within sight of him and then runs faster then the sixe horses.' So hee stops the coach and inquires if any of us had a footman. I told him I had. 'Then,' said hee, 'pray make much of him, for I will bee answearble, hee is the best in England.' When I found hee could hold outt (as hee did all the way), I made him run by the coach, and hee was very usefull to all in itt.

That journy brought mee the aquaintance of Sir [ ] Witherington and his nephew Mr. Arington, who had one man, and my woman and my selfe was all wee had in the coach. I had discharged my woman and the footman to tell my name to any, butt tooke a borowed name. Sir [ ], beeing a very civill person, intertained mee with many handsome variety of discourses and related how hee had designed to goe for Flaunders and all his things a shipboard, and while hee was taking his leave, the ship sett saile from Newcastle; and so hee was forced to goe by land, which fell outt well for mee because I could nott have mett with civiller gentlemen, butt I regretted to find they were Roman Catholickes. And by my naming Mr. Fallowfield as one that I had seene, they presenttly knew who I was, and said they would inquire noe further, for they had heard him speake of mee as one hee had so great respect for as that they would have the same. This Mr. Fallowfield was an old priest that used sometime to come to Naworth Castle when I was there and had offten writt letters to mee for sicke persons and highly complemented mee upon there recovery. When I found they did know my name, I told them the reason why I concealed itt was because I had beene long absentt from my friends, and there had beene many changes since I left them, and therfore I resolved they should see mee before they heard of mee.

Wee came to High Gate aboutt 2 a clocke, where I desired to bee left, and writt a note in with the footman to an old servantt of my mother's to take a lodging in some private place in London and to come to mee the next morning with a coach; which accordingly hee did, and I wentt to White Fryars where my brother Newton's lodging used to bee, and most of those who desired nott to apeare puplickely. I then writt to my sister, who was then and her husband att Warwicke, by the footman Sir James H. had sentt her, aquainting her where I was and that I intended to bee knowne to very few till I heard what shee advised mee to doe. For though I knew the power that then governed did att that time indeavor to secure themselves rather by obleiging the Loyall Party then ruining them, yett itt was cheefely to such who could doe them most prejudice, and so that was noe security to mee; besides, the dept I had was considerable, and therfore, till I was sure they to whom itt was due would nott attempt any unhandsome action against mee, I thought itt was fitt upon both these considerations to conceale where I was till I had some way secured my selfe from the inconvience that I might suffer both upon a puplicke and private accountt.

My sister within 3 or 4 days returned backe the footman to mee againe with a very kind letter and twenty peeces, promising to bee with mee as soone as shee could, and till then thought itt best for mee nott to goe any where abroad. In the meane time I imployed my mother's old servantt to inquire of some that hee was aquainted with, who ruled much in those times, what there opinion was of my comming to London; butt there had beene so many changes among themselves, and some who they did much confide in who had left them, beeing convinced of there error, that they looked now the more favorable upon those who had never beene on there side and did more easily pardon what they acted against them. And this made mee the more secure as to the puplicke. And for my private troubles, there was nott one who I was really owing any thing to butt they were as civill as I could desire and as ready as ever to serve mee in what they had that could bee usefull to mee.

Having thus farre sattisfied my selfe, I only staid now till my sister came, that my going first abroad might bee with her, which was shortly affter. And having made some few visitts to some particular persons, I wentt with her and her husband to Charleton, which was a howse of thers within 5 or 6 miles of London. My brother, who lived then in the country with his familly, came to see mee and invited mee to his howse, where I wentt and staid sometime, butt my most constantt residence was with my sister, where I knew I was most wellcome to her and her husband; butt sometimes I wentt to London and had a lodging in Crew's mother's howse, where I staid when I had any persons to meett with in order to setle what I came there for.

One morning when I was there, they brought mee word there was two gentlemen desired to speake with mee who had brought a letter to mee from the Earle of Callander. I sentt for them up to my chamber and did something wonder to find the man tremble when hee gave mee the letter, and his lips quiver that hee could hardly speake. I tooke the letter and read itt, concerning a busynese his Lordship had recomended to my care. I asked who brought itt from Scottland. Hee was not well able to answeare mee, butt pointing to the other man, hee came and arrested mee. I was strangely surprised, having never mett with nothing like itt, and asked att whose instance. Hee pointed to the other who had given mee the letter and named him Mr. Maitland. I said I thought itt strange upon what accountt hee could doe itt, who I had never seene. Hee said itt was for a dept my brother Will owed his wife and I promised to pay. I said it was very strange I should promise to pay what I never till then knew was owing, nor did I ever heare of that woman's name till that time of my comming to London.

Yett though all this was true, I was forced to give baile and to answeare att Guild Hall, which I did by Atturny Allen. And though they had hired a man of there owne to come and sweare that I had promised to pay the dept, yett hee so farre contredicted himselfe that itt was visible itt was a cheat and the bill was flung over the barre; which so exasperated that wicked woman that there was nothing imaginable that is ill shee did nott say of mee puplickely in the street, and the interest shee had with the soldiers, who was dayly drinking in her howse att the Muse, made all people unwilling to medle with her. Butt I need nott insist upon this, which cost mee deare enough before I ended with her; butt itt hath cost her dearer since, if shee did nott repentt, and if shee did, since the Lord hath forgiven her, I blese Him for itt, and so did I as I sentt her word by her husband when I heard shee was dying.

I heard constantly once in a fortnight from Sir James, with many renued testimonys that neither time nor distance had power to change him.

I had nott beene long att London when I heard C.B. was come there, who sentt to mee severall times to have leave to come once butt to speake to mee, which I as offten positively denyed as hee earnestly asked itt. Butt one Sunday night, on the 10th of December, [16]54, affter I had suped and was walking alone in my chamber, hee came in, which I confese strangely surprised mee, so that att first I was nott able to speake a word to him. Butt a litle beeing recollected, I said I thought hee had brought misfortune upon mee enough allready withoutt adding more to it by giving new occation of my beeing censured for conversing with him. Hee intreated mee to give him leave butt to sitt downe by mee a litle and hee would imediately leave mee, which I did, and hee begun to vindicate himselfe as hee had done often; butt I interupted him and told him though my charity would induce mee to beleeve him inocentt, yett that could bee noe argumentt why I should now allow him liberty to visitt mee, since hee could nott pretend ignorance of that which made mee thinke allowable once what were hainously criminall now. Hee said hee desired mee only to resolve him one question, which was whether or not I was maried to Sir J. H. I asked why hee inquired. Hee said because if I was nott, he would then propose something that hee thought might bee both for his advantage and mine, butt if I were, hee would wish mee joy, butt never trouble mee more. I said nothing a litle while, for I hated lying and I saw there might bee some inconvenience to tell the truth, and (Lord pardon the equivocation) I said, 'I am' (outt aloud, and secrettly said, 'nott').

Hee imediately rose up and said, 'I wish you and him much hapinese together.' And taking his leave, from that time to this I never saw him nor heard from him, only when hee had gott my writtings (of what concerned mee left to mee by my mother which I had left with him when I wentt outt of London, and hee had taken for security with him when hee wentt first to Holland affter his escape outt of prison) that hee sent them to mee with a letter. The liberty hee tooke in comming outt from his concealed lodging upon Sunday was upon an act made by the Usurper, which was that none upon any accountt (what ever was there crime) should bee aprehended upon that day, butt should have liberty to goe to any church they pleased or any other place; which shewed a veneration hee had for that day, though in other things hee forgott obedience where itt was due by the same Authoraty that comanded that day to bee kept holy. Butt when that hipocritte raigned the people were insnared.

The first post affter C.B. had beene with mee I gave Sir Ja. an accountt of itt, who was so farre from beeing unsattisfied with itt that hee writt mee word if itt were nott that itt might doe me more prejudice in other people's thought then itt would doe in his, hee would nott care though I dayly conversed with him, so litle did hee aprehend any unhandsome action from mee; and therfore itt had beene the highest unworthynese and ingratitude to have beene falce to so great a trust as hee reposed in mee.

I was above a twelvemonth indeavoring all I could so to setle my affaires that I might have given Sir James some incouragement to come to mee, which hee offten designed to doe; butt I diswaded him from itt till itt might bee with more sattisfaction to himselfe, for I knew itt would bee butt a trouble to him to stay long att London or returne withoutt mee, and the ill succese I had (in my proposalls to my brother) would make one of them nesesary. Butt Sir James' patience beeing long tried, hee would nott bee hindred any longer, butt towards the latter end of the yeare 1655 hee came to London, where I att that time had come for two or three days, and hee returned with mee to Charleton to my sister's howse where hee staid for the most part while hee continued in England. The constancy of his affection and the urgency of his desireing mee to marry made mee now unite all the interest I had either by relation or freindship to gett mony, if nott to pay all I owed, yett such as was most presing, and to accomodate my selfe in some way suitable for what I designed.

I imployed some againe to try my brother, who (though one of the best natured men living) could nott bee prevailed with either to lend or ingage for one peny for mee, butt I did nott blame him since the hindrance was from another hand. And that disapointmentt came to make mee more highly value the kindnese of my brother Newton, who volontarily lentt mee three hundred pound, and the Countese of Devonshire two hundred, which was an obligation that I shall never forgett; nor what paines Mr. Neale tooke for mee to perswade her Ladyship and was bound with mee to her for the mony. I wish I had as much power to requite as I have memory to retaine the sence of those undeserved favors, and that my reflecting upon them may raise up my thoughts to the adoration and praise of Him who is the fountaine of mercy and from whom only all blesings are derived.

Affter this mony was receaved and paid where itt was most nesesary, and that I had sattisfied all that I knew any thing was due to, I wentt to London for some few days, where Sir James came to mee in order to conclude our mariage, which I could nott now in reason longer deferre; since the greatest objections I had made against itt was removed, and that I was fully convinced noe man living could doe more to deserve a wife then hee had done to obleige mee. And therfore I intended to give him my selfe, though I could secure him of nothing more, and that was my regrett that I could nott bring him a fortune as great as his affection to recompence his long expectation.

Itt was nott withoutt many debates with my selfe that I came att last to bee determined to marry, and the most prevalentt argument that perswaded mee to incline to itt was the extreordinary way that Sir James took even in silence to speake what hee thought nesesary to conceale, till itt apeared to bee fitt for avowing. And then nott to bee discouraged from all the inconveniences that threatned his pursuit was what I could nott butt looke upon as ordered by the wise and good providence of the Allmighty, whom to resist or nott make use of so good an opertunity as by His mercy was offred to mee I thought might bee offencive to His Devine Majesty, who in justice might deliver mee up to the power of such sins as might bee a punishment for nott making use of the offer of grace to preventt them. And this consideration, beeing added to Sir James'es worth, ended the contraversy.

However, lest I might have been mistaking, or Mr. Dickson in his opinion who thought itt lawfull for mee to marry, I entred nott into that state withoutt most solemne seeking the determined will of God; which by fasting and prayer I suplicated to bee evidenced to mee either by hedging up my way with thornes that I might nott offend Him, or that Hee would make my way plaine before His face and my paths righteous in His sight. And as I beged this with the fervor of my soule, so itt was with an intire resignation and resolution to bee content with what ever way the Lord should dispose of mee. To this I may add St. Paul's attestation, '*The God and Father of our Lord Jesus Christ*, *which is blesed for evermore*, *knoweth that I lie nott*' (2 Cor. xi. 31).

Affter this day's devotion was over, every thing that I could desire in order to my mariage did so pleasingly concurre to the consumation of itt, and my owne mind was so undisturbed and so freed of all kind of doupts, that with thankefullnese I receaved itt as a testimony of the Lord's aprobation and a presage of my future hapinese; and, blesed bee His name, I was nott disapointed of my hope.

Upon Satturday the first of March, 1655/6, Sir James and I wentt to Charleton and tooke with us Mr. Gaile, who was chaplaine to the Countese of Devenshire, who preached (as hee sometimes used to doe) att the church the next day; and affter super hee maried us in my brother Newton's closett, none knowing of itt in the familly or beeing presentt butt my brother and sister and Mr. Neale. Though [to] conforme to the order of those that were then in power, who allowed of noe mariage lawfull butt such as were maried by one of there Justices of Peace, that they might object nothing against our mariage, affter the evening sermon my sister pretending to goe see Justice Elkonhead, who was nott well, living att Wollwitch, tooke Sir James and mee with her in the coach and my brother and Mr. Neale wentt another way affoott and mett us there; and the Justice performed what was usuall for him att that time, which was only holding the Derectory in his hand, asked Sir James if hee intended to marry mee. Hee answeared, 'Yes'; and asked if I intended to marry him, I said 'Yes.' 'Then,' says hee, 'I pronounce you man and wife.' So calling for a glass of sacke, hee dranke and wished much hapinese to us, and we left him, having given his clarke mony, who gave in parchmentt the day and wittneses and attested by the Justice that hee had married us. Butt if itt had nott beene done more solemnly affterwards by a minister, I should nott beleeved itt lawfully done.

Affter I was maried I staid butt a short while with my sister and concealed my mariage from all except some particular persons that either relation or freindship made mee have confidence of, for itt was nott a time for any that honored the King to have any puplicke celebration; and another reason for performing itt privately was that aboutt ten days before I was maried, Mrs. Cole, who was Maitland's wife, had arested mee againe, and I was forced to give in new baile, who were such as I owned my intention of marying and going imediately affter for Scottland and obliging my selfe to keepe them harmelese. I left the managementt of itt to him who before I had imployed for my atturny, who was so confidentt shee could never recover two pence of mee that hee said hee would bee content to pay whatever should bee determined by the judges against mee; for hee said hee could prove by very good wittneses that she said (when her former bill was cast over the barre), 'Well, I will have one that shall sweare to the purpose, though I should give him ten pound for his paines.'

Hee, beeing an understanding, active man and giving mee such assurance, made mee with the lese desturbance leave London, for if I had had any aprehension of whatt affter fell outt, I might have easily prevented the prejudice shee did mee; for 3 yeare affter my atturny died, and my baile beeing in the country, shee gott outt a judgementt against mee privately so that none ever heard of itt that was concerned in mee. And though itt cost mee a great deale of trouble and expence (which to this day I am owing for to Mr. Neale) to have that judgement reduced, yett [I] found itt imposible, because itt was confirmed by the Act of Indempnity made by the King when His Majesty first came home, which was much outt of my way as well as injurious to many others. Butt that was my misfortune, which I had felt the weight of more heavily if, att the same time, the King had nott beene graciously pleased to grant mee 500 pound outt of the Exchequer. Butt of this I shall have more occation to speake hereaffter.

Sir James and I, having taken leave of our friends, came safe withoutt any ill accidentt (in the post coach) the lengh of Bow Bridge within —— mile of Yorke. And there wee had so remarkable a deliverance that I cannott omitt the relation of itt. There was none in the coach butt Sir James and I, his man and my woman, and a big fatt gentleman whose name I forgott, butt hee was one that had imploymentt under the Bishop of Durham. Aboutt a quarter of a mile before wee came to the bridge that gentleman had lighted outt to walke a litle and came in and satt on the side of the coach which was contrary to the place hee was in before, which contributed much to our safety; for Sir James and hee beeing on the one side of the coach and his man in that boot, Crew's weight and mine was the lese considerable, who were next to the danger. Butt all of us had unevitable beene drowned and had our neckes broke withoutt an extreordinary providence, for 6 horses beeing in the coach and the postillion nott carefull how hee entred the bridge, which was butt narrow withoutt any ledges upon itt and built of the fashion of a bow from which itt had the name, hee driving carelesly, both the wheeles of that side where I satt wentt over the bridge; which the coachman seeing, cried outt, 'Wee are all lost', and flung himselfe outt of the coachboxe, and to escape hurt his leg very ill, so that hee could hardly gett up to pull the horses to him, nor was there scarce roome upon the bridge to give any assistance. But that which was our preservation was some good angell, I thinke (sentt by his Master), who, seeing the danger wee were in, held the coach behind all the way till itt was off the bridge.

Itt was so extreordinary a deliverance that wee knew nott how to bee thankefull enough to God Allmighty who had given itt, butt resolved to reward the man who had beene instrumentall in itt, butt when wee all came outt of the coach att the end of the bridge and inquired for the man, there was none to bee seene. Nor had wee all that day mett or overtaken any travailer; only that man was seene by Hary Macky and the coachman to hold up the coach along the bridge, butt they both declared they never saw him before nor affter the danger, and that which made itt apeare the more strange was that hee seemed to bee butt a poore man and such doth nott usually doe any service withoutt seeking a recompence. Butt what ever hee was, itt was hee the Lord made use of as a meanes of our safety, and the lese wee knew of his comming, the more wee had reason to bee thankefull to Him who brought him there.

When we came to Yorke and related what wee had escaped, itt was the admiration of all that heard itt. The coach man and postillion was very penitentt for there fault, and therfore wee forgave them, butt would make noe more use of them. For wee hired another coach to Newcastle, wher Sir James had apointed his owne horses and servants to meett him because hee intended to see his sisters as hee wentt home; which he did, and wee came safe withoutt any other accidentt to the Cavers, where I was receaved with much kindnese by all, butt most from Sir James'es daughter, who I had left there and was very well pleased to returne home with mee, which shee did affter some days' stay att Cavers.

When wee came to Edinburgh, I sentt my excuse for nott beeing fitt then to waite upon my Lady Broghill, who was then there with her Lord who was Presidentt of the Councill, butt resolved to come there againe only to pay that respect which I had for them both; nott as they were then imployed, butt as I had long beene intimately aquainted with them before and knew that what they acted now was more outt of a good designe then an ill, as was evident by the civility they shewed to all the Royallists.

Affter wee came home and had receaved a very kind wellcome from all

Sir James his friends and neibours and that wee were a litle setled, hee thought itt convenientt for us to goe over as I promised to waite upon my Lady Broghill. And the reason which made Sir James the sooner doe itt was that severall gentlemen who had ingaged to serve under the English power in puplicke imploymentt as Justices of Peace had presed to have Sir James one of that number, butt hee declining, they made his name bee inserted in the list, with this certification: that who ever refused to act in that station who was nominate should bee sentt to the Castle att Edinburgh. This made us hasten our journy, and as soone as wee came there a gentleman (who I will nott now name, because I hope hee repents what hee then did) that had beene very urgentt with Sir James to accept the imploymentt came and importunatly presed him againe and, to make mee the better sattisfied with the proposall, told mee many advantages hee would receave by itt, and was very desirous that hee might goe with mee to make my aquaintance with my Lady Broghill. I excused my going att such times as hee mentioned only because I would nott have him with mee, nor did I take notice as if I had ever seene her. Butt as soone as I was free of him, I wentt presently affter dinner.

They lay then in the Earle of Muray's howse in the Canongate, and just as I came in att the gate my Lord Broghill was going outt, and with him a great attendance, and amongst the rest that gentleman who had beene so forward to have Sir James putt in to bee a Justice of Peace. Hee was a litle surprised when hee saw my Lord Br. come with so much freedome and kindnese and bid mee wellcome and, bringing me to the staires, asked if I had any service for him. I said, 'My Lord, though there hath beene many sad changes since I saw your Lordship, yett I still looke upon you as the same person you were, and therfore, in short, I am come to beg your Lordship's faver to Sir James, who I heare is in the list.'

'Why,' said hee, 'hath hee nott a mind to bee a Justice?'

'Noe, my Lord, so farre from itt that hee will goe to the Castle first.'

'Well, my word for itt,' replied hee, 'you shall never heare of itt more.'

Beeing then in hast going up to some committee, hee left mee with his lady and ingaged mee to dine with them the next day, which I did, and had all the assurance I could desire that Sir James should bee free from having any thing imposed upon him that was contrary to the duty and loyalty that became a faithfull subject.

Affter two or three days' stay in Edinburgh, wee returned home, and presently affter came the order to Sir James either to joyne with the other Justices of Peace or goe to the Castle. When I saw itt, I confese I was much disordered, and the more because I had such confidence of my Lord B.'s word. I desired Sir James to tell the mesenger that the next weeke hee would doe one of them if desired, and imediately I writt a letter to my Lord B. telling how much I was surprised with that order, affter I had his Lordship's promise to have . . .

THE MEMOIRS OF

Ann, Lady Fanshawe

A NOTE ON THE TEXT

THE TEXT is based on a manuscript 'Transcribed this presant May 1676'—as a note on a preliminary page signed by Lady Fanshawe states. This manuscript, in a handsomely bound volume, is now in the British Library (Add. MS. 41161), having been purchased, 29 July 1924, at Sotheby's. The volume is succinctly described in the catalogue of the Library:

Paper; ff. vii+124. Folio. A.D. 1676. Contemporary binding of red leather, gilt-tooled, in the centre of both covers a device of arms, Fanshawe impaling Harrison.

The manuscript is not in Lady Fanshawe's hand, though she made frequent corrections in it and added occasional comments. She also deleted with vigorous overscorings certain passages that, to judge from the nature of most of them, seemed to her indecorous, or too personal. That she was responsible for the deletions may be assumed from the fact that in one instance (p. 190 in this edition) she added a phrase in her own hand needed to complete a sentence, the latter part of which she had cancelled. One leaf in the manuscript (165–166 in the original pagination; folio 91 in a later numbering of leaves) is out of order: obviously the amanuensis she employed copied an earlier manuscript that was not bound. The existing manuscript is incomplete, breaking off abruptly at the end of a page with a reference to King Charles II's stopping payments by the Exchequer, 27 January 1672—though Lady Fanshawe mistakenly predates the event by a week. Following the Memoirs in the bound volume appear, in Lady Fanshawe's hand, a prayer used by her husband's chaplains in Portugal and Spain; a prayer used, presumably in the embassy in Madrid, after her husband's death; a list of his chaplains; and, finally, a list and brief account of Sir Richard and Lady Fanshawe's children born before 1659, most of whom died in infancy. A list of the children born after 1659 is added in a much later hand, probably of the nineteenth century.

The passages in the Memoirs which were cancelled are impossible, or almost impossible, to read, so thorough was the overscoring. However, the cancelled passages are supplied by recopyings, in handwriting much later than the seventeenth century, on blue slips of paper pasted into the volume after the folio leaves were bound. Probably the readings of these passages were taken from some other manuscript of the Memoirs—perhaps the one from which the amanuensis employed by Lady Fanshawe copied in May 1676. Conceivably the readings were taken from this manuscript by some person equipped with a magnifying glass and infinite patience. In any event, the passages, in part because of their personal and unguarded nature, hold particular interest, and I have felt no hestitation in including them. They were first printed in 1907 by H. C. Fanshawe in his edition of the Memoirs. Even if Lady Fanshawe were not protected by the three intervening centuries, there would be little in the cancelled passages, except perhaps a very severe reference to the Earl of Shaftesbury (p. 189), that could embarrass her. Yet it is easy to understand why, with her intense pride in her family and in her husband's career, she might have cancelled the passages. I have identified them in the textual notes.

Although extracts from the Memoirs had been printed earlier,[1] they did not appear in approximately their full length until 1829, in an edition in modern spelling by Sir Harris Nicolas, with a dedicatory epistle addressed to the Duchess of Clarence signed by Charles Robert Fanshawe, the head of the family.[2] The following year, 1830, Nicolas published a new edition, almost identical in its text with that of 1829. Although he had not identified himself in the previous edition, this time he signed the preface with his initials, 'N.H.N.'. The dedication to the Duchess of Clarence was omitted, probably because, in 1830, she became Queen as the wife of William IV. Sir Harris Nicolas is pointedly non-committal about the reasons the Memoirs had not been published prior to 1829. But he describes with precision the provenance of his text: 'The MS., from which this volume is printed, was copied, in 1786, from one written in 1766, by Lady Fanshawe's great granddaughter, Charlotte Colman, from the original, which was written under her Ladyship's inspection about four years before her death [i.e. 1676].'[3] The original from which Charlotte Colman copied is the manuscript now in the British Library. The edition of 1829, based at one remove on her transcription, includes the marginal and interlinear additions in Lady Fanshawe's hand; it omits the names and inventory of property on the misplaced leaf of the manuscript, which are meaningless out of proper sequence; it breaks off in mid-sentence at the same place as the manuscript of 1676.

Of particular significance, the edition of 1829 omits the passages that are deleted from the manuscript of 1676—the passages that are now restored in transcriptions on the interleaves pasted in the bound volume. We may therefore assume that when Charlotte Colman copied that manuscript in 1766 the interleaves were not present. The handwriting on the interleaves looks as though it is of nineteenth-century origin. In

1. In [William Seward], *Anecdotes of Distinguished Persons*, 4th edn. (London, 1798), ii, 43–52, 57–82; and Robert Clutterbuck, *The History and Antiquities of... Hertford* (London, 1827), iii, 314–16.

2. *Memoirs*, ed. H. C. Fanshawe (London, 1907), p. 222.

3. Edition of 1829, p. x.

any event, the interleaves were present in 1907 when H. C. Fanshawe prepared his edition, in modern spelling.[4]

Presumably the interleaves were present in 1905 when an edition of the Memoirs in modern spelling had been published 'With an Introduction by Beatrice Marshall and a Note Upon the Illustrations by Allan Fea', but the cancelled passages are not printed. Although the edition of 1905 includes some new emendations of proper nouns, the text is apparently based on that established by Sir Harris Nicolas, even though Allan Fea refers to the manuscript now in the British Library, and includes a photograph of it.

In so far as is consistent with presenting a text that is immediately intelligible to a modern reader, I have followed the spelling, capitalization, punctuation, and paragraphing of the manuscript of 1676. But I have frequently found it necessary to depart from the manuscript in such matters as punctuation and paragraphing in order to achieve ready intelligibility. I have regarded the more common abbreviations, such as the ampersand, 'y^{e}', 'y^{t}', 'S^{r}', and 'L^{d}', as a form of shorthand, which I could silently expand. Apart from expansions of unambiguous abbreviations, I have placed additions to the text within square brackets. I have also used square brackets to mark the few blank spaces left for words that were never inserted and to indicate corrections of dates from those in the manuscript. When Lady Fanshawe writes about events on the Continent, she often uses double dates, Old and New Style. When she uses the Old Style calendar alone, as when she writes about her life in England, I follow the customary modern practice of retaining her dates of the months but considering a new year as beginning 1 January rather than 25 March. In instances in which proper names are not recognizable in the original spelling even with reference to the index, I have changed them, using square brackets to mark departures from the manuscript, and recording the manuscript readings in the textual notes.

4. Mr. H. C. Fanshawe mistakenly considered the deleted passages that have been restored by the transcriptions in a hand much later than the seventeenth century on the small interleaves to be transcriptions of additions Lady Fanshawe made 'to the faired MSS. of the *Memoirs*'. (Cf. edition of 1907, p. 415, in a comment on the passage, 'We praised God . . . fall a sleep'. In this edition, p. 131, ll. 23–9.) In his account of the manuscript of 1676, Mr. Fanshawe writes (p. 222) that 'Besides her signature on the first page there are a few additions to the written text in the handwriting of Lady Fanshawe. . . . Most of the additions have been recopied on blue slips in a handwriting of a much later date than 1676.' There are indeed, as recorded in the textual notes of this edition, additional comments written by Lady Fanshawe in her own hand. But it is not these comments that have been recopied on the interleaves but rather passages of the original text that were vigorously deleted in an ink of the same colour as that of the original text. In one instance of deletion, Lady Fanshawe was forced to complete a sentence in her own hand.

A CHRONOLOGY OF SIR RICHARD FANSHAWE AND ANN, LADY FANSHAWE

In his edition of Lady Fanshawe's *Memoirs* published in 1907, Mr. H. C. Fanshawe included a 'Chronological Table' twenty-seven pages in length, in which by the use of double columns he presented the major events in the lives of Sir Richard and Lady Fanshawe and the historical events relevant to their lives. In the brief space available to me, and without access to family records he used, it would be unwise for me to attempt an independent chronology. Accordingly, in preparing this chronology I have drawn heavily on his.

		Age	
		Sir R.	*Lady F.*
1608	Sir Richard Fanshawe born, Ware Park, Hertfordshire, June (baptized 12 June), son of Sir Henry Fanshawe, third King's Remembrancer, and Elizabeth, daughter of Customer Smythe		
1616	Death of Sir Richard Fanshawe's father	7	
c. 1620	Sir Richard Fanshawe enters Thomas Farnaby's School, Cripplegate	12	
1623	Enters Jesus College, Cambridge. Reveals aptitude for classical studies and for writing poetry	15	
1625	Ann Harrison, later Lady Fanshawe, born, Hart Street, St. Olave's, London, 25 March, daughter of Sir John Harrison of Balls, Hertfordshire, and Margaret, daughter of Robert Fanshawe of Fanshawe Gate	17	
1626	Sir Richard Fanshawe enters the Inner Temple	18	1
1631	Death of his mother	23	6
1632–4	He travels in France and Spain	24–26	7
1635	Appointed secretary by Lord Aston, Ambassador to Spain. Goes to Madrid	27	10
1638	*Chargé d'affaires* in Madrid, between the departure of Aston and the arrival of his successor. Returns to England	30	13

1639–41	Secretary to the Council of War, Ireland	31–33	14
1640	Death of Ann Harrison's mother	32	15
1641	Sir John Harrison supports the Crown with a loan and is knighted. Sir Richard Fanshawe appointed fifth King's Remembrancer	33	16
1642	Sir John Harrison imprisoned by the Parliamentarians and deprived of his property	34	17
1643	Sir John Harrison goes to Oxford with his daughters. Sir Richard Fanshawe goes there also to join the King	35	18
1644	Appointed Secretary for War to the Prince of Wales. Marries Ann Harrison, near Oxford, 18 May	36	19
1645	Son, Harrison, born 23 February. Dies 10 March. Sir Richard Fanshawe goes from Oxford to Bristol with the Prince's retinue (March). Lady Fanshawe follows (May). Further journeys for them both	37	20
1646	They go with the Prince to Jersey. Daughter Ann (first of two given that name) born 7 June (died 1654). Sir Richard and Lady Fanshawe go to Caen to visit his brother, Thomas. She returns to London (August). Resides with his sister, Lady Boteler	38	21
1647	Sir Richard Fanshawe returns to England (January) and 'compounds' for £300. They live privately in London. Son Henry (first of two given that name) born 30 May (died 1649). *Pastor Fido* and poems by Sir Richard published. Sir Richard and Lady Fanshawe visit Charles I at Hampton Court (September or October), where the King gives Sir Richard letters for the Queen. They go to France	39	22
1648	Return to England. Son Richard (first of three given that name) born 8 June (died 1659). They go separately to Paris (November). Sir Richard goes to Ireland and is made Treasurer of the Navy	40	23

1649	Lady Fanshawe travels to Calais and London (January). Sir Richard visits Charles II at the Hague and returns to his duties in Ireland (March or April). Lady Fanshawe goes to Cork (May). Sir Richard and Lady Fanshawe are in Limerick (November and December)	41	24
1650	In Galway (January). On orders from Charles II Sir Richard and Lady Fanshawe proceed to Madrid with despatches requesting financial aid from the Spanish king (April). Daughter Elizabeth (the first of three given that name) born and dies in July. Sir Richard and Lady Fanshawe depart from Madrid (August), are nearly shipwrecked near Nantes, and reach Paris (November). Sir Richard made a baronet (September)	42	25
1651	Lady Fanshawe goes to London. Sir Richard goes to Scotland by way of Holland. Daughter Elizabeth (second of three given that name) born 24 June (died 1656). Sir Richard captured after the Battle of Worcester and imprisoned at Whitehall (September). Lady Fanshawe visits him regularly before dawn, and obtains from a physician a statement about his ill health which she presents to the Council of State, requesting his release. Sir Richard released on bail (November)	43	26
1652	His translations of Horace published. Daughter, Katherine, born 30 July	44	27
1653–4	Sir Richard and Lady Fanshawe reside at Tankersley Park, Yorkshire. Daughter, Margaret, born 9 October	45–46	28–29
1654–5	Sir Richard and Lady Fanshawe reside in Hamerton, Huntingdonshire	46–47	29–30
1655	They reside in Chancery Lane, London. Daughter Ann (second given that name) born 22 February. Sir Richard's translation of Camoens's *The Lusiads* published	47	30

1656	Daughter, Mary, born 12 July (died 1660). Sir Richard and Lady Fanshawe reside near Ware Park, Hertfordshire	48	31
1657	They visit Bath (August). Son Henry (second of two given that name) born (died 1658)	49	32
1658	Sir Richard's *La Fida Pastora* published. Sir Richard permitted to go abroad	50	33
1659	Lady Fanshawe and her children go to Paris (June). Lady Fanshawe returns to England (December)	51	34
1660	Sir Richard and Lady Fanshawe in Flanders. Sir Richard appointed Latin Secretary and Master of Requests. Knighted at Breda (April). Returns to England in the King's ship (May). His family returns in the *Speedwell*. They reside in Portugal Row	52	35
1661	Sir Richard elected Member of Parliament for Cambridge University. Sent to Portugal to complete arrangements for Charles II's marriage to Catherine of Braganza (September). Returns (December)	53	36
1662	Daughter, Elizabeth (third of three given that name) born, 22 February. Sir Richard attends the marriage of Charles II and Catherine of Braganza (21 May). Lady Fanshawe presented to the Queen. Sir Richard, appointed Ambassador to Portugal, leaves with his family for Lisbon (August)	54	37
1663	Son Richard (second of three given that name) born. Dies. Sir Richard recalled to England and made Privy Councillor	55	38
1664	Appointed ambassador to Spain, Sir Richard leaves for Madrid with his family (January). Takes up residence in Madrid (June)	56	39
1665	Son Richard (third of three given that name) born, Madrid, 6 August (died 1694). Conditional treaty between Spain and England negotiated by Sir Richard Fanshawe and the Duke of Medina de las Torres	57	40

1666	Sir Richard learns that he has been recalled as ambassador (March). Dies, 16/26 June. Lady Fanshawe and her family leave Madrid (July) and arrive at London (November). Sir Richard buried, All Hallows Church, Hertford. Lady Fanshawe claims payment of her husband's salary and money spent in the public service	58	41
1669	Death of Sir John Harrison. Lady Fanshawe receives partial payment from the Crown of money owed her husband		44
1670	Reburial of Sir Richard in St. Mary's Chapel, Ware Church, Hertfordshire		45
1671	Sir Richard's translations of *Querer por solo querer* and *Fiestas de Aranjuez* published		46
1676	Lady Fanshawe writes her Memoirs		51
1680	Death of Lady Fanshawe, January. Burial in Ware Church, 20 January, next to her husband		

THE MEMOIRS OF ANN, LADY FANSHAWE

Lord prosper Thou the works of our hands upon us,
prosper Thou our handy works.

Transcribed this presant May

1676

Ann Fanshawe

Glorey be to God, Amen

I have thought it convenient to discourse to you (my most dear and only son) the most remarkable actions and accidents of your family, as well as those of more eminent ones of your father and my life, and neceseity, not delight nor revenge, hath made me insert some passeges which will reflect on their owners, as the praises of others will be but just, which is my intent in this narrative. I would not have you be a stranger to [it], because by the example you may imitate what is applyable to your condition in the world, and indeavour to avoyd those misfortunes we have passed through, if God pleases.

Indeavour to be innocent as a dove, but as wise as a serpent, and let this lesson direct you most in your greatest extreams of fortune.

Hate idlenesse, and courbe all passions, be true in all words and actions. Unnecessarily deliver not your opinion but when you doe let it be just, and considered, and plaine.

Be charitable in thought, word, and deed, and ever ready to forgive injury don to yourself, and be more pleased to doe good than to receive good. Be civill and obliging to all, dutifull where God and nature command you, but friend to one, and that friendship keep sacred as the greatest tye upon earth, and be sure to ground it upon virtue, for no other is either happy or lasting.

Indeavour always to be content in that estate of life which it hath pleased God to call you to, and think it a great fault not to imploy your time either for the good of your soul or improvement of your understanding, health, or estate, and as these are the most pleasant pastimes, so it will make you a cheerfull old age, which is as necessary for you to designe, as to make provision to support the infirmitys which decay of strength brings, and it was never seen that a vicious youth terminated in a contented, cheerfull old age, but perished out of countenance.

Ever keep the best qualifyed persons company, out of whom you will find advantage, and reserve some hours daily to examine yourself and fortune; for if you embark yourself in perpetuall conversation or recreation, you will certainly shiprack your mind and fortune. Remember the proverbe, 'Such as his company is, such is the man', and have glorious actions before your eyes, and think what shall be your portion in heaven, as well as what you desire on earth.

Manage your fortune prudently, and forget not that you must give God an account here after, and upon all occasions.

Remember your father, whose true image though I can never draw to the life unless God will grant me that blessing in you, yet because you were but ten months and ten days owld when God took him out of this world, I will for your advantage show you him with all truth and without partiality.

He was of the highest sise of men, strong, and of the best proportion, his complexion sanguin, his skinne exceeding fair, his hair dark brown, and very curling, but not very long, his eyes gray and penetrating, his nose high, his countenance gracious and wise, his motion good, his speech cleare and distinct. He never used exercise but walking, and that generally with some book in his hand, which often-times was poetry, in which he spent his idle houres. Sometimes he would ride out to take the air, but his most delight was to goe only with me in a coach some miles, and there discourse of those things which then most pleased him of what nature soever. He was very obliging to all, and forward to serve his master, his country and friends, cheerfull in his conversation, his discourse ever pleasant mixt with the sayings of wise men, and their histories, repeated as occasion offered; yet so reserved that he never shewed the thought of his heart in his greatest sence, but to myself only, and this I thank God with all my soul for, that he never discovered his trouble to me but went from me with perfect cheerfulness and content, nor revealed he his joyes and hopes, but would say that they were doubled by putting them in my brest.

I never heard him hold dispute in my life, but often he would speak against it, saying it was an uncharitable custome, which never returned to the advantage of either party. He would never be drawn to the faction of any party, saying he found it sufficient honestly to preforme that imployment he was in. He loved and used clearness in all his actions, and professed his religion in his life and conversation. He was a true Protestant of the Church of England, so borne, so brought up, and so dyd.

His conversation was so honest, that I never heard him speake a word in my life that tended to God's dishonour or incouragement of any kind of debauchery or sin. He was ever much esteemed by his two masters, Charles the First, and Charles the Second, both for great parts and honesty, as for his conversation, in which they took great delight. He being so free from passion, that made him beloved of all that knew him, nor did I ever see him moved but with his master's concerns, in which he would hotly pursue his intrest through the greatest difficultys.

He was the tendrest father imaginable, the carefullest and most generous master I ever knew. He loved hospitality, and would often say it was wholy essentiall for the constitution of England. He lov'd and kept order with the greatest decency possible, and though he would say I managed his domesticks wholy, yet I ever governed them and myself by his commands, in the managing of which I thank God I found his approbation and content.

Now you will expect I should say something that may remain of us jointly, which I will doe, though it makes my eyes gush out with tears, and cuts me to the soul, to remember and in part express the joys I was blessed with in him.

Glory be to God we never had but one mind through out our lives, our soules were wrapped up in each other, our aims and designs one, our loves one, and our resentments one. We so studyed one the other that we knew each other's mind by our looks; what ever was reall happiness, God gave it me in him; but to commend my better half (which I want sufficient expression for) methinks is to commend myself and so may bear a censure; but might it be permitted I could dwell eternally on his praise most justly, but thus without offence I doe, and so you may imitate him in his patience, his prudence, his chastity, his charity, his generosity, his perfect resignation to God's will, and praise God for him as long as you live here, and with him hereafter in the kingdome of heaven. Amen.

Your father was born in Ware Park in the month of June, in the year of our Lord God 1608, and was the tenth child of Sir Hinery Fanshawe, whose father bought Jenkins in Essex, and Ware-Park in Hertfordshire. This your great grand father came out of Darbyshire from a small estate, Fanshawe-Gate, being the principal part that then the family had, which exceeded not above two hundred pounds a year, and about so much more they had in the town and parish of Drawnfield, within two miles of Fanshawe-Gate, where the family had been some hundreds of years, as appears by the church of Drawnfield, in the chancell of which church I have seen severall grave-stones, with the names of that family, many of them very antient, and the chancell, which is very old, was and is kept wholy for a burying place for that family.

There is in the town a free-schoole, with a very good house and noble endowment, founded by your great grand-father, who was sent for to London in Henry the Eighth's time by an uncle of his, and of his own name, to be brought up a clerck under his uncle Thomas Fanshawe, who procured your great grand father's life to be put with his in the patent of Remembrancer of His Majesty's Exchecker, which place he enjoy'd after the death of his uncle, he having left no male issue, only two daughters who had both great fortunes in land and mony, and marryed into the best familys in Essex in that time. This was the rise of your greatgrandfather, who, with his office and his Darbyshire estate, raised the family to what it hath been and is now. He had one only brother, Robert Fanshawe, who had a good estate in Darbyshire and liv'd in Fanshawe-Gate which he hired of his eldest brother, your great grandfather.

In this house my mother was borne, Margarett, the eldest daughter of Robert, your great great uncle. He marryed one of the daughters of Rowland Eyrs of Bradway in the same county of Darby, by whom he had 12 sons and 2 daughters. That family remains in Drawnfield to this day.

Your greatgrandfather married Alice Boucher of the last Earl of Bath's family, by whom he had onely one son that lived, Henery, which was your grand father; afterwards, when he had been 2 years a widower, he married one of the daughters of Costomer Smith, who had 6 sons and 6 daughters. His sons were Sir John Smith, Sir Thomas Smith, Sir Richard Smith, Sir Robert Smith, Mr. William Smith, and Mr. Edward Smith, who dy'd young. Two were knighted by Queen Elizabeth and 2 by King James. The eldest was the grandfather of the now Lord Strankford. The second has been severall times Ambassador, and all married into good familyes and left great estates to their posterity, which remains to this day. The daughters were Mrs. Fanshaw, your great grandmother-in-law; the second married Sir John Scott of Kent; the third married Sir John Daveis of the same county; the fourth married Sir Robert Poyns of Lestershire; the fifth married Thomas Buttler of Harald, Esq.; and the sixth married Sir Henry Fanshawe, your grandfather. These all left a numerous posterity but Daveis, and this day they are matched into very considerable familys.

Your great grand father had, by his second wife, Sir Thomas Fanshawe, Clerck of the Crown and Survayer Generall to King James. To him he gave his mannour of Jenkins in Essex, vallued at near 2 thousand a year. His second son by the same wife (William) he procured to be auditor of the duchy, whose posterity hath in Essex at Parsles about 7 or 8 hundred pounds a year.

His eldest daughter married Sir Christopher Hatton, heir to the Lord Chancellor Hatton; his second married Sir Benjamin Alofe of Bracksted in Essex; the third married Mr. Bulluck of [Darley] in Darbyshire—all men of very great estates.

As your grandfather inherited Ware-Parke and his office, the flower of his father's estate, so did he of his wisdom and parts, and both were happy in the favour of the princes of that time, for Queen Elizabeth said that your great grand father was the best officer of accounts she had and a person of great integrity, and your grandfather was the favorite of Prince Henry and, had the Prince lived to be king, had been Secretary of Estate, as he would often tell him. Mr. Camden speaks much in the praise (as you may see) of Sir Henry Fanshawe's garden of Ware-Park, none excelling it in flowers, phissicke-herbes, and fruit, in which things he did greatly delight. Also he was a great lover of musick and kept many gentlemen that were perfectly well qualified both in that and the Italian tongue, in which he spent some time. He likewise kept severall horses of manadge and rid them himself, which he delighted in, and the Prince would say none did it better. He had great honour and generosity in his nature, to show you a little part of which I will tell you this of him.

He had a horse that the then Earle of Execter was much pleased with, and Sir Henry esteemed because he deserved it. My Lord after some apolegy desired Sir Henry to let him have his horse and he would give him what he would. He replied, 'My Lord, I have no thoughts of selling him, but to serve you. I bought him of such a person and gave so much for him, and that shall be my price to you, as I paid, being 60 pieces.' My Lord Ex[eter] said, 'That's too much, but I will give you, Sir Henry, 50'; to which he made no answer. Next day my Lord sent a gentleman with 60 pieces. Sir Henry made answer, that was the price he had pay'd and once had offered him my Lord at, but not being accepted, his price now was 80. At the receiving of that answer my Lord Ex[eter] stormed and sent his servant back with 70 pieces. Sir Henry said that since my Lord would not like him at 80 pieces, he would not sell him under 100 pieces, and if he returned with less, he would not sell him at all, upon which my Lord Exeter sent 100 pieces and had the horse.

His retinue was great and that made him stretch his estate, which was near if not full foure thousand pounds a year, yet when he dy'd he left no debt upon his estate. He departed this life at the age of fourty eight years and lyes buryed in the chancell in a vaulte with his father in the parish church of Ware. He was as handsome and as fine a gentleman as England then had, a most excellent husband, father, friend, and servant to his prince.

He left in the care of my Lady, his widow, five sons and five daughters. His eldest son succeeded him in his land and office, and after the restoration of the King was made Lord Vicount of Drommore in Irland. He did ingage his person and estate for the Crown and fought in the Battle of Edgehill, and this ruined his estate and was the cause of his son's selling Ware-Park. Afterwards he tryed by the King's assistance to be reimburst, but could not prevail. I guesse his wound was too wide to be closed.

He was a very worthy, valiant, honest, good natured gentleman, charitable and generous, and had excellent naturall parts, yet cholerick and rash; which was onely incommode to his own domestick family. He was a very pretty man (for he was but low) of a sanguine complexion, much a gentleman in his mine and language; he was 69 years of age when he dy'd, and is buried with his ancestors in Ware Church.

He married first the daughter of Sir Giles Allington, by whom he hath a daughter called Ann, who remains a maid to this day. His second wife was Elizabeth, daughter to Sir William Cokin, Lord Maior of London. She was a very good wife, but not else qualified extraordinary in any thing. She brought him many children, wherof now remains 3 sons and five daughters. Thomas, Lord Viscount Fanshawe, his eldest son, dy'd in May 1674; he was a handsome gentleman of an excellent understanding and great honour and honesty. He married the daughter and sole heir of Knitton Ferres of Beefordberry in the county of Hertfort Esqr. by which he had no child. After his father's death he married the daughter of Sir John E[velyn], widow to Sir John [Wray] of Lincolnshire. By this wife he had severall children, of which only two survived him: Thomas, now Lord Vicount Fanshaw, and Katharine. His widow is lately married unto my Lord Castelton of Senbeck in Yorkshire. He lies buried with his ancestors in the parish church of Ware.

Your uncle Henry, that was the second son, was killed in fighting gallantly in the Low Countrys with English colours in his hand. He was very handsom and a very brave young man, beloved and lamented of all that knew him. The 3d died a bachellor. I knew him not.

The fourth is Sir Simon Fanshawe, a gallant gentle man, but more a libertin than any one of his family. He married a very fine and good woman, and of a great estate. She was daughter and co-heir to Sir William Walter and widow to Knitton Ferres, Esqr., son to Sir John Ferres of Hertfordshire.

Your father, Sir Richard Fanshaw, Knight and Baronnett, one of the Masters of the Requests, Secretary of the Latin Tongue, Burgesse for the University of Cambridge, and one of His Majestye's most honorable Privy Councell of England and Irland, and His Majesty's Embassadour to Portugall and Spaine, was the fifth and youngest sonn. He married me, the eldest daughter of Sir John Harrison Knight, of Balls in the county of Hertford. He was married at thirty-five years of age and lived with me but 23 years and 29 days. He lies buried in a new vault I purchassed of Humfrey, Lord Bishop of London, in St Mary's Chappell in the church of Ware near his ancestors, over which I built him a monument.

My dear husband had six sons and eight daughters borne and christned, and I miscarryed of 6 more, 3 at severall times and once of 3 sons when I was about half gone my time. Harrison my eldest son, and Henry my second son, Richard my third, and Henery my fourth, and Richard my fifth are all dead. My third lyes buried in the Protestant Churchyard in Paris, by the father of the Earl of Bristol.

My eldest daughter Ann lyes buried in the parish church of Tankersley in Yorkshire, where she dyed. Elizabeth lyes in the chappell of the French Hospitall at Madrid, where she dyed of a feavor at 10 days old. My next daughter of her name lyes buryed in the parish of Fotts Cray in Kent near Frogpool, my brother Warrick's house, where she dyed, and my fourth daughter Mary lies in my father's vault in Hartford with my first son Henry. My eldest lyes buried in the parish church of St. John's Colledge in Oxford, where he was born; my second Henry lyes in Bengey Church in Hartfordshire, and my second Richard in the Esperance in Lisbone in Portugall, he being borne 10 weeks before my time when I was in that court. I praise God I have living yourself and foure sisters: Katharin, unmarried; Margarett married to Vincent Grantham, Esqr., of Gaultho in the county of Lincoln; Ann; and Elizabeth.

Now that I have shewed you the most part of your family by the male line, except Sir Thomas Fanshawe of Jenkines, who hath but one child and that a daughter, and 2 brothers, both unmarried. Their father as well as themselves, was a worthy, honest gentleman, and a great sufferer for the Crown, wholy ingaging his estate for the maintenance thereoff, and so is my cousin, John Fanshaw of Parsles in Essex, who hath but 2 sons, one (unmarried) by his first wife, who was the daughter of Sir William Kinsmall, and the other is a child whom he had by his last wife, the daughter of my cousin, Thomas Fanshaw of Jenkins. I confess I owe to Sir Thomas Fanshaw as good a caracter as I can express, for he fully deserves it both for his true honour and most excellent acquired and naturall parts; and that which is of me most esteemed, he was your father's intimate friend as well as near kinsman, and during the time of the war he was very kind to us by assisting us in our wants, which were as great as his supports, which, though I thank God I have fully repay'd, yet must ever remain obliged for his kindness and esteeme he hath for us. He married the daughter and heir of Sir Edward Heath, a pretty lady and good woman.

But I must here with thankfullness acknowledge God's bounty to your family, who hath bestowed most excellent wives on most of them, both in person and fortune; but with respect to the rest I must give with all reverence justly your grandmother the first and best place, who being left a widow at 39 years of age, handsom with a full fortune, all her children provided for, kept her self a widow, and out of her jointure and revenue purchased six hundred pounds a year for the younger children of her eldest son. Besides she added five hundred pounds a piece to the portions of her younger children, having nine, whereof but one daughter was married before the death of Sir Henry Fanshawe, and she was the second. Her name was Mary, married to William News, Esqr., of Hadham in Hartfordshire. The eldest daughter married Sir Capell Bedells of Hammerton in Huntingtonshire; the 3d never married; the fourth married Sir William Buttler of Tesin in Kent; the fivet dyd young.

Thus you have been made acquainted with most of your nearest relations by your father, except your cousin germains, which are the 3 sons of your uncle, Lord Fanshawe, and William News, Esqr., and his 2 Brothers, and Sir Oliver Buttler and my Lady Cam[pbell] of Essex and 3 maiden sisters of hers, and my Lady Loventhorp of Blacksware in Hertfordshire. There was more, but they are dead, and so is the most part of them I have named, but their memories will remain as long as their names for honest, worthy, vertuous men and women who served God in their generations in their severall capacitys. And without vanity none exceeded them in their loyalty, which cost them dear, for there was as many fathers, sons, uncles, nephews, cousin germains, and those that matched to them, ingaged and sequestred for the Crown in the time of the late rebellion, as their revenue made near eighty thousand pounds a year, and this I have often seen a list off and know it to be true. The use of which to you is that you should not omit your duty to your king and country, nor be lesse in your industry to exceed, at least not shame, the excellent memory of your ancestors. They were all eminent officers, and that, I believe, keeping them ever imployed, made them so good men. I hope in God the like paralell will be in you, which I heartly and dayly pray for.

I was borne in St. Olives, Heart-Street, London, in a house that my father took of the Lord Dinguell, father to the now Duchess of Ormond, in the year 1625, on Our Lady Day, the 25 day of March. Mr. Hide, Lady Astion, Lady Wolstolholme were my godfather and godmothers. In that house I lived in the wintertime untill I was fifteen years old 3 months, with my ever honoured and most dear mother, who departed this life on the 30th day of July, 1640, and now lies buried in Hallows Church in Hartford. Her funerall cost my father above a thousand pounds, and a Doctor Howlsworth preached her funerall sermon, in which upon his own knowledge he told before many hundreds of people this accident following. That my mother being sick to death of a feavour 3 months after I was borne, which was the occasion she gave me suck no longer, her friends and servants thought to all outward appearance that she was dead, and so lay almost two days and a night, but Doctor Winston coming to comfort my father went in to my mother's chamber and, looking earnestly on her face, sayd, 'She was so handsome, and now looks so lovely, I can not think she is dead'; and suddenly took a lancet out of his pocket and with it cut the sole of her foot, which bled. Upon this he immediatly caused her to be lain upon her bed again, and to be rubb'd, and such means used as she came to life, and opening her eyes saw 2 of her kinswomen stand by her, my Lady Knowells and my Lady Russell, both with great white sleeves as the fashon was then, and said, 'Did ye not promiss me 15 years? and are you come again?', which they not understanding persuaded her to keep her spirits quiet, in that great weaknesse wherin she then was. But some few houres after she desired my father and Doctor Howlsworth might be left alone whith her, to whom she sayd, 'I will acquaint you that during the time of my trance I was in great quiet, but in a place I could neither distinguish nor describe; but the sence of leaving my girle, which is dearer to me than all my children, remained a trouble upon my spirit. Suddainly I saw two by me cloathed in long white garments, and methought I fell down with my face in the dust, and they asked why I was troubled in so great happines. I replyed, "O let me have the same grant given to [Hezekiah], that I may live 15 years to see my daughter a woman." To which they answered, "It is done"; and then at that instant I awaked out of my trance.' And Dr. Howlsworth did then affirme that that day she dyed made just 15 years from that time.

My dear mother was of excellent beauty and good understanding, a loving wife and most tender mother, very pious, and charitable to that degree that she reliev'd (besides the offall of the table which she constantly gave the poore) many with her own hand dayly out of her purse, and drest many wounds of miserable people when she had health, and when that fall'd, as it did often, she caused her servant to supply that place. She left behind her 3 sons, all much older than myself. The eldest, John, married 3 wives. By his last, which was the daughter of Mr. Ludlow, a very antient and noble family, he left 2 daughters, which are both unmarried. My second brother, William, dyed at Oxford with a bruise on his side caused by the fall of his horse, which was shot under him as he went out with a party of horse against a party of the Earle of Essex in 1643. He was a very good and gallant young man, and they are the very words the King say'd of him when he was told of his death. He was much lamented by all that knew him. The 3rd, Abraham, hath left no issue. I was the fourth, and my sister Margarett the fifth, who married Sir Edmund Turner of Southstock in Lincolnshire, a worthy, pious man.

My father in his old age married again, the daughter of Mr. Shatbolt of Hartfordshire, and had by her a son, Richard, and a daughter, Mary. The son marryed the eldest daughter of the now Lord Grandeson, and the daughter married the eldest son of Sir Rowland Litton of Knebworth in Hartfordshire. My father lived to see them both married, and injoy'd a firm health untill above 80 years of age. He was a handsom gentleman, of great naturall parts, a great accomptant, vast memory, an incomparable penman, of great integrity and servise to his Prince, had been a member of five Parliaments, a good husband and father, especially to me, who never can sufficiently praise God for him nor acknowledge his most tender affection and bounty to me and mine; but as in duty bound I will for ever say none had ever a kinder and better father than myself. He dyed on the 28th day of September, 16[69], and lyes buried by my mother in his own vault in Allhollows Church in Hartford.

My father was born at Bemond in Lancashire, the 12th son of his father, whose mother was the daughter of Mr. Hiessom, cosen garman to the old Countess of Riveres. I have little knowledge of my father's relations, more than the families of Aston, Irland, Sandis, Bemond, and Courwin, who brought him to London and placed him with my Lord Treasurer Salsbury, then Secrettary of Estate, who sent him into Sir John Wolstolholm's family, and gave him a small place in the Custome House to inable him for that imployment. He, being of good parts and capacity, in sometime raised himself by God's help to get a very great estate, for I have often heard him say that besides his education, he never had but 20 marks, which his father gave him when he came to London, and that was all he ever had for a portion. He made it appeare with great truth that during the time of the war he lost by the rebells above an hundred and thirty thousand pounds, and yet he left his son 1600 a year land and gave his daughters about 20000lb.

Now it is necessary to say something of my mother's education of me, which was with all the advantages that time afforded, both for working all sorts of fine works with my needle, and learning French, singing, lute, the virginalls, and dancing; and, not withstanding I learned as well as most did, yet was I wild to that degree that the houres of my beloved recreation took up too much of my time, for I loved riding in the first place, and running, and all acteive pastimes; and in fine I was that which we graver people call a hoyting girle. But to be just to myself, I never did mischief to myself or people, nor one immodest action or word in my life, but skipping and activity was my delight. But upon my mother's death I then begun to refflect, and as an offering to her memory, I flung away those little childnesses that had formerly possest me, and by my father's command took upon me the charge of his house and family, which I so ordered by my excellent mother's example, as found acceptance in his sight. I was very well beloved by all our relations and my mother's friends, which I payd a great respect to; and I ever was ambitious to keep the best company, which I have done, I thank God, all the days of my life. My father and mother were both great lovers and honourers of clergemen, but all of Cambridge, and chiefly Dr. Bamberdg, Doctor Howlsworth, Broanbricke, Walley, and Mickellthite, and Sanderson, with many others. We lived with great plenty and hospitality, but no lavishness in the lest, nor prodigality, and I believe my father never drunk 6 glasses of wine in his life in one day.

About [16]41 my brother William Harrison was chosen Burges of [Queensborough] and sett in the Commons House of Parliament, but not long. For when the King sat up his standard, he went to him to [Nott]ingham. Yet he, during his setting, undertooke that my father should lend 50000 pounds to pay the Scots, who had then entered England, and as it seems was to be both payd and prayd to goe home. But afterwards their plague infected the whole nation, as to all our sorrows we know, and this debt of my father remained to him untill the restoration of this king.

In [16]42 my father was taken prisonner at his house, called Mountegue House in Bishop Gate Street, and threatned to be sent a bord a ship into the plantations, with many more of his own quality. And then they plundered his house, but he getting loose under pretence to fetch some writings they demanded in his hands concerning the publick revenue. He went to Oxford in [16]43, and thereupon the Long Parliament (of which he was a member for the town of Lankester) plundered him out of what remained, and sequestred his whole estate, which continued out of his possession until the happy restoration of the King.

My father commanded my sister and myself to come to him to Oxford where the court then was; but we, that had till that hour lived in great plenty and great order, found ourselves like fishes out of the water and the sene so changed that we knew not at all how to act any part but obedience; for from as good houses as any gentleman of England had we came to a baker's house in an obscure street, and from roomes well furnished to lye in a very bad bed in a garrett, to one dish of meat and that not the best ordered; no mony, for we were as poor as Job, nor clothes more than a man or two brought in their cloak bags. We had the perpetuall discourse of losing and gaining of towns and men; at the windows the sad spectacle of war, sometimes plague, sometimes sicknesses of other kind, by reason of so many people being packt together, as I believe there never was before of that quality; alwaies want, yet I must needs say that most bore it with a martyrlike cheerfulness. For my owne part I begun to think we should all like Abraham live in tents all the days of our lives.

The King sent my father a warrant for a baronnett, but he returned it with thanks, saying he had too much honour of his knighthood which His Majesty had honoured him with some years before for the fortune he now possessed. But as in a racke the turbulence of the waves disperses the splinters of the rock, so it was my lot; for having buried my dear brother Will Harrison in Exeter Colledge Chappell, I then married your dear father in [16]44 in Wolvercot Church, 2 miles from Oxford, upon the 18th day of May. None was at our wedding but my dear father (who by my mother's desire gave me her wedding ring, with which I was married), and my sister Margarett, and my brother and sister Buttler,

Sir Edward Hide, afterwards Lord Chancellor, and Sir Geffrey Palmer, the King's Atturny. Before I was married my husband was sworn Secrettary of War to the Prince, now our King, with a promise from Charles the First to be prefer'd so soon as occasion offered it, but both his fortunes and my promised portion, which was made 10000lb, were both at that time in expectation, and we might truely be called marchant adventurers, for the stock we sett up our trading with did not amount to 20 pounds betwixt us. But, however, it was to us as a little piece of armour is against a bullet, which if it be right placed, though no bigger than a shilling serves as well as a wole sute of arms; so our stock bought pens, ink, and paper, which was your father's trade, and by it I assure you we liv'd better than those that were born to 12000lb a year as long as he had his liberty. Here stay till I have told you your father's life untill I married him.

He was but 7 years old when his father died, and his mother, my Lady, designed him for the law, having bred him first with that famous school-master Mr. Farneby, and then under the tuition of Doctor Beall in Jesus Colledge in Cambridge; from whence, being a most excellent Latinist, he was admitted into the Inward Temple; but it seemed so crabbed a study and disagreable to his inclinations that he rather studyed to obey his mother than to make any progress in the law.

Upon the death of his mother, whom he dearly loved and honoured, he went into France, to Paris, where he had 3 cousin germains: Lord Strangford, Sir John Baeker of Kent, and my cousin Thornell. The whole stocke he carryd with him was 80 pieces of gold, and French silver to the value of 5 pounds in his pockets. His gold was quilted in his doublett. He went by post to lodgings in the Fauxbourg St. Germain with an intent to rest that night and the next day to find out his kindred, but the Devil that never sleeps so ordered it that 2 friers entered the chamber where in he was, and wellcoming him, being his countrymen, invited him to play; he innocently, only intending diversion untill his supper was ready. But that was not their design, for having ingadged him, they left him not as long as he was worth a grot; which when they discovered, the one gave him five pieces of his mony untill he could recruit himself by his friends, which he did the next day, and from that time forward never playd for a piece. It came to pass that seven years after, my husband being in Huntingtonshire at a bowling green with Sir Cappell Beddels and many other persons of quality, one in the company was called Captain Taller. My husband, who had a very quick and persing eye, marked him much as knowing his face, and found through his perrwig, and scarlett cloak, and buff sute, that his name was neither Captain nor Taller, but the honest Jesuite called Frier Sherwood that had cheated him of the greatest part of his mony, and after had lent him the five pounds. So your father went to him and gave him his 5 pieces and said, 'Father Sherwood, I know you, and you know this.' At which he was extreamly surprised and begg'd of your father not to discover him, for his life was in danger.

After a year's stay in Paris he travelled to Madrid in Spain, there to learn that language. At the same time for that purpose went the late Earle of Carnarvan, and my Lord of Bedford, and Lord John B[erkeley], and severall other gentlemen. Afterward, having spent [about two] years abroad, he returned to London, and gave so good an account of his travells that he was about the year 163[5] made Secrettary of the Ambassy, when my Lord Aston went ambassador. During your father's travells he had spent a considerable part of his stock which his father and mother left him. In those days, where there was so many younger children, it was considerable, being 50 pounds a year and 1500lb in money. Upon the return of the Embassador, your father was left resident untill Sir Arthur Hopter went embassador, and then he came home about the year [16]37 or [163]8.

And I must tell you here of an accident that your father had coming out of Spaine in this journy poste. He, going into a bed for some few houres to refresh himself in a village fivetey leagues from Madrid, he slept so soundly that, not with-standing the house was on fire, and all the people of the village there, he never awaked, but the honesty of the owners was such that they carryd him and set him asleepe upon a piece of timber on the high way, and there he awaked and found his portemanteau and clothes by him, without the lest loss—which is extraordinary considering the possession of his landlord, who had at that time his house burnt to the ground.

After being here a year or 2, and no preferment coming, Secrettary Window Banke calling him Puritan, being his enemy because himself was a Papist, he was by his eldest brother put into the place of the King's Remembrancer, absolutely, with this proviso, that he should be accomptable for the use of the income, but if in 7 years he would pay 8000lb for it to his brother, then it should be his with the whole revenue of it. But the war breaking out presently after put an end to this design; for being the King's sworn servant, he went to the King in Oxford, as well as his fellows, to avoyd the fury of the madness of the people; where having been almost a year, we married, as I sayd before, and I will continue my discourse where we left.

Now we appeared upon the stage to act what part God desined us, and as faith is the evidence of things not seen, so we upon so righteous a cause cheerfully resolved to suffer what that would drive us to, which afflictions were neither few not small, as you will find.

This year the Prince had an established Councell which were Earl Barkshire, Earl of Brandford, Lord Cappell, Lord Culpeper, Lord Hopton, and Sir Edward Hide, Chancellor of the Exchecker. My husband was then, as I said, newly entered into his new office of Secrettary of the Councell of War, and the King would have had him then to have been sworn His Highness's Secretary. But the Qween, who was then no friend to my husband because he formerly had made Secret[ary] Windowbanke appeare in his colours, who was one of Her Majesty's favorites, wholy obstructed that then, and placed with the Prince Sir Robert Long, for whom she had a great kindnesse; but the consequence will show the man.

The beginning of March [1645], your father went to Bristol with his new master, and this was his first journy, which because he left me behind him, I then lying in of my first son Harrison Fanshaw, who was borne on the 22nd of February last, as for that it was the first time we had parted a day since wee maried, he was extreamly afflicted even to tears, though passion was against his nature. But the sence of leaving me with a dying child, which did dye 2 days after, in a garrison town, extream weake and very poor, were such circumstances as he could not beare with, onely the argument of necescity. And for my own part, it cost me so dear that I was 10 weeks before I could goe alone, but he by all opportunitys writ to me to fortify myself and to comfort me in the company of my father and sister, who were both with me, and that so soon as the Lords of the Councell had their wives come to them, I should come to him, and that I should receive the first mony he got and hoped it would be suddainly. By the help of God, with these cordialls, I recovered my former strength by little and little. Nor did I in my distressed condition lack the conversation of many of my relations then in Oxford and kindnesses of very many of the nobility and gentry, both for goodness' sake, and because your father being there in a good imployment, they found him serviceable to themselves or friends, which friendships none better distinguished between his place or person than your father.

It was in May [16]45, the first time I went out of my chamber and to church, where after service Sir William Parceust, a very honest gentleman, came to me and said he had a letter for me from your father, and 50 pieces of gold, and was coming to bring them me. I opened first my letter and rid those unexpressable joys that most overcame me, for he told me that I should the Thirsday following come to him, and to that purpose he had sent me that mony, and would find 2 of his men with horse and all accommodation both for myself, my father, and sister, and that Lady Cappell and Lady Brandford would meet me on the way. But that gold your father sent me when I was ready to perish did not so much revive me as his summons. I went immediately to walke, or at lest to sett, in the air (being very weake) in the gardon of St. John's Colledge, and there with my good father communicated my joy, who took great pleasure to hear of my husband's good success and likewise of his journy to him.

We all of my household being present heard drums beat in the high way under the garden wall. My father asked me if I would goe up upon the mount and see the souldjers march, for it was Sir Charles Lee's company of foot, an acquaintance of ours. I sayd yes, and went up, laining my back to a tree that grew on the mount. The Commander, seing us there, in compliment gave us a volly of shott, and one of their muskets being loden shot a brace of bullets not 2 inches above my head as I lained to the tree; for which mercy and deliverance I praise God.

And next week we were all on our journy for Bristol, very merry and thought that now all things would mend and the worst of my misfortunes past, but little though[t] I to leap into that sea that would tosse me untill it had racked me, but we were to ride all night by agreement for feare of the enemies surprising us as we pased, they quartering in the way. About nightfall, having travailed about 20 miles, we discovered a troop of horse coming towards us, which proved Sir Marmaduke Royden, a worthey commander and my countryman. He told me that hearing I was to pass by his garrison, he was come out to conduct me, he hoped, as far as there was danger, which was about 12 miles. With many thanks we parted and, having reffreshed ourselves and horses, we sett forth for Bristol where we arrived the 20th of May.

My husband had provided very good logings for us, and as soon as he could come home from the Councell, where he was at my arrivall, he with all expressions of joy received me in his arms and gave me an hundred pieces of gold, saying, 'I know that thou that keeps my heart so well will keep my fortune, which from this time I will ever put into thy hands as God shall bless me with increase.' And now I thought myself a qween, and my husband so glorious a crown that I more valued myself to be call'd by his name than borne a princess, for I knew him very wise and very good, and his soule doted on me, upon which confidence I'll tell you what happened.

My Lady Rivers, a brave woman and one that had suffered very many thousand pounds loss for the King, and that I had a great reverence for and she a kindness for me as a kindswoman, in discourse she tacitly commended the knowledge of state affaires and that some women were very happy in a good understanding there of, as my Lady [Aubigny], Lady [Isabella] Thine, and divers others, and yet none was at first more capable than I; that in the night she knew there came a post from Paris from the Qween, and that she would be extream glad to hear what the Qween commanded the King in order to his affairs, saying if I would ask my husband privatly, he would tell me what he found in the packett, and I might tell her. I that was young, innocent, and to that day had never in my mouth, 'What news', begun to think there was more in inquiring into buseness of publick affaires than I thought off, and that it being a fashonable thing would make me more beloved of my husband (if that had been possible) than I was. When my husband returned from

Councell, after wellcoming him home, as his custome ever was, he went with his handfull of papers into his study for an houre or more. I followed him. He turning hastyly sayd, 'What wouldst thou have, my life?' I told him I heard the Prince had received a packett from the Qween, and I guessed it that in his hand, and I desired to know what was in it. He smiling replyed, 'My love, I will immediatly come to thee. Pray thee goe, for I am very busy.' When he came out of his closet I revived my sute. He kissed me and talked of other things. At supper I would eat nothing. He as usually sat by me and drunke often to me, which was his custome, and was full of discourse to company that was at table. Going to bed I asked again, and said I could not belive he loved me if he refused to tell me all he knew, but he answered nothing, but stopped my mouth with kisses, so we went to bed. I cryed and he went to sleep; next morning very early, as his custome was, he called to rise, but begun to discourse with me first, to which I made no reply. He rose, came on the other side of the bed and kissed me, and drew the curtaine softly and went to court. When he came home to dinner, he presently came to me as was usuall, and when I had him by the hand I sayd, 'Thou dost not care to see me troubled.' To which he, taking me in his armes, answered, 'My dearest soule, nothing upon earth can afflict me like that; and when you asked me of my busines, it was wholy out of my power to satisfy thee. For my life and fortune shall be thine, and every thought of my heart, in which the trust I am in may not be revealed; but my honour is my own, which I can not preserve if I communicate the Prince's affaires, and pray thee with this answer rest satisfyed.' So great was his reason and goodness, that upon consideration it made my folly appeare to me so vile that from that day untill the day of his death I never thought fit to aske him any business, but that he communicated freely to me, in order to his estate or family.

My husband grew much in the Prince's favour, and Mr. Long not suffered to execute the business of his place, the Councell suspecting that he held private intelligence with the Earl of Essex, which when he perceived, he went into the enemys' quarters and so to London, and then into France, full of complaints of the Prince's Counsell to Qween Mother. When he was gone, your father supplyd his place.

About July this year the plague increased so fast in Bristol that the Prince and all his retinue went to Barstable, which is one of the finest towns I know in England, and your father and I went 2 days after the Prince; for during all the time I was in court I never journyed but either before him, or when he was gone, nor ever saw him but at church, for it was not in those days the fashon for honest women, except they have business, to visit a man's court. I saw there, at Mr. Pamer's where we lay, who was a merchant, a parrat above an hundred years old. They have neer this town a fruit called a massard, like a cherry, but different in tast, and makes the best pyes, with their sort of cream, I ever eat. My Lady Cappell here left us, and with a passe from the Earl of Essex went to London with her eldest daughter, now Marquesse Woster. Sir Allan Apsley was Governor of the town, and we had all sorts of good provision and accommodation, but the Prince's affaires calling him from that place, we went to Lanstoen in Cornwall, and thither came very many gentlemen of that county to doe their dutys to His Highness. They were generally loyall to the Crown and hospitable to their nighbours, but they are of a crafty and sensorious nature, as most are so far from London.

That country hath great plenty, especially of fish and fowl, but nothing near so fatt and sweet as within 40 miles of London. We were quartered at Truerow, 20 miles beyond Lanston, in which place I had like to have beene rob'd one night, haveing with me but 7 or eight persons, my husband being then at Lanston with his master. Some had discovered that my husband had a little trunke of the Prince's in keeping, in which were some jewells that tempted them to this assay. But, praysed be God, I deffended, with the few servants I had, the house so long that help came from the towne to my rescue, which was not above a flit shott from the place where I dwelt. And the next day, upon my notes, my husband sent me a guard by His Highness's command.

From thence the court remov'd to Pendenees Castle, some times commanded by Sir Nicholas Slaning, who lost his life bravely in the King's servise and left an excellent name behind him. In this place came Sir John [Grenvile] into His Highness's servise, and was made a gentleman of his bed chamber. His father was a very honest gentleman, and lost his life in the King's servise, and his uncle, Sir Richard, was a good commander, but a little too severe. I was at Pensance with my father, and in the same town was my brother Fanshawe and his lady and children. My father and that family imbarked for Morlais, in Brittany, with my father's new wife, which he had then married out of that family. My cousin Fanshawe of Jenkins and his eldest son, being with them, went also over, but being in a small vessel of that port, and surprised with a great storme, they had all like to have been cast away, which forced them to land in a little creek 2 leagues from Morlais upon the 28th of March, 1646.

5 days after, the Prince and all his Councell imbarked themselves in a ship called the *Fenixe* for the Ile of Silly. They went from the Land's End, and so did we, being accompanyed with many gentlemen of that country, among whom was Sir Francis Bassett, Governor of the Mount, an honest gentleman, and so were all his family, and in particular we received great civility from them. But we left horse and furniture with Captain Bluett, who promised to keep them untill such a time as we could dispose of them, but when we sent he said he had been plundered of them, not with standing it was well known he lost nothing of his own

at that time. This loss went deep with us, for we lost to the value of 200lb and more. But as the proverb saith, an evil chance seldome comes alone, we having put all our present estate into two trunks and carryed them abord with us in a ship commanded by Sir Nicholas Crispo, whose skill and honesty the master and seamen had no opinion off. My husband was forced to appease their mutiny which his miscariage caused, and taking out money to pay the seamen, that night following they broke open one of our trunks and took out a bag of 60lb and a quantity of gold lace, with our best clothes and linnin and all my combs, gloves, and ribonds, which amounted to near three hundred pounds more.

The next day, after having been pillaged and extreamly sick and bigg with child, I was sett a shore almost dead in the Iland of Silley. When we had got to our quarters near the castle where the Prince lay, I went immediatly to bed, which was so vile that my foot men ever lay in a better, and we had but 3 in the whole house, which consisted of 4 rooms, or rather partitions, 2 low rooms and 2 little lofts, with a ladder to goe up. In one of these they kept dry fish, which was his trade, and in this my husband's two clercks lay; one there was for my sister, and one for myself, and one amongst the rest of our servants. But when I awaked in the morning, I was so cold I knew not what to doe, but the daylight discovered that our bed was neer swimming with the sea, which, the owner told us afterwards, it never did so but at spring tides. With this we were destitute of clothes, and meat or fewell for half the court, to serve them a month, was not to be had in the whole iland. And truly we begg'd our dayly bread of God, for we thought every meal our last. The Councell sent for provisions into France, which served us, but they were bad, and a little of them. Then, after 3 weeks and odd dayes, we sat saile for the Ile of Jarsey, where we safely arrived, praised be God, beyond the belief of all the beholders from that iland; for the pylott, not knowing the way into the harbor, sailed over the rocks, but being spring tides and by chance high water, God be praised, His Highness and all of us came safe a shore through so great a danger.

Sir George Carteright was Lieutenant Governor of that iland under my Lord St. Albans, a man formerly bred a sea boy and borne in that iland, the brother's son of Sir Philip Cartright, whose younger daughter he after wards married. He indeavoured with all his power to entertaine His Highness and court with all plenty and kindness posible, both which the iland afforded, and what was wanting he sent for out of France.

There is in this iland two castles, both good, but St. Marie's is the best, and hath the largest reception. Ther is many gentleman's houses at which we were entertained. They have fine walkes along to their dores of double elmes or oakes, which is extream pleasant, and ordinary high ways are good walks by reason of the shadow. The whole place is grass, except some small parcels of corne ground. Their chieffest imployment is knitting. They neither speak English nor good French. They are a cheerfull, good natur'd people and truly subject to the present Governour. We quarterd at a widow's house in the markett place, Madame the Dipommes, a stocking merchant here. I was upon the seventh of June, 1646, delivered of my second child, a daughter christned Anne.

And now there begun great disputes about the disposall of the Prince, for the Qween would have him to Paris, to which end she sent many letters and messengers to His Highness and Councell, who were for the most part against his going, both to the Qween, his mother, and his going to France for reason of estate. But the French and Qwene having an excellent sollicitor of the Lord Culpeper, it was resolved by His Highnesse to goe, upon which Lord Capell, Lord Hopton, and [the] Chancellor stayed at Jarsey, and with them my husband, whose imployment seased when his master went out of his father's kingdoms; not that your father sided with either party of the Councell, but having no inclination at that time to go to that court, and because his brother Lord Fanshaw was desperate sick at Ca[en], he intended to stay some time with him.

About the beginning of July the Prince, accompany'd with the Earl of Brandford, a souldjer of fortune, and Lord Culpeper, and Earle of Barkshire, and most of his servants, went to Cotanville, and from thence to Paris, where he remained some little time by his mother the Qween's councell, and afterward went into Holland.

Your father and I remained 15 days after in Jersey, and resolved that he would remaine with his brother in Caen whilst he sent me into England, whether my father was gone a month before to se if I could procure a sum of money. The beginning of August we took our leaves of the Governor's family and left our child with a nurse under the care of the Lady Cartrit, and in 4 days we came to Cain, and myself, sister, and maid went from Mr. Sanborne's house (where my brother and all his family lodged) a boord a small merchant man that lay in that river, and upon the 30th of August I arrived in the coves near South-Hampton, to which town I went that night, and came to London two days after.

This was the first time that I had taken any journy without your father, and the first manage of business hee ever put into my hand, in which I thank God I had good success. For lodging in Fleet Street at Mr. East's, the watch maker, with my sister Buttler, I procured by the means of Colonell Coply, a great Parlement man whose wife had formerly been obliged to our family, a pass for your father to come and compound for 300lb hundred a year, which was a part of my portion; but it was onely a pretence, for your grand father was obliged to compound for it, and deliver it us free. And when your father was come, he was very private in London, for he was in dayly fear to be imprisonned in London before he could raise money to go back again to his master, who then was not in a condition to maintaine him. Thus upon thorns he stayd the October, [16]47. In the October before ([16]46) my brother Richard Harrison was borne, and this year my sister Buttler married Sir Philip Warricke, her second husband; for her first, Sir William Buttler, was killed at Cropley Bridge, commanding a part of the King's army. He was a most gallant, worthy, honest gentleman.

In that year, being bigg with child, I fell down one pair of stairs and never hurt myself in the least, but upon the 30th of July I was delivered of a son called Henry, in lodgings in Portugall Row in Lincolnsinfields.

This was a very sad time for us all of the King's party, for by their folly (to give it no worse name) Sir John B[erke]ley, since Lord B[erke]ley, and Mr. John Asbornham of the King's bedchamber, who were drawn in by the cursed crew of the then standing army for the Parlement to perswade the King to leave Hampton Court (to which they had then carryed him) to make his escape; which design falling, as the plott was layd, he was tormented and afterwards shamefully and barbarously murdered as all the world knows.

During his stay at Hampton Court my husband was with him, to whom he was pleased to talk much of his concerns and gave him there credentialls for Spaine with private instructions and letters for his servise, but God for our sins disposed His Majesty's affaires otherwise. I went 3 times to pay my duty to him, both as I was the daughter of his servant and wife to his servant. The last time I ever saw him, when I took my leave, I could not refraine weeping. When he had saluted me, I prayd to God to preserve His Majesty with long life and happy years. He stroked me on my cheek and sayd, 'Child, if God pleaseth, it shall be so, but both you and I must submitt to God's will, and you know in what hands I am in.' Then turning to your father, he sayd, 'Be sure, Dick, to tell my son all that I have sayd, and deliver those letters to my wife. Pray God blesse her. I hope I shall doe well'; and taking him in his arms sayd, 'Thou hast ever been an honest man, and I hope God will bless thee and make thee a happy servant to my son, whom I have charged in my letter to continue his love and trust to you,' adding, 'And I doe promiss you both that if ever I am restored to my dignity, I will bountifully reward you both for your servise and sufferings.' Thus did we part from that glorious sun that within a few months after sett, to the grief of all Christians that were not forsaken by God.

In October, as I told you, my husband and I went into France by the way of Portesmouth, where, walking by the sea side about a mile from our lodging, 2 ships of the Dutch then in war with England shot bulletts at us so near that we heard them wiss by us, at which I called to my husband to make haste back, and begun to run. But he altered not his pace, saying if we must be kill'd, it were as good to be kill'd walking as running. But escaping, we imbarked the next day, and in that journy fetcht home our girle we had left in Jarsy. And my husband was forced to come out of France to Hammerton in Huntingtonshire to my sister Beadell's to the wedding of his nephew, the last Lord Thom[as] Fanshawe, who then married the daughter of Mr. Fearers, as I have sayd before. She was a very great fortune, and a most excellent woman, and brought up sometimes after her mother's death with my sister Bedell's.

About 2 months after this, in June, I was deliverd of a son on the eighth day of June, 1648. In the latter end of July I went to London, leaving my little boy Richard at nurse with his brother at Hatonfortbery. It happened to be the very day after that the Lord Holland was taken prisoner at St. Need and Lord Francis Villers was killed, and as we passed through the town we saw Collonell Montagu, afterwards Earl of Sandwich, spoiling the town for the Parlement and himself. Coming to London, I went to welcom the Marquess of Ormond to town, that then was newly come out of France, who received me with great kindness as she ever had done before, and told me she must love me for many reasons, and one was that we were both borne in one chamber. When I left her she presented me with a ruby ring set with 2 diamonds which she prayd me to wear for her sake, and I have it at this day.

In the month of September my husband was commanded by the Prince to waite on him in the Downs, where he was with a very considerable fleet; but the fleet was divided, part being for the King and part for the Parlement. They were resolved to fight that day, which, if they had, would have been the most cruell fight that ever England knew; but God by His will parted them by a storme, and afterwards, as it was sayd, Lord Culpeper and one Low, a surgion that was a reputed knave, so ordered the business that for mony the fleet was betrayd to the enemy. During this time my husband writ me a letter from a boord the Prince's ship full of concern for me, believing they should ingadge on great odds; but if he should lose his life, he advised me to patience, and this with so much love and reason that my heart melts to this day when I think of it; but God be praysed, he was reserved for better things.

In [Nov]ember my husband went to Paris on his master's business and sent for me from London. I carryed him 300lb of his money. During our stay at Paris I was highly oblidged to the Qween Mother of England. We passed away 6 weeks with delight in very good company. My Lady Morton that was governess to the Lady Henrietta, Charles the First's youngest daughter, was very kind, and I had the honour of her company both in my own lodging and in the Pallais Royall, where she attended her charge. My eldest daughter by her favour was admitted to play with the Princess dayly, and presented with many toys. Likewise my Lady Denby and her daughter, my Lady Gilford, with many other of our nation, both in the court and out of it, amongst whom was Mr. Waller the poet and his wife. They went with us to Callis. Upon the 25 of December, 164[8], I with my husband kissed Qween Mother's hand, who promissed her favour with much grace to us both, and sent letters to the King then in Holland by my husband from Her Majesty. We waited on the Princess, and afterwards took our leaves of all that court. When we came to Callais we met the Earle of Strafford and Sir Ke[nelm] Digby, with some others of our countrymen. We were all feasted at the Govenour's of the castle, and much excellent discourse passed; but, as was reason, most share was Sir Kellan Digby's, who had enlarged somewhat more in extraordinary stories than might be averr'd, and all of them passt with great applause and wonder of the French then at table. But the concluding was that barnackells, a bird in Jarsey, was first a shell fish to appearance and from that sticking upon old wood became in time a bird. After some consideration they all unanimously burst out into laughter, believing it altogether false; and to say the truth, it was the only thing true he had discoursed with them. This was his infirmity, though otherwise a person of most excellent parts and a very fine bred gentleman.

My husband thought it convenient to send me into England again there to try what sums I could raise both for his subsistance abroad and mine at home; and though nothing was so grievous to us both as parting, yet the necessity both of the publick and your father's private affaires obliged us often to yeld to the trouble of absence, as at this time. I took my leave with a sad heart and imbarked myself in a h[oy] for Dover with Mrs. Waller, and my sister Margarett Harrison, and my little girle Nan. But a great storm arising we had like to be cast away, the vessell being half full of water, and we forced to land at Deale, every one carried upon men's backs and we up to the middle in water, and very glad to scape so.

About this time the Prince of Orange was borne.

My husband went from thence by Flanders into Holland to his master, and in February following your father was sent into Ireland by the King, there to receive such monys as Prince Rupert could raise by that fleet he then commanded of the King's. But a few months put an end to that design, though it had a very good aspect in the beginning, which made my husband send for me, and the little familly I had, thither. We went by Bristoll very cheerfully towards my North Starr, that only had the power to fix me, and because I had had the good fortune (as I then thought it) to sell 300lb a year to him that is now Judge Archer in Essex, for which he gave me near 4000lb which at that time I thought a vast sum. But be it more or less, I am sure it was all spent in 7 years' time in the King's servise; and to this hour I repent it not, I thank God. 500lb I carried my husband; the rest I left in my father's agent's hands, to be returned as we needed it. I landed at Yachall in Monster, as my husband directed me in hopes to meet me there, but I had the discomfort of a very hasardous voyage, and the absence of your father, he then being upon business at Corke. So soon as he heard I was landed, he came to me, and with mutuall joy we discoursed those things that were proper to entertaine us both. And thus for 6 months we liv'd so much to our satisfaction that we begun to think of making our abode there during the war, for the country was fertil and all provisions cheap, and the houses good, and we were placed in Red Abby, a house of Dean Boyl's, in Corke. And my Lord of Ormond had a very good army, and the country seemingly quiet, and to compleat our content, all persons very civill to us, especially Dean Boyl, now Lord Chancellor of Ireland and Arch Bishop of Dublin, and his family, and the Lord Inchequin, whose daughter Elhena I christned in 1650. But what earthly comfort is exempt from change, for here I heard of the death of my second son, Henry; and within few weeks of the landing of Cromwell, who so hotly marched over Ireland that the fleet with Prince R[upert] was forced to set sale; and within a small time after, he lost all his richess, which was thought to be worth hundreds of thousands of pounds, in one of his best ships commanded by his brother Maurice who, with many a brave man all sunk, being lost in a storme at sea.

We remained sometime behind in Ireland untill my husband could receive His Majesty's command how to dispose of himself. During this time I had, by a fall of a stumbling horse (being with child), broke my left wrist, which because it was ill set put me to great and long pain; and I was in my bed when Corke revolted. By chance my husband that day was gone upon business to Kingsale. It was in the beginning of [Octo]ber, 16[49], at midnight, I heard the great guns goe off, and there upon I called my family to rise, which they and I did, as well as I could in that condition. Hearing lamentable scricks of men and women and children, I asked at a window the cause. They told me they were all Irish, stript and wounded, turned out of the town, and that Collonell Jefreis, with some others, had possessed themselves of the town for Cromwell. Upon this I immediatly write a letter to my husband, blessing God's providence that he was not there with me, perswading him to patience and hope that I should gett safely out of the town by God's assistance, and desired him to shift for himself for feare of a surprise, with promiss I would secure his papers. So soon as I had finished my letter, I sent it by a faithfull servant, who was lett down the garden wall of Red Abby, and sheltered by the darkness of the night he made his escape. Immediatly I packed up my husband's cabeenet, with all his writings, and near a 1000lb in gold and silver, and all other things both of clothes, linnin, and household stuff that were portable and of value; and then, about 3 a clock in the morning, by the light of a tapour and in that pain I was in, I went into the market place, with onely a man and maid, and, pasing through an unruly tumult with their swords in their hands, searched for their chief commander, Jeffreys, who whilst he was loyall had received many civilitys from your father. I told him that it was necessary that upon that change I should remove, and desired his pass that would be obey'd, or else I must remain there. I hoped he would not deny me that kindness. He instantly writt me a pass, both for myself, family, and goods, and said he would never forgett the respects he owed your father.

With this I came through thousands of naked swords to Red Abbey and hired the next nighbour's cart, which carryed all that I could remove. And myself, sister, and little girle Nan, with 3 maids and 2 men, sett forth at 5 a clock in [Octo]ber, having but 2 horses among us all, which we ridd on by turnes. In this sad condition I left Red Abby, with as many goods as was worth 100lb, which could not be removed, and so were plundered. We went 10 miles to Kingsale in perpetuall fear of being fetched back again, but by little and little, I thank God, we got safe to the garrison where I found your father the most disconsolate man in the world for fear of his family, which he had no possibility to assist; but his joys exceeded to see me and his darling daughter, and to hear the wounderfull escape we through the assistance of God had made.

But when the rebells went to give an accompt to Cromwell of their meritorious act, he immediatly asked them where Mr. Fanshawe was. They replyed, he was that day gone to Kingsale. Then he demanded where his papers and his family were, at which they all stared one at an other, but made no reply. Their Generall sayd, 'It was as much worth to have seised his papers as the town; for I did make account by them to have known what these parts of the country were worth.'

But we within a few days received the King's command, which was that my husband should upon sight therof go into Spaine to Philip the 4th, and deliver him His Majesty's letters, and by my husband also His Majesty sent letters to my Lord Cottington and Sir Edward Hide, his Embassadors Extraordinary in that court. Upon this order we went to Macrom to the Lord Clancartie, who married a sister of the Lord Ormond. We staid there 2 nights, and at my coming away after very noble entertainment, my Lady gave me a great Irish gray hound, and I presented her with a very fine besser stone.

From thence we went to Limbrick, where we were entertained by the Maior and Aldermen very nobly, and the Recorder of the town was very kind, and in respect they made my husband a freeman of Limbrick. There we met the Bishop of Londonderey and the Earl of Rosscomon, who was Lord Chancellor of that kingdom at that time. These 2 persons with my husband, being together writing letters to the King to give an account of that kingdome, when they were going down stairs from my Lord Roscomon's chamber, striving to hold the candle at the stairs' head because the privacy of their dispatch admitted not a servant to be near, my Lord Roscomon fell down the stairs, and his head fell upon the corner of a stone and broke his scull in 3 places, of which he dyed 5 dayes after, leaving the broad Seal of Irland in your father's hands untill such time as he could acquaint His Majesty with this sad accident and receive orders how to dispose of the seales. This caused our longer stay, but your father and I being invited to my Lord Inchequin's, there to stay until we heard out of Holland from the King, which was a month before the messenger returned, we had very kind entertainment and vast plenty of fish and fowle.

By this time my Lord Lieutenant the now Duke of Ormond's army was quite dispersed and himself gone for Holland, and every person concerned in that intrest shifting for their lives, and Cromwell went through as bloodily as victoriously, many worthy persons being murdered in cold blood, and their familys quite ruined. From thence we went to the Lady Honor O'Brien's, a lady that went for a maid, but few believed it; she was the youngest daughter of the Earle of Toumment.

There we stayd 3 nights, the first of which I was surprised by being layd in a chamber where about 1 a clock I heard a voice that awaked me. I drew the curtain, and in the casement of the window I saw by the light of the moon a woman leaning into the window through the casement, in white, with red hair and pale, gastly complexion. She spake loud and in a tone I never heard, thrice, 'Ahone', and then with a sith more like wind than breath she vanished, and to me her body looked more like a thick cloud than substance. I was so much affrighted that my hair stood an end and my night clothes fell off. I pulld and pinched your father, who never awaked during this disorder I was in, but at last was much surprised to find me in this fright, and more when I related the story and showed him the window opened; neither of us slept more that night; but he entertained me with telling how much more those apparitions were usuall in that country than in England, and we concluded the cause to be the great superstition of the Irish and the want of that knowing faith that should deffend them from the power of the Devill, which he exercises amongst them very much.

About 8 a clock the lady of the house came to see us, saying she had not been abed all night because a cousin O'Brien of hers, whose ancestors had own'd that house, had desired her to stay with him in his chamber, who dyed at 2 a clock, and, said she, 'I wish you to have had no disturbance; for it is the custome of this place that when any dye of the family, there is the shape of a woman appears in this window every night untill they be dead. This woman was many ages agoe got with child by the owner of this place, and he in his garden murdered her and flung her into the river under your window. But truly, I thought not of it when I lodged you here, it being the best roome I had.' We made little reply to her speech, but disposed ourselves to be gone suddenly.

By this time my husband had received order from the King to give the Lord Inchequin the Seal to keep until further order from His Majesty. When that business was settled we went, accompany'd with my Lord Inchequin and his family, 4 or five miles towards Galloway, which we did by force and not by choise; for the plague had been so hott in that city the summer before that it was almost depopulated, and the haven as much as the town. But your father, hearing that by accident there was a great ship of Amsterdam bound for Malegoe in Spaine, and Cromwell pursuing his conquests at our backs, resolved to fall into the hands of God rather than into the hands of men, and with his family of about 10 persons came to the town at the latter end of February, where we found guards placed that none should enter without certificats from whence they came. But understanding that your father came to imbark himself for Spaine, and that there was a merchant's house took for us that was near the seaside and one of their best, they told us if we pleased to light, they would wait on us to the place, but it was long from thence and no horses were admitted into the town.

An Irish footman that heard this and served us, sayd, 'I liv'd here some years and know every street, and I likewise know a much nearer way than these men can show you, Sir. Therefore come with me, if you please.' We resolved to follow him, and sent our horses to stables in the suburbs. He led us all on the backside of the town under the walls over which the people during the plague, which was not yet quite stopped, had flung out all their dung, deart, and rags, and we walked up to the middle of our leggs in them, for being ingaged we could not get back.

At last we found the house by the master standing at the doore expecting us, who sayd, 'You are wellcome to this desolate city, where you now see the streets grown over with grass, once the finest little city in the world.' And indeed it was easy to think so, the buildings being uniformely built and a very fine markett place, and walkes arched and paved by the sea side for their merchants to walk on, and a most noble harbour. Our house was very clean; onely one maid in it besides the master. We had a very good supper provided and, being very weary, we went early to bed, but we could not rest very well, fancying our legs bit.

The next morning, as soon as my husband had put on his gown and begun to put on his stockings, he called me, saying, 'My heart, what great spots are these on my legs? Sure, this is the plague, but I am very well and feel nothing.' At which I ran out of the bed to him and saw my own legs in the same condition, and upon examining the cause we found that the sheets being short and the blanketts full of fleas, we had those spots made by them.

The owner of this house entertained us with the story of the last Marques of Woster, who had been there sometime the year before. He had of his own and other friends jewells to the value of 8000lb which some merchant had lent upon them. My Lord appointed the day of receiving the mony and delivering his jewells. Being met, he shews them all to these persons, then seals them up in a box and delivered them to one of these merchants, by consent of the rest, to be kept for one year, and upon the then payment of the 8000lb by my Lord Marquis to be delivered him. After my Lord had received this mony, he was entertained at all these persons' houses and nobly feasted, staing with them near a month. Then he went from thence into France. When the year was expired they, by letters into France, pressed the payment of this borrowed mony severall times, alledging that they had great necessity of their mony to drive their trade with, to which my Lord Marquis made no answer, which did at last so exasperate these men that they broke open the seales, and opening the box found nothing but rags and stones for their 8000lb, at which they were highly inraged, and in this case I left them.

The beginning of February we took ship, and our kind hoste with much satisfaction in our company pray'd God to bless us and give us a good voyage. 'For,' sayd he, 'I thank God you are all gone safe a boord from my house, not withstanding I have buryed 9 persons out of my house within these 6 months'; which saying much started us, but God's name be praised, we were all well and so continued.

Here now our scene was shifted from land to sea, and we left that brave kingdom fallen in 6 or 8 months into a most miserable sad condition, as it hath been many times in most kings' reigns. God knows why, for I presume not to say, but the natives seem to me a very loving people to each other and constantly false to all strangers, the Spaniards only excepted. The country exceeds in timber and seaports, and great plenty of fish, fowle, flesh, and by shipping wants no forein commoditys.

We pursued our voyage with prosperous winds, but with a most tempestuous master, a Duchman, which is enough to say, but truly I think the greatest beast I ever saw of his kind. When we had just passed the Straights, we saw coming towards us with full saile a Turkish galley well man'd, and we believed we should all be carried away slaves, for this man had so loaden his ship with goods for Spaine that his guns were useless, though the ship carried 60 guns. He called for brandy, and after he had well drunken and all his men, which were neare 200, he called for armes and cleared the deck as well as he could, resolving to fight rather than lose his ship that was worth 30000lb. This was sad for us passengers, but my husband bid us be sure to keepe in the cabine and not appear (no woman), which would make the Turks think we were a man of war; but if they saw women, they would take us for merchants and boord us. He went upon the decks and took a gun and bandoliers and sword, and with the rest of the ship's company stood on the deck expecting the arrival of the Turkish man-of-war. This beast captain had locked me up in the cabine. I knocked and called long to no purpose, untill at length a cabine boy came and opened the doore. I, all in teares, desired him to be so good as to give me his blew throm cap he wore and his tarred coat, which he did, and I gave him half a crown, and putting them on and flinging away my night's clothes, I crept up softly and stood upon the deck by my husband's side as free from sickness and fear as, I confess, from discretion; but it was the effect of that passion which I could never master. By this time the 2 vessels were ingaged in parley and so well satisfyd with speech and sight of each other's forces that the Turk's man-of-war tacked about and we continued our course. But when your father saw it convenient to retreat, looking upon me he blessed himself and snatched me up in his armes, saying, 'Good God, that love can make this change!' And though he seemingly chid me, he would laugh at it as often as he remembred that voyage.

In the beginning of March we all landed, praysed be God, in Malegoe, very well, and full of content to see our selves delivered from the sword and the plague, and living in hope that we should one day return happily to our own country; notwithstanding we thought it great odds, considering how the affaires of the King's 3 kingdomes stood. But we trusted in the providence of Almighty God and proseeded. We were very kindly entertained by the English merchants and by them lodged in a merchant's house, where we had not been with our goods 3 days, but the vessell that brought us thither, by the negligence of a cabine boy, was blown up in the harbor with the loss of above 100 men and all her lading.

After we had reffreshed ourselves some dayes, we went on our journey towards Madrid, and lodged the first night at Velez Mallegoe, to which we were accompanied by most of the merchants. The next day we went [to] Granatha, having passed the highest mountaines I ever saw in my life; but under this lyeth the finest vally that can be possibly described, adorned with high trees, rich grass, and beautifyed with a large, deep, clear River. Over the town and this standeth that goodly vast pallace of the kings called the Allhambray, whose buildings are, after the fashon of the Moores, adorned with vast quantitys of jasper stone, many courts, many fountains, and by reason that it is situated on the side of a high hill and not built uniformly, many gardens with ponds in them, and many baths made of jasper, and most of their principall roomes ro[ofed] with mosaik work which exceeds the finest enamell I ever saw. Here I was shewed, in the midst of an exceeding large piece of rich imbrodery made by the Moores of Granada, in the middle, as long as half a yard of the true Teyrian dey, which is so glorious a colour that it cannot be expressed. It hath the glory of scarlet, the beauty of purple, and is so bright that when the eye is removed upon any other object it seems as white as snow.

The entry into this great pallace is of stone for a porter's lodge, but very magnificent (though the gate be low), which is adorned with figures of forest work, in which the Moores did transcend. High above this gate was a bunch of keyes cut in stone, and many yards under them perpendicularly was a hand, cut in stone like-wise, with this moto: 'UNTILL THAT HAND HOLD THOSE KEYS THE CHRISTIANS SHALL NEVER POSSESS THE ALLHAMBRAY'. This was a prophesy they had, in which they animated themselves, by reason of the impossibility that ever they should meet; but see how true, ther'is a time for all things. It happened that when the Moores were besieged in that place by Dom Fernando and his Queen Isabella, the King with an arrow out of a bow, which they then used in war, shooting the first arrow as their custom is, cut that part of stone that held the keys, which was in fashion of a chain, and the keys falling remained in the hand underneath. This strange accident preceded but a few days the conquest of the town of Granada and kingdom.

They have in this place an iron gate fixed into the side of a hill that is a rock. I did lay my head to the key-hole and heard a noise like clashing of armes, but could not distinguish other shrill noises I heard with that. But tradition says it could never be oponed since the Moores left it, notwithstanding severall persons had indeavoured to rench it open, but that they perished in the attempt. This truth of this I can say no more to, but that ther'is such a gate and I have seen it.

After 2 days we went on our journy, and on the 13th of Aprill, 16[50], we came to the court of Madrid, where we were the next day visited by the English Embassadours, and afterwards by all the English merchants. Here I was delivered of my *first* daughter that was called Elizabeth, upon the 13 of July. She lived but 15 days and lyes buryed in the chappell of the French Hospitall.

Your father had great difficulty to carry on his businesse, without intrenching upon the Extraordinary Embassadors' negotiation, and the performance of his master's commands to shew his present necessitys, which he was sent to Philip the Fourth for, in hopes of a present supply of mony which our king then lacked. But finding no good to be done upon that arrand, he and I accompanied with Doctor Bell, master of Jesus Colledge in Cambridge (who had been his tutor), went a day's journy together towards St. Sebastians, there to imbarke for France. Whilst we stayd in this court we were kindly treated by all the English, and it was no small trouble to your father's tutor to quit his company; but having undertaken the charge of that family of the Embassadors as their caplain, he sayd he held himself obliged in conscience to stay; and so he did, for within a few months after he dyed there, and lyes buried in the garden of the house where they then livd.

Whilst we were in Madrid there was sent one As[cham] as resident from the then Governor of England. He lay in a common eatinghouse where some travellers used to lye, and being one day at dinner, some young men meeting in the street with Mr. Prodgers, a gentleman belonging to the Lord Embassador Cottington, and Mr. Sparks, an English merchant, discoursing of news, begun to speak of the impudence of this As[cham] to come a publick Minister from rebells to a court where there were 2 embassadors from his king. This subject being handled with heat, they all resolved without more consideration to goe immediatly into his lodging and kill him. They came up to his chamber doore and finding it open, and he sett at his dinner, seased him and so killed him, and went their severall wayes. Afterwards they found Mr. Sparkes in a church for rescue. Notwithstanding it was contrary to their religion and laws, they forced him out from thence, and executed him publickly; their fear of the English power was then so great.

There was at that time the Lord Goring, son to the Earl of Norwich. He had a command under Philip the 4th of Spain against the Portugueses. He was generally esteemed a good and great commander (and had been so brought up in Holland in his youth) of vast naturall parts, for I have heard your father say he hath dictated to severall persons at once that were upon severall dispaches, and all so admirably well that no one of them could be mended. He was exceeding facetious and pleasant company, and in converse, where good manners were due, the civilest person imaginable, so that he would blush like a girle, which was naturall to him. He was very tall and very handsom. He had been married to a daughter of the Earl of Cork, but never had a child by her. His expences were what he could gett, and his debauchery beyond all presedents, which at last lost him that love the Spaniards had for him, and that country not admitting his constant drinking, he fell sick of a hectick feavor, in which he turned his religion; and with that artifice could scarce get to keep him whilst he lived in that sickness, or to bury him when he was dead.

We came to St. Sebastian about the beginning of September and there hired a French small vessell to cary us to Nance. We embarked within two days after our coming into this town. I never saw so wild a place, nor was the inhabitants unsutable, but like to like, which made us hasten away with the first, and I am sure to our cost we found the proverb true, for our haste brought us woe. We had not been a day at sea before we had a storme begun, that continued 2 days and 2 nights in a most violent manner, and being in the Bay of Biskey, we had a huricane that drew the vessel up from the water, which neither had saile nor mast left, and but 6 men and a boy. Whilst they had hopes of life, they ran about swearing like devils, but when that failed them, they ran into holes and let the ship drive as it would. In this great hasard of our lives we were the beginning of the 3d night, when God in mercy seaced the storm of a sudden, and there was a great calme, which made us exceeding joyfull; but when those beasts, for they were scarce men that manned the vessell, begun to rummedge the barke, they could not find their compass no where, for the loss of which they begun again such horrible lamentations as was as dismall to us as the storme past. Thus between hope and feare we past the night, they protesting to us they knew not where they were, and truely we believed them; for with fear and drink I think they were bereaved of sense.

So soon as it was day, about 6 of the clock, the master cryed out, 'The land, the land.' But we did not receive that news with the joy belonging to it, but sithing sayd, 'God's will be done.' Thus the tide drives us untill about 5 a clock in the afternoon, and drawing near the side of a small rock that had a crick by it, we ran on ground; but the sea was so calme that we all got out without the loss of any man or goods, but the vessel was so shattered that it was not afterwards servisable.

Thus, God be praised, we escaped this great danger and found ourselves near a little viladge, about 4 leagues from Nance. We hired there 6 asses upon which we rode, as many as could, by turnes, and the rest carryed our goods. This journey took us up all the next day; for I should have told you that we stured not that night, because we sat up and made good cheere, for beds they had none, and we were so transported that we thought we had no need of any, but we had very good fires and Nance white wine, and butter and milk, and wall nuts and eggs, and some very bad cheese. And was not this enough with the escape of shiprack to be thought better than a feast? I am sure untill that houre I never knew such pleasure in eating, between which we a thousand times repeated what we had spoke when every word seemed our last. We praised God; I wept, your father lifting then up his hands admired so great a salvation. Then we often kissed each other, as if yet we feared death, sithed, and complained of the cruelty of the rebells that forced us to wander. Then we again comforted ourselves in the submitting to God's will for his laws and our country, and remembered the lott and present sufferring of our king. The much discourse and wearynes of our journey made us fall a sleep.

As soon as it was day we begun our journy towards Nanse, and by the way we passed by a little poor chappell, at the dore of which a frier begged an almes, saying that he would shew us there the greatest miracles in the world. We resolved to goe with him. He went before us to the altar and out of a cupboord with great devotion he took a box, and crossing him self he opened it. In that was another of cristall that contained a little silver box. He, lifting this cristall box up, cryed, 'Behold in this the hem of St. Joseph which was taken as he hewed this timber.' To which my husband replyed, 'Indeed, Father, it is the lightest, considering the greatness, that I ever handled in my life.' The ridiculousnes of this, with the simplicity of the man, entertained us until we came to Nanse. We met by the way good grapes and wall nuts growing, of which we culled out the best.

Nants is a passable good town, but decay'd; sum monasterys in it, but none good nor rich. There was in a nunnery when I was there a daughter of Secretary Windebank. There is English provisions and of all sorts, cheap and good. We hired a boat to carry us up to Orleans, and we were towed up all the river of Loire so far. Every night we went a shoare to bed, and every morning carryed into the boat wine and fruit and bread, with sum flesh which we dressed in the boat; for it had a hearth on which we burned charcoale. We like wise caught carpes, which were the fattest and the best I ever eat in my life. And of all my travells none was for travell's sake, as I may call it, so pleasant as this; for we saw the finest cityes, seats, woods, medows, pastures, vineyards, and champain that ever I saw in my life, adorned with the most pleasant river of Loire, of which at Orleans we took our leaves, and arriving about the beginning of November, 1650, at Paris, we went, so soon as we could get cloaths, to waite on Qwen Mother and the Princess Henrieta.

The Qween entertained us very kindly, and after many favours done us and discourses in privat with your father about affairs of state (he receiving Her Majesty's letters to send the King, who was then on his way for Scotland), we kissed her hand and went to Callais with resolution that I should goe for England to send my husband more mony; for this long journy cost us all we could procure. Yet this I will tell you, praysed be God for his peculiar grace herein, that your father nor I never borrowed mony, nor owed for cloathes, or diett, or lodging beyond sea in our lives, which was very much, considring the straights we were in many times, and the bad custom which our countrymen had that way, which did redound much to the King's dishonour and their own discredit.

When we came to Callais my husband sent me to England and stayd himself there, intending as soon as he had received mony to go and live in Holland untill such time as it should please Allmigty God to enable him to wait again on his master, now in Scottland, both to give him an account of his journy into Spaine, as of the rest of his imployments since he kissed his hand. But God ordered it other wise; for the case being that the 2 partyes in Scotland being both unsatisfyed with each other's ministers, and Sir E[dward] Hide and Secretary Nicholas being excepted against and left in Holland, it was proposed, the state wanting a secrettary for the King, that your father should be immediatly sent for, which was done accordingly; and he went with letters and presents from the Princess of Orange and the Princess Royall.

Here I will shew you something of Sir Edward Hide's nature. He being surprised with this news and suspecting that my husband might come to a greater power than himself, both because of his parts and integrity, and because himself had been sometimes absent in his Spanish embassy, he with all the humility possible, and earnest passion, begged my husband to remember the King often of him to his advantage, as occasion should serve, and to procure leave that he might waite on the King; promissing, with all the oaths that he could express to cause belief, that he would make it his business all the days of his life to serve your father's interest in what condition soever he should be in. Thus they parted, with your father's promisses to serve him in what he was capable off; upon which account many letters passed between them.

When your father arrived in Scotland he was received by the King with great expressions of great content, and after he had given an account of his past imployments, he was by the King recommended to the Kerke party, who received him very kindly and gave him both the broad seale and signet to keep. They severall times pressed him to take the Covenant, but he never did; but followed his business so close, with such diligence and temper, that he was beloved of all sides, and they reposed great trust in him.

When he went out of Holland he writ to me to arme myself with patience in his absence, and like wise that I would not expect many letters as was his custome, for that was now impossible; but he hoped that when we did meet again, it would be happy and of long continuance; and bid me trust God with him, as he did me, in whose mercy he hoped; being upon that duty he was obliged to, with a thousand kind expressions. But God knows how great a surprise this was to me, being great with child, and two children with me, not in the best condition to maintain them, and in dayly fear of your father's life upon the publick account of war and upon the private account of animositys amongst them selves in Scotland. But I did what I could to arme myself, and was kindly visited by both my relations and friends.

About this time my cousin Eveling's wife came to London, and had newly bury'd her mother, my Lady Brown, wife to Sir Richard Brown, that then was resident for the King at Paris: a little before she and I and Doctor Stuard (Clarke of the Closett to King Charles the First) christned a daughter of Mr. Waller's, near a year old. About this time my Lord Chief Justice Heath dyed at Callais, and severall of the King's servants at Paris, amongst others, Mr. Henry Morey, of his bed chamber, a very good man.

I now settled myself in a lodging in Hunsdon House in London with a heavy heart. I stay'd in this lodging almost seven months, and in that time I did not goe abroad 7 times, but spent my time in prayers to God for the deliverance of the King and my husband, whose danger was ever before my eyes. I was seldom without the best company in the town, and some times my father would stay a week, for all had compasion for my condition. I removed to Qween Street and there in very good lodging I was upon the 24 of June delivered of a daughter.

In all this time I had but 4 letters from your father, which made the paine I was in more difficult to bear. I went with my brother Fanshaw to Ware Parke, and my sister went to Balls to my father's, both intending to meet in winter, and so indeed we did with tears, for upon the 2 day of

September following was fought the Battle of Woster, when the King being missed and nothing of your father being dead or alive for 3 days heard of, it is unexpressible what affliction I was in. I neither eat nor slept, but trembled at every motion I heard, expecting the fattal news which at last came in their newsbook, which mentioned your father a prisonner; then with some hopes immediatly I went to London, intending to leave my little girle Nan, the companion of my troubles, there, and so find out my husband where soever he was carryed. But upon my coming to London, I met a messenger from him with a letter which advised me of his condition, and told me he was very civilly used, and sayd little more but that I should be in some roome at Chering Cross, and he had promiss from his keeper that he should rest there in my company a dinner-time. This was ment to him for a great favour.

I expected with impatience and on the appointed day provided a dinner and roome as I was ordered, in which I was with my father and some more of our friends, where about eleven of the clock we saw hundreds of poore souldjers, both English and Scotch, march all naked on foot and many a horseback. At last came the Captaine and 2 souldjers with your father, who was very cheerefull in appearance; who, after he had spoke and saluted me and his friends there, sayd, 'Pray let us not lose time, for I know not how little I have to spare. This is the chance of war: nothing venture, nothing have; and so let us sett down and be merry whilst we may.' Then taking my hand in his, and kissing me, sayd, 'Cease weeping. No other thing upon earth can move me. Remember wee are all at God's dispose.' Then he begun to tell how kind his captain was to him, and the people as he passed offered him mony and brought him good things, and particularly my Lady Denham at Boston House, who would ha[ve] given him all the mony she had in her house, but he returned her thanks and told her he had so ill kept his own that he would not tempt his governor with more, but if she would give him a shirt or two and some handkerchiefs he would keep them as long as he could for her sake. She feched him 2 smocks of her own and some handkerchiefs, saying she was ashamed to give him them, but having none of her sonns at home she desired him to weare them.

Thus we passed the time untill order came to carry him to White Hall, where in a little room yet standing in the bowling green he was kept prisonner, without the speech of any so far as they knew, 10 weeks, and in expectation of death. They often examined him, and at a last he grew so ill in health by the cold and hard marches he had undergone, and being pent up in a room close and small, that the scurvey brought him almost to death's doore. During this time of his imprisonment I failed not constantly to goe when the clock struck 4 in the morning, with a dark lanterne in my hand, all alone and on foot from my lodging in Chancery Lane at my cosin Yong's to White Hall in at the entry that went out of

King's Street into the bowling ground. There I would goe under his window and softly call him. He, that after the first time expected me, never failed to put out his head at first call. Thus we talked together, and sometimes I was so wet with rane that it went in at my neck and out at my heels. He directed how I should make my adresses, which I did ever to their Generall Cromwell, who had a great respect for your father and would have bought him off to his servise upon any termes.

Being one day to solicit for my husband's liberty for a time, he bid me bring the next day a certificate from a pysitian that he was really ill. Immediatly I went to Doctor Batters, that was by chance both physitian to Cromwell and to our family, who gave me one very favorable in my husband's behalf. I delivered it at the Councell Chamber doore at 3 of the clock that afternoon to his own hand, as he commanded me, and himself moved that seing they could make no use of his imprisonment where by to lighten them in their business, that he might have his liberty, upon 4000lb bale, to take a course of physick, he being dangerously ill. Many spake against it, but most Sir Henry Vane, who sayd he would be instrumentall, for ought he knew, to hang them all that sat there, if ever he had opportunity; but if he had liberty for a time, that he might take the ingagements before he went out. Upon which Cromwell sayd, 'I never knew that the ingagement was a medecine for the scorbute.' They hearing their General say so, thought it obliged him, and so ordered him his liberty upon bale. His eldest brother and sister Bedels and self was bound in 4000lb bound, and so the latter end of November he came at my lodgings at my cousin Yong's. He there met many of his good friends and kindred, and my joy was unexpressable, and so was poore Nan's, of whom your father was very fond.

I forgot to tell you that when your father was taken prisonner of war, he, before they entered the house where he was, burned all his papers, which saved the lives and estates of many a brave gentleman. When he came out of Scotland he left behind him a box of writings in which his patent of baronnett was, and his patent of additional armes; which was safely sent him after the happy restauration of the King. You may read your father's demeanour of his self in this affaire, writ by his own hand in a book by it self amongst your books, and it's a great masterpiece, as you will find.

Within 10 days he fell very sick, and the feavour settled in his throat and face so violently that for many days and nights he slept no more, but as he lained on my shoulders as I wa[ked]. At last, after all that the doctor and surgion could doe, it broke, and with that he had ease and so recovered, God be praysed.

In [16]52 he was advised to goe to the Bath for his scorbute that still hang on him, but he deffered his journy untill August, because I was delivered on the 30th of July of a daughter.

At his return we went to live that winter following at Beaford in Hartfordshire, a house of my niece Fanshaw's. In this winter my husband went to waite on his good friend the Earle of Straford in Yorkshire, and there my Lord offered him a house of his in Tankersly Parke, which he took and payd 120lb a year for. When my husband returned, we prepared to goe in the spring to this place, but [were] confined that my husband should not stir five miles from home without leave. About February following my brother Nues dyed at his house at Much-Hadame in Hartfordshire. My sister Margarett Harrison desired to go to London, and there we left her. She soon after married Mr. Edmond Turner, afterwards Sir Edmond Turner.

In March we with our 3 children, Ann, Richard, and Betty, went into Yorkshire, where we livd an innocent country life, minding only the country sports and the country affairs. Here my husband translated Luis de Camoens, and in October the 8th, 1653, I was delivered of my daughter Margarett. I found all the nighbourhood very civil and kind upon all occasions, the place plentyfull and healthfull and very pleasant; but there was no fruit untill we planted some; and my Lord Straford says now that what we planted is the best fruit in the north. The house of Tankersly and parke are both very pleasant and good, and we livd there with great content. But God had ordered that it should not last, for upon the 20th of July, 1654, at 3 a clock in the afternoon, dyed our most dearly beloved daughter Ann Fanshawe, whose beauty and wit exceeded all that ever I saw of her age. She was between 9 and 10 years old, very tall, and the dear companion of our travells and sorrows; she lay sick but five dayes of the small pox, in which time she expressed so many wise and devout sayings as is a miracle from her years. We both wished to have gone into the grave with her. She lyes buryed in Tankersly Church, and her death made us both desirous to quit that fatall place to us. And so, the week after her death, we did, and came to Hamerton and were half a year with my sister Bedell.

Then my husband was sent for to London, there to stay by command of the High Court of Justice, and not to goe five miles of that town, but to appeare once a month before them. We then went to my cousin Yong's again, in Chancery Lane, and about Christmas my husband got leave to go for some time to Frogg Poul in Kent to my brother Warick's, where upon the 22nd of February, [1655], I was delivered of a daughter whom we named Ann, to keep in remembrance her dear sister which we had newly lost. We returned to our lodgings in Chancery Lane, where my husband was forced to attend untill Christmass [16]55, and then we went down to Jenkins to Sir Thomas Fanshawe's. But upon New Year's Day my husband fell very sick, and the scorbute again prevailed so much that it drew his upper lip arye. Upon which we that day came to London into Chancery Lane, but not to my cousin Yong's, but to a house we tooke of Sir George C[arey] for a year. There by the advise of Dr. Battharst and Doctor Ridgley my husband took physick for 2 months together, and at last, God be praysed, he perfectly recovered his sickness, and his lip was as well as ever. In this house, upon the 12th day of July, I was delivered of a daughter named Mary, in 1656, and in this month dyed my second daughter Elizabeth, that I had left with my sister Buttler at Froggpool to see if this would recover her, but she dyed of a hecktick feaver and lyes buried in the church of Fottscray.

My husband, weary of the town and being advised to goe into the country for his health, procured leave to goe in September to Benngey in Hartfordshire, to a little house lent us by my brother Fanshawe. It happened at that time there was a very ill kind of feaver of which many dyed, and it ran generally through all familys. This we and all our small family fell sick off, and my husband's and mine after some months turned to quartaine agues. But I being with child, none thought I could live; for I was brought to bed of a son in November, 10 weeks before my time, and thence forward untill Aprill [16]58 I had 2 fits everyday. That brought me so weake that I was like an anatomy. I never stirr'd out of my bed in 7 months, nor during that time eat flesh, or fish, or bread, but sack, possett drink, and pancake or eggs, or now and then a turnip or carrot. Your father was likewise very ill, but he rose out of his bed some houres dayly and had such a greedyness upon him that he would eat and drink more than ordinary persons that eat most, though he could not stand upright without being held, and in perpetual sweats, and that so violently that it ran down like water day and night. This I have told you that you may see how near dying we were, for which recovery I humbly praise God. This son Henry lyes buryed in Benngey Church.

We got leave in August to goe to the Bath which, God be praised, perfectly recovered us, and so we returned into Hartfordshire to the Friery of Ware, which we hired of Mrs. Heyden for a year. This place we accounted happy to us because in October we heard the news of Cromwell's death, upon which my husband began to hope that he should get loose of his fetters in which he had been seven years. And going to London in the company of my Lord Philip, Earl of Pembrock, he lamented his case of his bounds to him that was his old and constant friend. He told him if he would dine with him the next day he would give him some account of that business. The next day he sayd to him, 'Mr. Fanshawe, I must send my eldest son into France. If you will not take it ill that I desire your company with him and care of him for one year, I will procure you your bonds within this week.'

My husband was overjoy'd to get loose upon any termes that were innocent; so having seen his bonds cancelled he went into France to Paris, from whence he by letter gave an account to Lord Chancellor Claren[don] of his being got loose, and desired him to acquaint His

Majesty with it, and to send him his command, which about Aprill [16]59 he did, to this effect: that His Majesty was then going a journey, which afterwards proved to Spaine, but upon his return, which he supposed would be about the beginning of winter, my husband should come to him, and that he should have in present the place of one of the Masters of Requests and the Secretary of the Latin Tongue. Then my husband sent me word of this and bid me bring my son Richard and my 2 eldest daughters with me to Paris, for that he intended to put him into a very good schoole that he had found in Paris.

We went as soon as possibbly I could accommodate myself with mony and other necessarys, with my 3 children, one maid, and one man. I could not goe without a pass, and to that purpose I went to my cousin Henry Nevel, one of the High Court of Justice, where he then was sitting at White Hall, and told him that my husband had sent for me and his son, to place him there, and that I desired his kindness to help me to a pass. He went into the then Masters, and returned to me saying that by a trick my husband had got his liberty, but for me and his children upon no conditions we should not stir. To this I made no reply, but thanked my cousin Henry Nevel, and took my leave. I sett me down in the next room, full sadly, to consider what I should doe, desiring God to help me in so just a case as I then was in. I begun, and thought if I were denyed a passedge, then they would ever after be more severe upon all occasions, and it might be very ill for us both. I was ready to goe (if I had a pass) the next tide, and might be there before they could suspect I was gone.

These thoughts put this invention in my head. At Walingford House the office was kept where they gave passes. Thither I went, in as plain a way and speech as I could device. Leving my maid at the gate, who was much a finer gentlewoman than myself, with as ill mine and tone as I could express, I told a fellow I found in the office that I desired a passe for Paris to goe to my husband. 'Woman,' says he, 'what is your husband, and your name?' 'Sir,' sayd I, with many courtesys, 'he is a young merchant, and my name is Anne Harrison.' 'Well,' says he, 'it will cost you a crown.' Say'd I, 'That is a great sum for me, but pray put in a man, my mayd, and 3 children.' All which he immediatly did, telling me that a Malignant would give him 5lb for such a pass. I thanked him kindly, and so immediatly went to my lodging, and with a penne I made the great *H* of Harrison 2*ff*, and the 2 *rr*'s an *n*, and the *i* an *s*, and the *s* an *h*, and the *o* an *a*, and the *n* a *w*, so compleatly that none could find out the change. With all speed I hired a barge, and that night at 6 a clock I went to Gravesend, and from thence by coach to Dover; where upon my arrivall the searchers came and, knowing me, demanded my pass, which they were to keep for their discharge. When they had read it they sayd, 'Madam, you may goe when you please.' 'But,' says one, 'I little thought they would give pass to so great a Malignant, especially in such a troublesome time as this.'

About 9 a clock at night I went on boord the packetboat, and about 8 a clock in the morning landed safe, God be praised, at Callais. I went to Mr. Bothe's, an English merchant and a very honest man. There I rested 2 days, but upon the next day he had advise from Dover that a post was sent to stay me from London, because they had sent for me to my lodging by a messenger of their court, to know why and upon what business I went to France. Then I discovered my invention to him of the change of my name, at which as at their disappointment we all laughed, and so did your father, and as many as knew the deceit.

We hired a waggon coach, for ther'is no other at Callais, and begun our journy about the midle of June in [16]59, coming one night to Abeville. The Governour sent his lieutenant to me to let me know my husband was well the weeke before, that he had seen him at Paris, and had promissed him to take care of me in my going through his government, there being much robberys dayly committed; that he would advise to take a guard of the garrison soldjers and, giving them a pistole [a] piece, they would convey me very safely. This, he sayd, the Governor would have told me himself, but that he was in bed with the gout. I thanked him and accepted his proffer. The next morning he sent me 10 troopers well armed, and when I had gone about 4 leagues, as we assended a hill, says some of these, 'Madame, look out, but fear nothing.' They rid all up to a hill [and met] a well mounted troop of horse, about 50 or more, which after some parly wheeled about in the woods again. When we came upon the hill I asked how it was possible so many men so well armed should turne, having so few to oppose them; at which they laughed and say'd, 'Madame, we are all of a company and quarter in this town. The truth is, our pay is short, and we are forced to help ourselves this way, but we have this rule, that if we in a party guard any company, the rest never molest them, but let them pass free.' I having passed all danger, as they sayd, gave them a pistole each man, and so left them and went on my journy, and met my husband at St. Denis, God be praysed.

The 1[3]th day of October dyed my then only son Richard of the small pox. He lyes buryed in the Protestant Church near Paris, between the Earle of Bristol and Dean Steward. Both my eldest daughters had the small pox att the same time, and though I neglected them, and day and night tended my dear son, yet it pleased God they recovered and he dyed, the grief of which made me miscary and caused a sickness of 3 weeks.

After this, in the beginning of November, the King came to visitt his mother, who was at her own house at Collom, two leagues from Paris; and thither went my husband and myself. I had not seen him in almost 10 years. He told me that if God pleased to restore him to his kingdomes my husband should partake of his happyness in as great a share as any servant he had. Then he asked me many questions of England, and fell into discourse with my husband privatly 2 houres, and then commanded him to follow into Flanders. His Majesty went the next day. My husband that day month, which was the beginning of December, went with our family to Callais, and my husband sent me privatly to London for mony. In January I returned him 150 pounds with which he went to the King, and I followed to Newport and Bruges and Ghent, and to Bruselles, where the King received us very gratiously with the Princess Royall and the Duke[s] of York and Gloster. After staying 3 weeks at Bruxelles we went to Bredda, where we heard the happy news of the King's returne into England. In the beginning of May we went with all the court to the Hague, where I first saw the Qween of Bohemia, who was exceeding kind to all of us.

Here the King and all the royall family were entertained at a very great supper by the States, and now business of state took up much time. The King promissed my husband he should be one of the Secrettaryes of State, and both the now Duke of Ormond and Lord Chancellor Clar[endon] were witnesses of it. Yet that false man made the King break his word for his own accommodation, and placed Mr. Morice, a poor countrey gentleman of about 200lb a year, a fierce Presbiterian, and one that never saw the King's face, but still promisses were made of the reversion to your father.

Upon the King's return, the Duke of York, then made Admirall, appointed ships to carry over all the company and servants of the King, which was very great. His Highness appointed for my husband and his family a third-rate frigate called the *Speedwell*, but His Majesty commanded my husband to waite on him in his own ship. We had, by the States' order, sent a boord, to the King's most eminent servants, great store of provisions. For our family we had sent a boord the *Speedwell* a terse of clarett and a hogshead of Rhinish wine, 6 dozens of fowles, a dozen of gammons of bakon, a great baskett of bread, and 6 sheep, and 2 dozens of nets' tongues, and a great box of sweet meats. Thus taking our leaves of those obliging persons we had conversed with in the Hague, we went a boord upon the 23 of May about 2 a clocke in the after noone.

The King imbarked about 4 of the clock, upon which we sett saile, the shore being covered with people, and shouts from all places of a good voyage, which was seconded with many volleys of shott interchanged. So favourable was the wind that the ships' wherries went from ship to ship to visit their friends all night long. But who can sufficiently express the joy and gallantery of that voyage—to see so many great ships, the best in the world; to hear the trumpetts and all other musick; to see near an hundred brave ships saile before the wind with their wast clothes and streamers; the neatness and cleanness of the ships; the strength and jollity of the mariners; the gallantry of the commanders; the vast plenty of all sorts of provisions—but above all, the glorious

Majesties of the King and his 2 brothers was so beyond man's expectation and expression. The sea was calme, the moon shined at full, and the sun suffered not a cloud to hinder his prospect of the best sight, by whose light and the mercifull bounty of God hee was sett safely on shore at Dover in Kent upon the 25th of May, 1660. So great were the acclamations and numbers of people that it reached like one street from Dover to White Hall. We lay that night at Dover and the next day we went in Sir Arnold Brem's his coach towards London, where on Sunday night we came to a house in the Savoy. My neece Fanshaw lay then in the Strand, where I stood to see the King's entry with his brothers, surely the most pompous show that ever was, for the hearts of all men in this kingdom moved at his will.

The next day I went with other ladies of the family to congratulate His Majesty's happy arrivall, who received me with great grace and promissed me futur favours to my husband and self. His Majesty gave my husband his picture sett with small diamonds, when he was a child. It is a great rarity, because there never was but that one.

We took a house in Portugall Row in Lincoln's In Fields. My husband had not long entered upon his office, but he found an oppression from Secrettary Nickoles to his great vexation, for he as much as in him lay ingrossed all the petitions which really, by the foundation, belonged to the Masters of the Requests, and in this he was countenanced by Lord Chancellor Clar[endon], his great patron, notwithstanding he had married Sir Thomas Alsberey's daughter, that was one of the Masters of the Requests.

This year I sent for my daughter Nan from my sister Buttler's in Kent, where I had left her. And my daughter Mary dyed in Hartfordshire in August and lyes buried in Hartford Church in my father's vault. In the latter end of this summer I miscarryed, when I was near half gone with child, of 3 sons, 2 houres one after the other. I think it was with the great hurry of business I then was in, and perpetuall company that resorted to us of all qualitys, some for kindness and some for their own advantage. As that was a time of advantage, so it was of a vast expense, for in Aprill the 23 the King was crowned, and then my husband being in waiting rode upon His Majesty's left hand, with very rich foot clothes and 4 footmen in very rich liverys. And this year we furnished our house and payd all our debts which we had contracted during the war.

The 8th day of May following, the King rode to the Parliament, and then my husband rode in the same manner. His Majesty had commanded my husband to execute the place of the Chancellor of the Garter, both because he understood it better than any and was to have the reversion of it. The first feast of St. George my husband was proxy for the Earle of Bristol and was installed for him Knight of the Garter. The Duke of Buckingham put on his robes, and the Duke of Ormond his spur, in the stalle of the Earl of Bristoll.

Now it was the business of the Chancelor to put your father as far from the King as he could, because his ignorance in state affaires was dayly discovered by your father, who shewed it to the King. But at that time the King was so content that he should almost alone manadge his affairs, that he might have the more time for his pleasure, that his faults were not so visible as otherwise they would have been and afterwards proved. But now he sends for your father and tells him that he was by the King's particular choyce resolved on to be sent to Lisbone with the King's letter and picture to the Princess, now our Qween, which then indeed was an imployment any nobleman would be glad off; but the design from that time forth was to fixe him there.

When your father was gone on this arrand I stayd in our house in Portugall Row, and at Christmass I received the New Year's gifts belonging to his places, which is the custome, of 2 tunns of wine at the Custome House for Master of Requests, and 15 ounces of gilt plate at the Jewell House as Secretary of the Latin Tongue. At the latter end of Christmass my husband came from Lisbone and was very well received by the King. And upon the 22 of February following I was delivered of my daughter Elizabeth.

Upon the 8th of June [16]62 my husband was made a Privy Counsellor of Ireland; and some time after, my Lord and Lady of Ormond went into Ireland, and upon my taking leave of Her Grace she gave me a turquois and diamond bracelet and my husband a fosset diamond ring. I never parted from her upon a journy but she ever gave me some present. When her daughter the Lady Mary Ca[ve]ndish was married, none was present but his grandmother and father, and my husband and self. They were marryed in my Lord Duke's lodgings at Whitehall, and given by the King, who came privatly without any train.

As soon as the King had notice of the Qween landing, he immediatly sent my husband that night to wellcome Her Majesty on shore and followed himself the next day, and upon the 21 of May the King married the Qween at Portsmouth in the presence chamber of His Majestye's house. There was a raile cross the upper part of the roome into which entered only the King and Qween, the Bishop of London, and the Marquis de Sande, the Portugall Embassador, and my husband. In the other part of the roome were many of the nobility and servants to Their Majesties. The Bishoup of London declared them mared in the name of the Father, and of the Sonn, and of the Holey Goest, and then they caused the ribbons Her Majesty then wore to be cut in little pieces, and as far as it would goe every body had some.

Upon the 29 of May Their Majesties came to Hampton Court, where was all that pretended to Her Majesty's servise, and all the King's servants, ladys, and other persons of quality, who received Her Majesty in severall rooms according to their severall qualifications. The next morning about 11 a clock the Duchess of Ormond and her daughter, the now Lady Ca[ve]ndish, and myself, went to wait on Her Majesty as soon as Her Majesty was dressed, where I had the honour from the King, who was then present, to tell the Qween who I was, saying many kind things of me to ingratiate me with Her Majesty; where upon Her Majesty gave her hand to me to kiss with promisses of her future favour. After this we remained in Hampton Court in the Request lodgings, my husband being then in waiting, untill the 10th day of August, upon which day he received his dispatches for embassador to Portugall.

His Majesty was graciously pleased to promiss my husband his picture, which afterwards we received, set with diamond to the value of between three and foure hundred pounds, His Majesty having been pleased to give my husband at his first going to Portugall his picture, at length, in his Garter robes. My husband had also by His Majesty's order, out of the warderobe, a crimson velvett cloath of state fringed and laced with gold, with a chaire, a foot stoole, 2 cushions, and 2 other stooles of the same with a Persia carpett to lay under them, and a sute of fine tapestry hangings for that roome, with 2 velvett alter cloths for the chapell, and fringed with gold, with surplises, alter cloathes, and napkins of fine linnen, with a Bible in Oglosby's print and cuts, 2 Common Prayer Books in folio, and 6 in quarto, with 800 ounces of gilt plate, and 4000 ounces of white plate. But there wanted a velvett bed which he should have had by custome.

Thus having perfected the ceremonyes of taking our leave of Their Majesties and receiving their commands, and likewise taking our leaves of our friends, as I sayd, upon Sunday the 10th of August we took our journy for Portugall, carrying our 3 daughters with us, Katherine, Margaret, and Ann. This night we lay at Windsor, where on Munday the 11, in the morning, we went to prayers to the King's chappell with Doctor Heavers, my husband's chaplain. At our return we were visited with the Provost of Eaton, with divers others of the clergy of that place, and Sir Thomas Woodcock, the chief commander of that place in the absence of my Lord Mordaunt, Lord Constable of Windsor Castle. Upon the desire of some there, my husband left some of his coats of armes, which he carried with him for that purpose, as the custome of embassadors is to dispose off where they lodge.

That night we lay at Bagshott. Tuesday the 12th we dined at Basingstone and lay at Andivers. Wednesday the 13th we dined at Salisbury and there lay that night, and borrowed in the afternoon the Deane of Westminster his coach, willing to ease all our own horses for half a day, having a long journy to goe. We went in the Deane's coach to see Wilton, being but 2 miles from Salisbury. We found my Lord Herbert at home. He entertained us with great civility and kindness and gave my husband a very fine greyhound bitch, his father the Earl of Pembrooke being then at London. We visited the famous church, and at our returne to our lodging were visited by the Right Reverend Father in God, Dr. Henshaman, the Bishop of that place, and Dr. Hollis, the Deane of that place, and Dr. Earles, Deane of Westminster, since by the former Bishop's remove to the See of London, now Bishop of Salisbury.

On Thursday the 14 my husband and I, with our children, having begg'd of the then Bishop his blesing at his own house, tucke c[oa]ch and dined at Blankford in Dorsetshire. Sir William Portman hath a very fine seat within a mile of it. We lodged that night in Dorcester. On Friday the 15th we lay at Ackminstor, and Saturday the 16th at Exeter; and went to prayers to the Cathedrall Church, accompanied with the principal divines of that place, on Sunday the 17th, where we stayd all that day. And on Munday the 18th we lay at a very ill lodging of which I have forgott the name; and on Tuesday the 19th we went to Plymouth, where within 6 miles of the town we were mett by some of the chief merchants of that place and of the chief officers of that garrison, who all accompanied us to the house of one Mr. Tyler, a merchant. Upon our arrivall the Governor of that garrison, one Sir John Skelton, visited us and did us the favour to keep us company with many of his officers during our stay in that town. Sir John Heele, as soone as he heard of our being there, sent my husband a fat buck. And my cousin Edgecomb, of Mount Edgecomb, a mile from Plymouth, sent him an other buck, and came so soone as he heard we were there, from a house of his which is 12 miles from Mount Edgecombe, to which he came only to keep us company, from whence the next day after his arrival he, with his lady and Sir Richard Edgecombe, his eldest son, and others of his children, came to visit us at Plymouth; and the day after we dined at Mount Edgecomb, where we were very nobly treated; where at our coming home, they would needs accompany us over the river home to our lodgings. The next day the Mayor and Aldermen came to visit my husband, and on Saturday we had a great feast at Mr. Seale's house, the father of our land lady. Our being so well lodged and treated by the inhabitants of this town was upon my father's score, whose deputyes some of them were (he being one of the farmers of the Custome House) to receive the King's customes of that part.

On [Satur]day the 30th the wind coming faire, we imbarked, accompanyed with my cousin Edgecombe and all his family, and with much company of the town that would shew their kindnesse untill the last. Taking our leave of our land lord and land lady, we gave her 20 pieces in gold to buy her a ring, and they presented my children with many pretty toys. Thus on [Satur]day at 9 a clock in the morning we were received on boord the *Ruby* fregate, commanded by Captain Robinson. We had very many presents sent us on boord by divers gentlemen, amongst which my cousin Edgecomb sent us a brace of fatt bucks, 3 milk goats, wine, ale, and beere, with fruit of severall sorts, biscake, and sweet meats.

On [Su]nday the 31st of August, 1662, we sett sayle for Lisbone, and landed the 14 of September, our style, between the Conde de St. Laurenso, his house, and Belline: God be praised, all in good health. As soon as we had ancored, the English Consull, with the merchants, came on boord us, but we went presently to a country house of the Duke of Avero's, where my husband was placed by His Majesty when he was there before, in which he had then left his chief secretary, and one other, with some others of his family.

The first that visited my husband incognito there (for he was not to own any till he had made his entry) was the King of Portugall's secretary, Antonio de Sousa. There came about that time also the Earle of Insequeen and Count Scomberg to visit us. The $\frac{28}{18}$th day my husband went privatly on boord the fregate in which he came, with all his family, to whom the King sent a nobleman to receive him on shoare, with his own and Qween Mother's and very many other coaches of the nobilityes. As soon as they met, there passed great salutations of canons from the ships to the fregate in which my husband came, and from our ships to the King's forts, and from all the forts innumerable shott returned again. So soon as my husband landed, he entered the King's coach, and the nobleman that fetched him (whose name I have forgot). Before him went the English Consull, with all the merchants; on his right hand went foure pages; on the left side the coach, by the horses' heads, 8 footmen all clothed in rich livery. In the coaches that followed went my husband's own gentlemen (after the coach of state, empty), and those that did him the favour to accompany him.

Thus they went to the house where my husband was lodged. 3 suppers and 3 dinners the King entertained him, with great plenty of provisions in all kinds, and all manner of utensiles belonging there unto, as the custome of that country is. Their Majestys did for sometime furnish the house till my husband could otherwise provide himself in town. The Abadessa of the Alcantra, neece to the Qween Mother, naturall daughter to the Duke de Medina Sidonia, sent (to wellcome mee into the country) a very noble present of perfums, waters, and sweet meats, and during my abode in Lisbone we often made visits and enterchanged messages to my great content, for she was a very fine lady. On the $\frac{19}{29}$ one Mr. Bridgewood, a merchant, sent me a silver bason and ewry for a present.

On the 10th of October (Stilo Novo) my husband had his audience of His Majesty in his pallace at Lisbone, going into the King's coach with the same nobleman and in the same forme as he made his entry. The King received him with great kindness and respect, much to his satisfaction. On the 11th Don Juan de Sousa, the Qween's viador, came from

Her Majesty to us both, to wellcome us into the country. On the 13th Her Majesty sent her chief coach, accompanyed with other coaches, to fetch my husband to the audience of Her Majesty, where she received him very graciously; and the same day he had audience of Dom Pedro, the King's brother, at his owne pallace. Saturday, the 14th, Her Majesty sent her best coach for me and my children. When wee came there the Captaine of the Guard received me at the foot of the stairs, all my people going up before me, as the custome is. On each side were the guards placed with halberds in their hands, as far as the presence chamber doore. There I was received by the Qween's Lord Chamberlaine, who carryed me to the dore of the next roome where the Qween was. There the Qween's principall lady (as our Groom of the Sto[le]) received me, telling me she had commands from the Qween to bid me welcome to that court, and to accompaney me to Her Majesty's presence. She sat in the next roome, which was very large, in a black velvett chaire with armes, upon a black velvett carpett, with a state of the same. She had caused a low chaire without armes to be sett some distance from her, about 2 yards on her left hand, on which side stood all the noblemen, on her right all the ladys of the court. After making my reverences due to Her Majesty according to custome, and sayd those respects which became me to Her Majesty, she sat down and then I presented my daughters to her. She, having expressed much grace and favour to me and mine, bid me sett down, which at first I refused, desiring to waite on Her Majesty as my Qween's mother, but she pressing me again, I sat down, and then she made her discourse of England, and questions of the Qween's health and liking of our country, with some little hints of her own and her family's condishon, which having continued better than half an hour, I took my leave. During my stay at court I severall times waited on the Qween Mother. Truly she was a very honorable, wise woman, and I believe had been very handsome. She was magnificent in her discourse and nature, but in the prudentest manner. She was ambitious, but not vain. She loved government, and I doe believe the quitting of it did shorten her life. After saluting the ladys and noblemen of the court, I went home as I came.

The next day the Secretary of State and his lady came to visit me. She had at my arrivall sent me a present of sweet meats. My husband had left in this person's family one of his pages to improve himself in writing and reading the Spanish tongue untill his returne again to that court, when he went the last year for England, in consideration of which we presented his lady with a piece of India plate of about 20lb sterlings. They were both very civill, worthy persons, and had formerly been in England, where the King, Charles the First, had made his son an English baron.

She told me in discourse one day this of a French embassador, that lately had been in that court and lodged next to her. There was ever a numerous sort of people about the Embassador's dore, as is usuall, amongst whom a poore little boy that his mother had animated dayly to cry for relief so troublesomely that at last the Embassador would say, 'What noise is that at the gate of perpetuall screaking? I will have it so no more.' Upon which they carried the child to his mother and bid her keep him at home, for it screaked like a divell, and if it returned the porter swore he would punish him severely. Not many days after, according to his former custom, this child returned, louder than before if possible. The porter, keeping his word, took this boy and pulled off his rags and annointed him all over with hony, leaving no part undone and very thick, and then threw him into a tub of fine feathers, which as soon as he had done he sett him on his leggs and frighted him home to his mother, who seing this thing, for non living could ghess him a boy, ran out into the city, the child squeaking after her, and all the people in the streets after them, thinking it was a divell or some strange creature.

But to returne to the business; we were visited by many persons of the court, some upon business and others upon compliment, which is more formall than pleasant, for they are not generally a cheerful people. About February the King intended to goe into the field and lead his army himself. During this resolution my husband prepared himself to wait on His Majesty, which cost him much, those kind of expenses in that place being scarce and very dear. But the Councell would not suffer him to goe, and so that ended. The King loved hunting much, and ever when he went would send my husband some of what he killed, which was stag and wild boare—both excellent meat.

We kept the Qween's birthday with great feasting. We had all the English merchants.

There was during my stay in this town a Portugall merchant jalous of his mistris favouring an English man, whom he entertained with much kindness, hiding his suspition. One evening he invited him to see a country house and eat a collation, which he did; after which the merchant with 3 or 4 more of his friends for a rarity shewed him a cave hard by the house, which went in at a very narrow hole but within was very capatious, in the side of a high mountaine. It was so dark that one carried a torch. Says one to the Englishman, 'Did you ever know where batts dwell?' He replyd, 'No.' 'Then here, sir,' say they, 'you shall see them.' Then holding up the light to the roof they saw millions hanged by their legs. So soon as they had done, they, frighting the birds, made them all flye about him, and put out the light, ran away, and left the Englishman there all night to gett out as well as he could, which was not untill the next morning.

This winter I fell sick of an aguish distemper, being then with child, but I believe it was with eating more grapes than I am accustomed to eat, being tempted by their goodness, especially the Frontigniack which exceeds all I ever eat both in Spaine and France.

The beginning of May [16]63 there happened in Lisbone an insurrection of the people in the town, about a suspition, as they pretended, of some persons disaffected to the publick, upon which they plundered the Arch Bishop's house and the Marquis of Marialva's house, and broke into the treasure. But after above 10 thousand of these ordinary people had run for 6 or 7 houres about the town, crying, 'Kill all that is for Kastill', they were appeased by their priests, who carried the sacrement amongst them, threatning excommunication, which, with the night, made them depart with their plunder. Some few persons were lost in the number, but not many.

Upon the 10th of June came the news to this court of the totall rout of Don John de A[ustria] at the Battle of Ev[ora], after which our house and tables were full of distressed, honest, brave English souldjers, who by their and their fellows' valor had got one of the greatest victorys that ever was. These poor but brave men were most lost between the Portugese's poverty and Lord Chancellor Hide's neglect, not to give it a worse name. While my husband stay'd there he did what he could, but not proportionably either to their merits or wants. About this time my husband sent great assistance to the Governor of Tanger, the Earle of Petterborow then being Governor, whose letters of supplication and thanks for the kindness and care of my husband I have yett to shew.

June the 26 I was delivered of a son 10 weeks before my time. He liv'd some houres and was christened Richard by our chaplain Mr. Marsden, who performed the ceremonyes of the Church of England in his buriall and then layd him in the parish church in which we lived, in the principall part of the chancell. The Qween sent to condole with me for the losse of my son, and the Marquis de Castell-Melhor, the Marquis de Nica, the Condesa de Villa Franca, the Condesa de Abatha, the Condesa de Telegare, Doña Maria de Antonia, with many other ladys, and severall good gentlewomen that were English merchants' wives.

Severall times we saw the feasts of bulls, and at them had great voyders of dryed sweetmeats brought us upon the King's account, with rich drinke. Once we had sum dispute about some English commanders that thought themselves not well enough placed at the show, according to their merit, by the King's officers, which they did so ill represent to my husband that he was extreamly concerned at it; upon which, notice being given to the chief minister, the Counde de Cassell-Malhor came from the King to my husband after having examined the businesse, and desired that there might be no misunderstanding between the King and him, that the business was only the impertinence of a servant and that it might so pass. My husband was well satisfyed, and presented his most humble acknowledgements to the King for his care and favour to him, as well as the honor he had received. The Counde de Cass [tel-Melhor], when he had finished his visit to my husband, he came to my appartement and told me that he hoped I tooke no offence at what had passed at the feast, because the King had heard I was sad to see my husband troubled, assuring me that His Majesty and the whole court desired nothing more than that we should receive all content imaginable. I gave him many thanks for the honour of his visit, and desired him to present my most humble servises to the King, assuring him that I and my husband had all the respects imaginable for His Majesty. True it was, according to the English fashion, I did make a little mine when I saw my husband disordered, but I should forever remain His Majestye's humble servant with my most humble thanks to His Excellency, and so he returned well satisfyed when he left us.

The 14th, the chieff ministers met my husband, in order to his returne home for England, and expressed a great trouble to part from him. They from the King presented my husband with 12000 crowns in gold plate, with many compliments and favours from the King, whom my husband waited on the next day to receive His Majestie's commands for his master in England. After giving His Majesty many thanks for the many honours he had received from His Majesty, the greatest of which he esteemed His Majesty's kind acceptation of his servise, then he thanked His Majesty for his present, saying that he wished His Majesty's bounteous kindness to him might not prejudice His Majesty in this example by the next coming embassador. To which His Majesty replyed, 'I am sure it can not, for I shall never have such an other embassador.' Then my husband took his leave, performing all those ceremonies with the same persons and coaches as he made his entry.

Upon the 19th of August, my husband and I tooke our leaves of the Qween Mother at her house, who had commanded all her ladyes to give attendance, though Her Majesty was then in a retired condition. Her Majesty expresed much ressentment for our leaving that court, and after our respects payd to Her Majesty, and I receiving Her Majesty's commands to our Qween, with a present, took my leave with the same ceremonys of coaches and persons as I had waited on Her Majesty twice before. Upon the 20th my husband took his leave of Dom Pedro, His Majesty's brother. The 21st of August the Secretary of State came to visit me from the King and Qween, wishing me a prosperous voyage, and presented me with a very noble present. The same day I took my leave of my good nighbour the Condessa de Palma, as I had done to all the ladyes of my acquaintance before, who all presented me with fine presents, as did my good nighbour the Countes of [Santa Cruz], who had with her when I went to take my leave many persons of quality that came on purpose there to take their leaves of me, from whom I received great civility, and the Countesse gave me a very great banquett. On the 23 of

August, 1663, we, accompanyed with many persons of all sorts, went on board the King of England's fregate, called the *Reserve*, commanded by Captaine Holmes; where, so soone as I was on boord, the Conde de Cassell-Melhor sent me a very great and noble present, a part of which was the finest case of waters that ever I did see, being made of Brasill wood garnished with silver; the bottles of cristall garnished with the same and filled with rich amber water.

Lisbone with the river is the goodlyest situation that ever I saw; the city old and decayd, but they are making new walls of stone which will containe six times their city. Their churches and chappells are the best built, the finest adorned, and the cleanlyest kept of any churches in the world. The people delight much in quintes, which are a sort of country houses, of which there are aboundance within few leagues of the city, and those that belong to the nobility very fine, both houses and gardens. The nation is generally very civill and obliging; in religion divided between Papists and Jews; the people generally not handsom. They have many religious houses and bishopricks of great revenue; and the religious of both sects for the most part very strickt. Their fruit of all kinds is extraordinary good and faire; their wine rough for the most part but very whole some; their corne dark and gritty; water bad, except some few springs far from the city; the flesh of all kinds indifferent; their mules and asses extraordinary good and large, but their horses few and naught; they have little wood and less grass.

At my coming away I visited severall nunneryes, in one wher'off I was told that the last year there was a girle of 14 years of age burned for a Jew. She was taken from her mother so soon as she was borne in prison (her mother being condemned) and brought up in the Esperance; [she] never heard, as they to me did afferme, what a Jew was, yett she did dayly scratch and whip the crucifixes and run pins into them in private, and when discovered confessed it and sayd she would never adore that God.

On Thursday the 25th, 1663, we sett sayle for England, and the 4th of September, our stile, being on Friday, we landed at Deale, all in good health, praised be God. Saturday the 5th we went to Cantorbery and there tarryed Sunday, when we went to church; and very many of the gentlemen of Kent came to wellcome us into England. And here I cannot omitt the relating the ensuing story confirmed by Sir Thomas Batten, Sir Arnold Breames, the Deane of Cantorbery, with very many more gentlemen and persons of this town.

There lives not far from Cantorbery a gentleman called Colonell Culpepper, whose mother was a widow unto the Lord Stragford. This gentleman had a sister that liv'd with him, as the world sayd, in too much love. She married Mr. Porter. This brother and sister, being both atheists and living a life according to their proffession, went in a frolick into the vault of their ancestors, where, before they returned, they pulled some of their father's and mother's hairs. Within a very few dayes after, Mrs. Porter fell sick and dyed. Her brother kept her body in a coffin sett up in his buttry, saying it would not be long before he dyed, and then they would be both buried together; but from the night after her death untill the time that we were told this story, which was 2 months, they say that a head as cold as death, with curled haire like his sister's, did ever lye by him where ever he slept, notwithstanding he removed to severall places and countrys to avoyd it; and severall persons told us they had felt this apparition.

On Monday the 7th of September we went to Gravesend and from thence by water to Dorset House in Salisbery Court, where we stayd 15 dayes. The 18th of September, 1663, within 2 houres after our arrivall, we were visited with very many kindred and friends, amongst which His Grace of Cantorbury, who came the next day and dined with us. The same day came the Bishop of Winchester, as did many others of the greatest clergy in England. Upon the 10th of September my husband went to Bath to waite on His Majesty, who was then there. His Majesty graciously received him, and for a confirmation that he approved his servise of his negotiation in Portugall, he was pleased to make him a Privy Councellor. He was also very graciously received of Her Majesty the Qween.

Being indisposed with a long journy my husband fell sick, but it continued but 2 days, thanks be to God. On the 17th he went by Corneborow, where my Lord Chancellor then was, and so to London. And in his absence, on the 16th I tooke a house in Boswell Court near Temple Bar for 2 year; immediatly removing all my goods thereto, as well those, which were many, that I had left with my sister Turner in her house in my absence, as those that I brought with me out of Portugall, which were 17 carte loads. Upon Saturday the 19th my husband returned from His Majesty and met me at our new house in Boswell Court. On Munday the 21st, being at a great feast at my sister Turner, where there met us very many of our friends upon the same invitation, wher'off Sir John Cutler was one; who after dinner brought me a box saying, 'Madame, this was to goe to Portugall, but that I heard your Lady ship was landed.' In it there was a piece of cloth of titio—— forme, and ribbons and gloves for my children. Whilst we were at dinner there came an express from court with a warrant to swear my husband a Privy Councellor, from Sir Henry Bennett. The 22nd we went down for Hartfordshire to my brother Fanshawe. The 24th we dined at Sir John Watt, where we were nobly feasted with great kindness, and to add to my content, I there met with my little girle Betty, whom I had left at nurse within 2 miles of that place, at my going to Portugall. After being entertained at Sir Francis Butler's, our very good friend, we went to St. Albans to bed, where next day we bought some coachehorses, and on the 26th we returned to London. On

Tuesday the 29th we went again to St. Albans, where my husband bought 8 more coach horses. The same night we returned to London.

On the 1st of October the King and Qween came from the Baths, and on the 2d of October my husband was sworn a Privy Councellor in the presence of His Majesty, His Royall Highnesse, and the greatest part of His Majesty's most honourable Privy Councell. On the 3d my husband waited on Her Majesty the Qween Mother, who received him with great kindness. The 4th I waited on Her Majesty at Whitehall, and there delivered the present that the Qween Mother of Portugall had sent Her Majesty, who received both them and me in Her Majesty's bed chamber with great expressions of kindness. I stayd with Her Majesty about an houre and a half, which time Her Majesty spent in asking questions of her mother, brothers and country; after which I waited on Her Majesty into the drawing roome, where into the King entered presently after; and I, seeing the King, retired to the side of the roome, where His Majesty came to me presently, saluting of me, and bad me welcome home with great grace and kindnesse, asking me many questions of Lisbone and the country.

On Sunday the 4th of October my husband took his place in the King's chappell as Privy Councellour in the Lord's seate. Likewise this day His Grace of Cantorbury took his seat, and the Bishop of Winchester, both in the same place. His Grace of Cantorbury did his homage to the King the same day that my husband was sworne a Privy Councellor. I waited on the Qween Mother at Sommersett House, and the Duke and Duchess of York at St. James's, who all received me with great cheerfullness and grace. On the 7th the Lord Mayor invited all the Lords of the Privy Councell to dinner, amongst which was my husband for one. The first of January, New Year's Day, my husband (as the custome of Privy Councellors is) presented His Majesty with 10 pieces of gold in a purse, and the person that carrys it hath a ticket given him of the receit thereoff from the cabboord of the Privy Chamber, where it is delivered to the Master of the Jewell House, who is thereupon to give him 20 shellings for his pains, out of which he is to give to the servant of the Master of the Jewell House eighteen pence. We received, as the custome is, 15 ounces of gilt plate for a Privy Councellor, and 15 ounces for Secrettary of the Latin Tongue. Likewise we had the impost of 4 tuns of wine, 2 for a Privy Councellor and 2 for a Master of Requests.

January the 16th I took my leave of the King and Qween, who with great kindnesse wished me a good voyage for Spain. Then I waited on the Qween Mother at Sommersett House. Her Majesty sent for me into her bed chamber, and after some discourse I took my leave of Her Majesty. Afterwards I waited on Their Royall Highnesses, who received me with more than ordinary kindness; who after an houre and a half discourse with me saluted me and gave me leave to depart. Going along the matted gallery from His Highnes the Duke of York his lodgings, entering into His Majesty's withdrawing room, I found a twenty shillings piece of gold, which nobody owning that was by, I kept. On Tuesday, January the 19th, my husband carryed the Speaker Sir Edward Turner's eldest son and my brother Turner to the King at White Hall, who conferred the honour of knighthood on them both, my husband particularily recommending my brother Turner to His Majesty's grace and favour.

On the 20th of January my husband took his leave of His Majesty and all the royall family, receiving the dispatches and their commands for Spain; from which hour to our going out of towne, day and night our house was full of kindred and friends taking leave of us; and on Thursday, January the 21st, 166[4], in the morning at 8 a clock, we did rendezvous at Dorset House in Salisbury Court, in that half of the house which Sir Thomas Fanshawe of Essex then lived in, who entertained us with a very good breakfast and banquett. The company that came thither was very great, as was like wise that which accompanied us out of town.

Thus with many coaches of our family and friends we took our journy at 10 of the clock towards Portsmouth.

The company of our family was

My husband, and myself, and foure daughters
Mr. Barte, son to the Earle of Lyndsey, Lord Great-Chamberlaine of England
Mr. Newport, second son to the Lord Barone Newport
Sir Benjamin Right, Baronnett
Sir Andrew King
Sir Edward Turner, Knight, son to the Speaker of the Commons House of Parliament
Mr. Francis Godolphin, son to Sir Francis Godolphin, Knight, of the Bath
Mr. Fanshawe, Chief Secretary
Mr. Witcherly
Mr. Lovin
Mr. Hatton
Mr. Geffreys
Mr. Smith
Mr. Price, Under Secretary
Mr. Creeton
Mr. Cooper, Gentleman of the Horse
Mr. Carey, Under Gen. of the Horse
Mr. Weeden }
Mr. Jamett } Pages
Mr. Broomstead }
Mr. Le Blanc }

Mr. Helloe, Chief Butler
Mr. Broom, Chief Cook
Two Undercooks
Two Coachmen
Two Grooms
Two Footmen
Mrs. Kesten, Governess to the children
Mrs. Elizabeth Kesten, House keeper
Mrs. Le Blanc, Waiting Gentlewoman
Mrs. Ursula Fossett, Servant to the young gentlewomen
Mrs. Francis, Chambermaid
Ann Piquett, Washmaid
A Coach of State of crimson velvett, laced and fringed with silver and gold and richly gilt, cost a thousand pounds
A green velvett coach, cost 200lb
Liverys of green velvett, richly laced, for 8 pages
Twelve liverys of the same colour, cloath laced, for 12 footmen, 3 coachmen, 3 postillons and 2 grooms
Two close wagons with our coat of armes above them, with trunks and cloathes
Ten coach horses, the worst cost above 30lb, all bred in Hertfordshire
Two saddle geldings for my husband and my self, besides the servants of the gentlemen

The most part of them went by water.

We lay the first night at Gildford; the second night at Petersfield; and the third at Portsmouth, where we stayed till the 31st of the same month, being very civilly used there by the Mayor and his brethren, who made my husband a freeman of the town, as their custome is to doe to persons of quality that pass by that way. And like wise we received many favours from the Lieutenant Governour, Sir Philip Honywood, with the rest of the commanders of that garrison. As I sayd, on the 31st, being Sunday, we went on boord the Admirall of that fleet, then setting out, Sir John Lawson, Chief Commander (in His Majesty's ship called the *Resolution*). There was Captaine B[erke]ley, Commander of the *Bristoll* frigate; Captaine Utbert, Commander of the *Phoenix*; Captaine Torne, Commander of the *Portsmouth*; Captaine Moone, Commander of the *Yorke*; and Sir John Lawson's catch, commanded by Captaine King. Thus at 10 a clock we sett sayle with a good wind, which carryed us as far as Tar Bay, and then failed us. There we lay till Munday the 15th of February at 9 a clock at night, at which houre, it pleasing God to give us a prosperous wind, we set saile, and on the 23d of February, our style, we cast anker in Cadis roade in Spaine.

So soon as it was knowne that we were there, the English Consull with the English merchants all came on boord to welcome us into Spaine, and presently after came the Lieutenant Governour and the Governour, for the time being Don Diego de Iubara, to give us the joy of our arivall, and to ask leave of my husband to visit him, which Don Diego did within 2 houres after upon the Lieutenant's returne. The next morning [the 6th of March], Stylo Novo, came in a Levant wind which blew so forcibly that we could not possibly land untill Fryday the 7th of March, at 10 a clock in the morning. Then came the Governour Don De Iuara a boord, accompanyed with most of the persons of quality of that town, with many boats for the conveyance of our family, and a very rich barge covered with crimson damaske, fringed with gold, and Persia carpetts under foot. So soon as it was day, in the morning we sett saile to goe nearer to the shore. We were first saluted by all the ships in the roade, and then by all the King of Spaine's forts, which salutation we returned again with our guns. My husband received the Governour upon the deck and carried him into the round house, who, so soon as he was there, told my husband that contrary to the use of the King of Spaine, His Majesty had commanded that his ships and forts should first salute the King of England's Embassadour, and that His Majesty had commanded that both in that place of Cadiz and in all others belonging to the court of Madrid, my husband and all his retinue should be entertained upon the King's account in as full and ample manner, both as to persons and conveyances of our goods and persons, as if His Majesty were there in person.

My husband and self and children went in the barge, the rest in other barges provided for that purpos. At our setting off Sir John Lawson saluted us with very many guns, and as we went neer the shore the canons saluted us in great numbers. When we landed we were carryed on shore in a rich chaire supported with 8 men. We were wellcomed with many vollys of shott, and all the persons of quality of that town by the sea side, amongst whom was the Governour's lady with a coach to receive me and to conduct me to the house provided for us, as the Governour did conduct my husband with all his traine. There were infinite numbers of people, who with the souldjery did shew us all respect and welcome imaginable. I was received by His Excellency Don Melcha de la Cueva, the Duke of Alberquerce his brother, and the Governour of the garrison, who both led me 4 or 5 paces to a rich sidan, which carryed me to the coach where the Governour's lady was, who came out immedi[atly] to salute me, and after some complements I took in the coach with me and my children.

When we came to the house where we were to lodge, we were nobly treated and the Governour's wife did me the honour to sup with me. That afternoone the Duke of Alberquerce came to visit my husband and afterwards me with his brother Don Milcha de la Cueva; and here I must tell you a Spanish compliment. As soone as the Duke was sett and covered, he said, 'Madame, I am Don Juan de la Cueva, Duke of Alberkerce, Viceroy of Milan, of His Majesty's Privy Councell, Generall of the Galleys, twice a grandee, the first Gentleman of His Majesty's Bedchamber, and neer kinsman to his Catholic Majesty, whom God long preserve.' And then rising up and making me a low reverence, with his hat off, sayd, 'This, with my family and life, I lay at Your Excellency's feet.' They were accompanied with a very great traine of gentlemen. At his going away he told me his lady would suddenly visit me.

We had a guard constantly waited on us, and centryes at the gate below and at the stair's head above. We were visited by all the persons of quality of that town. Our house was richly furnished, both my husband's quarter and mine (the worst bed and chamber of my apartement being furnished with damask, in which my chambermaide lay), and all the chambers through[ou]t the floores of them covered with Persia carpets. The richnesse of the guilt and silver plates which we had in great aboundance, as we had like wise of all sorts of very fine househould linnen, was fit onely for the entertainment of so great a prince as His Majesty, our master, in the representation of whose person my husband received this great entertainment. Yet I assure you, notwithstanding this temptation, that your father and myself both wisht our selves in a retired country life in England, as more agreable to both our inclinations.

I must not forget here the ceremony that the Governor used to my husband. After supper the Governor brought the keys of the towne to my husband saying, 'Whilst Your Excellency is here, I am no Governour of this towne, and therefore desire Your Excellency from me your servant to receive these keys and to begin and give the *word* to this garrison this night.' My husband, with all the demonstra[ti]ons of sense of so great an honour, returned His Chatholick Majesty by him his humble thanks, refusing the keys and wishing the Governor much prosperity with them, who so well deserved that honour the King had given him. Then the Governor prest my husband againe for the word, which my husband gave, and was this: '*Long live His Chatholick Majesty*.' Then the Governor took his leave, and his lady of me, whom I accompanied to the stair's head.

The next day we were visited by the Mayor and all the Burgesses of the town. On the same day, Saturday the 8th, the Governor's lady sent me a very noble present of India plate and other commoditys ther'off. In the afternoone the Dutchesse of Alberquerce sent a gentleman to me to know if with conveniency Her Excellency might visit me next day, as the custome of this court is. On Sunday the 9th Her Excellency with her daughter, who was newly marryed to her uncle Don Milchal de la Cueva, visited me. I met them at the stair's head, and at Her Excellency's going, there parted with her. Her Excellency had on, besides other very rich jewells, as I guesse, about 2000 pearls, the roundest, the whitest, and the biggest that ever I saw in my life. On Thursday, the 13th present, the English Consull with all the merchants brought us a present of 2 silver basons and ewres with a hundred weight of chocaletta, with crimson taffeta cloathes laced with silver lace, and voyders which were made in the Indies, as were also the basons and ewres.

This afternoon I went to pay my visite to the Duchess of Alberquerce. When I came to take coach the souldjers stood to their armes, and the Lieutenant held the colours after displaying them, which is never done to any but to kings or such as represent their persons. I stood still all the while. Then, at the lowring of the colours to the ground, they received for them a low courtesy from me and for himself a bow. Then, taking coach with very many persons both in coaches and on foot, I went to the Duke's palace, where I was again received by a guard of His Excellency's with the same ceremony of the King's colours as before. Then I was received by the Duke's brother and neare an hundred persons of quality. I laying my hand upon His Excellency's wrist of his right hand, he putting his cloak there upon (as the Spanish fashion is) went up the staires, upon the top of which stood the Duchesse and her daughter, who received me with great civility, putting me into every doore, and all my children, till we came to sit down in Her Excellency's chamber, where she placed me on her right hand upon cushions, as the fashion of this court is, being very rich and layd upon Persia carpets. At my returne the Duchesse and her daughter went out before me, and at the doore of Her Excellency's chamber I met the Duke, who with his brother and the rest of the gentlemen that did accompany our gentlemen during their stay there, went down together before me. When I tooke my leave of the Duchesse (in the same place where Her Excellency received me), the Duke led me down to the coach in the same manner as his brother led me up the staires, and having received the ceremony of the souldjers, I returned home to my lodgings, where, after I had been an hour, Don Antonio de Pimentell, the Governor of Cadis (who that day was newly come to town), after having been in visite with my husband came to visit me, with great complements on the part of His Chatholick Majesty, and afterwards upon his own score, he sent me a very rich present of perfumes, both skinnes, gloves, and purses imbrodered, with other knacks of the same kind.

Sir John Lawson being now ready to depart from Cadiz, we presented him with a paire of flaggons, £100, and a tun of Lusena wine that cost us 40lb, and 140 pieces of 8 for his men. We sent Captaine Terne 200 pieces of 8, and to his men 40 pieces of 8, he being very carefull of our goods, the most of which he brought. We sent Captaine Ber[keley] 100 pieces of 8, and to his men 20. He carryed part of our horses as did Captaine Utbert, to whom we sent the like summe.

On the 19th March we took our leave of Cadiz, where we gave at our coming away to persons that attended on us in severall offices 280 pieces of 8. We were accompanied to the water side in the same manner as we were received on shoare, with all points of formalities, and having taken our leaves with many thanks and complements to the Governor and Don Diego de Juara, his Lady, with all the rest of those persons there to whom we were so much beholding for their civility, we entered the King's barge, which was newly trimmed up for the purpose by the Duke de Medina Celi at Puerta St. Maria. No person ever went in it before but the King. The Governor, Don Antonio de Pimentel, went with us in the barge, and many other barges were provided by him for all our traine. At our going we had many volleys of shott and after wards many canons, and as we went, the guns of all the ships in the harbour. When we were come over the barr, all the forts by St. Mary's port saluted us, and when we came to the shore side we found many thousand souldjers in armes in very great order, with their commanders, and a bridge made on purpose for us, with great curiosity, so far into the river that the end of the bridge touched the side of the barge. At the end of the bridge stood the Duke de Medina Celie and his son, the Duke of Alcala. During the time of our landing we had infinite vollyes of shot presented with drum beating and trumpets sounding, and all the demonstrations of hearty welcome imaginable. The 2 Dukes embraced my husband with great kindness, welcoming him to the place, and the Duke de Medina Celi led me to my coach, an honour he said that he never had done any but once, that he waited on the Qween to help her in the like occasion. The Duke de Alcala led my eldest daughter, and the younger son led my second, and the Governor of Cadis, Don Antonio de Pimontel, led the third. Mrs. Kestian carried Betty in her armes.

Thus I entered the Duchesse of Alcala's coach, which conveyed me to my lodging, the ceremony of the King's colours being performed as at Cadis. We passed through the streets, in which were infinite numbers of people, to a house provided for us, the best of all the places, which was caused to be glazed by the Duke on purpose for us. At our lighting out of the coaches, the Duke led me up into my apartement with infinite number of noblemen and gentlemen of his relations. There they took their leaves of me, conducting my husband to his quarter, with whom they stayed in visit about half an houre, and so returned to his house. After I had been there 3 houres the Duchesse of Alcala sent a gentleman to say Her Excellency welcomed me to the place, and that as soon as I was reposed after my long voyage she would waite upon me. In like manner did the Marques of Bayon and his lady, and son with his lady. I must not passe by the description of the entertainment which was vastly great, tables being plentifully covered every meale for above 300 persons. The furniture was all as rich: tapestry, embroyderys of gold and silver upon velvet, cloath of titius both gold and silver, with rich Persia carpets on the floare, none could exceed this, with very delicate fine linnen of all sorts both for table and beds, never washed, but new cut out of the piece, and all things there unto belonging. The plate was vastly great and beautyfull, nor for ornament were they fewer than the rest of the bravery, there being very fine cabinets, looking glasses, tables and chaires.

On Thursday the 2[oth] in the afternoon, the Duchess of Alcala came to visit me, who had layn in but 3 weeks of a daughter. The day before she performed all the ceremonyes and civilityes, which is the custome of this court, to me and mine. On the [22nd] I was visited by the Marquessa of Byona and all that noble family. On the 23rd I went to repay to the Duchess of Alcala Her Excellencye's visite and to give her thanks for my noble entertainement, a part thereoff being provided under the care of Her Excellency. I went likewise to pay the visit to the Marquessa de Byona.

On Munday the 24th we begun our journy from Port Santa Maria to Madrid, and taking leave of all the company, we gave 100 pieces of 8 to the servants of the family, 50 pieces of 8 to the Dukes' coachmen and footmen. The Duke accompanied me to the coach side on the same manner as he did when he brought me to the coach side when we landed, and afterwards my husband and the dukes entering the Duke's coach brought us a mile out of town, as did also the Marquess of Bayone and his lady, with infinite numbers of persons of the best quality of that place. That night we went to [Jerez], being met a league before we came to town by the Corijedio, accompanied with many gentlemen and coaches of that place, with many thousands of common people, who conducted us to a house provided for us, as the King had commanded, with much plenty of all sorts of accommodation. My husband made his entry in the town in the Corijedoe's coache, as he did in all places up to Madrid. At this town I was visited by my Lord D[ongan]'s lady who lives there, whose visite I repayd next day, and before I went out of the town. We received letters by a gentleman sent express from the Duke of Medina Celi and the Duke of Alcala, who both wrote to my husband, and his Duchess to me, all of them expressing great civility and kindness. By the bearer of these letters we returned the aknowledgement of their favours in our letters to all Their Excellencys, and presented the knight that brought them with a chaine of gold, cost 30lb sterling.

At 9 of the clock we left the pleasant town of [Jerez] and lodged the next night at Lybria, and the next night at Utrera, where we saw the ruines of a brave town, nothing remaining extraordinary but the fineness of the situation. We were met there by Don Lopus, who was sent with his troope of horse from Siville by the command of the Assistant of that city, the Conde de Molina. There came out to meet us also the Corijedoe of Utrera, with infinite number of persons of all qualityes, and met us a league from the town, as did also the English Consull of Sevill, with many English merchants, who had cloathed 12 foot men in new liverys for to shew the more respect to my husband. We were lodged in a priest's house, which was very nobly furnished for our reception, and our treatment was answerable thereunto.

Thursday the 27th of March we entered Sivilla, being met a league of the city by the Assistant, the Conde de Molina, with many hundred coaches with nobility and gentry in them, and very many thousands of the burgeses and common people of the town. My husband after usuall complements past went into the Conde's coach, I following my husband in my own coach, as I ever did in all places, all the pages going next my coach on horseback, and then our coach of state and other coaches and litters behind, many of the gentlemen and servants riding on horseback, and many of the gentlemen did ride before the first coach. Thus we entered the great city, that had been, of Sivilla, though now much decayd. We lay in the King's pallace, which was very royally furnished on purpos for our reception and all our treatment during our stay. We were lodged in a silver bedstead guilt, and the curtains, and vallans and counterpan of crimson damask, embossed richly with flowers of gold; the tables of precious stones, and the looking glasses bordered with the same; the chaires the same, with the bed and the floore covered with rich Persia carpets, and a great brasera of silver filled full of delicate flowers, which was replenished every day so long as we stayed. The hangins were of tapestry full of gold, all which furniture was never layen in but two nights when His Majesty was at Sivilla.

Within my chamber was a dressing roome, and by that a chamber very richly furnished in which my children lay, and within them all my women. On the other side of the chamber as I came in was my dining room in which I did constantly eat, I and my children eating at a table alone all the way without any company, till we came to our journey's end, where we provided for ourselves, at [V]allecas, within a league of Madrid. In this pallace the chiefe roome of my husband's quarter was a gallery, wherein were 3 paire of India cabinetts of Japan, the biggest and beautifullest that ever I did see in my life. It was furnished with rich tapestry hangings, rich looking glasses, tables, Persia carpets, and cloath of tisua chaires. This pallace hath many princely rooms in it both above and underneath the ground, with many large gardens, tarras walkes, fish ponds, and statues, many large courts, and fountaines, all which were as well drest for our reception as art or mony could make them. During our stay in this pallace we were every day entertained with variety of recreations, as shows upon the river, stage plays, singing, dancing, men playing at legerdemain, which were constantly ushered with very great banquets, and so finished.

On the 30th of this present the Malagoe merchants of the English presented my husband with a very fine horse, cost them 300lb, and on the first of March the English merchants, with their Consull of Seville, presented us with a great quantity of chocaletta and as much of sugar, with 12 fine sasnett napkings laced, there unto belonging, with a very large silver pot to make it in, and 12 very fine cups to drink it in, made of fillagrana, with covers of the same, with 2 very large salvers to set them upon, of silver.

On Thursday the 3rd of Aprill, 1664, we tooke our leaves of the Assistant and the rest of that noble company at Sevilla. The Conde de Molina who was Assistant of Sevill presented me with a young lyon, but I desired His Excellency's pardon that I did not accept of it, saying I was of so cowardly a make I durst not keep company with it. In the same manner as they received us, so they accompanied us a league onward of our way, where upon my husband's lighting out of the Conde's coach, and having with me taken leave of all the company, both he and I got up on horseback, and here we took our leave of my Lord D[ongan], who with great kindnese brought us so far from [Jerez]. Some of the Malago merchants, and of those of Sevilla, accompanyed us forward on our journey. That night we lay at Carmona and on the 4th of Aprill at Fuentes, the honor of the Marquis who is now at Paris, Ambassadour from the King of Spaine to the court.

On the 5th we lay at E[cija], where we received noble entertainment from the noblemen and gentlemen of that town, with whom we stayd till Tuesday the 8th day of Aprill; and then, after paying thanks to these persons that had so well ordered that noble entertainment with great civility to us, we went that night to Corduba, where a league before we came to the town we were met by the Corrijodor, with near an hundred coaches; and a foot company of soldjers stood on each side of the way giving volleys of shott with display colours and trumpets, with many thousands of people, who by fire works and other expressions, shewed much joy. Here we parted with Don Lopas, a gentleman sent from the Conde de Molina to this place to accompany us. We were lodged at a very brave house, and as bravely furnished. At night we had a play acted, and during our stay there we saw many nunneries and the best churches, as we had likewise done at Sevilla and all other towns thorough which we had passed in our journy from the seaside. We had there the feast of the bulls, called in the Spanish tongue jogo de los toros. We had likewise another sport called jogo de canas, in which appeared very many fine gentlemen, fine horses, and very fine trappings. We had the aboundance of noble entertainment that was imaginable, and yet their civilitys and good manners exceeded it all, as likewise the fame of that place, which is so highly renowned in the world for noble and well bred gentlemen. The Corrijedor presented me with 12 great cases of amber and orange water, which is reputed the best in the world, with 12 barrells of olives, which have also the like fame.

Upon Tusday the 15th of Aprill we took our leave of Corduba and all those noble persons ther'in, lodging that night at Carpio, the Marquis-ship of Don Lewis de Haro; and on the 16th we lodged at Anduxar, and on Thursday the 17th at Linaries. Friday the 18th we entered the Siera Morena and lodged at St. Estevan, the honor of a conde that is at present Vice King at Peru; and on Saturday the 19th we came out of the Siera Morena and lodged that night at La Tore de Juan Abad. On Sunday the 20th we lay at Membrilla, and there stayed all day; on Monday and Tuesday the 22nd at Villa Harta. Here rises the River Guadiana that goes under ground 7 leagues before. On Wednesday the 23rd we lay at Corsuegra. Here Don Juan de Austria was nursed. Thursday the 24th we lay at Mora.

On Friday the 25th we lay at the famous city of Toledo. 2 leagues from that town, the Marquesse of [ ], Governor of Toledo, met us, into whose coach my husband went with him towards the town, where within half a league he was met by 4 persons that represented the city, and all the city of Toledo with all the noblemen and gentlemen of that towne. A little farther the Marquis his lady met me, who lighting out of her coach, and I to meete her, after some complements passed, entered her coach with my children, and so passing through the street in which there was both water works and fireworks, and many thousands of people of all sorts, and companies of soldjers giving us volleys of shotts. We alighted at the gate, the Marquis leading me up into my lodgings. This house, next the King's pallace at Sevilla, was both the largest and the noblest furnished that I did see in all my journy; as like wise all the streets of this city were hung with rich tapestry and other rich things of silver and gold and embroydery, through which we passed. We were ther entertained during our stay with comedyes and musick and jogo de toros, and with great plenty of provisions of all sorte that were necessary to demonstrate a princely entertainment. I eat constantly at a table on purpos provided for me, at which the Marquesse kept me company; as she did like wise where ever I went to visite any remarkable place, of which there be many in Toledo; but none comparable to the great church, which, for the greatness and beauty of it, I have not seen many better, but for the riches ther'in, never the like. Here my husband received an other message from the Duke de Medina les Tores, desiring him to meet him at Valldamora the Friday following, His Catholick Majesty being then at Aranjuez. This message was sent by a gentleman of his own; the other that he sent to welcome us into the country being Under-gentleman of the Horse to Her Majesty. Upon Tuesday the 29th of Aprill we took our leaves of the Marquis and his lady, giving 180 pieces of 8 among the servants of that family.

That night we lay at [Il]lescas, and on the 30th we came to [V]allecas where we found a house provided for us. Here the King's entertainment ceased, and we provided for all the accommodations of all our family, the bare house onely excepted. We continued at [V]allecas till the 8th of June following, during which time there happened nothing extraordinary, the Duke often sending his secrettary to my husband about busenesse, and the Master of the Ceremonys, and our constant endeavouring for a house; though at last we were glad to goe to a part of a house of the Conde de Irvias, where the Duke of St. Germain had lived before.

Here we did receive many messages of welcome to this court from all the ambassadores and all the grandees, and I from the German Ambassadore's Lady, the Duchess De Medina Les Tores, with great numbers of the greatest persons of quality in Madrid. The men visited my husband, but I could not suffer the ladys to visit me (though they much desired it), because I was so straitoned in my lodgings that in no sort were they convenient to receive persons of that quality, in not being capacious enough for our own family, for whose accommodation we took Count Marsin's house close by this.

On Wednesday the 18th of June my husband had his audience of His Chatholick Majesty, who sent to conduct him the Marquis de Melpique, and brought with him an horse of His Majesty's for my husband to ride on, and 30 more for his gentlemen, and His Majesty's coach with the guard that he was captaine of. No ambassadore's coach accompanyed my husband but the French, who did it contrary to the King's command, who had before, upon my husband's demanding the custome of ambassadors accompanying all other ambassadores that came into the court at their audience, replyed that although it had been so, it should never be againe; saying it was a custome brought into this court within less than these 25 years; and that it caused many disputes for which he would no more suffer it. To this order all the ambassadores in the court submitted, but the French, whose secretary told my husband at his coming that morning that his master the Ambassadore said that His Chatholick Majesty had nothing to doe to give his master orders, nor would he obey any of them; and so great was this work of super arrogation on the part of the French, that they waited on my husband from the pallace home, a complement till that time never seen before.

[My husband] about 11 of the clock sett forth out of his lodgings thus: first went all those gentlemen of the town and pallace that came to accompany my husband; then went 20 foot men all in new liveryes of the same colour we used to give, which is a dark green cloath with a frost upon green lace; then went all my husband's gentlemen, and next before himself his camaradoes, two and two:

Mr. Wicherly Mr. Lovin
Mr. Godolphin Sir Edward Turner
Sir Andrew King Sir Benjamin Right
Mr. Newport and Mr. Barte,

then my husband in a very rich suite of cloathes of a dark fillemoate imbrocad laced with silver and gold lace, nine laces, every one as broad as my hand, and a little silver and gold lace layd between them, both of very curious workmanship. His sute was trimed with scarlet taffeta ribbon, his stockings of white silk upon long scarlett silk ones, his shoes black with scarlett shoes' strings and garters, his linnen very fine laced with very rich Flanders lace, a black beavour button on the left side, with a jewell of 1200lb, a rich curious wrought gold chaine made in the Indies, at which hung the King his master's picture richly sett with diamonds, cost 300lb, which His Majesty in great grace and favour had been pleased to give him at his coming home from Portugal. On his fingers he wore two very rich rings, his gloves trimed with the same ribban as his cloathes. All his whole family was very richly cloathed according to their severall qualityes. Upon my husband's left hand rode the Marquis of Malpique, Captain of the German guard, and the Mayor Domo to His Majesty being that week in waiting. By him went all the German guard, and by them my husband's 8 pages cloathed all in velvet, the same colour as our liveries. Next them followed his Chatholick Majesty's coach, and then my husband's coach of state, with 4 black horses, the finest that ever came out of England (none going in this court with 6 but the King himself). The coach was of rich crimson velvet laced with a broad silver and gold lace fringed round with a massey gold and silver fringe, and the falls of the bootes so rich that they hung almost down to the ground. The very fringe cost almost 400lb. The coach was very richly guilt on the outside and very richly adorned with brasse work, with rich tassells of gold and silver hanging round the top of the curtains round about the coach. The curtains was of rich damask fringed with silver and gold. The harness for 6 horses was richly embossed with brass work, with reines and tassells for the horses of crimson silk, silver and gold. That coach is said to be the finest that ever entered Madrid with any embassadour whatsoever. Next to this followed the French Ambassador's coach, then my husband's second coach, which was of green figured velvett with green damask curtains, handsomly gilt and adorned on the outside with harness for 6 horses suitable to the same. The 4 horses were fellows to those that drew the rich coach (when we went out of town using always six). After this followed my husband's 3d coach with foure mules, being a very good one according to the fashion of this country. Then followed many coaches of perticular persons of this court.

Thus they rode through the greatest streets of Madrid, as the custome is; and all lighting within the pallace, my husband was conducted up by the Marquis (all the King's guard attending, thorough many roomes in which there was infinite numbers of people, as there was in the streets to see him passe to the pallace) up to a private withdrawing room of His Catholick Majesty, where my husband was received with great grace and favour by His Majesty. My husband being covered delivered his message in English, interpreted afterwards by himself in Spanish. After this my husband gave His Catholick Majesty thanks for his noble entertainment from our landing to this court. To which His Catholick Majesty replyed that as well for the great esteem he had ever had of his person, as the greatness of his master whom he served, he would be always glad to be serviceable to him. After my husband's obeissance to the King, and saluting all the grandees there waiting, he was conducted to the Qween, where having stayed in complements with Her Majesty, the Empresse, and the Prince, took his leave, making his obeissance to all the ladys there waiting. He returned home in his Majestye's coach with the Marquis de Malpique sitting at the same end on his left hand, accompanyed with the same persons that went forth with him, having a banquett ready for them at their returne. That day in the evening my husband visited His Excellency the Duke De Medina de las Torres, and then the next morning all the Councell of State as the custome of this court is.

Upon the 21st all the ambassadores at the court one after another visited my husband, as did alsoe all the grandees and nobles, His Excellency the Duke de Medina de las Torres beginning. On the 24th my husband had a private audience with His Catholick Majesty. On the 27th I waited on the Qween and the Emperesse with my 3 daughters and all my traine. I was received at the Buen Retiro by the guard, and afterwards, when I came upstaires, by the Marquesse of Hinoesser, the Qween's Carmareiro Mayor, then in waiting. Through infinite number of people I passed to the Qween's presence where Her Majesty was seated at the upper end under a cloath of state, upon 3 cushins, and on her left hand the Emperesse, and 3 more. The ladyes were all standing. After making my last reverence to the Qween Her Majesty, and the Emperesse rising up and making me a little curtsy, sate downe—again. Then I, by my interpreter Sir Benjamin Right, said those complements that were due from me to Her Majesty; to which Her Majesty made a gracious and kind reply. Then I presented my children, which Her Majesty received with great grace and favour. Then Her Majesty speaking to me to sitt, I sate down upon a cushion lay'd for me above all the ladys who sate, but below the Camerera Mayor (no woman taking place of Her Excellency but princesses). The children sate on the other side, mingled with court ladys that are maides of honour. Thus after having passed half an houre in discourse, I tooke my leave of Her Majesty and the Emperesse, making reverences to all the ladyes in passing. I returned home in the same order as I came. The next day the Camerera sent to see how I did, in complement from Her Majesty.

On the 9th of July my husband sent Don Pedro Ro[jas], Master of the Ceremonyes, a gold chaine, cost foure score pounds, and on the 22 of July the merchants of Alicant sent us a piece of purple damask of 130 yards for a present.

On Saturday the 16 of August we came to the House of Sietta Chimineas, which His Majesty did give us to dwell in, having been the house where the Venetian Ambassadour dwelt, and went out for our accommodation by the King's command. We settled now our family in order, and tables. Our own consisted of 2 courses of 8 dishes each, and the steward's of foure. We had our mony returned from England by Mr. Godhard, an English merchant living in Madrid, a very honest man and an able merchant.

Tuesday the 2[6]th we dined at the Casa del Campo, a house of His Majesty's, in the garden of which stands a very brave statue of Philip the [Third] on horseback. October the fourth we dined at the Parda, another house of His Majesty's, which is very fine, and hath a very fine parke, well stored with deare, belonging to it.

October the 10th we went privatly to see Aranjuez, which was most part of it built by Philip the Second, husband to Qween Mary of England. There is the highest trees, and grow the evenest, that ever I saw. Many of them are bored through with pipes for water to ascend and to fall from the tops down, one against an other; and like wise there is many fountaines in the side of this walke, and the longest walkes of elmes that ever I saw in my life. The parke well furnished with English oakes and elmes, well stored with dear; and the Tagus makes it an iland. The gardens are vastly large, with the most fountaines and the best that ever I did see in my life. As soone as the Duke heard we were gone thither, he immediately sent orders after us for our entertainment by a post, but we were gone before, going home by Escivias, where we saw those famous reputed cellers which are 44 steps downe, where that admirable wine is kept in great tanajas, which are pots holding about 500 gallons each. And to lett you know how strangely they clear their wine, it is by putting some of the earth of the place in it, which way of refining their wines is done no where but there.

October the 14th the King proclaimed the lowering of the vellon money to the half; and the pistol that was this morning at 82 ryalls was now proclaimed to goe but for 48, which was above 800lb loss to my husband.

October the 21st we went to see the Buen Retiro. The Duke de Medina de les Torres, who hath the keeping of this house of the King's from His Majesty, sent 2 of his gentlemen to shew us all that belongs thereunto.

The place is adorned with much water and fountaines, trees and fine gardens, with many hermitages scatered up and down the place, and a very good house for His Majesty. Yet the pictures there in did far exceed the rest, they being many and all very curious, done by the best hands of the world in their times.

On the 27th of October we went with all our traine to see the Escuriall, the Duke de Medina de las Torres having procured a letter here from the Pope's Nuncio to give me leave to see the convent there, which cannot be seen by any woman without his leave. Likewise the Duke did send letters to the Prior, commanding him to assist in shewing all the principall parts of that princely fabrick, and to lodge us in the lodging of the Duke de Montalto, the Mayor Dome Mayor to Her Majesty. We were near 80 persons in company and five coaches. So soone as we were arrived there, the Prior sent two of his chief fryers to welcome us to the Escuriall. The fryer who met us by command, a league before, at a grange house of His Majestye's, and accompanyed us to the Escuriall, being returned, these fryers from the Prior brought us a present of St. Martine's wine and mellons, a calfe, a kidd, 2 great turkies, fine bred, apples, peares, creame, with some other fine things of that place. On the 28th, being St. Simon and Jude's Day, we all went early in the morning to see the church, where we were mett by the Pryor at the doore, with all the fryers on both side, who received us with great kindnesse and respect; and all the quires singing till we came up to their high altar. Then all of them accompanyed us to the Pantheon, which was for that purpose hanged full of lights in the branches. There saw I that most glorious place for the covering of the bones of their kings of Spaine as is possible to imagine.

I will briefly give you this small description. The descent is about 30 steps, all of polished marble, and arched and lyned on the sides with jaspar polished. Upon the left hand, on the middle of the staires, is a large vault in which the bodyes of their kings, and qweens that have been mothers of kings, lye in silver coffins for one year untill the moisture of their bodies be consumed. Over against this is an other vault in which lyes buried the bodies of those qweens that had no sons at their death, and all the children of their kings that did not inherit. At the bottome of the staires is the Pantheon, built eight squares, and as I guesse about 60 foot over. The whole lyning of it in all places is jaspar, very curiously carved both in figures, and flowers, and imagery; and a branch for 40 lights, which is vastly rich, of silver and hangs down from the top in a silver chaine within 3 yards of the bottome, and is made with so great art, as is also this curious knott of jaspar on the floare, that the reflection of the branch and lights is perfectly there to be seen. The bodies of their kings lye in jaspar stones, supported every coffin with 4 lyons of jaspar at the 4 corners. 3 coffins and 3 broad stones are set in every arch, which arch [is] curiously wrought in the roof and supported with jaspar pillars.

There is 7 arches, and one in the middle at the upper end, and over against the coming in, that contains a very curious alter and crucifix of jaspar. From thence we saw all the convent, and the sacristiana, in which there was the principall pieces that ever Titian made, and the hands of many others of the most famous men that then were in the world.

After seing the convent and every part thereoff, we saw the King's pallace, with the apothecary's shop, and the stillitoryes, and all belonging thereunto. The Escuriall stands under the side of a very high mountaine. It hath a fair river and a very large parke well stored with deare. It is built upon a hill, and you ascend above half a mile through a double row of elme trees to the house, which is aboundantly served with most excellent water and wood for their use. The front hath a large platforme paved with marble, and rayled with a stone ballaster round about. The entry of the gate is supported with 2 marble pillars, each of them of one entire marble, which are near 12 foot high. It is built with 17 courts and gardens there unto. Every court contains a different office. The whole is built of rough marble with pillars of the same round the cloysters, and the walls thereoff are made so smooth that famous Titian hath painted them with storys all over, with the story of the Battle of Lepantho, and the galleryes of the pallace also. They have infinite numbers of fountaines both within and without house. It containes a very fair pallace, a convent, and a colledge, and hospitall; all which are exactly well kept and royally furnished. But I cannot omitt saying that the finest stillitory I ever saw is there, being a very large roome shelved round, with glasses sized and sorted upon the shelves, many of crystall gilt and the rest of Venice glasses, and some of vast sizes. The floare is paved with black and white marble and in the middle stands a furnace with 500 stills round it, with glasse like a pyramide, with glasse heads. The apothicary shop is large, very richly adorned with paint and gilding and marble. There is an inward roome in which the medecines are made, as finely furnished and beautifyed as the shop. All the vessels are silver and gilt, and so are all the instruments for surgery. Nothing is wanting there for that purpose that invention or money can produce.

We were entertained with a banquett at the Pryor's lodging and afterwards returned, accompanied with the fryers, to our own lodgings, where the Prior made a visite to my husband, and my husband offered to repay it againe, sending to him to know if His Reverentissima Sennoria would give him leave to waite on him that night to thank him for his noble entertainment, although both he and I had done it. The Pryor excused the visite and so we rested that night.

I would not have you that reade this book admire that I should not more largely describe this so unparallelld fabrick of the world, but I doe purposely omitt the particulers, because it is in every particuler exactly described in a book writ by the fryers and sold in that place, with all the cuts of every particuler of that place, and you have it amongst your father's books. The fryers of this convent are of the Order of St. Laurence.

On the 29th we returned home to our house at Madrid, where on Saturday after my little child Betty fell sick of the small pox, as had done my daughter Anne in the month of September, but both of them (God's name be praysed) recovered perfectly well without blemish. But as I could not receive (for want of capacity of roome) the ladys of this court in my lodgings at the Conde de Irvia's, so I could not receive them here by reason of the small pox in the family, and they having twice a piece offered to visite me and I refused it, upon that account.

Thursday the 27th of November I went to waite upon the Emperor's Ambassador's lady at her house. Upon the 28th I went to waite upon the Duchesse De Medina de les Torres, and upon the 29th the Emperor's Ambassador's lady came to see me in the afternoone. The same day the Duchess de Medina de les Torres sent to excuse by Don Alonso, one of the Duke's secretaryes, that she could not visite me that day by reason her youngest daughter was fallen sick of a feaver. Sunday the 30th of November I sent to thanke the Emperor's Ambassador's lady for her visit the day before, and to see how she did.

Upon the first of December, 1664, being Monday, we lett our dispense for 72000 Rlls vellon a year, which at 48 ryalls a pistole is 125 pistolles a month. He paid me this sum this day as he is obliged to doe on the first day of every month, and likewise to give me for the arrears of the dispence (which was neare 11 weekes) 14000 Rlls within 2 months beginning this day.

Upon the 15th of December was seen here at Madrid a very great blazing star, which to our vew appeared with a traine of 12 or 14 yards long. It rose at first in the south south east, about 12 a clock at night, but altered its course during the continuance thereof, and within a fortnight of its expiration it appeared at 6 a clock at night with the rays reversed. It continued in our vew till the 23rd of January.

[Nov]ember the 22nd, which is the Qween of Spaine's birthday, I went to give Her Majesty the joy thereoff, and to the Emperesse and the Prince of Spaine, in such formes as the custome of this court is. About this time I had sent me by a Genovas merchant that was a banker in Madrid a box of about a yard and half long and all most a yard and half broad and a quarter and half deep, covered with green taffety and bound with a silver lace with lock and key within. It was divided into many partitions garnished with gilt papers and fill'd all full of the best and choycest sweet meats, all dry. I never saw any so beauty full and good before or since, besides the curiosity.

On the 23rd we were invited to see a show performed by 48 of the chiefest of the nobility of this court, who ran 2 and 2 on horseback as fast as the horses could run, in walkes, railed in on purpose on both sides, before the pallace gate, over which in a balcony sat the King, Qween, and Emperesse. Round about in other balconys sate the nobility of the court, and in an entresuelo at the King's left hand sate the chief of the ambassadors. My husband and I were with the Duke and Duchess de Medina de les Torres in their own particuler quarter in the pallace, which we chose as the best place and having the best view, where upon we refused the belcony. The sight was very fine and the noblemen and the horses very rich attired.

Upon the 1st of January I received of our dispensiero, as was my due, 6000 Rlls for the month's dispence, and 6000 Rlls more in part of the arrears. Upon the 4th of January I waited on the Qweene, Prince, and Empress, to give them the buenas pasquas, as the custome of this court is. On the 5th here came, among other diversions of sports we had this Christmass, Juan Arana, the famous comedian who here acted above 2 houres to the admira[ti]on of all that beheld him, considering that he was near upon 80 years of age. About this time the Duke of Alva sent my husband a fatt buck. I never eat any better in England. We doe take it for granted in England that there is nothing good to eat in Spaine, but I will assure you the want is money only.

The 11th of December the President of Castille gave a warrant to an officer to execute upon Don Francisco de Ayala to carry him prisonner for some offences by him committed. This gentleman lived in a house within the protection of my husband's barriers, very near to his own dwelling house, for which reason no person can give or execute a warrant for what crime soever without the leave of the ambassador. But notwithstanding, the officer who executed this warrant, being backed by the President of Castille, did seize the person of Don Francisco de Ayala in his own house and carryed him to prison. Notice where of being given to my husband from him, my husband immediatly wrote a letter to the President of Castille demanding the prisonner to be immediatly brought home to his house, that he would not suffer the priviledge of the King his master to be broke, making farther great complaints of this usage to him, to which the next day in a letter the President replyed that an ambassadour had no power to protect out of his own house and household with many other ridiculous excuses. But all his allegations being proved against him both by antient and moderne custome, by hundred of examples, and nothing left him to defend himself but his own peevish wilfullnesse, my husband pursued the business with much vigor, telling the gentleman that brought him the President's letter that his master the President, as to him, had been once very civill but, as to the King his master most uncivill, both in the acting and defending so undecent a business; for which reason he would not give an answer by letter to the President, because his to the Ambassadour did not deserve one. All which my husband desired the gentleman to acquaint the President his master with.

Then my husband visited the gentleman in prison, a thing never before known of an ambassadour, telling the prisonner openly before many gentlemen that were there accompanying of him that he would have him out or else that he would immediatly leave the court. (The great number of gentlemen and servants of my husband's family gave apprehensions to the keepers of the prison, when my husband demanded leave to visite the prisonner.) The next day, being the 16th, Don Francisco de Ayala was visited (by my husband's example) by most of the Councel and nobility of this court. In the evening, in a letter to the Duke of Medina de les Torres, my husband inclosed a memoriall to His Catholick Majesty demanding the prisonner, saying he was very sorry that at one time a few years agoe sacriledgeously (in the year 1650) some English gentlemen, whereof Mr. Sparkes was one, did kill one As[cham], an agent of Oliver's to the Catholick King. When they had thus done, all these persons by degrees made their escape, but Mr. Sparks, who tooke sanctuary in one of their churches; notwithstanding which, the priviledge thereof being defended both by the Archbishop of Toledo and the greatest prelates of this kingdom, he was by the King and Councell pulled out of the church and executed, so great at that time was the fear that this court then had of Oliver; and now violation of priviledges should onely have been used to His Majesty the King of England, assuring His Majesty he neither could nor would put it up without ample restitution made. Upon the perusall of which memorialls His Catholick Majesty did immediately command the President of Castile to send his warrant the next day, and to release Don Fran[cis]co de Ayala and to send him home immediately to my husband, which was accordingly done that night, and my husband with all his coaches and family, which were near an hundred persons, carryed him and placed him in his own house, before the officers' faces that brought him home from prison. All this you will find in your father's transactions in his Spanish embassey. In this action my husband did not receive so much content in the victory, as the Spaniards of all sortes, in whom it made a very great impression; though the chief minister of state in our countrey did not value this nor give the incouragement to such a noble action as was due.

And I will here impartially say what I observed of the Spanish nation, both in their customes and principles and countrey. I find it a received opinion that Spaine affords not food either good or plentifull. True it is that strangers that neither have skill to choose nor money to buy will find themselves at a loss, but there is not in the Christian world better wines than their midland wines are especially, besides Sherrey and Canary. Their water tasts like milk; their corne white to a miracle; and their wheat makes the sweetest and best bread in the world. Bakon beyond belief good; the Segovia veal, much larger, whiter and fatter than ours; mutton most excellent; capons much better than ours. They have a small bird that lives and fattens on grapes and corne, so fatt that it exceeds the quantity of flesh. They have the best partridges I ever eat, and the best saucidges, and salmon, pikes and sea-breams, which they send up in pickle called oskeveche to Madrid; and dolphins, which are excellent meat; besides carpes and many other sorts of fish. The creame called nattuos is much sweeter and thicker than ever I saw in England. Their eggs much exceed ours; and so all sorts of sallets and roots, and fruits. That I most admired is mellons, peaches, Burgemoti peares, and grapes, oranges, lemmons, citrons, figgs, pomegranates. Besides that I have eat many sorts of biskets, cakes, cheese, and excellent sweetmeats. I have not here mentionned especially manger blanc. And they have olives which are no where so good. Their perfums of amber excell all the world in their kind, both for cloathes, houshold stuff, and fumes, and there is no such waters made as in Siville. They have dayly curiositys brought from Italy and the Indies to this court, which (though I gott my death's wound in) without partiality I must say it is the best established court but our own in the Christian world that ever I saw, and I have had the honour to live in seven. All embassadours live in as great splendor as the most ambitious can desire, and if they are just and good, with as much love as they can deserve. In the palace none serves the King or Qween but the chiefest of the nobility and antientest families; no, not in the meanest offices.

The nation is most superstitiously devout in the Roman Catholick religion; true in trust committed to them to a miracle, withstanding all temptations to the contrary. And it hath often been tryed, and particularly in poor men about Cadis and St. Lucar, that for 8 or 10 pieces of eight will undertake stealing f[rom] the merchants their silver aboord when their shipping coms in, which sometimes by the watch for that purpose are taken; and after their examination and refusall to declare whose the silver is, or who imployed them to steal this custome, they are often times racked, which they will suffer with all the patience imaginable; and notwithstanding their officers mingle great promisses of rewards if they will confess as they execute their punishments, yet it was never known that ever any confessed. And yet these men are not worth 10 pounds in the world. They are civill to all, as their qualityes require, with the highest respects; so that I have seen a grandee and a duke stop his horse, when an ordinary woman passeth over a kennel, because he would not spoyle her cloathes, and put off his hat to the meanest woman that makes reverence, though it be their footmen's wives. They meddle with no nighbour's fortune or persone, but their owne familys'. They are puntuall in visits, men to men, and women to women. They visit not together, except their greatest ministers of state to [wives of] publick ministers from princes. If they have animosityes concerning place, they will by discretion avoyd ever meeting in a third place, and yet converse in each other's house all the dayes of their life with satisfaction on both sides. They are generally pleasant and facetious company, but in this their women exceed, who seldome laugh, but never aloud, but the most witty in repartyes and storys and notions in the world. They sing, but not well, their way being between Italian and Spanish. They play of all kinds of instruments likewise, and dance with castelliates very well. They work little, but that rarely well, especially in monasterys. They all paint white and red, from the Qween to the cobler's wife, old and young, widows excepted, which never goe out of close mourning, nor weare gloves, nor shew their hair after their husband's death, and seldome marry. They are the finest shaped women in the world, not tall. Their hair and teeth are most delicate. They seldome have many children. There is none love cleanlyness more, in dyett, and cloathes, and houses, than they doe. They dress up their little oratoryes very fine with their own work and flowers. They have a seede which they sow in the latter end of March, like our sweet basill, but it grows up in their pots, which are often of chenny, large for their windows, so delicately that it is all the summer as round [as] a ball and as large as the circumference of the pot, of a most pleasant green and very good sent.

They delight much in the feasts of bulls, and in stadge plays, and take great pleasure to see their little children act before them in their own houses, which they will doe in perfection. But the children of the greatest are kept at great distance from conversing with their relations or frends, never eating with their parents but at their birth[day]s. They are caryed into an apartement with a priest that sayes dayly the office of their church, a governess, nurse, and under servants, who have their allowances according to the custome of great men's houses, so many pounds of flesh, fruit, bread, and the like, with such a quantity of drink and so much a year in mony. Untill their daughters marry, they never stir so much as down stairs, nor [marry] for no consideration under their own quality, which to prevent, if their fortunes will not procure, they make them nuns. They are very magnificent in houses, furniture, pictures of the best, jewells, plate and cloathes, most noble in presents, entertainment, and in their equipage; and when they visite, it is with great state and attendance. When they travell they are the most jolly people in the world, dealing their provisions of all sorts to every person they meet, when they are eating.

One thing I had like to have forgot to tell you. In the palace there never lyes but one person in the King's apartement, which is a nobleman to wait the King's commands. The rest are lodged in apartements at farther distance, which makes the King's side most pleasant, because it is so airy and sweet. The King and Qween eat together twice a week in publick, with their children; the rest privately and asunder. They eat often, but flesh is their breakfast, which is generally, to persons of quality, a partridge and bacon, or capon, or some such thing, ever rosted; much chocalatey and sweet meats, and new eggs; drinking water, either cold with snow or lemonathay, or some such thing. Seldome their women drink wine, their maids never. They all love the feasts of bulls and strive to appeare gloriously fine when they see them.

Upon February the 11th the Emperor's Ambassador's lady visited me. Upon Thursday the 19th of February went from us to England Mr. Charles Bartell, Mr. Francis Newport, Sir Andrew King, Sir Edward Turner, Mr. Francis Godolfin, Mr. Wicherly, Mr. Hatton, Mr. Smith, with all their servants. This day likewise we received letters of the arrival of Mr. Price from Elvas, a gentleman of my husband's which had been sent by him on the 28th of January last past to the King of Portugall upon business of state.

Upon the 2nd of March we went to see a country house of the Marquis de Liche, who presented me with a dog and a bitch, perfect grayhounds, and I could put each of them into my pockett.

On Thursday the 5th I returned the visite of the Emperor's Ambassador's lady. March the 8th we went to see a house of Don Juan de Gongra at Cham[artín]. On Wednesday the 18th we went to take the ayr and dined at Vicalvero. Mr. Price came from Lisbone this day to Madrid.

Upon the 20th of March, 1665, Stylo Novo, upon desire of the Duchesse de Medina de les Torres (who was then sick and had long kept her bed) I visited Her Excellency, taking all my children with me. After I had been there a litle while, passing those complements, Her Excellency told me that Her Catholick Majesty had commanded her to assure me that Her Majesty had a very high esteeme for me, not onely as I was the wife of a great king's ambassadour, for whom Her Majesty had much respect, but for my person and the delight that Her Majesty took in my conversation, assuring me from Her Majesty that upon all occasions I should find her most cheerfully willing to doe me all possible kindness in her crout. And for a token there off Her Majesty had here with sent me a jewell of diamonds that cost the Qween 8550 ducats plate, which is about 2000lb sterling, which then Her Excellency did deliver me, saying she thought herself much honoured, and much contented, that Her Majesty had imployed her in a business in which she took so great a delight. I desired Her Excellency to lay me at the feet of Her Majesty and to tell Her Majesty that I esteemed the honour according as I ought; of whose bounty and graces I, and mine, had aboudantly received ever since our coming into this kingdome; that the ribbon wherewith the jewell was tyed, coming from Her Majesty, was a favour of which I should have bragg'd all the dayes of my life, though I could never have deserved it. Much more I did esteem so rich a jewell Her Majesty was pleased to send me; but above all, Her Majesty's gracious acceptance of my service, and Her Majesty's promiss of her grace and favour to me, in which I desired I might live; giving Her Excellency many thanks for the kindness on her part therein, believing that Her Excellency had upon all occasions made my best actions seem double, and winked at my imperfections; but that which I did certainly know and desired Her Excellency to believe was that I was Her Excellency's most humble servant.

On Tuesday the 24th of March, the Marqueza de Liche visited me, who had not made a visite before in 7 years. On Thursday the 26th I returned the visite to Her Excellency the Marquesa, who entertained me with a very fine banquet, and gave to my youngest girle Betty a little baskett of silver plate very richly wrought. On [Wednes]day the 8th of Aprill, being His Catholick Majestye's birthday, I went to give the Emperesse and Her Catholick Majesty the parabien thereof, and likewise my thanks to Her Majesty for the many honors she had done me, and particularily for that of the jewell.

Upon the 5th of Aprill here appeared a new blazing starr, rising in the east about 2 a clock in the morning, rising every day a quarter of an hour later than the former, so that it appeared to our view but about 3 weeks, because the day light obscured it.

Thursday the 23rd of Aprill we dined at a pleasure house of the King's, 3 leagues from Madrid, called the Torre de la Prada.

Munday the 2[7]th of Aprill we went to see a garden house of the Murquis de Liche, which had been the Marquis de Fuentes'. The house is very finely adorned with curious pictures painted on the wall, with a very fine and large garden there unto belonging, in which on May Day following we dined.

On Sunday the 3rd of May we heard by letters from my father the sad news of the death of my good brother-in-law, my Lord Fanshawe, and at the same time of his son's being happily marryed to one of the daughters and heirs of Sir John Ev[elyn] of Wilkeshire, and widdow to Sir John Ray of Lincolnshire.

May the $\frac{28}{18}$th, 1665, we went to see the feasts of bulls, in a balcony made at the end of a street that looked in even with the rows of houses on the King's right hand, just below the Counsell's, which is over against all other embassadours; because there sat the Pope's Nontio and the rest of the embassadors below him; but we not owning the Pope's priority, your father was placed by himself.

June the 20th came to this court by an expresse the news of the totall route of the King of Spaine's army, under the command of the Marquis of Carasena, by the Portugezes.

Upon the 6th of July we went to the feast of bulls again. Upon the 7th, anno 1665, came to my husband the happy news of our victory against the Dutch, fought upon the 13th of June, S. N.

August the 6th at 11 a clocke in the morning was borne my son Sir

Richard Fanshawe (God be praised), and christned at 4 of the clock that afternoon by our chaplain, Mr. Bagshawe; his godfathers, my cousin Fanshawe, Chief Secretary, Mr. Cooper, Gentleman of the Horse; his godmother, Mrs. Kestian, one of my gentlewomen. The same day the Duke of Medina and his Duchesse sent to give us the joy. Upon the 7th the Duke came in person to give us the joy with all his best jewells on, as the custome of Spaine is to shew respect.

Upon Thursday the 10th of [August] the Qween sent one of Her Majesty's Major Domos, the Marquis of [Aitona], to visite me from Her Majesty, and give me the joy. The next day her Majesty's Camerera Major and the Princess Alva gave me the joy, as did likewise most of the others of the greatest ladyes at court.

O ever living God, through Jesus Christ, receive the humble thanks of thy servant for the great mercy to us in our son; which I humbly desire, O Jesus, to protect, and to make him an instrument of thy glory. Give him thy Holy Spirit, O God, to be with him all the dayes of his life. Direct him through the narrow path of righteousness, in faith, patience, charity, temperance, chastity, and a love and liking of thy blessed will in all the various accidents of this life. This with what outward blessings thou, O Heavenly Father, knowest needfull for him, I begg of thee, not remembring his sins, nor the sins of us his parents, nor of our fore fathers, but thy tender mercy which thou hast promissed shall be over all thy workes; and for the blessed merits of our onely Lord and Saviour Jesus Christ, to whom with thee and the blessed Spirit be all honour and glory, as it was in the beginning, is now, and ever shall be Amen.

On Thursday the 17th of [Septem]ber dyed Philip the 4th of Spaine, having been sick but 4 dayes, of a flux and a feavour. The day before his death he made his will, and left the governement of the King and kingdome in the hands of his Qween, Dona Anna of Austria, and to assist Her Majesty he did recommend for her Councell therein the President of Castille, Conde de Cast[rillo], the Cardinall of Toledo, the Inquisitor Generall, the Marquis of Aytona, the Vice Chancellor of Aragon, and the Conde de Penaranda. He did declare for his successor, Charles the 2d, that now reigns; then in case that he should dye without issue, the Emperor if he marries the Infanta, now called the Emperesse, to whom he is affianced; but if not, then the Infanta before himself; after the Emperor, the Duke of Savoy; the Qween of France to inherit next to the Infanta, in case she be a widow, and all her children successively by an other husband; but neither she can inherit or any child of France.

The body of Philip the 4th lay exposed from Friday morning the 18th of September till Saturday night the 19th, in a great roome in his pallace at Madrid, where he dyed; in which roome they used to act playes. The roome was hung with 14 pieces of the King's best hangings, and over them rich pictures round about, all of one size, placed close together. At the upper end of the roome was raised a throne of 3 steps, upon which there was placed a bedstead, boarded at the bottom, and raysed at the head therewith. The throne was covered with a rich Persia carpett; the bottome of the bed stead with a counterpoint of cloath of gold. The bedstead was of silver; the vallens and head cloth (for there was no curtaines) was cloath of gold wrought in flowers with crimson silk. Over the bed-stead was placed a cloth of state of the same, with the vallens and headclothes of the bedstead, upon which stood a silver gilt coffin, raised about a foot or more higher at the head than at the feet, in which was layd a pillow; and in the coffin lay Philip the 4th with his head on the pillow; upon it a white beaver hat; his haire combed, his beard trimed, his face and hands painted. He was cloathed in a musk coloured silke sute, embroydered with gold, a gollila about his neck; cuffs on his hands, which were clasped on his breast, holding a globe and a crosse on it therein. His cloake was of the same, with his sword on his side; stockings and garters and shoe strings of the same, and a paire of white shoes on his feet. In the roome were erected 7 altars for the time, upon the which stood 6 candlesticks with 6 wax candles lighted; and in the middle of each altar a crucifix. The forepart of each altar was covered with black velvett, embroydered with silver. Before the throne a rayle went cross from one side of the roome to the other. At the two lower corners of the throne at each side stood a noble man, the one holding an imperiall crown, the other the scepter; and on each side of the throne 6 high candlesticks with 6 tapers in them. The doores of that roome were kept by the Major Domo of the King and Qween, then in waiting, and the outward by the Italian guard.

On the Saturday night he was carryed upon a beere hung betwixt 2 mules, upon which the coffin with the King's body was layd, covered with a covering of cloth of gold, and at every corner of the beere was placed a high crystall lanterne, with lighted tapers in them. He was attended by some grandees, who rode next after him, and other noblemen in coaches, with between 2 and 300 on horseback, of which a great part carryed tapers lighted in their hands. This was the company, besides footmen. When the King's body came to the convent of the Escuriall the fryers of that convent stood at the gates, and there according to the institution of the place performed the ceremonyes as followeth. The priors askt the grandees, who carryed the King on their shoulders (for none other must touch him), who is in that coffin, and what they doe there demand. Upon which the Sumiller de Corps (which is the Duke de Medina de les Torres) answered, 'It is the body of Philip the Fourth of Spaine, whom we here bring for you to lay in his own tombe.' Upon which the Duke delivered the Qween's letter as Regent of the kingdom, to testifye that it was Her Majesty's command that the King's body should be there buryed.

Then the Prior read the letter and accompanied the body before the high altar, where it was for some time placed, till they had performed the usuall ceremonys for that time appointed. After which the grandees took up the corps again, and carried it down to the Pantheon; into which as soon as they were entered the Prior demanded of the Duke the covering of the King's coffin as his fee; then demanded the keys; upon which the Duke delivered him his as Sumillo de Cuerpo, and then the Prior's own, sent him by the Qween; and [the] Mayor Domo then in waiting delivered him his. The Prior having received these 3 keyes demanded franca of the Duke and Mayor Domo that in that coffin was the body of Philip the 4th, which when they had done, they there left the body with the Prior, who after sometime of the bodye's lying in the place where the infants are buried, placed it in his own tombe. My husband, with all his family and coaches, were put into mourning for Philip the 4th of Spaine.

October the 4th following I waited upon the Qween to give Her Majesty pessaine of the King's death, who received me with great grace and favour, as likewise did the King and the Emperess who were both present.

On the 8th of October, 1665, my husband and I with all our family and sonn, being the first time we went out of doores, [went] to the Placa Mayor to hear and see the King Charles the 2d of Spaine proclaimed by the Duke de Medina de les Torres, who was very richly apparelled in a silk sute embroydered with silver and gold sett with dyamond buttons. He was accompanyed with most of the nobles in the town on horseback, as hee himself was. In his right hand he carryed the King's royall standard, and by his left side rode the Mayor of the town. The heralds that rode before went first upon the scaffold, which was there made for that purpose before the King's balcony, where he was want to see juego de torres. The scaffold was covered with carpets. On the Duke's both sides stood the heralds, and on his left hand the Mayor, and by the heralds 2 notarys. The King was proclaimed in 5 places, at the court above named; at the Discaelas Raeles; at the House of the Town; at the Gate of Gadajara; and the pallace.

November the 9th I went to give the Qween the parabien of the King's birthday, who the 6th of this month compleated 6 years of age. Her Majesty received me with great grace and favour, causing the King to come in and receive of me the parabien of his años likewise.

The 14th of this month I went to waite on the Camerera Mayor, and the Marques de la Vel[ez], the King's a[y]a, from both whom I received great kindnesses.

December the 17th, 1665, my husband, upon the part of our King his master, and the Duke de Medina de les Torres, on the part of His Catolick Majesty, did conclude and signed together the peace between England and Spaine, and the articles for the ajustement between Spaine and Portugal; which articles were cavilled at by the Lord Chancellor Clarendon and his party, that they might have an opportunity to send the Earl of Sandwiche out of the way from the Parlement which then sat, and as he and his friends feared, would be severely punished for his cowardise in the Dutch fight. He neither understood the customes of the court, nor the language, nor indeed anything but a vitious life, and thus was he shuffled into your father's imployment to reap the benefit of his five years' negotiation of the peace of England, Spaine, and Portugall, and after above 30 years studying estate affairs, and many of them in the Spanish court. So much are embassadors slaves to the publick ministers at home, who often through ignorance or envy ruine them.

December the 23rd I went to give the Qween the parabien of her años, wher'of she had then compleated 31. I likewise gave the joy to the Emperess and the King who were both then present.

The 6th of January, 1666, twelve day, Stil[o] N[ovo], my husband sent Mr. John Price, one of his secrettarys, to Lisbone, to advertize the King by the Conde de Castell Melhor of his intended journey the week following.

On the 14th of this present January, the Duke of Medina de les Torres wrote a letter to my husband by the command of Her Catholick Majesty which said that for his great kindness and paines he had and did take for the accommodating a peace between England and Spaine, and procuring a truce of 30 years between the crowns of Spaine and Portugall, that on the day of the ratification thereof Her Majesty did give him an hundred thousand pieces of 8, and likewise for a further expression of Her Majesty's kindnesse, to me 50 thousand pieces of 8.

Thes gratifications weare never payd, becaus Lord San[dwich] was sent to receive what advantag hee could make; but the body of the peace being concluded before by my husband, hee received very small advantage therby. But had my hus[band] lived, hee had through their justis and kindnes to him for his great wisdom and in[de]fatigable payns in procuering a triple peace betwen the 3 crouns of Ingland, Spain, and Portugall received a sum.

The 16th of January, 1666, being 12th day, English accompt, my husband begun his journy from Madrid to Portugall.

The day before he went, Her Catholick Majesty sent to the Marquess Itonia to offer a sett of Her Majesty's machos to carry his litter, and an other sett for his coach; but my husband refused both, with many humble thanks to Her Majesty for so great grace and honour done him, which he refused upon no other score, but the consideration of the length of the journy, and illness of the way, which the time of the year caused, which would expose the beasts to that hazard as he could not satisfy himself to put them in; and although my husband was next day pressed again to receive this favour, yet he refused it with much respect to Her Majesty, upon the fore-named reasons.

Likewise the Duke de Medina de les Torres sent 2 setts of very brave machos to convey my husband to Portugall, which he refused, with many thanks to His Excellency, upon the same acco[un]t he had done those formerly to Her Majesty. My husband carryed none of his own horses or mules, but hired all he used for himself and retinue. He went in his owne litter and carryed one of his own coaches with him, [and] five sumpters covered with his own sumpter cloathes. His retinue were:

Mr. Fanshawe, Chief Secretary
Mr. Price, gone before to Lisbone
Mr. Cooper, Gentleman of the Horse
Mr. Bagshawe, Chaplain
Mr. Asburnham
Mr. Parry
Mr. Creyghton
Mr. Ayres, Steward
Mr. Weedin }
Mr. Jemmett } Pages
Mr. B[room]stead }
Mr. Hellowe, Butler
William, Cook
Francis, a groome
Frances, a laundresse
4 Spanish footmen

To every five mules went a mo[z]o and a sobrestante over all. Her Majesty sent an alquazil of the court with my husband through Spaine to provide him lodgings, and to assist him in all other occasions belonging to his journey. I accompanyed my husband a league out of town in our coach of state. Then he entered his litter and so begun his journey.

Within an hour after I was returned to my house, the Duke and Duchesse of Medina de les Torres sent each of them a gentleman with very kind messages to me on the part of Their Excellencyes.

The 17th came the Master of the Ceremonyes to see me, and offered me the service of the court with high complements and much kindness. The 18th came the Duke of Avero to see me, and afterwards the Marquis of Trusifall. The 19th came to see me the Baron of Lisola's lady.

The 20th of January I received a letter from my husband from Toledo. The 26th the Marquis de Liche came to visit me. The 28th the Duchesse de Aveyro sent a gentleman to me to excuse her not coming to see me by reason of her being with child and not having stirred out of her chamber from the time she had conceived with child.

The 29th I received a letter from my husband from Frexinall.

The 2d of February the Duke De Medina de les Torres sent to me Don Nicholas Navas with letters from Her Catholick Majesty and himself to my husband; and put up the packett here before me inclosing my letters therein, I giving it a covert, and sealing it with my seal; and a pastport to the post that carryed it to come and goe; all which was required of me by His Excellency, who was pleased to continue this forme every post that he sent during my husband's stay in Portugal.

The 12th of February the Duchess of Alberquerque sent a gentleman to excuse her not visiting me, Her Excellency being sick of a feavour. This night likewise the Duke sent second post to my husband as before. The 13th Father Patricio came to visite me from the Duke. The 17th dyed the Qween Mother of Portugall. The 20th the Duke dispatched a 3d post to my husband. The 23 the Duke and his Duchess came to visite me in very great state, having 6 coaches and 2 siddans to waite on them, and above 100 gentlemen and attendants.

The 27th of February one of the three posts returned from my husband. Another on the second of March. The 3d on the 5th.

On the 8th of March, 1666, S.N., returned my husband from Lisbone to this court, with all his family in very good health (God be praised). I went with my children 2 leagues out of town to [Aler]con to meet him. He brought in his company Sir Robert Southwell, an envoyado from our King to Portugall and Spaine, if need so required. My husband entertained him at his house 3 weeks and odd dayes.

Upon the 26th of March came a letter from C[oruña], advertising this court of the Earl of Sandwich's arrivall, Extraordinary Embassador from our King to His Catholick Majesty. Sunday the 12th of Aprill I tooke my leave of the Qween of Spaine, and Emperess, and the King, and the next day of the Camerera Mayor, and of the King's aya.

The 13 of Aprill returned from hence to the [ ] a gentleman named Mr. Werden, who came hither on the 6th of the same month bringing letters to the court, and my husband, from his Lord, the Earl of Sandwich, and likewise a list of the Extraordinary Embassador's family, which were as followeth.

Mr. Sydney Mountague, his son
Sir Charles H[arbord]
Mr. Stewart
Mr. Godolphin, Secretary to the Embassy
Mr. Worden
Mr. Beadles
Mr. Cotrel
Mr. Bridges

Mr. Clerck
Mr. Melham
Mr. Stuard
Mr. Linch
Mr. Boddie, Interpreter
Mr. Parker
Mr. Shere
Mr. Moore, Chaplain

The steward
Captaine Ferrer, Gent. of Horse
Mr. William Ferrer

Mr. Kerke
Mr. Churchill
Mr. Jeffrys

Mr. Gately, Chirurgeon
Mr. Gibbs
Mr. Boreman, Clerck of the Kitchin
Mr. Loud
Mr. Veleam
Mr. Mallard
Mr. Richard Jarrald, Mr. Joseph Chawmons } Under Secretarys
Francis Parton, Confectioner
Henry Pyman, Butler
Gentleman, Mr. Cooke
Balfoure, Allenchip } 2 Cookes
Albion Tompson, Trump[eter]

Mr. Crown { Pages, 10 in all
Mr. Nicho. Nieto
Mr. Righton
Edward Hooton
Richard Russell
Andrew Daniell
Peacock, Dennis } footmen
Thomas Gibson
Thomas Williams
Josias Brown
Gaspar, El Negro
Nathaniel Bennet

William Killegrew
Thomas Rice
William Roch
Francis Warrington
Jo. Ashton
Mr. Place
John Beverly
Briggs
Richard Cooper

The nurse
Her husband
2 maydes
Nicholas Bennet
Henry Mitchell
Jo. Goodes

On the 14th I tooke my leave of the Duchess de Medina de les Torres and the Marques de Trucifall and the Condessa Torres Vedras. On the 15th I tooke my leave of the Duchess de Aveiro, who gave my daughter Katherine a jewell of 27 emeralds; and to my daughter Margaret a crystall box sett in gold, and a large silver box of amber pastills to burn; and to my daughter Ann a crystal bottle with a gold neck full of amber water, and a silver box of philagrania; and to my daughter Betty a little trunk of silver wyer made in the Indias. This day I likewise visited the Marques de Liche, and the daughter-in-law of the Almirante of Castile, the Baron de Lisola's lady, and Don Diego Tinojo's lady, who all had visited me.

On the 16th I tooke my leave of the Duchesse of Alberquerque, and Her Excellency Dona Maria de la C[ueva]. The Duchess shewed me a large roome full of gilt and silver plate, which they sayd did cost an hundred thousand pistolls, though to my eye it did not seem of half the worth. It was made for the Duke's journey into Germany, being the principall person intrusted to dispose of Her Imperiall Majesty's family and mony, for his voyadge to that court, and afterwards he and his lady is to returne to Scicily, and there to remain Viceroy. The same day I took my leave of the German Ambassador's lady.

Easter Day, being the 25th of Aprill, 1666, the Infanta Dona Maria was marryed to the Emperor by proxy, viz. the Duke De Medina de les Torres. The ceremony thus: First went a great high coach of the Duke's drawn by foure black Flanders maires. In it were the Duchesse's 2 sons, with other persons of quality. In Madrid none can goe with 6 horses but the King or Qween, as I sayd before. Then went the coach of the Duke's (a most exceeding rich one drawn by 4 gray Flaunders mares), in the upper end whereof the Duke himself sat with the German Ambassador on his right hand, and the Duke of Alva on his left; in the other end, the Conde de Peneranda, between the Duke of Pastrane and his son; after this coach followed immediately the Duke of Medina's Gentleman of the Horse upon a very fine white one. Then went a very rich new coach, empty, of the German Ambassadour, made on purpose for that day and drawn by 4 horses. Then followed another of the Duke's coaches, with some of his gentlemen in it. Then the German Ambassador's second coach, with some of his gentlemen in it. Then one of the Duke's coaches, in which was the Baron de Lisle, Envoy Extraordinary from the Emperor, and one person with him. Then another of the Duke's coaches, with more of his gentlemen. Then an other of the German Ambassador's coaches, with more of his family in it. The Duke's pages walked by his coach and had gold chaines crosse their shoulders. The Baron de Lisle's gentlemen went in some of the before-named coaches.

On Munday the 26th Don Juan de Austria came to court to give the Emperess the joy, but that ceremony performed, returned immediatly the same day to a retiring place His Highness hath at Ocana, near Aranjuez, which famous seat of royall recreation, for a farewell, the Emperess lay at that night, being to take in her way to Denia where she was to embarque. Don Juan, from Ocana aforesaid, accompanied Her Imperiall Majesty 2 or 3 days' journey.

On Tuesday the 27th my husband (invited thereto by the Master of the Ceremonys, and then to come in short mourning with something of jewells) gave to the Empresse the joy in his master's name, also to the Qween jointly present, and then giving her daughter the hand. Sir Robert Southwell was admitted to accompany him in like manner and performe the same function.

On Wednesday, the $\frac{18}{28}$ of Aprill, 1666, Her Imperiall Majesty went from the pallace to the Descalsas Reales, and from thence to the Atocke, from whence she began her journey for Viena. Her passing through the town was in this manner: First past severall persons of quality in their coaches, intermixt with others. Then the 2 Lieutenants of Her Catholick Majesty's guards on horse back. Then the 2 Captaines of the said guards, the Marquis de Salina and the Marques de Malpica, also on horseback. Then a coach of respect, lined with cloath of gold mixed with green. Then a litter of respect, lined with the same stuff. Then 4 trumpetters on horseback. Then the Duke of Alberquerke in a plain coach. Then 24 men upon horses, and mules with portemantuas before them. Then 2 trumpeters more. Then the Emperesse and her Camerera Mayor (Condesa de Benevente) in a plaine, large coach. Then 8 men without cloakes on horseback, who I presume were pages to Her Catholick Majesty. Then the Emperesse's nurse, and 4 or 5 pretty children of hers, in a coach. Then 4 young ladys with caps and white feathers with black specks in them in an other coach. Then duenas, or antient ladies. Then more young ladys with caps and black hats pinned up with rich jewells. Then an other coach with young ladyes. Then followed many other coaches irregularily.

The Duke De Medina de les Torres, as also the German Ambassador and many of the nobility of Spaine, went out of towne and stayed about a league of for the Emperesse's coming that way. All the meaner sort of Her Imperiall Majesty's trayne, and her carriages, as also the Duke of Alberquerque's, went before.

On Munday the 26th I wrote to the Camerera Mayor and the Emperesse's aya, giving both Their Majestys the joy of this marriage.

May the 5th we dined at Salva Tiera, 2 leagues from Madrid, and returned again at night.

On Friday the $\frac{28}{18}$ of May, 1666, came to Madrid the Earl of Sandwich, Ambassador Extraordinary from our King to the Qween Regent of this kingdome. My husband went with all his train two leagues to welcome him and conduct him to this court. This day 22 years we were married.

The 29th my Lord of Sandwich delivered my husband the King's letters of revocation, and there with a private letter from His Majesty of great grace and favour. This afternoon my Lord Sandwich, with most part of his traine, came to visit me.

June 9th, S.N., being our King's birthday, my husband made an entertainment for my Lord of Sandwich, with all his retinue, and the rest of the English at Madrid. The next Sunday, being White Sunday, my husband went with the Earle of Sandwich to a private audience, where my husband introduced him to the King of Spaine. (This was the last time my husband received the communion. A.F.) Munday the 14th my husband went with the Earle of Sandwich to the Duke de Medina de les Torres.

On the $\frac{15}{5}$, being Tuesday, my husband was taken sike like an ague, but turned to a malignant inward feavour, of which he lay untill the 26th of the same month, being [Satur]day, untill 11 of the clock at night, and then departed this life 15 days before his intended journy for England.

Lollio Thou art a man hast skill
To fathome things: that being tride
In either Fortune, couldst abide
In both up-right, and *Lollio* still.

Of covetous Fraud a scourge severe:
On whom the All attracting Gold
Could with its Tenters ne'r take hold:
Nor Consul of one year. When ere
A vertuous Magistrate, and true,
Shall call good, gain, bid Bribes Avaunt:
Upon Opposers bellies plant
His conqu'ring Flags: *Lollio* That's You.
He is not happy that hath much:
But who so can his mind dispose
To use aright what Heav'n bestows,
He justly is accounted such:
If he know how hard want to bear:
And fear a crime, more then his end.
If for his Country, or his Friend
To stake his life he doth not fear.

O all powerfull Lord God, look down from heaven upon me, the most distressed wretch upon earth. See me with my soule divided, my glory and my guide taken from me, and in him all my comfort in this life. See me staggering in my path, which made me expect a temporal blessing for a reward of the great integrity, innocence, and uprightnesse of his whole life, and his patience in suffering the insolencyes of wicked men, which he had to converse with upon the publick employment which thou thoughtest fit in thy wisdome to exercise him in. Have pitty on me, O Lord, and speak peace to my disquieted soul now sinking under the great weight, which without thy support cannot sustaine itself. See me, O Lord, with five children, a distressed family, the temptation of the change of my religion, the want of all my friends, without counsell, out of my country, without any means to returne with my sad family to our own country, now in warr with most part of Christendom. But above all, my sins, O Lord, I doe lament with shame and confusion, believing it is them for which I receive this great punishment. Thou hast shewed me many judgements and mercyes which did not reclaime me nor turne me to the holey conversation which the example of our Blessed Savior taught. Lord, pardon me; O God, forgive whatsoever is amisse in me; break not a bruised reed. I humbly submitt to thy justice. I confesse my wretchedness, and know I have deserved not onely this, but everlasting punishment. But, O my God, look upon me through the merits of my Saviour, and for His sake save me. Doe with me and for me what thou pleasest, for I doe wholly rely upon thy mercy, beseeching thee to remember thy promisses to the fatherlesse and widow, and enable me to fullfill thy will cheerfully in the world. Humbly beseeching thee that when this mortall life is ended, I may be joyned with the soule of my dear husband,

and all thy servants departed this life in thy faith and fear, in everlasting prayses of thy Holy Name. Amen.

The next day my husband was embalmed. The 28th I begun to receive messages from the Qween and the court of Spaine.

July the 4th, S. N., 1666, my husband was buryed by his own chaplaine, with the ceremonyes of the Church of England, and a sermon preached by him. In the evening I sent the body of my dear husband to Bilbao, intending suddainly to follow him. He went out of town privately, being accompanyed onely with a part of his retinue (his body arived safe at Bilbao on the 14th of July, 1666, and was layd in the King's house):

Mr. Cooper, gentleman of his horse
Mr. Jemett, who waited on him in his bedchamber
Mr. Rookes
Mr. Weedon
Mr. Carew
Richard Batha
Francis

The 5th of Ju[ly], 1666, St.N., the Qween Mother sent the Master of the Ceremonyes of Spaine to invite me to stay with all my children in her court, promissing me a pension of 30 thousand ducats a year, and to provide for my children, if I and they would turne our religion and become Roman Catholicks. I answered, I humbly thanked Her Majesty for her great grace and favour, the which I would ever esteeme and pay with my service, as far as I was able, all the days of my life. For the latter I desired Her Majesty to believe that I could not quitt the faith in which I had been borne and bred in, and which God had pleased to try me for many years in the greatest troubles our nation hath ever seen, and that I do believe and hope in the profession of my own religion God would hear my prayers and reward Her Majesty, and all the princes of that royall family, for this so great favour which Her Majesty was pleased to offer me in my greatest afflictions.

The 6th and seventh day of this month I was visited by the German Ambassador's lady, and severall other ladys, also by the Ambassador, and the Duke de Medina de Les Torres, de Avero, Marquis de Trucifall, Conde de Montery, with severall others of that court.

The Qween sent me for a present 2000 pistolls, which Her Majesty sent me word was to buy my husband a jewell, if he had lived to the week following. I gave the Secretary of State a gold watch and chaine worth about 30lb. I gave the Master of Ceremonys at my coming away a clock cost me 40lb. I sold all my coaches and horses and lumber of the house to the Earle of Sandwich for 1380 pistolles. I likewise sold there 1000lb worth of plate to severall persons, all the mony I could make being little enough for my most sad journey for England.

The 8th of July, 1666, at night I took my leave of Madrid and of the

Sietey Chimineas, the house so beloved of my husband and me formerly. I carryed with me all my jewells, and the best of my plate, and other pretious rarityes, all the rest being gone before to Bilbao with part of my family. All the women went in litters and the men on horseback.

Myself, my son, and my foure daughters
One gentlewoman
One chambermaid
Mr. Fanshawe, my husband's secretary
Secretary, Mr. Price
The Chaplaine, Mr. Bagshawe
Mr. Creyton
Mr. White
Mr. Hellowe
John Burton
William, the cook, besides other Spanish attendants

My Lord Sandwich came in the afternoone to accompany me out of town, which offer, though earnestly pressed by my Lord, as well as by other persons of quality, I refused, desiring to goe out of that place as privately as I could possibly, and I may truly say, never any ambassadoure's family came into Spaine more glorious or went out so sad.

July the 21st, after a tedious journy we arrived at Bilbao, to which place my dear husband's body came the 14th of this month, and was lodged in the King's house, with some of his servants to attend him. But I hired a house in the town during my stay there, in which time I received severall letters from Madrid, from England, and from Paris. The Qween Mother was graciously pleased to procure me passes from the King of France, which I received the 21st of September, S.N., accompanied with a letter from my Lady Gilford, and severall others of Her Majesty's court. Likewise I did receive a pass from the Duke of Beauford, then at Lixa.

October the 1st I sent answers of letters into Ingland to my Lord Arlington, brother Warwick, my father, and to several other persons. Here I heard the sad news of the burning of London.

October the 3d, being Sunday, 1666, I begun my journy from Bilbao, with the body of my dear husband, all my children, and all my family but 3, whom I left to come with my goods by sea. The 7th of October we came to Bayone in France, having had a dangerous passage between Spaine and France. October the 9th we begun our journey from Bajona toward Paris, where we arrived the 30th of October, being Saturday.

November the 2d the Qween Mother sent my Lady Gilford to condole my loss and welcome me to Paris. Many of Her Majestie's family of their own accord did the same. On the 26th Her Majesty sent Mr. Church in one of her coaches to convey me to Shalliott, a nunnery where the Qween then was, who received me with great grace and favour, and promissed me much kindnesse when Her Majesty returned for England. Her Majesty sent by me letters to the King, Qween, Duke, and Duchesse of York, with a box of writings to Her Majesty's secretary, Sir John Winter.

November the 11th we begun our journey towards Callice, and upon the 11 of November, Old Stile, we embarqued at Calais in a little French man-of-war which carryed me to Tower Wharfe, where I landed the next day at night, being Tuesday, at 12 of the clock. I made a little stay with my children at my father's house on Tower Hill. The next day, being the 13th, we went all to my owne house in Lincolne's In Fields, on the North side, where the widow Countesse of Middlesex had lived before; and the same day likewise was brought the body of my dear husband.

On Saturday following, being the 1[7]th of November, 1666, I sent the body of my dear husband to be layd in my father's vault in Alhollows Church in Hertford. None accompanyed the hearse but 7 of his own gentlemen, which had taken care of his body all the way from Madrid to London; being Mr. Fanshawe and Mr. Bagshawe, Mr. Cooper, Mr. Preyer, Mr. Creghton, Master Jarret, and Mr. Rookes.

On the 18th my Lord Arlington visited me, proffering me his friendship to be shewn in the procuring the arrears of my husband's pay, which was 2000lb, and to reimburse me 5815lb my husband had layen out in His Majesty's service. Likewise I was visited to welcome me into England, and to condole my losse, by very many of the nobility and gentry, and also by all my relations in these parts.

November the 23d I waited on the King and delivered His Majesty my whole accompts. He was pleased to receive me very gratiously and promissed me they should be paid, and likewise that His Majesty would take care for me and mine. Then I delivered His Majesty the letter I brought from Qween Mother. Then I did my duty to the Qween, who with great sence condoled my losse. After which I delivered Qween Mother's letter sent to Her Majesty by me. After staying 2 houres longer in Her Majesty's bed chamber, I waited on His Royall Highness who having condoled with me my loss of my dear husband, and promissed me a ship to send for my goods and servants to Bilbao; then I waited on the Duchesse, who with great grace and favour received me, and having been with Her Highnesse about an hour, I delivered a letter from Qween Mother. I took my leave. I presented the King, Qween, Duke of York, and Duke of Cambridge with two dozens of amber skins and 6 dozens of gloves. I likewise presented my Lord Arlington with amber skinnes, gloves, chocalaty, and a great picture, a copy of Tishine's, to the value of an hundred pounds; and I made presents to Sir William Coventre and severall other persons then in office. In February the Duke ordered me the *Victory* fregat to bring the remainder of my goods and people from Bilbao in Spaine, which safely arrived in the latter end of March, 1667.

I spent my time much in petitioning and solliciting my Lord Treasurer

Southhampton for the present dispatch of my accounts, which did pass the Secretary then Lord Arl[ington], and within 2 months I gott a Privy Seal for my mony, without either fee or present, which I could never fasten on my Lord. Now I thought my self happy, and feared nothing less than further trouble. God, that only knows what is to come, so disposed my fortune, that losing that excellent good man and friend my Lord Southhampton, my mony, which was 5600lb, was not paid me untill December, 1669, notwithstanding I had tallys for my mony above 2 years before. This was above 2 thousand pounds loss to me; besides these Commitionners by the instigation of one of their fellow Commissionners, my Lord Shafesbury (the worst of men), [were] perswaded that I might pay for the embassy plate, which I did, 2000lb; and so maliciously did he oppress me as if he hoped in me to destroy the whole stock of honesty and innocence which he mortally hates. I have been told that he did this to have a bribe. Only I wish I had given one, though I had *poured* it down his throat, for the benefit of mankind.

In this great distress I had no remedy but patience. How far this was from a reward, judge ye, for near 30 years suffering by land and sea, and the hasard of our lives over and over, with the many services of your father, and the expence of all the monyes we could procure, and 7 years' imprisonment, with the death and beggery of many eminent persons of our family, that when they first entered the King's service had great and clear estates. Adde to this the carefull manadgement of the King's honor in the Spanish court after my husband's death, which I thought my self bound to maintain, although I had not, God is my witnesse, above 25 doublons by me at my husband's death to bring home a family of threscore servants, but was forced to sell 1000lb worth of our own plate, and to spend the Qween's present of 2000 doublons in my journy into England; not oweing or leaving a shilling debt in Spaine, I thank God; nor did my husband leave any debt at home, which every embassador cannot say. Neither did thees surcomstances folowing prevaile to mend my condition; much less found I that compassion I expected upon the vew of my self, that had lost at onece my husband and fortune in him, with my son of but 12 months old in my armes, 4 daughters, the eldest but 13 years of age, with the body of my dear husband dayly in my sight for near 6 months together, and a distressed family, all to be by me in honor and honesty provided for; and to add to my afflictions, neither person sent to conduct me, either pass, or ship, or mony to cary me 1000 miles, but some few letters of complement from the Chief Ministers, bidding God helpe me, as they do to beggers; and they might have added, they had nothing for me, with great truth. But God did hear, and see, and help me, and brought my soule out of trouble; and by his blessed providence I and you live, move, and have our being, and I humbly pray God that that blessed providence may ever supply our wants. Amen.

Seing what I had to trust to, I begun to shape my life as well as I could to my fortune, in order whereto I dismissed all my family, all but some few persons about me. I did at my arrivall give them all mourning, and five pounds the piece, and put most of them into a good way of living, I thank God. Then in [16]67 I took a house in Holborne Row, in Lincoln's In Fields, for 21 years of Mr. Colle. This year I crisened a daughter of my Lord Fanshawe with Lady Lev[enthorpe] and Sir P[hilip] W[arwick]. Here in this year I onely spent my time in laments and dear remembrances of my past happiness and fortune, and though I had great graces and favours from the King and Qween and whole court, yet I found ⟨at the present no remedey.⟩ it impossible to find my bread in a stone, and therefore I had a thousand contrivances in my head to increase my fortune for the advantage of my children, but none did succeed to my wish.*

I often refflected how many miscariadges and errors the fall from that happy estate I had beene in would throw me, and, as it is hard for the rider to quit his horse in a full carrier, so I found my self at a loss that hindred me settling myself in a narrow compass suddenly, though my small fortune required it. But I resolved to hold me fast by God, untill I could digest in some measure my afflictions. Sometimes I thought to quitt the world, as a sacrifice to your father's memory, and to shut my self up in a house for ever from all people; but upon the consideration of my children, who were all young and unprovided for, being wholy left to my care and dispose, I resolved to suffer as long as it pleased God the stormes and flowes of fortune.

As soon as I had got my talleyes placed again by the Commissioners, I sold them for 500lb less than my assignment to Alderman Backwell, who gave me ready mony, and I put it out upon a morgage of Sir William Allofe's estate in Essex at Braxted. In [16]68 I hired a house and grounds of 60lb a year at Hattenfortbery in Hertfordshire, to be near my father, being but two miles from Balls, both because I would have my father company and because the aire was very good for my children. But when God took my father, I lett my time in it, and never saw it more.

About this time Sir Philip Waricke retired himself from publick business to his house at Froggpool in Kent. He had his son and daughter-in-law liv'd with him some time untill this year [16]69 they went into France. She was the daughter and coheir of the Lord Frechwell. In my brother Warick's house at London in [16]66 dyed my sister Bedells and was carryed down into Huntingtonshire, to Hammerton, and was there buryed by her husband in the chancell. She was a most worthy woman and eminently good, wise, and handsom. She never much injoyed herself since the death of her eldest daughter, who marryed Sir Francis Compton, and in her right he had Hamerton, in Huntington sheere. She dyed

*See Textual Notes, 190: 11–14.

5 years before my sister, a most dutifull daughter, and a very fine bred lady, and excellent company and very vertuos. In this yeare I crisened a daughter of my sister Turner's with Sir Ed[ward] and Lady Kilmorey.

About this time dyed my brother Lord Fanshaw's widow. She was a very good wife and tender mother, but else nothing extraordinary. She was buryed in the vault of her husband's family in Ware Church. Within a year after that her son the Lord Fanshawe sold Ware Park for 26 thousand pounds to Sir Thomas Bide, a bruer of London.

Thus in the fourth generation of the chief of our family since the[y] came in to the south, they, for their sufferings for the crown, sold the flower of their estate and of near 2000 a year more; there remains but the Remembrancer place of the Exchequer office, and very patheticall is the moto of our armes for us:

THE VICTORY IS IN THE CROSS.

I had about this time sum trouble with keeping the lordships of Tring and Hiching, which your father held of Qween Mother, but I, not being able to make a considerable advantage of them, gave them up again. And then I sold a lease of the manner of Burstallgarth for 31 year to your father from the King. Deane Hich bought it, it being convenient for him, lying upon Humber. There was a widow, one Mrs. Hiliard, hired this mannour and had so done long. She was very earnest to buy it at a very under rate. When she saw it sold she, as was suspected, fired the house, which was burnt down to the ground within two months after I had sold it.

In this year my brother Harrison married the eldest daughter of the Lord Viscount Grandeson. I lett in this year a lease for 11 years of F[rin]ton Hall in Essex to Jonathan Wier, which I hold of the Bishoprick of London. This lease we bought the first year the King came home of Doctor Shelden, then Bishop of London, who was exceeding kind to us, and sold it for half the worth, which I will ever aknowledge with thankfullness.

My dear father departed this life upon the 28th of September, 16[69], being above 80 years of age, in perfect understanding, God be praysed. He left me 500lb to everyone of my 4 daughters, and gave me 3000 pounds for a part of the mannor of Scalls How, near Linn in Norfolk, but the year before he dyed, to make my sister Harrison a jointer. In [16]71 I crisened the eldest sonn of my brother Harrison with my Lord Grandeson and Sir Edmond Turner.

The death of my father made so great an impression in me that with the grief I was sick half a year almost to death; but through God's mercy and the care of Doctor Jasper Nedham, a most worthy and learned physitian, I recovered; and so soon as I was able to think of business I bought ground in St. Mary's Cappell in Ware Church, of the Bishop of London, and there made a vault for my husband's body, which I had there layd in by the most of the same persons that had layd him before in my father's vault in Hertford Church, deposited untill I could make this vault and monument, which cost me 200lb; and here, if God pleases, I intend to lye my self.

When I sett up this monument there was omitted this, *and Burgess for the University of Cambridge*; which fault I doe mean to repair by adding this inscription at the bottom of the tombstone, if God permit; the omission of it being really a trouble to me, because they chose him of their unanimous desire, without my husband's knowledge untill the Vice Chancellor sent him a letter by an officer of theirs to his house in Portugall Row, in Lincoln's Inn Fields, to acquaint him with it. And he had the fortune to be the first chose and the first returned member of the Common House of Parlement in England, after the King came home; and this cost him no more than a letter of thanks, and 2 braces of bucks, and 20 broad pieces of gold to buy them wine.

Upon St. Steven's Day, 1671, the King shut up the . . .

EXPLANATORY NOTES

Lady Halkett, *Memoirs*

The numerals preceding the colons refer to pages; the numerals following, to lines.

9: 14–15 *Lady of the Bedchamber to Queen Henrietta Maria:* No corroborating evidence for this assertion is known. 'S.C.' in *Life* (1701) omits reference to any such position and in fact comments (pp. 30–1) on the ingratitude Lady Halkett encountered at the time of the Restoration. Anne Murray was nineteen when Queen Henrietta Maria left London in 1642, and it is not impossible she held the position at that time. Two of her brothers, Henry and Charles, were Grooms of Charles I's Bedchamber.

9: 16 *Pitfirren:* Pitfirrane (spellings of the place name, as of Sir James's surname, differ), the family seat, was in Fife, two and a quarter miles south-west of Dunfermline.

10: 6–7 *the Earle of Tillibardin's familly . . . the Earle of Perth's:* The earldoms of Tullibardine and of Perth were not created until 1606 and 1605 respectively. But Lady Halkett writes merely of a kinship with the families of the earls.

10: 11 *temptations of Spaine:* Charles I as Prince of Wales had travelled to Madrid in 1623 as a suitor of the Infanta, sister of Philip IV.

10: 27–30 *the Countese of Roxbery . . . under the signett:* the second wife (married 1614) of the first Earl of Roxburghe (*c.* 1570–1650). Mary, the Princess Royal (1631–60), was married in England, 2 May 1641, to William, the grandson of Frederick Henry, Prince of Orange (d. 1647). When her mother, Queen Henrietta Maria, left England in February 1642, she took Mary—and presumably the Countess of Roxburghe—to Holland. Because Lady Roxburghe died 7 October 1643, she could not have attended Princess Mary until the Princess was old enough, in 1644, to assume her conjugal role.

Anne Murray's mother presumably was governesss to the Royal children during much of 1642 and perhaps part of 1643 and again from June 1645 probably until her death, 28 August 1657. The 'signett' (i.e. a letter bearing Charles I's royal seal) to which Lady Halkett refers was written a short time before 8 June 1645, when it is mentioned in the 'Proceedings at the Committee of both kingdoms' (*Calendar of State Papers, Domestic, 1644–45*, pp. 576–7).

11: 7–8 *usurped power . . . Church of England:* Anglicans were subjected to increasingly severe restrictions in the 1640s. The use of the Book of Common Prayer in religious services was prohibited in 1645.

11: 21 *Spring Garden:* at the south-west corner of what is now Trafalgar Square. It was then a part of St. James's Park.

11: 24 *my sisters:* Lady Halkett had only one sister, Elizabeth, who married Sir Henry Newton. However, in using the plural form she may refer also to her sister-in-law, Anne, daughter of Paul, Viscount Bayning of Sudbury, the wife of her brother Henry, who was married 26 November 1635 (*Scots Peerage*, iii. 398–400).

11: 32 *I gave way to the adrese of a person:* Thomas Howard (24 October 1625–24 August 1678), son of Edward, first Lord Howard of Escrick. It is significant that he was two and a half years younger than Anne Murray.

11: 33–4 *discharged:* 'discharge', 'to charge or command not to do something; to prohibit, forbid' (*OED*).

11: 36 *fudged:* 'fudge', 'to fit in with what is anticipated' (*OED*).

11: 37 *his sister:* Anne Howard, daughter of Lord Howard of Escrick.

11: 38–9 *my sister's howse att Charleton:* Lady Halkett's brother-in-law, Sir Henry Newton, had an estate at Charlton, near Woolwich, in Kent.

12: 4–5 *my Lady Anne, his cousin german:* Lady Ann Howard, daughter of the second Earl of Suffolk, who later married Thomas Walsingham.
12: 9–10 *turne Capucin:* 'become a Capuchin', a Roman Catholic 'friar of the order of St. Francis, of the new rule of 1528' (*OED*). Cf. Thomas Howard's threat below, p. 13, to 'goe imediately into a conventt'.
12: 17–20 *his father . . . howse and k*[*in*]*:* The father was Edward, first Lord Howard of Escrick, son of Thomas, first Earl of Suffolk. Lord Howard had been in a position to intercede with the Parliamentarians to reduce the very heavy fines levied on Anne Murray's brother-in-law, Sir Henry Newton, who had fought in the King's army. An eighteenth-century historian writes that Lord Howard, after the death of his patron, the first Duke of Buckingham,

> having no proper Qualifications of his own to advance him, he gradually sunk from his Attendance upon the Court, and even his good Wishes towards it, implicitly devoting himself to its most violent Opposers; insomuch that after the Dissolution of the House of Lords, he was one of those few, who so far demeaned themselves, as to sit as Members in that of the Commons (Robert Masters, *The History of the College of Corpus Christi*, Cambridge, 1753, pp. 315–16).

13: 10 *though:* 'even if; even supposing that' (*OED*).
14: 2 *lengh:* 'Length (of time or space)' (*OED*, which cites Lady Halkett's use of the word, on p. 76 of this edition). See also pp. 58 and 85.
14: 25–7 *a more considerable portion . . . ruine his younger chilldren:* Lord Howard had five children, of whom Thomas was his eldest son and heir. Anne Murray's mother perceived that it was necessary for Thomas to marry an heiress if the younger children were to be provided for.
16: 25 *I was neere to take the start:* 'to decamp, run away' (*OED*).
16: 37 *Mr. T. . . . his governer:* John F. Tindall, who had been Thomas Howard's tutor at Corpus Christi College, Cambridge (Masters, *History of Corpus Christi*, p. 315; Appendix, 'A List of the Names, . . . etc.', p. 48).
17: 4 *Musgrove:* a tenant farmer at Sir Henry Newton's estate at Charlton.
17: 20 *stonished:* 'stonish', 'to stun mentally, shock, surprise' (*OED*).
17: 26 *Deepe:* Dieppe.
18: 3 *banketting howse:* presumably a garden house used for banquets.
20: 8–9 *Sir Patrick Drumond . . . Conservator in Holland:* Drummond was an influential and widely-respected man. (Cf. Sir James Balfour, *The Annales of Scotland*, in *Historical Works*, London, 1825, iii. 284.) A 'Conservator' was 'an officer appointed to protect the rights and settle the disputes of Scottish merchants in foreign ports or places of trade' (*OED*).
20: 13 *advertisement:* 'The action of informing or notifying' (*OED*).
20: 18 *ingeniously:* 'ingenuity', 'freedom from dissimulation; honesty, straightforwardness, sincerity' (*OED*, which alludes to the confusion in the seventeenth century between *ingenuity* and *ingenuous*). Cf. below, p. 36, *ingenuity*; and p. 39, *ingenious*.
21: 3 *my Lord H. had a sister in France:* Elizabeth (Howard) Knollys Vaux, Countess of Banbury, was in France, 1643–4 (*DNB*, s.v. Knollys, William, Earl of Banbury (1547–1632)).
21: 30 *my Lady Anne W.:* Lady Ann Walsingham.
22: 8 *my Lady E. M.:* Lady Elizabeth Mordaunt, daughter of John, first Earl of Peterborough (1599–1643). She and Thomas Howard were married, 21 July 1646.
23: 5 *the Countese of B.:* Elizabeth (Howard) Knollys Vaux, Countess of Banbury. See above, p. 21 and n. 21: 3.
23: 8 *my brother Will:* William Murray (1617–49), her youngest brother. It is evident from Lady Halkett's Memoirs that he was active in Royalist intrigue for several years before his death.
23: 9 *This gentleman:* It is scarcely surprising that a leaf is missing from the manuscript at the point in her narrative when Lady Halkett writes about meeting Colonel Joseph Bampfield, an enigmatic—and unscrupulous—figure who dominates much of the

surviving portion of her Memoirs. Added to her sense of guilt arising from her relations with him—a married man, though he told her that his wife had died—would have been embarrassment arising from her knowledge, when she wrote her Memoirs in the 1670s, of his activities in the service of Oliver Cromwell's government in the 1650s and his treasonable service in the Dutch army during England's Second Dutch War in the 1660s. His record as soldier and secret agent for Charles I, culminating in his rescue of the Duke of York in 1648, is creditable. But thereafter his course was downward. For good reason Charles II did not trust him, and in time his actions were such as to force the Duke of York to abandon him, his service to the Duke in April 1648 notwithstanding.

23: 10 *St. Martin's Lane:* Anne Murray's mother resided in St. Martin's Lane (near the present Trafalgar Square) after her husband's death. The 'lane' 'served as the main road north out of Westminster until Charing Cross Road was formed' (Gillian Bebbington, *London Street Names*, London, 1972, pp. 289–90).

23: 35 *the Duke of Yorke's escape:* There are at least three other accounts of the escape. In order of importance they are J. S. Clarke, *The Life of James the Second*, 'Collected out of Memoirs Writ of His Own Hand', 2 vols. (London, 1816), i. 33–8; Clarendon, *History of the Rebellion*, xi. 19–20; and *Colonel Joseph Bamfeild's Apologie*, 'Written by himselfe and printed at his desire' (1685), pp. 41–2. These accounts are consistent with one another—and with what Lady Halkett writes—in the circumstantial details presented. The fact that Lady Halkett's narrative of the episode (which was not published until 1875) corresponds closely with that in *The Life of James the Second*, the reliability of which has been the subject of controversy, aids in establishing the accuracy of at least the early part of *The Life*.

For an account of the history of James II's autobiographical manuscript and of the controversy concerning *The Life* published in 1816 under the name of J. S. Clarke, see the Preface and the Translator's Introduction (pp. 13–47) to A. Lytton Sells, trans. and ed., *The Memoirs of James II: His Campaigns as Duke of York, 1652–1660* (Bloomington, Indiana, 1962).

23: 35 *St. James':* a royal palace since Henry VIII rebuilt it. The Prince of Wales and the Duke of York had been born there. The latter had resided in it most of his life. Charles I was to await execution in it.

23: 36 *the Duke of Glocester:* Henry, Duke of Gloucester (1639–60), the third son of Charles I. He was later permitted to go to the Continent, where he remained until the Restoration. He died of smallpox soon after returning to England.

23: 36–7 *the Princese Elizabeth:* the second daughter of Charles I. She died 8 September 1650 in Carisbrooke Castle on the Isle of Wight, where her father had been held after he left Hampton Court late in 1647. Clarendon writes that many persons believed she had been poisoned, adding, however, 'there was no appearance, nor any proof ever after made of it' (Clarendon, xiv. 86).

23: 37 *the Earle of Northumberland:* Algernon Percy, tenth Earl (1602–68). He had held high military and naval posts under Charles I and only gradually had become alienated from him and aligned with the Parliamentarians. Earlier, unsuccessful attempts having been made to rescue the Duke of York, Northumberland in February 1648 had requested that he be relieved of his guardianship of him.

A summary account of 'Proceedings at the Committee of both Houses', 19 February 1647–8 (*Calendar of State Papers, Domestic, 1648–49*, p. 19) includes an entry that suggests the difficult circumstances under which Colonel Bampfield two months later contrived the rescue of the Duke:

> That the paper now inserted containing what is yet known concerning the endeavours for the Duke of York's escape be reported to both Houses, likewise that the Houses would take some care for the safe keeping of the Duke, and that it is the desire of the Earl of Northumberland that he may not be held further accountable for him, for that it appears there is a design of taking him away, and that the Duke seems to be content with it.

23: 43 *Charles's preservation:* The King had compelling reasons for desiring the prompt rescue of the Duke of York. Cromwell and others were considering deposing the King, disinheriting the Prince of Wales, and crowning the Duke of York. S. R. Gardiner writes that 24 April 'seems to have been fixed on for a motion' in the House of Commons to bring all this about (*History of the Great Civil War*, London, 1894, iv. 99–100).

24: 1–2 *the King aproved of his choice of mee:* Charles I may not have known Anne Murray personally, but he was well acquainted with her family. Her father had been his tutor when he was Duke of York and his secretary when he was Prince of Wales. Her mother, who died less than eight months before the Duke of York's escape, had been under-governess and later governess of the King's children, the Duke of Gloucester and the Princess Elizabeth. Her brothers Henry and Charles had been Grooms of the King's Bedchamber. Her youngest brother William was active in the service of the Royal family until he was dismissed in 1649 by Charles II. (See below, p. 29.)

24: 11–12 *a gentleman attending His Highnese:* James II mentions 'the assistance of Mr. George Howard brother to the Earle of Suffolk who at that time was his Master of Horse' (Clarke, *James II*, i. 33–4). Howard later succeeded to his brother's title.

24: 20 *C.B. . . . all nesesary expence:* The 'nesesary expence' was very high: there is a record of receipts for £20,000 and of disbursements for £19,559 (Clarendon, *State Papers*, i. 462).

24: 22 *mohaire:* fabric made from the hair of the Angora goat, sometimes mixed with wool or cotton.

24: 35 *hide and seeke:* James II, who was fourteen years old at the time of his rescue, wrote that he had played the game 'for a fortnight together every night' (Clarke, *James II*, i. 34–5).

24: 39 *a treble key:* a key to be used to open a treble lock, i.e. 'a lock operating by three turns of the key' (*OED*), thus throwing three different bolts.

24: 40 *give him that key:* Clarendon comments on the freedom allowed the Royal children: 'The duke and his brother and sister were then kept at St. James', where they had the liberty of the garden and park to walk and exercise themselves in' (Clarendon, xi. 20).

25: 4–5 *the staires next the bridge . . . private howse:* on the north bank of the Thames. In his Memoirs James II mentions 'Mrs. Murray, who had women's cloths in a readines' (Clarke, *James II*, i. 35).

25: 26 *Woodstreet cake . . . hee loved:* That Anne Murray should know such a minor detail implies that she was familiar with the household in St. James's Palace. Probably she had heard much about it from her mother. She may indeed have resided in the Palace with her mother.

The name of the cake presumably derived from Wood Street in the Cheapside market.

25: 37 *some deficulty:* James II provides an account of the difficulties in his Memoirs (Clarke, *James II*, i. 36–8).

25: 37 *Graves-End:* a port twenty-four miles south-east of London, in Kent, on the south bank of the Thames near the estuary.

25: 38–9 *Collonell Washington's lady:* probably Elizabeth, the wife of Colonel Henry Washington (1615–64), who had served with distinction in the King's army during the Civil Wars. He was a first cousin of John and Lawrence Washington, who emigrated to Virginia (Charles Arthur Hoppin, *The Washington Ancestry*, Greenfield, Ohio, 1932, i. 106). Joseph Bampfield mentions a Colonel Washington—presumably Henry—as one of the Royalist officers who in the summer of 1648 were in the fleet that revolted against Parliament and sailed to the Netherlands, 'delivering themselves up to the Duke of York as their Admirall' (*Apologie*, pp. 43–4).

25: 42 *my brother's howse:* the house of her oldest brother, Henry Murray.

26: 7, 12 *scearch:* 'scearche', Scottish spelling of 'search' (*OED*). See also p. 31.
26: 9 *the Speaker:* The Speaker of the House of Commons was William Lenthall (1591–1662), Member of Parliament for Woodstock, Oxfordshire, 1640–53 (Keeler, p. 250).
26: 11 *Cinque Ports:* five ports on the coast of Sussex, Kent, and Essex, so called because they were the ports of an ancient jurisdiction for the protection of the southern coast of England.
26: 15 *infatuating:* 'that which infatuates or renders foolish' (*OED*).
26: 19 *Mr. N. . . . att that time:* 'Serjeant *Norfoulke*' was then mace-bearer (*Journals of the House of Commons From December the 5th 1646 . . . to September the 1st, 1648*, London, n.d., v. 259, 263).
26: 27–8 *the Prince imployed him:* Lady Halkett passes silently over one of the most controversial periods in Bampfield's career, the summer of 1648. Bampfield, according to Clarendon, used his influence with the fourteen-year-old Duke of York in an effort to persuade him to insubordination against the Prince of Wales. He also attempted to arouse support for the Duke, in opposition to the Prince, in the Royalist fleet that had revolted against Parliament and sailed to Holland (Clarendon, xi. 33–5). Although Bampfield's interpretation of his actions is very different from Clarendon's, he traces his subsequent misfortunes to his actions during this period (*Apologie*, pp. 43–5).
28: 14–15 *a good skollar . . . writting and speaking well:* Bampfield had been educated at Trinity College, Dublin. *Alumni Dublinenses*, ed. George Dames Burtchaell and Thomas Ulick Sadleir (London, 1924), p. 38, includes the following entry: 'Banfield, Joseph, 1631. B. A. Vern [Spring] 1638.

Clarendon refers to him as an Irishman, and although Clarendon for good reason did not like or trust him, he refers to Bampfield as a 'man of wit and parts' (Clarendon, viii. 10).
28: 30 *that execrable murder:* the execution of Charles I, 30 January 1649.
29: 21–3 *my brother Will . . . jelousye betwixt the King and Duke of Yorke:* See n. 23: 8 and n. 26: 27–8 above. It would appear not impossible that Will Murray was in some way implicated in his friend Colonel Bampfield's activities in support of the Duke in opposition to his older brother. In answer to his sister's question (p. 30) if he thought Bampfield had any responsibility for his dismissal by the King, Will answered cryptically that 'hee thought hee might say as much for him [Bampfield] as for himselfe'—scarcely a satisfactory answer in view of the convincing evidence that Bampfield had indeed encouraged the Duke in a jealous rivalry with his brother. The severe melancholy—or 'depression'—from which Will suffered could more plausibly be explained as the result of feelings of guilt than as merely the result of a rebuff by the King.
29: 41 *the Princese Royall's:* Charles II's sister, the Princess Royal, was married to the Prince of Orange. In 1650 she gave birth to the future William III of England.
30: 9–10 *Cobham . . . Duke and Duchese of Richmond:* Cobham is in Kent, five miles west of Rochester. The third Duke of Richmond, James Stuart (1612–55), was a devoted Royalist who had been given responsibility for the burial of Charles I (*Complete Peerage*).
30: 21 *Doctor Wild:* George Wilde or Wild (1610–65), Bishop of Derry after the Restoration. A devoted and courageous Anglican and an eloquent preacher, he had been chaplain to Archbishop Laud and had preached to Charles I at Oxford (*DNB*). William and Anne Murray wished him to attend William Murray on his death-bed because, among other reasons, Wild was willing to administer communion in the manner of the Church of England despite Parliamentary prohibitions.
31: 27 *the Savoy Church:* Now known as 'The Queen's Chapel of the Savoy', it was built in the thirteenth century. It is on Savoy Street in Westminster, just south of the Strand.
31: 28 *to my brother Murray's:* i.e. to the house of her oldest brother, Henry. Her biographer of 1701 writes that 'After her Mothers Death [in August 1647], She was

invited by her eldest Brother and his Lady, to live with them; where she had an apartment for herself and her Maid, and there stayed about a Year' (*Life*, p. 15).
31: 29 *my Lady H.:* Anne Howard, Anne Murray's friend at Charlton and the sister of her former suitor, Thomas Howard. She had married a cousin, Sir Charles Howard.
31: 31 *sodainly:* soon, speedily.
32: 2–3 *wee came to H., beyond Yorke . . . where his sisters lived:* Sir Charles Howard (*c.* 1629–85) of Naworth Castle in East Cumberland, the destination of the party, had a house at Hinderskelfe (or Hinderskelle), later to be the site of Castle Howard. The husband of Lady Howard, he had five sisters.
32: 9 *Sir Thomas Gore:* Sir Thomas Gower (*c.* 1605–72), second baronet, was the brother-in-law of Sir Charles Howard, having married Sir Charles's sister Elizabeth. He had raised a regiment in the service of the King (*Complete Baronetage*, i. 147).
32: 20–1 *there chaplaine:* Mr. Nicolls. Lady Halkett's remarks about him here are consciously ironic. She was soon to suffer from his hypocrisy and dishonesty.
32: 34 *avealable:* variant spelling of 'available', meaning 'capable of producing a desired result; of avail, effectual, efficacious' (*OED*).
33: 11 *her father:* Edward, Lord Howard of Escrick.
33: 22 *gape:* to open the mouth as in yawning.
33: 23 *Mrs. Cullcheth:* wife of Sir Charles Howard's steward at Naworth Castle.
33: 44 *my sister Murray:* the wife of her brother Henry.
36: 1 *sise:* variant form of 'assize', a trial by jury.
39: 19 *wanted:* 'want', 'to be deprived of, to lose' (*OED*).
40: 15 *secretary:* 'one who is entrusted with private or secret matters; a confidant' (*OED*).
40: 27 *I told him I was maried:* It is curious that, even in the difficult circumstances in which she found herself, Anne Murray should tell a lie to a clergyman. That she said what she did lends support to what can only be conjecture: that Colonel Bampfield had deceived her into entering into a marriage which he knew to be invalid because his wife was alive.
41: 19 *exegentt:* 'exigent', 'a state of pressing need; a time of extreme necessity; a critical occasion' (*OED*).
43: 39 *ayreiest:* 'airy', 'vain, empty' (*OED*).
43: 39 *admired:* 'admire', to be surprised.
44: 20 *mose troopers:* 'moss-trooper', 'one of a class of marauders who infested the "mosses" of the Scottish border in the middle of the seventeenth century; a border freebooter' (*OED*).
48: 9–14 *My sister writtes . . . to releeve her:* Anne Murray's brother-in-law, Sir Henry Newton, wrote to his friend Sir Ralph Verney about this episode, recounting the abduction of his cousin Jane Puckering by a certain Joseph Walsh and his companions who took her to Holland. The crime understandably attracted much attention. Not long after Sir Henry's trip to Holland, the English Council of State sent a man-of-war which rescued her (Frances Parthenope, Lady Verney, and Margaret M., Lady Verney, comps., *Memoirs of the Verney Family*, 3rd edn., London, 1925, i. 463).

Jane (Puckering) Bale, daughter and heiress of Sir Thomas Puckering, died in childbirth, 27 January 1652. Sir Henry Newton, who was Sir Thomas's nephew, inherited the estate (which included a house near Warwick) and took the name Puckering (*Complete Baronetage*, i. 93, 141; ii. 214–15).
48: 14–29 *in the same ship . . . beleeved mee vicious:* In his letter to Sir Ralph Verney describing his trip to Holland, Sir Henry Newton alludes in a jocular vein to his duel with Bampfield:

> I mett at sea with a rencontre of a person who bored some few holes in mee at landing, which have done mee this only despight, that they kept me away so much longer then I intended from my Cosen, and you;

of two pricks scarcely worth the naming, one of them hath been kind to mee about the belly, but the other now seven weekes in cure I doubt will domineere among the sinewes a moneth longer before I gett my arme at Liberty (*Memoirs of the Verney Family*, i. 463–4).

The fact that Sir Henry Newton, a man of strong intelligence and good judgement, should feel compelled to challenge Bampfield while on such an urgent mission provides a measure of his belief that Bampfield had betrayed his sister-in-law.

48: 30 *an exprese:* a messenger sent for a specific purpose.

48: 40 *Collonel Loe:* Probably 'Colonel Hercules Lowe, who served K. Charles I' (*The Marriage, Baptismal, and Burial Registers of the . . . Abbey of . . . Westminster*, ed. Joseph L. Chester, London, 1876, Harleian Society, Registers, x. 190). If this was indeed the individual, he seems to have shared the moral turpitude of Colonel Bampfield. After having been commissioned soon after the Restoration to seize concealed property belonging to the King, he had his commission annulled as early as 27 June 1660 because of abuse of it (*Historical Manuscripts Commission, Seventh Report*, Appendix, London, 1879, pp. 92, 595).

49: 16–17 *my Lord Dunfermeline in Flanders:* Charles Seton, second Earl of Dunfermline (d. 1672), had gone to the Continent after the execution of Charles I. At the time of which Lady Halkett writes, he with other leaders of the Covenanting Scots was engaged in the negotiations with Charles II which had issue in the King's going to Scotland in June 1650. Lord Dunfermline accompanied him and entertained him at his seat in Dunfermline.

49: 24–5 *the recovery of my portion . . . in Scotch hands:* Lady Halkett's early biographer provides additional details about her financial difficulties:

She was no less unfortunat, in her own affairs, being deprived of an interest in *Barhamsteed*, to the value, of 412 *lib. Ster.* a Year: This was an House and Park of the Kings, of which her Mother had a lease (having payed a Fine for it to the Exchequer) and had left it to her Brother *William* [d. 1649] and her, dureing twelve Years, that were to run: and of the other part of her Patrimony the 2000 *lib. Ster.* [owed to her by the Earl of Kinnoull or his heirs] She could not command one Farthing (*Life*, p. 20).

See below, p. 64 and n. 64: 34–5.

Berkhamsted, in Hertfordshire, was in English hands. Hence, the Earl of Dunfermline referred to Anne Murray's claim on the estate of the Earl of Kinnoull.

After the Restoration, Lady Halkett, 17 June 1661, petitioned the King for '2,400 *l.*, due from the Exchequer, left her by her mother, and not daring to stay in England after the Duke of York's escape, lost the benefit of the lease of Berkhampstead, now otherwise disposed of . . .' (*Calendar of State Papers, Domestic, 1661–62*, p. 10).

49: 32–4 *my Lady H. very generously . . . what mony I desired:* The following entry is printed in Surtees Society, Vol. 168, *Naworth Estate and Household Accounts, 1648–1660*, ed. C. Roy Hudleston, London, 1958, p. 72: 'June 19. [1650] pd Mrs Murray at her goinge from Naward 44£ 5s. 6d.'

50: 37–8 *the Canongate:* The street, on which a number of noblemen and gentlemen then had town houses, is in the parish of the same name, about three-quarters of a mile east of Edinburgh Castle (*Cassell's Gazetteer of Great Britain and Ireland*, London, 1899–1900, i. 452).

50: 38 *discharged:* 'discharge', 'to charge or command not to do something', (*OED*).

51: 15–16 *my Lady Anne Campbell:* Anne Murray's interest in the beauty and demeanour of Lady Anne Campbell, the daughter of the Marquis of Argyll, may have been prompted by a knowledge that her father had proposed her to Charles II as a bride (Maurice Ashley, *Charles II: The Man and the Statesman*, New York, 1971, pp. 41–2).

51: 27 *Sir James Dowglas:* Later 11th Earl of Morton (d. 1686), he was the brother-in-law of both the Marquis of Argyll and the Earl of Dunfermline. His seat of Smithfield near Aberdour had been in the possession of his family since the fourteenth century.

51: 28–30 *Aberdour . . . Brun Island:* She crossed from Leith, near Edinburgh, on the south shore of the Firth of Forth, to Burntisland, a town about two and a half miles east of Aberdour.

51: 31–2 *the Laird of Maines:* the tenth Laird, Sir Archibald Douglas (*Burke's Landed Gentry*).

51: 32 *Fife:* Lady Halkett resided in Fifeshire, a county in eastern Scotland, after her marriage to Sir James Halkett in 1656.

51: 44 *the King . . . in the North:* Charles II landed in the Firth of Cromarty, 16 June 1650.

52: 20 *H. Seymour:* Henry Seymour (1612–86) had accompanied Charles II to Scotland in 1650. The cordial response Seymour conveyed to Anne Murray from him, as well as the King's subsequent reception of, and gift to her, implies that Charles II did not hold her responsible for the misdeeds of Bampfield or the alleged misdeeds of her brother Will.

52: 24 *her brother and his lady:* The brother of the Countess of Dunfermline was Sir James Douglas.

52: 39–40 *my Lady Anne Areskine:* Lady Anna Erskine, the niece of the Earl of Dunfermline.

53: 19 *Mr. Harding:* Richard Harding, an attendant of the King. He is mentioned frequently at this period in Clarendon, *State Papers*, ii.

54: 13–14 *The Humourous Lieutenant:* a reference to the opening scene of John Fletcher's *The Humorous Lieutenant* (*c.* 1619). Attending an audience at the court of King Antigonous, Celia is treated rudely until Prince Demetrius, her lover, kisses her. She then comments ironically on the abrupt change in demeanour of the company towards her.

54: 20–1 *Cromwell comming in . . . devissions both in Church and State:* Commanding the New Model Army, Cromwell invaded Scotland on 22 July 1650. He defeated the army of the Scottish Covenanters supporting Charles II at Dunbar on 3 September (precisely one year before he destroyed Charles's army at Worcester). During the winter of 1650–1, the English occupied all of Edinburgh except the castle.

For a concise analysis of the complex 'devissions' among the Scots to which Lady Halkett refers, see Ashley, *Charles II*, pp. 34–44.

55: 35 *wentt frankly:* a Scottish idiom. Although the *Scottish National Dictionary* includes no citation earlier than 1768, it lists as a meaning of the adjective 'frank', 'willing, ready . . . without restraint' and as an illustrative use of the word, '*frank to the road*, willing or eager to travel, of a horse'.

55: 38 *tuke:* 'tuck', a rapier (*OED*, which cites this use of the word).

55: 40 *prejudice:* injury, hurt.

56: 10–11 *my Lady . . . the Countese of Kinowle:* The Countess of Kinnoull was the widow of George Hay, the second earl (d. 1644). She was either the widow or the mother of the earl whose bond for £2,000 Anne Murray held. See below, p. 64 and n. 64: 34–5.

Lady Kinnoull and Lady Dunfermline were daughters of William Douglas, Earl of Morton (*Complete Peerage*; *Scots Peerage*).

56: 11 *my Lord Lorne:* son of the Marquis of Argyll.

56: 26 *Fivye:* The Earl of Dunfermline had an estate at Fyvie in Aberdeenshire, about twenty miles north-west of Aberdeen.

57: 15 *the conflict betwixt love and honor:* The troubled state of Anne Murray's mind—her sense of guilt—at the time of her residence at Fyvie is revealed in her devotional essay, *Meditations on the Twentieth and Fifth Psalm*, published posthumously (Edinburgh, 1701), which concludes with a statement (p. 48), '*Ended at* Fyvie *the first of* January 1651/2'.

57: 44–58: 1 *att Fyvie, which was neere two yeares:* Lady Halkett's biographer of 1701 explains Lord Dunfermline's interest in and hospitality to her, which made possible this prolonged visit to his estate at Fyvie:

The Earle of *Dunfermline's* Concern in her, was, That her Mother had been educated in his Fathers Family; and she, in duty and gratitude, had made His Lordship welcome to her House, at all times, when He came to Court' (*Life*, pp. 22–3).

58: 29 (*when His Majesty marched into England*): Charles II, leading his army, crossed the border into England, 6 August 1651.
60: 1–2 *Collonel Lilburne, Collonel Fitts, and Collonel Overton:* Colonel Robert Lilburne (1613–65) had taken a prominent part in the Second Civil War on the side of the army. He had been one of the signatories of the death warrant of Charles I, for which he was imprisoned from 1661 (*DNB*; C. H. Firth, assisted by Godfrey Davies, *The Regimental History of Cromwell's Army*, Oxford, 1940, *passim*). Colonel Thomas Fitch commanded a regiment of foot in Scotland during the period of Anne Murray's residence at Fyvie (Firth–Davies, *Regimental History*, pp. 509–11). Colonel Robert Overton (*fl.* 1640–68) had commanded a brigade of foot at the Battle of Dunbar (*DNB*; Firth–Davies, *Regimental History*, *passim*).
60: 4, 29 *pase:* a variant spelling of 'pass' (*OED*). See also p. 62.
61: 35–6 *I have now forgott:* Anne Murray's report of her conversation with Colonel Overton at Fyvie and her allusion to subsequent conversations in Edinburgh are consistent with what is known of him. A friend of Milton, he was a scholar, and he was deeply and disinterestedly committed to the cause for which he fought (*DNB*; Firth–Davies, *Regimental History*, pp. 550–1).

Anne Murray's part in the conversation expresses the intensity of her own Royalist convictions, which she appears to have held throughout her life. Her early biographer describes the emotional turmoil the Revolution of 1688 caused her, though—writing as he was during the reign of William III—he discreetly refrained from stating her final conclusions about the event. However, he circumspectly refers to her son Robert's service under James II in Ireland against William, and his subsequent capture and imprisonment (*Life*, pp. 45–9). It is reasonable to assume that the son acquired his political beliefs from his strong-minded mother.

Robert Halkett's militant Jacobitism is in marked contrast to his older half-brother Sir Charles Halkett's support of the Revolution. In 1689 Sir Charles, then a member of the Scottish Parliament for Dunfermline, was on the Parliamentary committee that resolved James had forfeited his crown (*Complete Baronetage*, iii. 334).
63: 8 *the late Lord Lyon:* the courtesy title of the chief herald of Scotland. The individual was Sir Charles Erskine of Cambo, who died in September 1677 (*Court of the Lord Lyon* . . ., ed. Sir Francis James Grant, Scottish Record Society, Edinburgh, 1946, lxxvii. 16).

Lady Halkett's reference to the death of Lord Lyon, in the recent past, is consistent with her marginal note stating that she was writing her Memoirs on 8 January 1677/8 (see above, Introduction, n. 5).
63: 10–11 *Northwatter Brig:* North Water Bridge, a hamlet three miles north of Montrose, on the border of Angus and Kincardineshire.
63: 14 *Sir Robert Moray:* Moray (1608/9–73), a first cousin of Sir James Halkett and a brother-in-law of the Earl of Balcarres, had served in the army of Charles I, who had knighted him in 1643. Active in planning the Royalist risings in the Highlands (see below, p. 66), he took part in the campaign of which Balcarres and the Earl of Glencairn were leaders. After the Restoration, he was one of the founders of the Royal Society (Alexander Robertson, *The Life of Sir Robert Moray, Soldier, Statesman and Man of Science*, London, 1922).
63: 14–15 *the Neither Bow:* the Netherbow, the name of the eastern extremity of a principal street in Edinburgh.
63: 21 *my Lord Belcarese:* Alexander Lindsay, first Earl of Balcarres, was at the time one of the most active of the Scottish Royalists. See below, p. 73 and n. 73: 6–7.
64: 7 *prejudice:* injury, loss.
64: 11 *W. Muray of Hermiston:* Hermiston is a village in Midlothian, slightly less

than two miles north of Currie. Hermiston House is west of the village. The person mentioned might have been a Sir William Murray, a Royalist who had served under the Duke of Hamilton. (Cf. *Burke's Landed Gentry*.)

64: 21 *my Lord Twedale:* probably John Hay, second Earl and first Marquis of Tweeddale (1626–97), though he did not succeed to the title of the first Earl until 1653 or 1654. He had served in the armies of both Charles I and the Scottish Covenanters. He had attended the coronation of Charles II at Scone, and over a number of years attempted to reconcile the Royalists and the Covenanters.

Lord Tweeddale's house was near the Netherbow, to the south (cf. Charles B. Boog Watson, 'Notes on the Names of the Closes and Winds of Old Edinburgh', *The Book of the Old Edinburgh Club*, xii (1923), 87).

64: 31 *prejudice:* injury, damage.

64: 34–5 *the suite in my name against Ar. Hay:* Lady Halkett's biographer of 1701 provides a few details:

> The ground of the Law Suit, in which She was engaged, was a Bond of 2000 *lib Ster.* due by the Earle of *Kinnoul*, and *Archibald Hay* his Cautioner [i.e. 'one who gives or becomes security for another' (*OED*)]; This Suit had been begun, some Years before, in her name, by M. *W. H.* Advocat against *Archibald Hay*: who, being dead, it is revived, and carried on against his Executors.

Lady Halkett's early biographer explains that a short time before her mother's death (in 1647), she 'made over to her, by Assignation, a Bond of the Earl of *Kinnoul* of 2000 *lib. Ster.*' (*Life*, pp. 13, 27).

The date of Anne Murray's mother's gift of the bond to her suggests that it was an obligation of either George Hay, second Earl of Kinnoull (d. 1644) or his son, George Hay, third Earl (d. 1649) (*Complete Peerage*, vii. 319–20). The surname 'Hay' of the 'caution' or 'Cautioner' implies that he was a member of the family of the Earls.

64: 39 *my Lord Newbeth and his father:* Sir John Baird of Newbyth (1620–98), an advocate in Aberdeenshire, was the son of James Baird, also an advocate. Sir John did not assume the title of Lord Newbyth until 1664, when 'he was created an ordinary lord of session' (*DNB*).

65:1 *Malignantt:* i.e. a Royalist.

65: 10 *my Lady Morton:* the Countess of Morton, *née* Anne Villiers (d. 1654). After her marriage to Robert, the son of William Douglas, eighth Earl of Morton, she was styled Lady Dalketh until the death of her father-in-law (*DNB*; *Complete Peerage*).

A widow at the time to which Lady Halkett refers, she had demonstrated ingenuity and courage in 1646 when, as governess to the two-year-old Princess Henrietta, she had disguised herself as a poor woman and the child as her son dressed in rags and conveyed the Princess to her mother in France.

65: 16 *Sir James Halkett:* Anne Murray's first sight of the man whom she married four years later. A middle-aged widower with four children, two sons and two daughters, he had long been active in Scottish affairs. (His name appears frequently in the indexes of the volumes of *The Register of the Privy Council of Scotland*.) A zealous Royalist, he was colonel of a cavalry regiment in the army of Scotland.

Sir James's birthdate is not known, though the circumstances of his life suggest a date in the latter part of the first decade of the century. He was knighted in 1633. He took an active part in military campaigns of the 1640s and 1650s. His older daughter had almost reached maturity when Anne Murray became her governess in 1653 (see below, p. 75). His younger son by his first marriage—James, later knighted for gallantry by Charles II—held a commission as Cornet in 1664 (Charles Dalton, *English Army Lists and Commission Registers, 1661–1714*, London, 1892–1904; reprinted, 1960, i. 42). Sir James appears to have enjoyed good health during the period prior to his death on 24 September 1670. As late as 28 November 1666, on the occasion of a minor rebellion, the Privy Council ordered 'Sir James Halkett to bring the presbytrie of Dumferlin to the rendezvous of the shyre of Fyff' (*Register of the Privy Council of Scotland*, 3rd series, ii. 227).

66: 3–4 *the Fleurs . . . the Countese of Roxbery:* the third wife and at this time the widow of the first Earl of Roxburghe (d. 1650). She resided in Floors, a house near Kelso, Roxburghshire, in south-eastern Scotland.

66: 35–7 *my chamber . . . to serve the King:* Ever adventurous, Anne Murray was thus a party to the Royalist intrigues preliminary to the risings in the Highlands of 1653 and 1654 which had as their objective—frustrated in the event—to arouse sufficient support in the North of Scotland to enable Charles II to return to that country. The biographer of 1701 remarks of Lord Tweeddale's house in Edinburgh, where Sir Robert Moray and his wife as well as Anne Murray were then residing, that it 'was the place of Rendez-vous to the best and most Loyal of the Kingdom, where were held frequent meetings of such who were contriving means to assert their Loyalty, and free their Country' (*Life*, p. 26).

68: 5–6 *hee came in . . . those persons mett:* That Colonel Bampfield should have been accepted into their secret councils by these Scottish Royalists of high rank and good character helps to explain how Anne Murray could continue to trust him despite the repeated warnings she had received. The Scottish leaders as well as Anne Murray were deceived by him. The Clarendon *State Papers* and the Thurloe *State Papers* include letters to and from Charles II and his advisors, some of them intercepted, that reveal they suspected Bampfield of treachery at least as early as 25 February–7 March 1653 when the King sent a despatch '*to the principal officers . . . in armes for us in the Highlands of Scotland*', warning them about Bampfield, who was falsely pretending to be acting on orders from the King (Clarendon Manuscripts, 45. 130; printed in *Scotland and the Commonwealth*, ed. C. H. Firth, Scottish Historical Society, Edinburgh, 1895, xviii. 94–5. Cf. Clarendon, *State Papers*, ii. 180). Later in March the King wrote to Lord Balcarres, replying to a letter from Balcarres commending Bampfield, saying he knew 'more ill' about Bampfield 'than anybody can know good' (Clarendon, *State Papers*, ii. 188).

A letter written from London, 21 July 1653, includes the ominous statement: 'I had almost forgot to acquaint you, that that arch-villaine Bampfield hath bin lately with Cromwell' (Thurloe, *State Papers*, i. 366–7). This letter was written just two months after Lord Dunfermline had sent Anne Murray in haste to warn Lord Balcarres that he was in imminent danger of arrest (see below, p. 73). An intercepted letter written from London, 11 December 1653, alludes to reports that Bampfield had betrayed the trust of the Scottish lords: 'I am told that Bampfylde hath been the parliament's good friend in counterfeiting the king's hand and seal, and getting the secrets of the lords designs in the Highlands, and discovered more than he knew, or they had courage or honesty to act' (Thurloe, *State Papers*, i. 630).

68: 9–11 *Sir G. Mackery . . . then very young:* Sir George Mackenzie of Tarbat (1630–1714); created Earl of Cromartie in 1703.

68: 19–22 *white inck . . . a booke:* The book may have been J.[ohn] W.[ilkins], *Mercury: or, The Secret and Swift Messenger* (1641), the fifth chapter of which includes a discussion of several kinds of invisible ink.

68: 30–1 *a safe hand . . . North of Scottland:* a safe-conduct pass, signed by a person of sufficient authority to ensure compliance with it.

68: 32 *Sir G. M.:* Sir G. 'Mackery', i.e. George Mackenzie.

69: 25–6 *my Lady Moray . . . died:* Sophia, Lady Moray (1624–53), the wife of Sir Robert and the sister of Lord Balcarres, died in childbirth at Edinburgh, 2 January. She was buried at Balcarres, the seat of her brother (*The Diary of Mr John Lamont of Newton, 1649–1671*, Edinburgh, 1830, Maitland Club Publications, No. 7, p. 52).

70: 6–7 *7 of February, 1652/3 . . . and C. B. began there journy:* An intercepted letter, dated 11 August 1653, by a Royalist seemingly with the King on the Continent, refers to this journey of Colonel Bampfield into Scotland:

> As concerning Bampfeild, he was heare five or six Moneths since meet by sir Will. Flemming [a Royalist], going into Scotland hence; to whom he said, that he had commissions from the king to Arguile and some

8

other lords; he then went by the name of Smith. Whether he hath since binn heare, I cannot of certainty learne; but tis by the Scotch prisoners believed, that he hath had late correspondence with us here' (Thurloe, *State Papers*, i. 408).

In an intercepted letter written by Charles II, 2 October 1653 (New Style: i.e. 23 September by the English calendar Lady Halkett used) to Lord Balcarres, in which the King warned Balcarres that Bampfield was not to be trusted, he wrote that Bampfield and two other officers whom Balcarres had in April sent to the King on the Continent had not arrived until after the middle of September (Thurloe, *State Papers*, i. 495).

For further comment on the King's letter, see below, n. 73: 6–7.

70: 26–7 *Blacke-fryar Wind:* a then aristocratic street near the Netherbow, leading southward from the thoroughfare of which the Netherbow was a part.

71: 1 *the Earle of Roxborough:* The second Earl (d. 1675) had succeeded to his grandfather's title in 1650. From 1648 or earlier, he had supported the Royalists in Scotland. Not long before, Anne Murray had visited the widow of his grandfather. See above, p. 66.

71: 29–30 *what the ground was . . . reflection upon him:* In 1650 Sir James Halkett had been accused of cowardice in battle. Balfour describes the episode and its aftermath:

> The last of Julij Sr James Hackett receauid a grate fryte at a skirmishe with the enmey; he should haue secondit the L. Generall bot turnid and neuer lowsid a pistoll against the enimey, bot tooke him to the speed of his horsse heiles. . . . (*Annales of Scotland*, in *Works*, iv. 86–7.)

Under date, 3 August 1650, Balfour adds:

> Sr James Hackett and Colonell Scotte, cleired by the comittee, zet that did litle salue ther honor amongest honest men and souldiours of worthe and reputatione. (ibid. iv. 88–9.)

71: 33–5 *the King . . . the whole proceedure:* Charles II was at Lord Balmerino's house at Leith, 29 July until 2 August 1650 (ibid. iv. 86). The King had watched the battle from the roof—the 'leads'—of the house.

72: 32 *misfortune so soone devulged?:* The context in which the missing leaf appeared suggests that it was removed, by Lady Halkett herself or some other person concerned to protect her reputation, because she had written forthrightly about her relationship with Colonel Bampfield. An enigmatic statement in the *Life* of 1701 suggests at least the possibility that she had at some time met him in, or accompanied him to, Holland, a country in which he spent much time. Referring to the hardships she experienced between the outbreak of war in 1642 and her marriage to Halkett in 1656, her biographer writes that she was 'pursued with a constant series of difficulties and incumbrances for the space of fourteen Years, both in *England* and *Holland*' (*Life*, p. 13). Yet in her manuscript as it survives, in which she relates the events of her life during those fourteen years, she includes no reference to travel except in England and Scotland.

73: 7–8 *take my Lord and bring him prisoner:* Presumably the Earl of Balcarres was to have been arrested because—along with the Earl of Glencairn—he was leading the movement to arouse support for the King in the Highlands. Although there is no direct evidence that Colonel Bampfield had a part in the planned arrest, Charles II himself had two months earlier, 18–28 March, attempted to warn Balcarres that he might be in danger because of his association with Bampfield (Clarendon Manuscripts, 45. 195; printed in Scottish Historical Society, xviii. 107). The King wrote again to Balcarres in September to warn him. But, Charles added, 'I found you had trusted Bamfield and others too farr, that it might not be safe for you to appeare to dissent from them' (Thurloe, *State Papers*, i. 495).

73: 15 *I landed safe and was att Belcarese:* Balcarres House was in East Fifeshire. three-quarters of a mile north-west of Colinsburgh. From Edinburgh, crossing the Firth of Forth in the hours before dawn, Anne Murray travelled rapidly to reach Balcarres by 10.00 a.m.

73: 38 *an exprese:* a messenger sent for a specific purpose.

73: 40–1 *wentt to the North . . . thence wentt abroad:* In the winter of 1653–4, Lord Balcarres, then in the remote Scottish Highlands, received a summons from the King to come to him in France to report on events in Scotland. Balcarres at once made the hazardous and arduous journey (Alexander Lindsay, 25th Earl of Crawford, *Lives of the Lindsays*, 2nd edn., London, 1858, ii. 97).
73: 43–4 *Dr. Cuningham:* Robert Cunningham (or Cuningham), an eminent doctor of medicine, had fought in the King's army at the Battle of Worcester. After the Restoration, he became Charles II's physician in Scotland. In 1673, the year before his death, he was created a baronet (*Complete Baronetage*, iv. 295). See also p. 78.
74: 9 *the Lady Ardrose:* probably Helen, eldest daughter of Sir Robert Lindsay, who in 1634 married Sir William Scott of Ardross (*Scots Peerage*, v. 401, 402).
74: 10 *Mr. D. Forett . . . Mr. H. Rimer:* clergymen of Fifeshire (see Balfour, *Annales of Scotland*, in *Works*, iv. 107).
75: 21 *his two daughters:* The biographer of 1701 provides information about Sir James's first marriage and his children born of his first wife, Margaret, daughter of Sir Robert Montgomery of Skelmorlie (*Complete Baronetage*, iii. 334):

Sir *James* had formerly been Married to an Excellent Lady, Daughter of *Skermorly*, and Niece to the Earle of *Argile*, of whom he kept a kind Remembrance, and spoke frequently of her, with great affection: He had by her, two Sons *Charles*, who succeeded to his fathers Honour, Inheritance and Vertue; and *James*, who, also for his worth and Valour was Knighted by K. *Ch.* II. And two Daughters, who proved very worthy Ladies; *Mary*, Married to Sir *William Bruce* of *Kinross*; and *Anna*, to Sir *Andrew Ker* of *Kavers* (*Life*, pp. 29–30).

75: 35–6 *there unckle and cousin, Sir R. Montgomery and Haslehead:* Lady Halkett's syntax is ambiguous, at least with respect to 'Haslehead'. Sir Robert Montgomery (d. 1684) had in 1651 succeeded his grandfather of the same name, his own father, also of the same name—the father of Sir James's first wife—having died earlier (Sir John Bernard Burke, *A Genealogical and Heraldic History of the Extinct and Dormant Baronetcies of England, Ireland, and Scotland*, London, 1841, 2nd edn.).

Presumably the cousin also had the name of Robert Montgomery: hence the need to identify him by the place name 'Haslehead'. At any rate, a 'Robert Montgomery of Haslehead' was married sometime after 10 April 1656 (*Scots Peerage*, v. 190).
78: 4 *my brother:* her oldest brother, Henry Murray.
78: 9 *the Countese of Morton:* See above, p. 65 and n. 65: 10. On p. 65 Lady Halkett writes that Sir James was 'much respected and very intimate with' Lady Morton.
78: 28 *Doctor Cunningham:* see p. 73.
79: 6 *Pincky:* Pinkie House, near Musselburgh in Midlothian, a mansion of the Earl of Dunfermline (*Cassell's Gazetteer*, ii. 152).
79: 9 *convenientt:* cf. 'convenience', 'means of living conveniently, competence' (*OED*).
79: 18 *the Cavers:* in southern Roxburghshire, five miles north-east of Hawick.
80: 19 *att Warwicke:* In 1654 Sir Henry Newton inherited from an uncle, Sir Thomas Puckering, an estate called the Priory near Warwick. Ten years later Newton, who had assumed his uncle's surname, sold his estate at Charlton. Cf. *The Diary of John Evelyn*, ed. E. S. de Beer, Oxford, 1955, iii. 66, 120, 377. Cf. n. 48: 9–14.
81: 14 *the Earle of Callander:* James Livingston, created Earl of Callendar in 1641, had been Lieutenant General of the Scottish army that had attempted to rescue Charles I and was defeated at Preston in 1648.
81: 19 *hee came and arrested mee:* Little can be added to Lady Halkett's account of this embarrassing episode and its sequel, the forfeiture of the money she was forced to post as bail, except that she was the executrix of the estate of her brother William, who had died in 1649. Her early biographer refers to her losses from 'the fraud and falseness of some Persons, whom (by his direction) She intrusted with managing affairs' (*Life*, p. 20).
81: 32 *flung over the barre:* '*To cast over the bar:* . . . to reject' (*OED*).
81: 35 *her howse att the Muse:* presumably a house near the Mews, 'the royal stables at

Charing Cross . . . so called because built on the site where the royal hawks were formerly mewed' (*OED*).

82: 3–4 *10th of December* [*16*]*54 . . . hee came in:* This meeting marks the end of Anne Murray's relationship with Colonel Bampfield. Although she had known past doubt for more than a year that he had betrayed her in falsely telling her that his wife was dead, reason enough for her to reflect on the misfortunes he had brought to her, she provides no hint that she knew he had treacherously deserted the Royalist cause and was then serving—again as a secret agent—the government of Cromwell. Her comment (p. 82) about the reason Bampfield left his place of concealment on Sunday implies that she did not have knowledge in 1654 of his reversal of political allegiance. By the end of 1656 Cromwell had employed him as a courier to Cardinal Mazarin (Wilbur Cortez Abbott, *The Writings and Speeches of Oliver Cromwell*, Cambridge, Mass., iv, 1947, 368–9).

83: 17–20 *my brother . . . from another hand:* her brother Henry. The 'hindrance' no doubt came from his wife, the mother of a large family.

83: 22 *the Countese of Devonshire:* Elizabeth (*c.* 1620–89), wife of William Cavendish, fourth Earl of Devonshire. She was a niece of Edward, Lord Howard of Escrick.

84: 39 *Derectory:* 'Directory', 'the set of rules for public worship compiled in 1644 by the Westminster Assembly, ratified by Parliament' (*OED*).

85: 1–2 *done more solemnly . . . lawfully done:* In 1645 an ordinance had prohibited the use of the Book of Common Prayer even for the marriage ceremony. The regulations enacted pertaining to marriage were bitterly resented by Anglicans (Godfrey Davies, *The Early Stuarts, 1603–1660*, 2nd edn., Oxford, 1959, pp. 201–3).

85: 27–8 *confirmed by the Act of Indempnity . . . when His Majesty first came home:* In 1660 the convention Parliament passed an Act of Indemnity 'pardoning all those who had taken part in the rebellion or the subsequent republican governments except some fifty named individuals' (Sir George N. Clark, *The Later Stuarts, 1660–1714*, 2nd edn., Oxford, 1955, p. 4).

Lady Halkett's meaning is obscure. She seems to imply that her alleged creditor, Mrs. Cole, was a republican who before the Restoration had employed political influence to bring about the forfeiture of Lady Halkett's bail; and that the Act of Indemnity prevented her from taking any retributive action after the Restoration.

85: 31–2 *500 pound . . . Exchequer:* The grant was made, 20 November 1662, 'to Lady Ann Hacket, in consideration of her zeal and sufferings' (*Calendar of Treasury Books, 1660–67*, i. 452).

85: 44 *boot:* 'an uncovered space on or by the steps on each side, where attendants sat, facing sideways' (*OED*).

86: 19 *Hary Macky:* presumably Sir James Halkett's 'man', mentioned in the preceding paragraph.

86: 34–5 *Sir James'es daughter:* It may be significant that, although Lady Halkett several times refers to one or both of Sir James's daughters, she never mentions either of his sons by his first marriage. The explanation could be merely that the sons were no longer residing in their father's household. Yet it is difficult to reconcile what is known of the prominence, and presumably the wealth, of the older of the sons, Sir Charles Halkett, with the financial hardship Lady Halkett suffered in her widowhood, as it is described by her biographer of 1701.

To be sure, the biography was dedicated to 'The Lady Dowager of Pitfirren', not more precisely identified but probably the widow of Sir Charles, who had died in 1697, two years before the death of Lady Halkett. In the dedicatory epistle as in the *Life* itself the biographer emphasizes the cordial relationship between Lady Halkett and the 'Honourable Family of *Pitfirren*'. Yet Sir Charles, who was created a baronet in January 1671, four months after he had succeeded to his father's estate, was one of the most influential men in Fifeshire, a member of the Scottish Parliament for some nine years. We cannot know the nature of the family relationships. But it appears curious that the stepmother of a man in Sir Charles's position should have been compelled at the age of sixty to support herself by teaching.

86: 38 *my Lady Broghill . . . her Lord:* Roger Boyle (1621–79), son of Richard, Earl of Cork, had as a child been created Lord Boyle, Baron of Broghill. He was subsequently, in 1660, created Earl of Orrery. At the time of which Lady Halkett writes, he was prominent in Cromwell's government: Member of Parliament at Westminster for Edinburgh and President of the Council in Scotland.

His wife Margaret (*c.* 1623–89) was the daughter of Theophilus Howard, second Earl of Suffolk (*Complete Peerage*). Lady Broghill was thus related to Edward, Lord Howard of Escrick, a circumstance that may account for Lady Halkett's earlier acquaintance with her.

87: 8–9 *the Castle att Edinburgh:* then used as a prison.

87: 19 *in the Canongate:* the name of a parish as well as a street in the Old Town of Edinburgh; then a fashionable area of residence.

EXPLANATORY NOTES

Lady Fanshawe, *Memoirs*

The numerals preceding the colons refer to pages; the numerals following, to lines.

104: 4–5 *patent of Remembrancer:* grant from the Crown, conferred by a legal document, of an office in the Court of Exchequer. In the Fanshawe family the office became hereditary.

105: 6 *Prince Henry:* King Charles I's older brother, who died in 1612 aged eighteen.

105: 7 *Mr. Camden:* As noted in *HCF*, p. 287, Lady Fanshawe is in error in referring to William Camden, who did not mention Ware Park; presumably she had in mind the laudatory account of the gardens and Sir Henry's expert cultivation of them in Sir Henry Wotton, *The Elements of Architecture* (London, 1624), pp. 110–11.

105: 41–2 *Battle of Edgehill:* the first important battle of the war, 23 October 1642.

106: 5 *mine:* mien, appearance.

108: 29 *Our Lady Day, the 25 day of March:* in the Old Style calendar, the first day of a new year.

109: 15 *grant given to* [*Hezekiah*]: Isaiah 38: 1–5.

109: 31 *the Earle of Essex:* third earl (1591–1646), the Parliamentary general, was the son of the second earl (the favourite of Queen Elizabeth I) and his wife Frances, the widow of Sir Philip Sidney.

109: 37–8 *the daughter of Mr. Shatbolt of Hartfordshire:* see below, p. 117.

109: 43 *accomptant:* an archaic form of 'accountant'.

110: 8 *cosen garman:* cousin-german, i.e. first cousin.

110: 29 *hoyting girle:* from 'hoit', a Northern dialect word, the expression here meaning 'an awkward silly girl, a hoyden' (*OED*, in which Lady Fanshawe is cited).

111: 1 *my brother William Harrison:* sat in the House of Commons from November 1640 until the start of the war (Keeler, p. 206).

111: 5–6 *to pay the Scots, who had then entered England:* On 20 August 1640 the Scots invaded England. By the terms of an armistice signed in October, 'The Covenanting forces were to occupy the six northern counties and to be paid the sum of £860 a day until peace was concluded' (C. V. Wedgwood, *The King's Peace, 1637–1641*, London, 1955, p. 355).

111: 38 *racke:* here meaning 'stress of weather; a storm' (*OED*).

112: 1 *Sir Edward Hide:* Hyde's presence at the wedding is noteworthy in view of the hostility Lady Fanshawe subsequently expresses toward him. Her husband seems never to have shared her hostility (*HCF*, p. 352). A series of letters written by Hyde to Fanshawe, April (New Style) 1659 to January 1660, printed in *Heathcote Manuscripts*, pp. 7–16, show the men to have been on terms of cordiality. Although Hyde (by then Earl of Clarendon) did not oppose the recall of Fanshawe from his embassy to Spain, in his Autobiography he wrote about him, after Fanshawe's death, with approbation (see below, pp. 178–9 and n. 178: 43–179: 3).

Lady Fanshawe regarded Clarendon as chiefly responsible for what she considered the ungenerous treatment of her husband and herself: for his failure to be appointed a Secretary of State; for his recall from Madrid in 1666; and for her difficulties in gaining financial compensation after his death. See pp. 132–3, 140, 141, 142, 171, and 178–9, for expressions of her hatred of Clarendon.

112: 17 *Mr. Farneby:* 'Thomas Farnabie [was] the most noted Schoolmaster of his time ...'. He taught 'in *Goldsmiths-rents* in *Cripplegate* Parish', London. 'He was the chief Grammarian, Rhetorician, Poet, Latinist and Grecian of his time...' (Anthony Wood, *Athenae Oxonienses*, London, ii, 1692, 53–4).

Presumably Fanshawe, appointed Latin Secretary at the Restoration, received his thorough classical training at Farnaby's school.

112: 17 *Doctor Beall:* Fanshawe's tutor, William Beale, D.D., was later to share the royal exile. Lady Fanshawe describes an affectionate meeting with him in Spain in 1650. See below, p. 129.

113: 4 *he travelled to Madrid: HCF*, pp. 339–43, provides additional information from diplomatic correspondence about Fanshawe's activities in Spain, 1635 to 1638.

113: 18 *poste:* i.e. travelling swiftly with letters and messages.

113: 27 *no preferment coming:* Fanshawe was more active in public affairs, 1638 to 1644, than his wife suggests (*HCF*, pp. 343–6). See the Chronology above, pp. 95–6.

113: 27–8 *Secrettary Window Banke:* Sir Francis Windebank, Secretary of State and a principal adviser to Charles I until late in 1640 when he came under attack by the House of Commons for alleged preferential treatment of Catholics. He then fled to France.

113: 29–30 *King's Remembrancer:* see above, n. 104: 4–5. The position had remained in the family.

114: 6–7 *Sir Robert Long . . . the consequence will show the man:* a reference to a charge that Long communicated with the Parliamentary general, the Earl of Essex. On p. 116 below, Lady Fanshawe refers to Long correctly as 'Mr Long'; he was not made a baronet until 1 September 1660.

114: 8–9 *March, [1645], your father went to Bristol with his new master:* On 4 March 1645 the Prince of Wales escorted by Sir Edward Hyde and others left Oxford for Bristol (C. V. Wedgwood, *The King's War, 1641–1647*, London, 1958, p. 426. Cf. Clarendon, viii. 279–86).

115: 11 *racked:* 'rack', here meaning 'to pull or tear apart' (*OED*).

115: 30 *My Lady Rivers:* the Countess Rivers, a distant cousin.

116: 44 *massard:* 'mazard', 'a kind of small black cherry', so called in the south-western counties (*OED*).

117: 18 *flit shott:* variant of 'flight shot' (*OED*): an idiom referring to the distance an arrow shot by a bow could travel.

117: 30 *which he had then married out of that family:* apparently meaning that Lady Fanshawe's father had married a gentlewoman who resided in the household of Sir Thomas Fanshawe (*HCF*, p. 327). See above, p. 109, where she is identified as 'the daughter of Mr. Shatbolt of Hertfordshire'.

119: 6 *disputes about the disposall of the Prince:* On 5 August 1645 the King wrote a letter to the Prince of Wales, ordering him to go to France if he found himself in 'apparent danger of falling into the rebels' hands' (Clarendon, ix. 74). The Prince's Council objected to his going to France, preferring Ireland or Scotland (Clarendon, ix. 77). On 29 September 1645 the King wrote to Lord Culpeper, a member of the Council, insisting that France be the destination (Clarendon, ix. 96–7).

119: 16–17 *his brother Lord Fanshaw:* see above, p. 117. Sir Thomas Fanshawe was not elevated to the peerage until 1661.

119: 23 *into Holland:* the Prince of Wales's sister was married to the son of the Prince of Orange. Her husband succeeded to the title in 1647.

119: 40–1 *compound for 300lb hundred a year:* The following entry appears in the *Calendar of the Proceedings of the Committee for Compounding*, &c., *1643–1660*, ed. Mary A. E. Green (London, 1891), p. 1649: 'RICH. FANSHAW, of the Remembrancer's Office in the Exchequer, and Brother of Sir Thos. Fanshaw, of Essex. 14 Jan. 1647. Begs to compound for delinquency in going into the King's quarters. Has returned from France with the Speaker's pass, presented himself to him, and been referred to the Committee at Goldsmiths' Hall.'

120: 15 *the King to leave Hampton Court:* Accompanied by Sir John Berkeley, John

Ashburnham, and William Legge, the King escaped from Hampton Court on the evening of 11 November 1647. He was captured on the Isle of Wight, 14 November, and taken to Carisbrooke Castle (S. R. Gardiner, *History of the Great Civil War*, London, 1894, iv. 17–19). For a judicious evaluation of the evidence concerning the allegations, which Lady Fanshawe apparently believed, that the Parliamentarians—and Cromwell—planned Charles I's escape and capture, see Abbott, *Writings and Speeches of Cromwell*, i. 554–5.

120: 19 *his stay at Hampton Court:* Charles I was at Hampton Court, 24 August to 11 November 1647.

120: 21–2 *credentialls for Spaine ... letters for his servise:* Charles I's instructions to Fanshawe, dated from Hampton Court, 9 October 1647, are printed in *Heathcote Manuscripts*, pp. 1–3.

120: 41 *the Dutch then in war with England:* Relations between the Dutch and the English were then uncertain and ambiguous, but the First Dutch War did not begin until 1652.

121: 4–5 *the last Lord Thom[as] Fanshawe:* By 'last' Lady Fanshawe means either the last to have the Christian name Thomas or, more likely, the 'last' in the sense of 'immediately preceding' the holder of the title at the time she was writing her Memoirs in 1676, i.e. Evelyn, third Viscount Fanshawe (grand-nephew of Sir Richard).

121: 14–15 *Collonell Montagu, afterwards Earl of Sandwich:* The animus Lady Fanshawe reveals towards Montague was no doubt intensified by her knowledge at the time she wrote her Memoirs that in 1666 he had replaced her husband as Ambassador to Spain. See below, pp. 184 ff.

121: 22–3 *September ... in the Downs:* Lady Fanshawe's is a simplified and misleading account of a narrowly-averted naval battle which reached a climax on 30 August 1648. A fleet of English ships had revolted from the Parliamentary government and sailed to Holland, where the Prince of Wales assumed command of it. In July the fleet sailed for the Downs and at the end of August encountered the Parliamentary fleet commanded by the Earl of Warwick. A battle did not occur because of a change in the wind. Lack of supplies compelled the Prince to lead his fleet back to Holland (Maurice Ashley, *Charles II*, New York, 1971, pp. 25–8).

122: 1–2 *Mr. Waller the poet:* Edmund Waller, who in 1643 had been captured by the Parliamentarians after leading an abortive Royalist plot, treacherously betrayed his accomplices and in return was allowed to go into exile.

122: 5 *the King:* the Prince of Wales until the execution of his father, 30 January 1649.

122: 7 *the Earle of Strafford:* the son of Charles I's executed Minister.

122: 11 *averr'd:* 'aver', to verify; prove true.

122: 13 *barnackells:* 'barnacle', 'English name of the penduculate genus of Cirripedes ... (This was the "shell-fish" out of which the Barnacle Goose was supposed to be produced ...)' (*OED*).

122: 25 *h[oy]:* a small sailing vessel with one mast.

122: 30 *Prince of Orange:* the future King William III of England was born at The Hague, 4 November 1650, after the death of his father. Because Lady Fanshawe is writing about events of 1648 and 1649, the context is misleading as to the date of the Prince's birth.

123: 16 *fleet with Prince R[upert]:* The nephew of Charles I, Prince Rupert had organized in foreign ports a fleet of English ships that had revolted against the Parliamentary government. On 14 September 1652 several ships, one of them commanded by his brother Prince Maurice, were lost near the Virgin Islands. (See *HCF*, p. 395, for additional details.)

123: 25 *Corke revolted:* The English garrison and the English residents of Cork revolted, 16 October 1649, in support of Parliament.

123: 31 *Collonell Jefreis:* The name is probably written in error for 'Gifford' (*HCF*, p. 397). If so, 'He was one of the officers who took the head in the revolt of the Munster garrisons to Cromwell' in October 1649 (Firth–Davies, *Regimental History*, ii. 640).

124: 27 *the King's command:* recorded in *Heathcote Manuscripts*, p. 3.

124: 30 *my Lord Cottington and Sir Edward Hide:* Hyde provides an account of his and Lord Cottington's embassy to Spain, 1649–50 (Clarendon, xii. 81–127; xiii. 9–31 *passim*).

124: 35 *besser stone:* 'bezoar stone', 'various substances formerly held as antidotes' (*OED*).

125: 2–3 *he dyed 5 dayes after:* The Earl of Roscommon died 8 November 1649.

125: 12–13 *Cromwell went through as bloodily as victoriously:* Having been appointed Lord Lieutenant of Ireland, Cromwell arrived in Dublin 15 August 1649. By the summer of 1650 he had put down significant resistance (C. V. Wedgwood, *Oliver Cromwell*, rev. edn., London, 1973, pp. 69–70).

125: 15 *a lady that went for a maid:* i.e. pretended to be a virgin.

125: 22 *sith:* 'sithe', meaning 'sigh' (*OED*). See below, 'sithing' and 'sithed', p. 131.

127: 14 *case:* state of mind.

127: 26 *exceeds:* surpasses.

127: 31 *the Straights:* presumably the Straits of Gibraltar.

127: 41 *bandoliers:* belts for carrying ammunition.

128: 2 *throm cap:* a cap 'made of thrums or waste threads of yarn (or something resembling it), or having thrums inserted in or projecting from it' (*OED*).

128: 14 *we all landed ... in Malegoe:* On 4 April 1650 Hyde wrote from Madrid to Secretary of State Nicholas: 'Dick Fanshaw has arrived at Malaga, and is coming with his wife, children, and a family of 12 persons ...'. Hyde adds that he does not know how Fanshawe will procure a livelihood nor does he himself 'know how to get either bread or money' (Clarendon, *State Papers*, ii. 51).

128: 27 *the highest mountaines:* the Sierra Nevada, the highest mountain range in Spain, rising to approximately 6,000 feet. Lady Fanshawe does not say they crossed this range; merely that they 'passed' it.

128: 31 *the Allhambray:* the Alhambra, the famous Moorish palace of Granada.

128: 39 *Teyrian dey:* tyrian purple, a bluish-red colour.

129: 1 *forest work:* according to *HCF*, p. 409, probably meaning 'fretwork'. This interpretation is supported by Washington Irving's description of the entrance to the palace (*The Alhambra*, rev. edn., New York, 1852, p. 35).

129: 13 *the conquest of the town of Granada and kingdom:* The last stronghold of the Moors in Spain, Granada was captured in 1492.

129: 28 *the Extraordinary Embassadors' negotiation:* Like Cottington and Hyde, Fanshawe had been sent to Madrid by Charles II to borrow money from Philip IV. On 27 July 1650 Cottington and Hyde wrote a letter to Charles II for Fanshawe, soon to go to France, to deliver to the King. They expressed their inability to gain support from the Spaniards (Clarendon, *State Papers*, ii. 70).

129: 37 *family of the Embassadors:* household of the English Ambassadors, Cottington and Hyde.

129: 38 *caplain:* chaplain.

129: 41–2 *one As[cham] as resident from the then Governor of England:* Antony Ascham, murdered in Madrid, 6 June 1650 (New Style). Hyde describes the episode and its sequel in detail (Clarendon, xiii. 8–16, 25).

130: 8–9 *Mr. Sparkes ... for rescue:* i.e. the Spaniards found William Sparks in a church to which he had gone to take sanctuary.

130: 25 *hectick feavor:* 'hectic fever', 'that kind of fever which accompanies consumption or other wasting diseases, and is attended with flushed cheeks and hot dry skin' (*OED*).

130: 26 *turned his religion:* George, Lord Goring (1608–57) became a Roman Catholic.

131: 7, 25 *sithing: sithed:* sighing, sighed. Cf. p. 125, 'sith'.

132: 16–17 *the King ... on his way for Scotland:* On 1 May 1650 (Old Style) Charles

II signed a treaty with the Scottish Covenanters, arriving in Scotland in June in his effort to recapture England with the military support of the Scots. The campaign reached its disastrous climax at the Battle of Worcester, 3 September 1651.

132: 31 *the 2 partyes in Scotland:* the Royalists, of whom the Marquis of Montrose (executed 21 May 1650) was the military leader, and the Covenanters or 'Kerke party' of Presbyterians.

132: 35–6 *the Princess of Orange and the Princess Royall:* the same person, Charles I's oldest daughter and the mother of the future William III (*HCF*, p. 416).

132: 37 *Sir Edward Hide's nature:* On Lady Fanshawe's hostility to Hyde, see above, p. 112, and n. 112: 1. Lady Fanshawe's account of the episode cannot be accurate because, among other reasons, Hyde was not then in Holland but still in Spain (*HCF*, p. 418).

133: 9 *the Covenant:* an agreement to defend Presbyterianism.

133: 44–134: 1 *2 day of September... Battle of Woster:* The Battle of Worcester, in which the Royalists were routed and from which the King himself had to flee in disguise, was fought on 3 September 1651.

134: 5–6 *their newsbook... a prisonner:* Fanshawe, who had been captured at Newport, 4 September 1651, was named among the prisoners in a list published by Parliament, 9 September, as well as in two journals published at about that time (*HCF*, p. 422).

134: 42–3 *dark lanterne:* 'a lantern with a slide or arrangement by which the light can be concealed' (*OED*).

135: 17 *Sir Henry Vane:* Lady Fanshawe refers to the younger—the son—of that name, who was a member of the Council of State at the time.

135: 20 *the ingagements:* a promise to be faithful to the Commonwealth.

135: 21 *scorbute:* scurvy.

135: 23 *liberty upon bale:* *HCF* (pp. 423–4) prints public records relevant to the government's actions against Fanshawe that substantiate and add detail to the account written by Lady Fanshawe.

135: 32 *patent of baronnett... patent of additional armes:* the latter dated 8 February 1650; the former, 2 September 1650.

135: 34–5 *writ by his own hand in a book:* Lady Fanshawe implies that Sir Richard wrote his own Memoirs. If so, I have found no trace of them.

136: 3 *the Earle of Straford:* the second earl, son of Charles I's executed Minister. See above, p. 122.

136: 6–7 [*were*] *confined... without leave:* presumably a condition of Sir Richard's release on bail.

136: 14–15 *translated Luis de Camoens:* Sir Richard's most important literary work, his translation of Camoens's *Os Lusiadas*, was published in 1655. While at Tankersley, he also translated a Spanish play and a Spanish dramatic entertainment.

136: 33 *five miles of that town:* i.e. out of London.

136: 41–2 *New Year's Day:* Presumably she means 1 January 1655/6. In referring to the date of her own birth, 25 March (above, p. 108), the beginning of a new year in the Old Style calendar, she identifies it as 'Our Lady Day'. On p. 152, below, she describes 1 January as 'New Year's Day'.

137: 8 *hecktick feaver:* see above, n. 130: 25.

137: 15 *quartaine agues:* fevers recurring every fourth day.

137: 18 *anatomy:* skeleton (*OED*).

137: 31–2 *October... news of Cromwell's death:* Cromwell died 3 September 1658. Lady Fanshawe must have written 'October' in error.

137: 34 *my Lord Philip, Earl of Pembrock:* The fifth Earl of Pembroke (1619–69) had taken the Parliamentary side and had held offices under Cromwell. It is perhaps a sign of his political allegiance that he does not address Fanshawe as 'Sir Richard', the baronetcy having been conferred by Charles II.

137: 42 *bonds cancelled:* On 24 September 1658 Sir Richard was granted a pass permitting him to travel abroad (*HCF*, p. 431).
138: 2–3 *journey . . . to Spaine:* In 1659 Charles II travelled by a circuitous route to Spain, for a diplomatic conference at Fuenterrabía near San Sebastían. Cf. *The Letters, Speeches and Declarations of King Charles II*, ed. Sir Arthur Bryant, rev. edn., New York, 1968, pp. 76–8.
138: 35–6 *a Malignant:* i.e. a Royalist.
138: 37–8 *great* H *of Harrison 2* ff*:* In signing her name, Lady Fanshawe customarily used two 'f's' in lower case rather than a single capital letter.
139: 18 *pistole:* a Spanish gold coin, *c.* 1600, worth from 16 shillings and sixpence to 18 shillings in seventeenth-century rates of exchange (*OED*).
139: 40 *in the beginning of November, the King came:* Charles II arrived at Colombe to visit his mother, 5 December 1659, New Style, or 25 November by the Old Style English calender (Clarendon, *State Papers*, iv. 456).
140: 12 *Qween of Bohemia:* James I's daughter (1596–1662). She had been married to the Elector Palatine Frederick V, who subsequently became King of Bohemia. He died in 1632.
140: 14 *the States:* the legislature of Holland.
140: 15–16 *one of the Secrettaryes of State:* Fanshawe expected the appointment. Clarendon, *State Papers*, iv. 470, records under date 5/15 December 1659, Colombe (presumably while Sir Richard and his wife were there to see the King and his mother), the following:

> *Draft* of a warrant for administering the usual oath to Sir Richard Fanshawe appointed to the office of one of the principal secretaries of state, surrendered by George, Earl of Bristol. 2 copies in Fanshawe's hand.

140: 18 *Mr. Morice:* William Morice (1602–76), knighted by the King on his landing in England, owed his appointment as Secretary of State to the recommendation of General Monck, who had consulted him about the restoration of the King (Clarendon, xvi. 162–4, 180, 204).
140: 29 *terse:* a cask holding about forty-two gallons (*OED*).
140: 31 *nets':* 'neats', cattle (*OED*).
140 41–2 *wast clothes:* 'waist-cloth', meaning 'Coloured cloths hung about the upper works of a ship as an adornment on occasions of ceremony . . .' (*OED*).
141: 19 *Secrettary Nickoles:* Sir Edward Nicholas, who had shared the royal exile, had been appointed Secretary of State by Charles II in 1654 (Clarendon, xiv. 106).
141: 21 *the Masters of the Requests:* Fanshawe was one of those who held this office.
141: 39 *Chancellor of the Garter:* Fanshawe became Deputy Chancellor of the Order of the Garter, 14 January 1661 (*HCF*, p. 444).
142: 4–5 *the King . . . his pleasure:* This is the single instance in which Lady Fanshawe even by implication is critical of the King.
142: 8–9 *the King's letter and picture to the Princess, now our Qween:* After prolonged diplomatic negotiations, the King was married to Catherine of Braganza *in absentia* by a treaty signed and ratified during the summer of 1661. In a letter of 2 July 1661 addressed to her in Lisbon, he refers to Fanshawe's imminent departure for Portugal (*Letters . . . of Charles II*, ed. Bryant, p. 115). Presumably Fanshawe's knowledge of Spanish, which would have been intelligible to the Portuguese, and his prestige as translator of *Os Lusiadas* were considerations in the selection of him for the mission.

The King's letter to his bride and his instructions to Fanshawe are printed in *Heathcote Manuscripts*, pp. 17–22.
142: 21 *my Lord and Lady of Ormond:* The Duke of Ormond was then Lord-Lieutenant of Ireland.
142: 23 *fosset:* facet.
142: 29–32 *the Qween landing . . . the King married the Qween:* Queen Catherine with her retinue arrived at Portsmouth 13 May 1662 in a squadron commanded by the Earl

of Sandwich. Although the marriage treaty had already been signed and ratified, Catherine and Charles were married, 21 May, in two religious ceremonies, one Roman Catholic and the other Anglican (David Ogg, *England in the Reign of Charles II*, Oxford, 1963, p. 188).

143: 9–10 *embassador to Portugall:* As Ambassador, Fanshawe had responsibility for ensuring Portugal's compliance with the terms of the King's marriage treaty, by which England gained major commercial advantages.

On 21 June/1 July 1662, Lionel Fanshawe, Sir Richard's nephew and secretary, had sent Fanshawe from Lisbon an account of the current state of affairs in the Portuguese Court. He referred to the military danger to Portugal from Spain (Clarendon, *State Papers*, v. 230–1).

143: 21 *a Bible in Oglosby's print and cuts:* John Ogilby (1600–76) specialized in fine printing and engraving.

143: 25 *perfected:* completed.

143: 31 *Doctor Heavers:* identified in the list of Sir Richard's chaplains following the Memoirs in the manuscript of 1676 as 'Preband & Vicar of Windser, and fellow of Eton College'.

143: 43 *my Lord Herbert:* presumably the eldest son of the fifth Earl of Pembroke, whom Sir Richard had escorted to France in 1658. See above, p. 137.

144: 4 *Dr. Hollis: HCF* (p. 456) notes that this name must have been written in error: Dr. Baylie was Dean of Salisbury at the time.

144: 34–5 *my father's score . . . farmers of the Custome House:* Her father, Sir John Harrison (*c.* 1589–1669), had accumulated great wealth before the Wars as a customs farmer. His war-time losses were heavy, but he recovered part of his fortune after the Restoration (Keeler, pp. 205–6).

145: 9 *where my husband . . . when he was there before:* in the autumn of 1661, when Sir Richard had been in Portugal to assist in preparations for Charles II's marriage to Catherine of Braganza. 'His Majesty' refers to the King of Portugal, Alfonso VI.

145: 10 *his chief secretary:* Sir Richard's cousin Lionel Fanshawe (*Heathcote Manuscripts*, pp. 25–6).

145: 14 *the Earle of Insequeen:* The Earl of Inchiquin was in command of a small body of English troops that Charles II had sent to aid Portugal in her war with Spain.

145: 15 *Count Scomberg:* Count Schomberg was in command of French troops sent by Louis XIV to aid the Portuguese. He subsequently commanded the English troops as well.

145: 17–18 *Qween Mother's:* The Queen Mother, Dona Luisa, was the mother of Charles II's wife as well as of the King of Portugal.

145: 39 *ewry:* ewer.

145: 40 *Stilo Novo:* New Style, referring to the Gregorian calendar in use on the Continent.

145: 44 *viador:* 'an official invested with inspecting or controlling power' (*OED*).

146: 1 *Her Majesty:* i.e. the Queen Mother.

146: 16 *with a state of the same:* a canopy of black velvet.

146: 32 *She loved government:* The Queen Mother had been Regent during the minority of her son.

146: 37 *one of his pages:* see above, p. 145.

146: 42–3 *his son an English baron: HCF* (p. 462) writes that Lady Fanshawe is in error in asserting that Charles I had made the Secretary of State's (Antonio de Sousa's) son an English baron.

147: 43 *aguish distemper:* an illness characterized by successive fits of chills and fever.

148: 1 *Frontigniack:* grapes of a variety grown in Frontignan.

148: 3–4 *an insurrection of the people in the town:* In a letter of 20/30 May 1663 to Sir Henry Bennet, Fanshawe described the insurrection in detail, suggesting that the motives leading to it were patriotic (*Heathcote Manuscripts*, pp. 92–7).

148: 17–18 *Portugese's poverty and Lord Chancellor Hide's neglect:* On 21/31 October 1662 Fanshawe wrote to Clarendon, expressing his lack of confidence in Portuguese military leadership and strength. The King of Portugal had stated that without English financial aid he could not maintain the English troops who were in the service of his country (*Heathcote Manuscripts*, pp. 37–9).
148: 21–2 *great assistance to . . . the Earle of Petterborow:* Apart from a letter of greeting Fanshawe wrote from Lisbon 19/29 June 1663 when the Earl of Peterborough put ashore briefly on the Portuguese coast as he returned to England (*Heathcote Manuscripts*, p. 120), Fanshawe's surviving diplomatic correspondence reveals no association between them at this period.
148: 33 *voyders:* 'voider', 'a tray, basket or large plate' (*OED*).
149: 10 *mine:* here used in a phrase which is a Gallicism, to make a 'mien': i.e. she expressed displeasure in her countenance.
149: 31 *ressentment:* sense of loss.
150: 12 *quintes*: *quinta*, a 'rural residence' or 'villa'.
150: 31–2 *the 4th of September . . . at Deale:* In September 1663 Sir Richard wrote a report to Charles II on his embassy to Portugal. He described the defeat of the Spanish army commanded by Don John of Austria, and he praised the courage shown by the English troops who had fought in support of the Portuguese (Clarendon, *State Papers*, v. 332).
151: 32 *upon the same invitation*: i.e. also upon her sister Turner's invitation.
151: 35 *titio:* probably meaning 'tissue' though *OED* does not record this spelling. In the seventeenth century, 'tissue' meant 'A rich kind of cloth, often interwoven with gold or silver' (*OED*). The word is used again, in variant spellings, on pp. 159 and 160.
152: 5 *His Royall Highnesse:* the Duke of York, later James II.
152: 31 *cabboord:* cupboard.
152: 39 *voyage for Spain:* Charles II's 'letter of credence for Sir Richard Fanshaw' addressed to Philip IV of Spain bears the date 13 January 1663/4 (*Heathcote Manuscripts*, p. 140).
153: 32 *Mr. Witcherly:* Although proof is lacking, this was probably William Wycherley the dramatist, whose first two plays, *Love in a Wood* (*c.* 1671) and *The Gentleman Dancing-Master* (*c.* 1672) include borrowings from plays by Calderón de la Barca that had not been translated into either English or French. See John Loftis, *The Spanish Plays of Neoclassical England* (New Haven, Conn., 1973), pp. 121–2.
154: 33 *Admirall of that fleet:* 'Admiral-ship: The ship which carries the admiral; the flagship' (*OED*).
154: 38 *catch:* 'ketch', 'a strongly-built vessel . . ., usually two-masted, and of from 100 to 250 tons burden' (*OED*).
154: 43 *roade:* roadstead; anchorage.
155: 6 *Levant wind:* wind from the east.
156: 2 *covered:* i.e. had his hat on.
156: 2–6 *I am Don Juan . . . whom God long preserve:* Wycherley in *Love in a Wood* (Act IV) includes a jocular allusion to the pomposity of the names and titles printed in 'Spanish Epistles Dedicatory'.
156: 9 *suddenly*: shortly.
156: 27 *word:* password.
157: 5 *voyders:* see above, n. 148: 33.
157: 20 *putting me into every doore:* letting me go first through every door.
157: 39 *flaggons:* large wine bottles.
157: 39 *Lusena wine:* 'came from a place of that name near Puerto Santa Maria' (*HCF*, p. 487).
157: 40 *pieces of 8:* large silver coins worth eight smaller coins called *reales*.
158: 33 *glazed:* fitted with glass windows.
159: 1 *titius:* probably 'tissue'. See above, p. 151, and below, p. 160.

159: 6 *bravery:* splendid and valuable objects.

159: 20 *Duke:* in the singular presumably referring to the father, the Duke of Medina Celi.

159: 26 *the Corijedio:* the *Corregidor* or chief magistrate.

159: 41 *brave:* excellent.

159: 43 *Assistant: Asistente*, at Seville, the chief officer of justice.

160: 16–17 *Sivilla, though now much decayd:* During the fifteenth and sixteenth centuries, the city port of Seville prospered because of its trade with America. After the reign of Philip II (d. 1598), it declined in importance and wealth.

160: 19 *vallans:* valance, a short drapery.

160: 23 *brasera: brasero*, brazier.

160: 34 *India cabinetts of Japan:* cabinets from India, varnished and perhaps ornamented in a Japanese manner.

161: 1 *30th of this present:* 30 March 1664.

161:1 *Malagoe merchants of the English:* The context implies that these were Spanish merchants of Malaga who traded with the English.

161: 5 *sasnett:* sarcenet, 'a very fine and soft silk material made both plain and twilled, in various colours' (*OED*).

161: 7 *fillagrana:* filigree, a delicate kind of jewel work.

161: 21 *honor:* 'a seigniory of several manors held under one baron or lord paramount' (*OED*).

161: 34 *brave:* splendid.

161: 38–9 *jogo de los toros . . . jogo de canas:* Sir Edward Hyde wrote a detailed account of these sports as he observed them in Madrid in 1649 (Clarendon, xii. 89–90).

161: 44 *amber and orange water:* perfume.

162: 5 *Don Lewis de Haro:* Don Luis de Haro had been the most influential figure in Spanish politics for nearly twenty years before his death in 1661.

162: 38 *the Duke de Medina les Tores:* Since the death of Don Luis de Haro in 1661, the Duke of Medina de las Torres had been one of the most powerful figures, if not indeed the most powerful, in the Spanish government.

162: 39 *Aranjuez:* site of one of the royal palaces. Sir Richard and his family visited the palace in October 1665.

163: 16 *so straitoned in my lodgings:* In a letter, 7 May 1664 (New Style), to Sir Henry Bennet, Fanshawe attributed the lack of an adequate residence for himself and his family to the shortage of houses in Madrid (Sir Richard Fanshawe, *Original Letters*, London, 1702, pp. 63–4; repr. in *N*, pp. 321–2).

163: 24–5 *No ambassadore's coach . . . but the French:* on 20 June 1664 (New Style) Fanshawe wrote at length about the episode to Lord Holles, English Ambassador to France. Fanshawe expressed his own gratitude to the French Ambassador, though he reported to Lord Holles that some observers in Madrid thought the French had an ulterior motive (Fanshawe, *Original Letters*, pp. 106–10; repr. in *N*, pp. 326–9). On 12 August (New Style) Fanshawe wrote to Sir Henry Bennet, reporting subsequent diplomatic exchanges resulting from the episode (Fanshawe, *Original Letters*, pp. 199–203; repr. in *N*, pp. 338–41).

163: 44 *camaradoes: camarada*, 'comrade', 'companion'.

164: 1 *Mr. Wicherly:* probably the dramatist, William Wycherley. See above n. 153: 32.

164: 5 *fillemoate:* a corrupted and anglicized form of the French *feuille morte*, here meaning 'brown or yellowish brown' (*OED*).

164: 11 *beavour button:* a button made of a heavy cotton or wool fabric.

164: 17 *family:* retinue.

164: 27 *falls of the bootes:* ornaments made of textiles attached to the steps of the coach.

165: 6–7 *being covered . . . his message:* Sir Richard wore his hat, as the representative of the King of England to the King of Spain.

165: 26 *private audience with His Catholick Majesty:* On 15 June 1664 (Old Style) Fanshawe wrote a report to Sir Henry Bennet of his private audience with the King. At this time Fanshawe opened discussion on the objectives of his embassy: the negotiation of a peace treaty with Spain and the resumption of trade between England and Spain. He reported to Bennet that he had been compelled to speak briefly because of the condition of the King's health (*N*, pp. 329–30).

165: 28 *Buen Retiro:* a palace built by Philip IV near the present site of the Prado museum.

165: 30 *Carmareiro Mayor:* principal chamberlain.

165: 35 *sate downe—again:* That Lady Fanshawe herself was still standing is implied by the Queen's telling her to sit, after she had presented her children.

166: 8–9 *the House of Sietta Chimineas:* 'the house of seven chimneys'. The Ambassador of Venice wished to retain it for his successor. In a letter to Sir Henry Bennet, 28 July 1664 (Old Style), Fanshawe states that the Duke of Medina de las Torres procured the house for him (Fanshawe, *Original Letters*, pp. 178–81; repr. in *N*, pp. 335–7).

166: 30 *the Duke:* the Duke of Medina de las Torres.

166: 34 *tanajas:* the Spanish word is *tinaja.*

166: 38–9 *the vellon money to the half:* The *vellón* was a copper coin. The drastic devaluation of currency is an indication of the financial weakness of the Spanish government at the end of Philip IV's reign.

167: 2 *hermitages:* secluded residences.

167: 6 *the Escuriall: El Escorial*, the famous palace of Philip II. Construction was begun in 1563 and completed in 1584.

167: 25 *branches:* chandeliers, especially of the kind used in churches (*OED*). See also l. 41.

167: 35–6 *eight squares . . . 60 foot over:* A 'square' was a hundred square feet (*OED*). The phrase '60 foot over' is ambiguous: perhaps it refers to the distance from floor to ceiling.

168: 7 *stillitoryes:* 'stillatory', a distillery (*OED*).

168: 16 *office:* a kitchen and adjacent rooms, such as a pantry and a scullery (*OED*).

168: 18–19 *Titian . . . Battle of Lepantho:* Lady Fanshawe was in error in attributing to Titian the painting of the Battle of Lepanto (*HCF*, p. 511). The battle was the famous victory of 7 October 1571 when a fleet commanded by Don John of Austria (1545–78), natural son of the Emperor Charles V, defeated a Turkish fleet.

168: 41 *admire:* regard with wonder.

168: 44 *described in a book:* The book is identified by *HCF* (p. 511) as written by 'El P. F. Francisco de los Santos', printed in Madrid, 1657, at the Royal Press.

169: 7 *could not receive . . . the ladys:* while residing at Vallecas. See above, p. 163.

169: 20–4 *we lett our dispense . . . beginning this day:* an obscure passage, elucidated by *HCF* (p. 159). Officials of the Court, including ambassadors, were entitled to a daily allowance of food. Lady Fanshawe refers to the entitlement as 'our dispense' and describes the financial terms of an agreement, made with an agent of the Court, in satisfaction of it.

169: 25–6 *a very great blazing star:* On 14 December 1664 (Old Style) Fanshawe described the comet in a letter to Sir Henry Bennet, assuming—correctly—that it was also visible in England (Fanshawe, *Original Letters*, pp. 375–7; repr. in *N*, pp. 346–7). Another comet came into view the following spring. See below, p. 175.

169: 41–3 *a show . . . the horses could run:* a 'jogo de canas' similar to that mentioned above, p. 161.

170: 2 *entresuelo:* mezzanine.

170: 11 *the buenas pasquas: dar las buenas pasquas* means, approximately, 'to wish a merry Christmas'.

171: 13–14 *one As*[*cham*], *an agent of Oliver's:* See above, p. 129.

171: 33 *the chief minister of state in our countrey:* the Lord Chancellor, Clarendon. Although there is no record of the response in London to this episode, after Sir Richard had had a similar dispute with the President of Castile in October 1665, Clarendon wrote to him, expressing disapproval of his course of action (*HCF*, pp. 515–16). Sir Keith Feiling considers such episodes to have been partially responsible for Fanshawe's recall: 'The [English] government found him tactless and unbusiness-like, particularly lamenting his zeal in pushing . . . a feud with the Madrid police' (*British Foreign Policy, 1660–1672*, London, 1930, p. 176).
172: 4 *oskeveche: escabeche*, pickled fish.
172: 6 *nattuos: nata*, cream.
172: 11 *manger blanc:* 'blancmange', a dessert made of milk and starchy or gelatinous food.
172: 27 *stealing . . . their silver aboord:* i.e. so that the merchants would not have to pay customs for it.
172: 37 *a kennel:* a gutter.
172: 43 *animosityes concerning place:* i.e. concerning rank or precedence.
173: 6 *castelliates:* castanets.
173: 7 *rarely well:* remarkably well.
173: 17 *chenny:* 'cheney', i.e. china (*OED*).
173: 20 *stadge plays:* This provides a reminder that the golden age of Spanish drama had not ended. (Calderón de la Barca lived until 1681.)
174: 9 *Mr. Wicherly:* See above, p. 153. If this man was indeed the dramatist, he spent approximately a year in Spain.
175: 13 *parabien:* congratulation.
175: 16 *a new blazing starr:* the second comet visible in Madrid in less than six months. See above, p. 169.
175: 28 *the death of . . . my Lord Fanshawe:* Sir Richard's oldest brother, the first Viscount Fanshawe, died 26 March 1665 (Old Style).
175: 38–9 *the totall route of the . . . army:* Lady Fanshawe does not exaggerate the extent of the defeat of the Spanish army by the Portuguese and their English allies. Philip IV was left with very little military power.
175: 42–3 *our victory against the Dutch:* In a naval battle during the Second Dutch War. The English fleet was commanded by the Duke of York.
176: 8 *Thursday the 10th of* [*August*]*:* The 10th (four days after the birth of the child) was a Thursday in the Old Style calendar.
176: 27–35 *dyed Philip the 4th . . . Charles the 2d:* On Philip's death at the age of sixty, his four-year-old son by his second wife (and niece), Maria Anna of Austria, succeeded him as Charles II. It is a consequence of Lady Fanshawe's reverence for royalty that at no time does she allude to the child-king's physical and mental weakness.

On the day of Philip IV's death, 7/17 September 1665, Sir Richard wrote a detailed account of it to Lord Arlington, as Sir Henry Bennet had become (B. L. Harleian MS. 7010, fos. 388–9; printed in *N*, pp. 352–4).
177: 14 *gollila: golilla*, a collar or ruff, worn in Spain by some magistrates.
177: 40 *the Sumiller de Corps:* the Lord Chamberlain.
178: 7 *Cuerpo:* Having used the French word *Corps* earlier in this paragraph, Lady Fanshawe here uses the Spanish equivalent, *Cuerpo*, meaning 'body'.
178: 9 *franca:* privileged or exempt. The context suggests that the Prior demanded assurance the body was 'privileged' to be buried in the Pantheon.
178: 12 *infants:* here presumably having the specialized meaning of *infantas*, daughters of kings of Spain, or *infantes*, sons of kings of Spain.
178: 16 *pessaine: pésame*, 'condolence'.
178: 32 *Discaelas Raeles: Descalzas Reales*, a convent built as a residence for dowager queens (*HCF*, pp. 181, 539).
178: 37 *parabien of his años:* birthday greetings.

178: 39 *a[y]a:* governess.
178: 43–179: 3 *the peace between England and Spaine . . . the Earl of Sandwiche:* The treaty of peace, 7/17 December, the negotiation of which was Sir Richard's primary mission in Spain, was a provisional one that was never ratified. It is a matter of dispute whether Sir Richard acted prematurely in signing the treaty when he did, a subject complicated by the extended time required for and the difficulties of communication with London. In any event, his signing the treaty was not the reason for his recall. As early as 6 December 1665, Samuel Pepys wrote in his diary that the Duke of Albemarle had told him that Lord Sandwich was soon to go to Spain as Ambassador (*Heathcote Manuscripts*, Introduction, pp. xv–xvii; *HCF*, pp. 234–51. Feiling considers Fanshawe to have acted injudiciously: *British Foreign Policy*, pp. 172–9).

Although Clarendon acquiesced in the recall of Fanshawe, he wrote what is—in the main—an approbatory account of Fanshawe's embassies to both Portugal and Spain, reporting that the Portuguese had wished Fanshawe to be sent as English ambassador to Spain (*The Life of . . . Clarendon . . . A Continuation*, 'Written by Himself', Oxford, 1759, pp. 307–9).

179: 5 *cowardise in the Dutch fight:* Lady Fanshawe refers to Lord Sandwich's alleged lack of success as commander of the English fleet against the Dutch in the summer and autumn of 1665. He had been accused of insufficient aggressiveness—or worse—in his command of the fleet. He had also been accused of appropriating, for himself and his fellow flag officers, valuable cargo taken from captured ships.
179: 22 *a truce . . . Spaine and Portugall:* Because of the alliance between England and Portugal that came with Charles II's marriage to Catherine of Braganza, a treaty of peace between England and Spain had to include terms relating to the continuing war between Spain and Portugal.
179: 23–5 *an hundred thousand . . . 50 thousand pieces of 8:* The terms of this large grant—which proved to be merely the promise of a grant—are confirmed in a letter of 4/14 January 1666 to Sir Richard by the Duke and Count of Oñate (*Heathcote Manuscripts*, p. 222).
179: 33–4 *12th day, English accompt . . . from Madrid to Portugall:* 6/16 January was 'Twelfth Night' in England. Sir Richard went to Portugal in an effort to persuade the Portuguese to accept the terms of the peace treaty. For a critical account of his mission, see Feiling, *British Foreign Policy*, pp. 177–8.
179: 36 *machos:* male mules.
180: 7 *sumpters:* beasts of burden such as mules or pack horses.
180: 25 *mo[z]o:* 'youth', here meaning a muleteer.
180: 25 *sobrestante:* overseer.
180: 26 *alquazil:* constable.
180: 37 *a letter from . . . Toledo:* Sir Richard's letter from Toledo, dated 8/18 January, expresses optimism concerning his forthcoming negotiations in Portugal for a peace with Spain. At that date he did not know of the decision made in London to send Lord Sandwich to replace him. However, Lady Fanshawe, writing to her husband 18/28 January, reported to him that she had heard rumours about the English decision from the Duke of Medina de las Torres (*Heathcote Manuscripts*, pp. 223, 224–7).
181: 19 *Sir Robert Southwell:* An able young diplomat whose father Sir Richard had known in Ireland, Southwell had been sent from London to provide assistance in the difficult negotiations for a peace between Portugal and Spain. He had arrived in Lisbon at the same time Sir Richard left Madrid for Portugal, and he accompanied Sir Richard on the latter's return to Madrid (*HCF*, pp. 545–7; Feiling, *British Foreign Policy*, pp. 177–8).
181: 23 *the Earl of Sandwich's arrivall:* On 11/21 February, before his return from his journey to Portugal, Sir Richard had written to the Duke of Medina de las Torres about Lord Sandwich's coming. He requested that the new ambassador be received as cordially as he himself had been (*Heathcote Manuscripts*, p. 236).

181: 32 *his son:* i.e. Lord Sandwich's son.
182: 28 *amber pastills:* rolls or cones of aromatic paste, burned as a disinfectant.
182: 30 *silver box of philagrania:* a silver box with delicate ornamentation, perhaps of beads.
182: 32 *Almirante:* admiral.
182: 40–183: 2 *Her Imperiall Majesty's family . . . the Emperor by proxy:* The Infanta was married by proxy to the Emperor Leopold I.
183: 37 *Descalsas Reales:* a convent. See above, n. 178: 32.
183: 37 *the Atocke:* a church, the Basilica de Nuestra Señora de Atocha (*HCF*, p. 557).
184: 21–3 *the Earl of Sandwich . . . to the Qween Regent of this kingdome:* On 22 May/1 June Sir Richard wrote to the Duke of Medina de las Torres, requesting that the Duke arrange a private audience for Lord Sandwich with the Queen Mother—the Regent—as soon as possible (*Heathcote Manuscripts*, p. 253). Sir Richard seems to have comported himself in an exemplary manner in what must have been an embarrassing situation for him.
184: 31 *White Sunday:* Whitsunday, the seventh Sunday after Easter.
184: 32 *the Earle of Sandwich . . . private audience:* In a letter to Clarendon, 5/15 July, Sandwich reported that he had discussed the proposed treaty of peace with Fanshawe before his death (Clarendon, *State Papers*, v. 550).
184: 38 *a malignant inward feavour:* In the same letter of 5/15 July, Sandwich attributed Fanshawe's fatal illness to 'a careless sleeping in cold air'.
184: 41–185: 16 Lollio *Thou art . . . doth not fear:* Sir Richard's own translation of Horace, *Odes* 4.9.34–52.
186: 5 *was buryed by his own chaplaine:* meaning that the chaplain conducted a funeral service. Sir Richard was not literally buried until his body reached England. The chaplain, the Rev. Dr. Henry Bagshawe, published his funeral sermon in 1667.
186: 21 *turne our religion:* It is presumably this offer by the Queen Mother to which Lady Fanshawe refers above (p. 185) when she writes that she was under 'temptation of the change of my religion'.
186: 33 *the Ambassador:* i.e. Lord Sandwich.
186: 40–1 *lumber of the house:* miscellaneous discarded household articles including furniture. In a letter to Clarendon, 5/15 July, Sandwich alluded to the purchase (Clarendon, *State Papers*, v. 550).
187: 26 *The Qween Mother:* presumably Henrietta Maria, the mother of Charles II of England, and the aunt of Louis XIV.
187: 33 *the burning of London:* the Great Fire of London, 2–6 September 1666 (Old Style).
188: 31–3 *His Royall Highness . . . a ship:* the Duke of York was Lord High Admiral.
188: 34 *the Duchesse:* the Duke of York's first wife, Anne Hyde, daughter of the Earl of Clarendon.
188: 37 *Duke of Cambridge:* the son of the Duke of York, born 1663 and died 1667.
188: 37 *amber skins:* The meaning is obscure. Probably Lady Fanshawe refers to small containers made of animal skin and filled with ambergis, a perfume.
189: 3–4 *which I could never fasten on my Lord:* In view of her hostility to Lord Arlington, she presumably means that she could not credit him with receiving authorization, 'without fee or present', for payment of the money due to her.
189: 6–7 *good man . . . my Lord Southhampton:* the Lord Treasurer, who died 16 May 1667. For details concerning the financial settlement made with Lady Fanshawe, see *HCF*, pp. 575–81.
189: 15–16 *though I had* poured *it down his throat:* The reason for her intense hostility to Lord Shaftesbury is not known. (The name *Fanshawe* does not appear in the index of the detailed and excellent biography of him by Kenneth H. D. Haley, *The First Earl of Shaftesbury*, Oxford, 1968.)

190: 7 *my Lord Fanshawe:* Sir Richard's nephew, the second Viscount.
190: 26 *my talleyes placed again by the Commissioners:* Lady Fanshawe apparently refers to an approval by the Commissioners of the Treasury of the warrant for payment to her. Probably the original authorization had been nullified by the death of the Lord Treasurer, 16 May 1667.
190: 32–3 *when God took my father:* Her father died in 1669 (Keeler, pp. 205–6). Lady Fanshawe twice misstates the date: on p. 110 above she gives it as 1671 and on p. 191 below as 1670. In each of these cases the date has been emended in this edition to 1669.
190: 34 *Sir Philip Waricke:* Lady Fanshawe's brother-in-law.
191: 7–8 *Lord Fanshawe sold Ware Park . . . a bruer of London:* Lady Fanshawe's simple statement provides a striking illustration of the irreversible consequences of the Civil Wars for many wealthy Royalists.
191: 15–16 *the lordships of Tring and Hiching . . . held of Qween Mother:* A record, dated 25 February 1669, of Lady Fanshawe's surrender of the leases of the two manors is printed in *Heathcote Manuscripts*, p. 256.
191: 34–6 *gave me 3000 pounds . . . to make my sister Harrison a jointer:* Apparently Lady Fanshawe means that her father gave her sister or one of her sisters-in-law the manor for a jointure or marriage settlement and in order to make equal his gifts to his daughters gave Lady Fanshawe £3,000.
192: 16 *the King shut up the:* Lady Fanshawe's narrative breaks off abruptly at this point, at the end of p. 216 in the original pagination. Although she misdates the event, she refers to a suspension of payments by the Exchequer, 2 January 1672.

TEXTUAL NOTES

Lady Halkett, *Memoirs*

The numerals preceding the colons refer to pages; the numerals following, to lines.

10: 8	f[ather]: *conjecture by JGN*
10: 10–11	the temptations: them temptations
10: 13	[unmove]able: *JGN*
12: 20	k[in]: k.
13: 8	conventt: conentt
13: 21	unreasonable: unreasonble
13: 35	scarce: scare
16: 8	[time]: *JGN*
17: 3	impertunity: *an interlineation over* deficulty, *which is cancelled*
17: 4	rogue: rouge
18: 5	intreat: *an interlineation under* desire, *which is cancelled*
18: 33	[have]: *JGN*
19: 8	all: *substituted for* both, *which is cancelled*
19: 12–13	(This was upon ... October, 1644.): *An asterisk is placed after* quiettly. *The sentence is written at the bottom of the page in Lady Halkett's hand.*
20: 1–2	fourteene: *The arabic numeral* 14 *is written above the word.*
20: 3	reproach: reprach
20: 6	and: an
23: 5	Countese of B.: *The full name* Banbury *is written, but all letters except* B *are cancelled.*
23: 6	[one leaf (two pages) missing]: *For discussion of the missing leaf, see the Introduction and the Note on the Text.*
23: 16	I approved of his advise: *The word* much *following* approved *is cancelled.*
23: 39	Majestie: Majesties
23: 40–4	I believe it ... what you doe: *The sentence is written in a script that is larger than usual.*
24: 6	stay: *an interlineation over* being, *which is cancelled*
25: 22	off: of
26: 8	and: an
27: 6	C. B.: *written as an interlineation over* him, *which is cancelled*
28: 32	of: off
30: 17	[he]: *JGN*
31: 1	scearch: scearh
31: 32	live with a gentleman: private *after the word* live *is cancelled.*
32: 4	[that]: *JGN*
34: 12	[him]: *JGN*
35: 30	given: giving
36: 27	too: two
36: 34	All I concluded att that time was: *Following* concluded, of was *is cancelled*; was *is written as an interlineation after* time.
36: 36	protestations: protestation
40: 16	too: to
41: 40	hapened: hapenened
43: 10	Mr. N.: *The full name* Nicolls *is written, but all letters except* N *are cancelled.*
43: 36	could: *an interlineation over* can, *which is cancelled*

44: 8 [the]: *JGN*
45: 22–3 strangenese from my Lady H. to mee: *altered by interlineations from* strangenese betwixt my Lady H. and mee
45: 34 whisper: whispers
46: 26 posess: poses
48: 17 fight: fights
48: 22 considerations: consideration
50: 36 Thursday, 6 June 1650: *written in the margin*
55: 27 [ ]: *left blank*
55: 39 [he]: *JGN*
56: 7 [it]: *JGN*
56: 16 an: and
57: 5 itt, [and though] hee: itt that hee
63: 2 having taken: having taking
63: 11 and: a
64: 33 lawier: lawiers
64: 37 too: to
65: 37 him: them
66: 18 Crew came backe: againe *following* backe *is cancelled.*
66: 34 anything: *changed from* something *by an interlineation*
67: 26 him, are: him and are
68: 4 Lord: Lords
68: 26 the English hands: *changed from* there hands *by an interlineation*
69: 21 Lady: Ladys
71: 34 Lord: Lords
72: 33 [one leaf (two pages) missing]: *For discussion of the missing leaf, see the Introduction and the Note on the Text.*
73: 7 next day to Belcarese: to goe *following* day *is cancelled.*
73: 23 [ ]: *left blank*
77: 7 pleaded, for hee: itt *following* pleaded *is cancelled.*
79: 37 [ ]: *left blank*
79: 41 [ ]: *left blank*
80: 28 considerations: consideration
81: 24 Will: Wills
82: 6 I said I thought: to him *following* I said *is cancelled.*
82: 14 nott pretend: now *following* pretend *is cancelled.*
82: 16 not: now
82: 25 from that time to this: *The date* Jan. 8, [16]77/8. *is written in the margin, apparently referring to the time at which Lady Halkett was writing this portion of her Memoirs.*
83: 20 was: *The word is written over* came.
83: 20 disapointmentt came to: from another *following* came *is cancelled.*
83: 43 nesesary: *written as an interlineation over* fitt, *which is cancelled*
84: 19 (2 Cor. xi. 31): *written in the margin opposite the quotation*
85: 26 to Mr. Neale): yet and he *following* Neale) *is cancelled.*
85: 26 to have: to had
85: 35 ——: *The number is missing.*
86: 19 travailer: *written as an interlineation over* passenger, *which is cancelled*
87: 44 promise to have: *Here the Memoirs breaks off, at the end of page 261 in the original pagination.*

TEXTUAL NOTES

Lady Fanshawe, *Memoirs*

For reasons that will be apparent from a reading of 'A Note on the Text' (above, pp. 91–93), it would not be profitable even if it were possible to undertake a systematic collation of my text with those prepared by the three earlier editors. However, the earlier editors, at least two of whom had access to family records that are no longer available, provide aid in emendation of certain words or passages, particularly in identifying proper names that are unrecognizable in the spelling of the manuscript. Accordingly, I list the readings of the earlier editors in instances in which I have adopted an emendation first proposed by one of them.

The numerals preceding the colons refer to pages; the numerals following, to lines.

102: 13 *After the word* occasions *a line is drawn across the page to mark a separation between Lady Fanshawe's personal address to her son and the beginning of the Memoirs.*

104: 43 [Darley]: *HCF*; Hardine *MS*, *N*; Harding *M*

106: 17 E[velyn]: *N*, *M*, *HCF*; Eulin *MS*

106: 17 [Wray]: *HCF*; Rey *MS*; Wrey *N*, *M*

107: 2 third: second *in MS. It is underlined and in the margin is corrected to* third.

107: 18 *An extra space follows this paragraph to indicate a change of subject.*

108: 10 Cam[pbell]: *M*, *HCF*; Camden *MS*, *N*

109: 15 [Hezekiah]: *N*, *M*, *HCF*; Ezekious *MS*

110: 5 16[69]: *HCF*; 1671 *MS*; 1670 *N*, *M*

111: 2 [Queensborough]: *HCF*; Garinborow *MS: left blank N*, *M*

111: 4 [Nott]ingham: *N*, *M*, *HCF*; Hollingham *MS*

111: 5 *The figure* 50000 *is carefully written, apparently by Lady Fanshawe, as an interlineation above a cancelled word that is illegible.*

113: 6 B[erkeley]: *M*, *HCF*; Bartly *MS*; Bartley *N*

113: 7 [about two]: seven *MS*, *HCF*; some *N*, *M*

113: 9 163[5]: *HCF*; 1630 *MS*, *N*, *M*

114: 8 [1645]: *N*, *M*, *HCF*; 44 *MS*

115: 34 [Aubigny]: *N*, *M*, *HCF*; Obeney *MS*

115: 35 [Isabella]: *HCF*; Esel *MS*; Isabel *N*, *M*

117: 24 [Grenvile]: *HCF*; Prinville *MS*; Greville *N*; Granville *M*

119: 5 1646: *The date is an interlineation, corrected from* 1644. *A note is written in the margin, in an early hand:* 2.1645. *After the word* my *an asterisk is inserted, referring to a note at the bottom of the page:* She means her first Daughter Vid. Page 65 [*present text, p. 129*] a similar mistake. *The note in the margin may refer to the birth date of her first son, 23 February 1645.*

119: 17 Ca[en]: *N*, *M*, *HCF*; Cane *MS*

120: 8–9 In that year . . . in the least, but upon: *The passage is cancelled. It is restored, in a much later hand, on a small interleaf.*

120: 12 B[erke]ley: *N*, *M*, *HCF*; Bartley *MS*

121: 35 [Nov]ember: *M*, *HCF*; December *MS*, *N*

121: 42–3 my eldest daughter . . . with many toys: *The passage is cancelled. It is restored, in a much later hand, on a small interleaf.*

122: 3 164[8]: *HCF*; 1649 *MS*, *N*, *M*

122: 7 Ke[nelm]: *N*, *M*, *HCF*; Kellam *MS*

122: 25 h[oy]: *N*, *M*, *HCF*; huye *MS*

123: 16 R[upert]: *N*, *M*, *HCF*; Robert *MS*

123: 26–7 [Octo]ber 16[49]: *HCF*; Nov. 1650 *MS*, *N*, *M*

124: 11 [Octo]ber: *HCF*; November *MS*, *N*, *M*

124: 13 worth 100 lb.: *The figure* 100 *is not clear. It seems to have been corrected from* 300. *HCF prints* three hundred pounds (*p. 55*).

126: 33–41 but we could not rest . . . spots made by them: *The passage is cancelled. It is restored, in a much later hand, on two small interleaves.*

128: 35 ro[ofed]: *N*, *M*, *HCF*; roughed *MS*

129: 3–5 'Until that hand . . . possess the Allhambray': *This passage, here within quotation marks, is written in a larger script than the usual.*

129: 21 16[50]: *N*, *M*, *HCF*; 1649 *MS*

129: 24 *first: The word is underlined and prefixed by an asterisk, referring to a note, in an early hand, at the bottom of the page:* She means her second Daughter. *Another note, in pencil and in a much later hand, is added:* She meant her *first* of the name of Elizabeth.

129: 41 As[cham]: *HCF*; Askew *MS*, *N*, *M*

131: 23–9 We praised God . . . discourse and wearynes: *The passage is cancelled. It is restored, in a much later hand, on a small interleaf.*

133: 40 24 of June: *In the margin the year is recorded in an early hand*: 1651.

134: 27 ha[ve]: *N*, *M*, *HCF*; had *MS*

135: 39 wa[ked]: *HCF*; walked *MS*, *N*, *M*

136: 6 [were]: *HCF*; *om. MS*; were so *N*, *M*

136: 15 1653: *The same date is written again, in an early hand, in the margin.*

136: 22 1654: *The same date is written again, in an early hand, in the margin.*

136: 37 [1655]: 54 *in MS. The date is written in the margin as* 1654/5.

136: 40 [16]55: *The date is written in the margin, in an early hand, as* 1655.

137: 1 C[arey]: *M*, *HCF*; Cuney *MS*, *N*

137: 5 1656: *The date is written again, in an early hand, in the margin.*

139: 18 [a]: *N*, *M*, *HCF*; y[e] [*for* the] *MS*

139: 24 a hill [and met] a well: *The MS. is incompletely amended by interlineations. The word* hill *is written above* well, *which is crossed out. This is followed by* a well *written as an interlineation.*

139: 34 1[3]th: 10th *MS*; *emendation from Lady Fanshawe's list of her children, in which the date of death is given in the New Style calendar as 23 October 1659*

141: 5 *The date* 1660 *is written again, in an early hand, in the margin.*

141: 33 Aprill the 23: *The year* 1661 *is written, in an early hand, in the margin.*

142: 6–7 and afterwards proved: *The phrase is added in Lady Fanshawe's hand.*

142: 25; 143: 2 Ca[ve]ndish: *N*, *M*, *HCF*; Candish *MS*

142: 37–8 The Bishoup . . . and then: *added at the top of the page in Lady Fanshawe's hand.*

143: 13 and foure hundred: *A single line is drawn through part of the phrase, perhaps signifying deletion.*

144: 8 tucke c[oa]ch: *an interlineation, in Lady Fanshawe's hand, spelled* tucke chouch

144: 37, 42 [Satur]day . . . [Satur]day: Sunday . . . Monday *MS*, *N*, *M*; Saturday . . . Monday *HCF*

145: 4 [Su]nday: *HCF*; munday *MS*, *N*, *M*

146: 12 Sto[le]: *N*, *M*, *HCF*; stool *MS*

148: 14 A[ustria] . . . Ev[ora]: *N*, *M*, *HCF*; Astrey . . . Everye *MS*

148: 34–5 with rich drinke: *phrase added in Lady Fanshawe's hand*

149: 41 the Countes of St. Acrusse [*Santa Cruz*] *is written as an interlineation, in Lady Fanshawe's hand, above a cancelled phrase, apparently* of whom I spoke.

150: 1 *The date* 1663 *is written again, in an early hand, in the margin.*

151: 35 *In MS a long dash follows* Titio.
152: 44–153: 3 Going along . . . I kept: *The passage is cancelled. It is restored, in a much later hand, on a small interleaf.*
153: 13 166[4]: *N, M*; 1663, *MS, HCF*
153: 21–154: 24 *The names and the inventory of property, beginning with* Mr. Fanshawe, Chief Secretary, *appear, through error, twenty-one and twenty-two pages later in the original pagination. At the end of the later list, the amanuensis employed by Lady Fanshawe wrote at the bottom of the page,* This leaf is lost. *Above this note is written, in a much later hand.* This should be page 125–126 [*present text, pp. 153–4*].
154: 25 *The phrase* Gentlemens men *is cancelled.*
154: 35 B[erke]ley: *M, HCF*; Bartley *MS, N*
155: 6 [the 6th of March]: *HCF*; *omitted MS, N, M*
157: 8 souldjers stood: *N, M, HCF*; souldjers that stood *MS*
157: 9 Lieutenant held: *HCF*; lieutenant that held *MS, N, M*
157: 42 Ber[keley]: *M, HCF*; Bertly *MS*; Bartley *N*
159: 8 2[oth]: *Only the 2 is visible, the remainder having been cut from the margin.*
159: 11 [22nd]: *HCF*; 21th *MS, N, M*
159: 25 [Jerez]: *HCF*; Xeres *MS, N*; Xerez *M*
159: 31 D[ongan]'s: *M, HCF*; Duncan's *MS*; Dunean's *N*
159: 39 [Jerez]: *HCF*; Xeres *MS, N*; Xerez *M*
160: 32 [V]allecas: *HCF*; Ballecas, *MS, N, M*
161: 9 1664: *The date is written again in the margin.*
161: 10 Assistant: *N, M, HCF*; assistants *MS*
161: 17 D[ongan]: *M, HCF*; Duncan's *MS*; Dunean's *N*
161: 18 [Jerez]: *HCF*; Xeres *MS, N*; Xerez *M*
161: 23 E[cija]: *HCF*; Escica *MS*; Ecica *N*; Ezija *M*
162: 6 Thursday: *This day, correct for 17 April 1664 (New Style) and consistent with the other days and dates given, is overscored and above it is written, in an early hand,* Saturday.
162: 6 Friday: *The word is lightly overscored and over it is written in pencil, apparently in a modern hand,* Sunday.
162: 16 [   ]: *A blank space is left for the name.*
163: 1 [Il]lescas: *HCF*; Lescas *MS, N*; Yllescas *M*
163: 1, 4 [V]allecas: *HCF*; Ballecas, *MS, N, M*
163: 38 [My husband]: *HCF*; *blank space MS*; *N and M insert* my husband *after* lodgings.
165: 15–16 his obeissance to . . . there waiting: *The passage is cancelled. It is restored, in a much later hand, on a small interleaf.*
166: 4 Ro[jas]: *HCF*; Roco *MS, N*; Rocca *M*
166: 16 2[6]th: *HCF*; 24th *MS, N, M*
166: 18 [Third]: *HCF*; Second *MS, N, M*
166: 33 44: *The number is changed by overscoring from* 49.
167: 6 to see the: *The word* the, *spelled* they, *is an interlineation in Lady Fanshawe's hand.*
167: 44 [is]: *N, M, HCF*; *missing or totally obscured in the tight binding*
169: 31 [Nov]ember: *HCF*; December *MS, N, M*
171: 13 As[cham]: *HCF*; Askew *MS, N, M*
172: 42 [wives of]: *omitted. However, the original amanuensis wrote* wifes (*and possibly* of, *though it is not visible in the tight binding*) *in the margin as though to supply an omission.*
173: 18 [as]: *N, M, HCF*; *omitted MS*
173: 23 relations or friends: *The phrase is written as an interlineation above the word* parents, *which is cancelled.*

173: 24 birth[day]s: *M*, *HCF*; births *MS*, *N*
173: 30 [marry]: *N*, *M*, *HCF*; *omitted MS*
174: 19 Cham[artín]: *M*, *HCF*; Cham St. Martin *MS*, *N*
175: 11 [Wednes]day: *HCF*; Thursday *MS*, *N*, *M*
175: 22 2[7]th: *HCF*; 26th *MS*, *N*, *M*
175: 30 Ev[elyn]: *N*, *M*, *HCF*; Evling *MS*
176: 8 [August]: *N*, *M*; July *MS*; 20th of July *HCF*
176: 9 [Aitona]: *HCF*; Estony *MS*, *N*; Aytona *M*
176: 27 [Septem]ber: *N*, *M*, *HCF*; 7ber *MS*
176: 32 Cast[rillo]: *HCF*; Castille *MS*; Castile *N*; Castilla *M*
178: 39 de la Vel[ez]: *HCF*; de la Vel *MS*, N; de los Veloz *M*
178: 39 a[y]a: *N*, *M*, *HCF*; aga *MS*
179: 26–32 Thes gratifications . . . received a sum: *This paragraph, in Lady Fanshawe's hand, is added in the margin.*
179: 36 Itonia: *The name is written, in Lady Fanshawe's hand, in a blank space left by the amanuensis.*
180: 3 acco[un]t: *spelled* accõpt *and written after* reason, *which is cancelled*
180: 19 B[room]stead: *HCF*; Bumstead *MS*, *N*, *M*
180: 25 mo[z]o: *HCF*; moco *MS*, *N*, *M*
181: 18 [Aler]con: *HCF*; Ricon *MS*, *N*, *M*
181: 22 C[oruña]: *M*, *HCF*; Croyne *MS*; Corunna *N*
181: 27 [ ]: *The space for the place name is left blank.*
182: 36 C[ueva]: *M*, *HCF*; Coyna *MS*, *N*
184: 33–4 (This was . . . received the communion.): *The sentence, signed by Lady Fanshawe with her initials, is written in the margin in her hand.*
184: 39 [Satur]day: *N*, *M*, *HCF*; Sunday *MS*
184: 41–185: 16 *Horace*, Odes *4.9.34–52. Translation by Sir Richard Fanshawe, deleted; transcribed, in a much later hand, on a small interleaf. Text corrected in accordance with 'Selected Parts of Horace', trans. Fanshawe (London, 1652), p. 60.*
186: 18 Ju[ly]: *N*, *M*, *HCF*; June *MS*
188: 12 1[7]th: *HCF*; 16th *MS*, *N*, *M*
189: 14–16 I have been . . . benefit of mankind: *passage deleted: restored, in a much later hand, on a small interleaf*
189: 37 and honesty: *added as an interlineation in Lady Fanshawe's hand*
190: 6–8 This year . . . Sir P[hilip] W[arwick]: *sentence added in Lady Fanshawe's hand. The persons whose names are abbreviated are identified by HCF, p. 206.*
190: 11–14 it impossible to . . . to my wish: *passage deleted: restored, in a much later hand, on a small interleaf. When Lady Fanshawe deleted the passage, she added an interlineation to complete her sentence:* at the present no remedey.
190: 43 in Huntington sheere: *an interlineation in Lady Fanshawe's hand*
191: 2–3 In this yeare . . . Lady Kilmorey: *sentence added in the margin in Lady Fanshawe's hand. The name* Ed[ward] *was spelled in full by HCF, p. 208.*
191: 9–10 since the[y] came in to the south: *an interlineation, in Lady Fanshawe's hand*
191: 27 F[rin]ton: *HCF*; Fanton *MS*, *N*, *M*
191: 32 16[69]: *HCF*; 1670 *MS*, *N*, *M*
191: 36–8 In [16]71 I crisened . . . Sir Edmond Turner: *sentence added in Lady Fanshawe's hand*
192: 5–11 When I sett up . . . him with it*; passage deleted; restored, in a much later hand, on a small interleaf*
192: 16 shut up the: *Here the Memoirs break off, at the end of page 216 in the original pagination. The notes in Lady Fanshawe's hand which follow in the bound volume are written on unnumbered pages.*

INDEX

The information supplied in this index has been gleaned principally from *Complete Peerage*, *Scots Peerage*, *Complete Baronetage*, and, in the case of persons and places mentioned by Lady Fanshawe, from the extensive notes supplied by Mr. H. C. Fanshawe in his edition of Lady Fanshawe's *Memoirs* published in 1907.

Where spellings differ greatly from present normalized spellings, the seventeenth-century spellings have been placed in square brackets following the main index entry. When necessary, seventeenth-century spellings have been cross-referenced to main entries. Spellings in parentheses following main entries are alternative spellings still in use.

The phrase 'not named' (also appearing as '(nn)' following particular page numbers) indicates that the subject is referred to on the pages cited, but that his name does not appear in the text on those pages.

The following abbreviations are used throughout the index:

AM: Anne Murray, before her marriage to Sir James Halkett (1656)
Lady H: Anne (*née* Murray), Lady Halkett
AH: Ann Harrison before her marriage to Sir Richard Fanshawe (1644)
Lady F: Ann (*née* Harrison), Lady Fanshawe
Sir RF: Sir Richard Fanshawe
young RF: Richard Fanshawe, only surviving son of Sir RF and Lady F
HCF: H. C. Fanshawe and his 1907 edition of Lady Fanshawe's *Memoirs*

Abatha, Countess of, Portuguese noblewoman: 148
Abbeville, France: 139
Aberdeen, Scotland: 56, 58, 200
Aberdour, Scotland: 199, 200
Act of Indemnity (1660): 85, 206
Aitona [Itonia], Don Fernando de Moncada y Castro, Marquis of; a *mayor domo* of the Queen of Spain; member of the Queen Regent's Council: 176, 179
Alba [Alva], Antonio Alvarez de Toledo, 7th Duke of (1612–90); Spanish nobleman: 170, 183
Albuquerque, Don Francisco de la Cueva, 8th Duke of; Spanish nobleman; Generalissimo of the Sea; Lady F is in error in calling him 'Don Juan' and in stating that he was 'General of the Galleys'; his daughter, Doña Ana, married his brother, Don Melchor de la Cueva: 155–6, 157, 182, 184
Albuquerque, Doña Juana Francisca Diaz y Aux, Marchioness of Cadereita, Duchess of; Spanish noblewoman; wife of the 8th Duke: 156–7, 181, 182
Alcalá, Doña Catalina Antonia de Aragon y Sandoval, Duchess of; daughter of the 6th Duke of Sergorbe and Cardona; Spanish noblewoman; wife of Don Juan Francisco Tomas Lorenzo de la Cerda, Duke of Alcala: 158, 159
Alcalá, Don Juan Francisco Tomas Lorenzo de la Cerda, Duke of (d. 1691); Spanish nobleman; son of the 7th Duke of Medina Celi, succeeded to his father's title (1671): 158, 159 (nn)
Alarcón, Spain, 181
Alfonso VI (1643–83), King of Portugal (1656–67): 145–9, 214; not named: 152, 174, 215
Alhambra, the, Moorish palace at Granada, Spain: 128–9, 211
Alicante, Spain: 166
Alington, Ann (1607–28), daughter of Sir Giles Alington, Knight, of Horseheath, Cambs.; married (1627), as his first wife, Sir Thomas Fanshawe, later 1st Viscount Fanshawe of Dromore; sister-in-law of Sir RF: 106 (nn)
Alington, Sir Giles, father of Ann Alington: 106

Allen, Mr., attorney in London (1654): 81, 85 (nn)
Allenchip, Mr., Cook on Lord Sandwich's staff in Spain (1666): 182
All Hallows Church, Hertford, Herts. *See* All Saints Church
Allofe. *See* Ayloffe
All Saints [Hallows] Church, Hertford, Herts.; burial place of Sir John Harrison of Balls and his second wife Mary, and of Lady F's and Sir RF's daughter Mary: 99, 107 (nn), 108, 110, 141, 188, 192
Alnwick [Anwicke], Northumberland: 66
Alonso, Don. *See* Carnero, Don Alonso de
Alsberey. *See* Aylesbury
Alva, Princess, at the Spanish Court: 176. *See also* Alba
Andover [Andivers], Hants: 143
Andújar [Anduxar], Spain: 162
Anna of Austria. *See* Maria Anna, Queen of Spain
Antonia, Dona Maria de, Portuguese noblewoman: 148
Anwicke. *See* Alnwick
Apsley, Sir Allan (1616–83), governor of Barnstaple (1645) and previously Lieutenant-Governor of Exeter; holder of minor offices of state after the Restoration: 117
Aragón, Don Pascual de, Spanish nobleman; Grand Inquisitor and Viceroy of Naples; member of the Queen Regent's Council: 176 (nn)
Aragón, Vice Chancellor of. *See* Crespi, Don Christoval
Arãna (or Raña), Juan; presumably Cosme Pérez, known as Juan Rana, the name of a comic type-character he often portrayed: 170
Aranjuez, Spain, royal palace at: 162, 166, 183, 216
Archer, John (1598–1682); justice of the common bench (1663) and later raised to the chief justiceship of the same bench; knighted (1663): 122
Ardross. *See* Scott of Ardross
Areskine. *See* Erskine
Argyll. *See* Campbell
Arington, Mr., nephew of Sir [ ] Witherington: 79–80
Arlington. *See* Bennet, Sir Henry
Aron, family servant of the Murrays: 16
Ascham, Antony (d. 1650); tutor to James, Duke of York; envoy from the Commonwealth of England to the Court of Spain; assassinated in Madrid: 129–30, 171, 211
Ashburnham, Mr., member of Sir RF's retinue on trip from Madrid to Portugal (1666): 180
Ashburnham, John (1603–71), Royalist; Groom of the Chamber of Charles I and Treasurer of his Army; managed escape of Charles I from Oxford; after the Restoration was Groom of the Bedchamber to Charles II and member of Parliament: 120, 209–10
Ashburton, Devon, not named; HCF identifies it as the site of the 'ill lodging' in Lady F's text: 144
Ashton, John, member of Lord Sandwich's staff in Spain (1666): 182
Aston, Gertrude (*née* Sadleir), Lady; only daughter of Sir Thomas Sadleir of Standon, Herts.; she married (1607) Walter Aston, 1st Lord Aston of Forfar; gentlewoman to Lady Christopher Hatton (daughter of Thomas Fanshawe of Ware); godmother of AH: 108
Aston, Walter (1584–1639), Lord Aston of Forfar; English Ambassador to Spain (1620–5; 1635–8); his mother's brother married Susannah, the younger daughter of Henry Fanshawe, 1st Queen's Remembrancer: 95, 113
Aubigny, Lady Catherine (*née* Howard), Seigneuress d'Aubigny (d. 1650); daughter of the 2nd Earl of Suffolk; widow of Lord George Stuart, Seigneur d'Aubigny, who was killed at the Battle of Edgehill (1642); married second (1649) Sir James Livingston, created Earl of Newburgh (1660); involved in several Royalist plots, she died in exile at the Hague: 115
Aveiro [Aveyro], Dona Maria de Guadalupe de Lancastre, Duchess of; Portuguese noblewoman; sister of the 17th Duke of Aveiro: 180, 182
Aveiro [Aveyro], 17th Duke of (d. 1665); Portuguese nobleman who had chosen the side of Spain in the dispute between the two countries; Admiral of the Spanish fleet, with Spanish titles including Duke of Arcos and Count of Bailen: 145
Aveiro [Avero], 18th Duke of; Portuguese nobleman; either successor to the 17th

Aveiro [Avero], 18th Duke of—*contd.* Duke of Aveiro or husband of the Duke's sister, who was a duchess in her own right: 180, 186
Axminster [Ackminstor], Devon: 144
Ayala, Don Francisco de, Spanish nobleman under Sir RF's protection: 170–1
Aylesbury [Alsberey], Sir Thomas, Bt. (1576–1657); father of Frances, second wife of Sir Edward Hyde, later Earl of Clarendon; Royalist; patron of mathematical learning; one of the Masters of Requests and of the Mint: 141
Ayloffe [Alofe], Sir Benjamin (d. 1663), 2nd Bt., of Great Braxted, Essex; husband of Margaret, youngest daughter of Thomas Fanshawe by his second wife, Joan (*née* Smythe); half-uncle of Sir RF: 104
Ayloffe [Allofe], Sir William (1618–75), 3rd Bt., of Great Braxted, Essex; son of Sir Benjamin Ayloffe, 2nd Bt., by Margaret (*née* Fanshawe); half-cousin of Sir RF: 190
Mr. Ayres, Steward on Sir RF's trip from Madrid to Portugal (1666): 180

B., Ned, Col. Bampfield's serving man: 29
Backwell, Edward (d. 1683), alderman; celebrated London goldsmith and principal founder of the banking system in England: 190
Bagshawe, Henry, D. D. (1632–1709); Sir RF's chaplain; younger son of Edward Bagshaw, treasurer of the Middle Temple: 175, 180, 186 (nn), 187, 188, 220
Bagshot, Surrey: 143
Bainbridge [Bamberdg], Thomas, D.D. (d. 1646); master of Christ's College, Cambridge University (1622–46): 110
Baird, James, of Byth in Aberdeenshire, advocate; father of Sir John Baird: 64, 202
Baird, Sir John, of Newbyth (1620–98), advocate; Lord of the Session; later (1664) Lord Newbyth: 64, 202
Baker, Sir John, of Sissinghurst, Kent (1608–53), son of Sir Henry Baker, Bt., by Catharine (*née* Smythe); notable Royalist; cousin of Sir RF's, who visited him in Paris: 112
Balcarres. *See* Lindsay
Balcarres House, East Fife, Scotland: 63, 69, 71, 72, 73, 74, 203, 204
Bale, Jane. *See* Puckering, Jane
Bale, John, of Carlton Curlieu, Leicester (d. before 1654); husband (*c.* 1651) of Jane Puckering; cousin-in-law of Sir Henry Newton: 198 (nn)
Balfoure, Mr., Cook on Lord Sandwich's staff in Spain (1666): 182
Balls, Herts.: 95, 133, 190
Balmerino. *See* Elphinstone
Bamberdg. *See* Bainbridge
Bampfield, Col. Joseph (*fl.* 1639–85), Royalist and (later) Commonwealth agent and intriguer; engineer of the escape of the Duke of York from St. James's Palace (1648): ix, x, xi–xiv, xix, 5–6, 23–34 *passim*, 41, 48–9, 52, 56–7, 66–76 *passim*, 81–2, 194–200 *passim*, 203–4, 206
Bampfield, Mrs., wife of Col. Joseph Bampfield: xii, xiii, 5, 6, 27, 29, 32–3, 34, 35, 44, 49, 52, 57, 67, 72, 76, 195, 206
Banbury. *See* Vaux
Barker, Dionis (d. 1597), daughter of Edward Barker of Rowley, Derby.; married (1567) Robert Fanshawe; Lady F's maternal grandmother, though Lady F confuses her with Margaret Eyre, Lady F's maternal great-grandmother: 104
Barnstaple, Devon: 116–17
Basingstoke [Basingstone], Hants: 143
Basset, Sir Arthur, Governor of St. Michael's Mount, Cornwall: 117
Bath. *See* Bourchier, Henry
Bath, Somerset: 98, 135, 137, 151, 152
Batha, Richard, accompanied Sir RF's body to Bilbao, Spain: 186
Bathurst [Batters], John, M.D. (1607–59); physician to Cromwell: 135, 137
Batten, Sir William (d. 1667), distinguished sailor with the Prince of Wales's fleet (1648); after the Restoration a commissioner of the navy; Lady F calls him Thomas in error: 151
Batters. *See* Bathurst
Bayfordbury [Beaford], Herts., site of the estate of Sir Thomas Fanshawe (later 2nd Viscount), nephew of Sir RF: 136
Baylie, Richard, D.D. (d. 1667); Master of St. John's College, Oxford; Dean of Salisbury (1635–67): 144, 214

Bayning, Paul (1588–1629), 1st Viscount Bayning of Sudbury (1628); married (1613) Anne, daughter of Sir Henry Glemham of Glemham, Suffolk; their daughter Anne married (1635) AM's brother, Henry Murray: 193
Bayona, Marquis of, General of the Galleys of Spain; connected with the family of Pimentel of Benevente: 158–9
Bayonne, France, 187
Beadles, Mr., on Lord Sandwich's staff in Spain (1666): 181
Beaford. *See* Bayfordbury, Herts.
Beale [Bell], William, D.D. (d. 1651), Royalist divine; fellow and master of Jesus College, Cambridge; nominated Dean of Ely (1646) but never inducted; went into exile and accompanied the embassy of Cottington and Hyde to Spain; died in Madrid; one of Sir RF's tutors at Jesus College: 112, 129, 209
Beaufort, François de Vendôme, Duc de (1616–69); French courtier and politician; natural grandson of Henri IV of France; exiled in 1652, he was later recalled and given command (1666) of the French fleet against the Turks and Barbary pirates: 187
Beaumont [Bemond], Lancs., birthplace of Lady F's father: 110
Bedell, Sir Capel, Bt. (1602–63) of Kirby, Northants; he married (1619) Sir RF's eldest sister, Alice; acquired land at Hamerton, Hunts.: 108, 112, 190 (nn)
Bedell, Elizabeth (d. 1661), eldest daughter of Sir Capel Bedell by Alice (*née* Fanshawe); married Sir Francis Compton; niece to Sir RF: 190
Bedell, Mary; daughter of Sir Capel Bedell by Alice (*née* Fanshawe); married (1654) Sir Thomas Leventhorpe; niece to Sir RF: 108, 190
Bedford. *See* Russell, William
Bell, Dr. *See* Beale
Benevente, Countess of; wife of the 12th Count, Don Francisco Pimentel de Quiñones y Benavides (a nobleman of Portuguese origin, who was *Sumiller de Corps* in 1699); *Camerera Mayor* to Margarita Teresa, Infanta of Spain: 184
Bengeo [Bengey], Herts., on the River Lea opposite Hertford; Sir RF's brother Sir Thomas owned property there; the Fanshawe's second son by the name of Henry is buried in the Bengeo church: 107, 137
Bennet, Sir Henry (*c.* 1620–85), created Baron Arlington of Arlington (1665); created 1st Earl of Arlington (1672); son of Sir John Bennet of Dawley, Middlesex, by Dorothy (*née* Crofts); knighted (1657); envoy to Madrid (1658–61); Secretary of State (1662–74); Lord Chamberlain (1674–85): 151, 187, 188, 189, 218, 220
Bennet, Nathaniel, on Lord Sandwich's staff in Spain (1666): 182
Bennet, Nicholas, on Lord Sandwich's staff in Spain (1666): 182
Berkeley, John (1607–78), 1st Baron Berkeley of Stratton (1658); Royalist, soldier, courtier, ambassador; son of Sir Maurice Berkeley: 113, 120, 209
Berkeley, Sir William (1639–66); Captain of the *Bristol* frigate, ship in the fleet taking the Fanshawes to Spain (1664); later Vice-Admiral and also Lieutenant-Governor of Portsmouth: 154, 157
Berkhampstead [Barhamsteed] Manor, Herts., estate leased to AM's mother: 199
Berkshire. *See* Howard
Bertie [Barte, Bartell], Charles (d. 1710); fifth son of Montagu Bertie, 2nd Earl of Lindsey, by his first wife, Margaret (*née* Cokayne) Ramsay, widow of the 1st Earl of Holdernesse; nephew by marriage of Sir RF, in Fanshawe retinue (1664): 153, 164, 174
Bertie, Montagu (1608–66), 2nd Earl of Lindsey (1642); Lord Great Chamberlain of England; father of Charles Bertie: 153
Beverly, John, on Lord Sandwich's staff in Spain (1666): 182
Bide. *See* Byde
Bilbao, Spain: 186, 187, 188
Biscay, Bay of: 130–1
Blakeware [Blacksware], Herts., manor half-way between Ware and Much Hadham, Herts.; purchased by Sir Thomas Leventhorpe (nephew-in-law of Sir RF) in 1660 and sold again in 1672: 108
Blandford [Blankford], Dorset: 144
Bluett, Captain, property owner near Pendennis Castle, Cornwall: 117

Boat-of-Bog [the Boge], ferry site on the lower part of the River Spey between Banffshire and Moray, Scotland: 62
Boddie, Mr., Interpreter on Lord Sandwich's staff in Spain (1666): 181
Bohemia, Queen of. *See* Elizabeth, Queen of Bohemia
Booth [Bothe], Henry, Charles II's agent at Calais (1649–59): 139
Boreman, Mr., Clerk of the kitchen on Lord Sandwich's staff in Spain (1666): 182
Boarstall [Boston] House, situated north-east of Oxford on the border of Bucks.; it formed one of the most important outlying military positions of that area and was held alternatively by Commonwealth forces and Royalists: 134
Boteler, Sir Francis (1610–90), of Watton Woodhall, Herts.; knighted (1642); friend of the Fanshawes: 151
Boteler, Joan (*née* Fanshawe), Lady. *See* Fanshawe, Joan
Boteler, Sir Oliver (b. 1636), of Teston, Kent; son of Sir William Boteler and Joan (*née* Fanshawe; sister of Sir RF); nephew of Sir RF and cousin of young RF: 108
Boteler, William, of Krytons, Beddenham, Beds.; second husband of Ursual (*née* Smythe) and thus brother-in-law of Thomas Fanshawe (great-grandfather of young RF) and of Sir Henry Fanshawe (grandfather of young RF); Lady F is in error as to his first name and estate: 104
Boteler, Sir William, Bt. (*c.* 1604–44); son of Sir Oliver Boteler of Teston, Kent; married (1631), as her first husband, Joan (*née* Fanshawe), fourth daughter of Sir Henry Fanshawe by Elizabeth (*née* Smythe); brother-in-law of Sir RF and Lady F: 108, 120
Boteler. *See also* Butler
Bothe. *See* Booth
Bourchier, Henry (1587–1654), 6th Earl of Bath (1637): 104
Bourchier, Mary (d. 1579), daughter of Anthony Bourchier of Barnsley, Glos.; married (*c.* 1568), as his first wife, Thomas Fanshawe of Fanshawe Gate; mother of Sir Henry Fanshawe (young RF's grandfather); Lady F calls her 'Alice' in error: 104
Bow Bridge, near York: 85–6
Boyle, Lady Elizabeth (*née* Feilding; d. 1667), Viscountess Boyle of Kinalmeaky; daughter of William Feilding, 1st Earl of Denbigh, by Susan (*née* Villiers); married (1639) Lewis Boyle, Viscount Boyle of Kinalmeaky; principal Lady of the Bedchamber to the Queen Dowager, Henrietta Maria; created (1660) Countess of Guildford: 121, 187
Boyle, Lady Lettice (1610–49); third daughter of Richard Boyle, 2nd Earl of Cork, by his second wife, Catherine (*née* Fenton); she married (1629) George Goring, styled Lord Goring: 130 (nn)
Boyle, Lady Margaret (*née* Howard; 1623–89), Baroness of Broghill; daughter of Theophilus Howard, 2nd Earl of Suffolk; married (1641) Roger Boyle, Baron of Broghill: 86, 87
Boyle, Michael (d. 1702); Dean of Cloyne and Chaplain-General to the King's army in Munster (1649); after the Restoration Bishop of Cork, Cloyne, and Ross; Archbishop of Dublin(1663); Archbishop of Armagh (1673); Lord Chancellor of Ireland (1665–85); he married, as his second wife, Mary (*née* O'Brien), daughter of the 5th Lord Inchiquin: 123
Boyle, Richard (1566–1643), 1st Earl of Cork (1620); Irish statesman; Lord High Treasurer of Ireland (1631–43); he married, as his second wife (1603), Catherine (*née* Fenton); father of Roger Boyle, Baron of Broghill, later Earl of Orrery, and of Lady Lettice Boyle: 130, 207
Boyle, Roger, Baron of Broghill (1621–79); created (1660) 1st Earl of Orrery; son of Richard Boyle, 1st Earl of Cork, by Catherine (*née* Fenton): 86, 87, 207
Bramhall, John (1594–1663); Bishop of Londonderry (1634); Archbishop of Armagh (1661): 124
Braxted [Bracksted], Great, Essex; site of the estate of Sir Benjamin Ayloffe, uncle-in-law of Lady F: 104, 190
Bream (or Braham), Sir Arnold (1601–81); Royalist; his father was Customs Agent at Dover: 141, 150
Brechin [Brighon], Scotland: 56

Breda, Netherlands: 98, 140
Brentford [Brantford; Brandford]. *See* Ruthven
Bridges, Mr., on Lord Sandwich's staff in Spain (1666): 181
Bridgewood, Edward, English merchant at Lisbon, Portugal (1662): 145
Briggs, Mr., on Lord Sandwich's staff in Spain (1666): 182
Bristol. *See* Digby
Bristol, frigate commanded by Capt. William Berkeley (1664): 154
Bristol, Glos.: 114, 115, 116, 122, 209
Broanbricke. *See* Brownrig
Broghill. *See* Boyle
Broom, Mr., Chief Cook in Fanshawe retinue (1664): 154
Broomstead, Mr., Page in Fanshawe retinue (1664): 153, 180
Brown, Josias, on Lord Sandwich's staff in Spain (1666): 182
Browne, Elizabeth (*née* Pretyman; d. 1652), Lady; daughter of Sir William Pretyman and granddaughter of William Bourchier of Barnsley, Glos., mother of Mary, who married John Evelyn; it was through Elizabeth that the relationship between John Evelyn and Sir RF occurred: 133
Browne, Mary. *See* Evelyn, Mary (*née* Browne)
Browne, Sir Richard, Bt. (1605–83); only son of Christopher Browne; succeeded his father as Clerk of the Privy Council; Resident Minister in France (1641–60); married Elizabeth (*née* Pretyman): 133
Brownrig [Broanbricke], Ralph, D.D. (1592–1659); Bishop of Exeter (1641): 110
Bruce, Sir William, of Kinross (d. 1710); created Baronet (1668); son-in-law of Sir James Halkett: 205
Bruges, Flanders: 140
Brussels, Flanders: 140
Buckingham. *See* Villiers
Bullock, John (*c.* 1578–1641), of Darley Abbey, Derby; Lord of the Manor of Norton; married (1608) Katherine, second daughter of Thomas Fanshawe and his second wife, Joan (*née* Smythe); half-uncle of Sir RF: 104
Burntisland [Brun Island], Scotland: 51, 63, 200
Burstall (or Bristol), Garth, Yorks.; a royal manor in south-east Yorkshire on the River Humber whose lease Sir RF acquired (1662) from Charles II; Lady F sold the lease (1668) to Dean Robert Hitch of York: 191
Burton, John, member of Lady F's retinue in her departure from Madrid (1666): 187
Butler, Eleanor, daughter of Thomas Butler, styled Viscount, by Elizabeth (*née* Poynts); married (before 1648) Donough Maccarty, later 1st Earl of Clancarty: 124 (nn)
Butler, Lady Elizabeth (*née* Preston; 1615–84), *suo jure* Baroness Dingwall, Duchess of Ormonde (1682); daughter of Richard Preston, 1st Earl of Desmond and Lord Dingwall, by Lady Elizabeth (*née* Butler); married (1629) her kinsman, James Butler, then styled Lord Thurles; she and AH were born in the same room of the same house in London: 108, 121, 141, 142, 143
Butler, James (1610–88), 1st Duke of Ormonde (1682); 1st Marquis (1642); 1st Duke, Irish Peerage (1661); Lord-Lieutenant of Ireland (1643–7, 1649–50, 1661–9, 1677–85); m. (1629) Lady Elizabeth (*née* Preston), daughter of the 1st Earl of Desmond: 123, 124, 125, 140, 141, 142, 213
Butler, Lady Mary (1646–1710), daughter of James Butler, 1st Duke of Ormonde, by Elizabeth (*née* Preston); married (1661 or 62) William Cavendish, eldest son of the 4th Earl of Devonshire; the marriage described by Lady F was apparently a clandestine one, the official public ceremony not occurring until 26 October 1662 when the Fanshawes were in Lisbon: 142, 143
Butler. *See also* Boteler
Byde, Sir Thomas (d. 1704), a brewer of Shoreditch; knighted (1661); Sheriff of Hertfordshire (1669); purchaser of Ware Park: 191

C., S., *The Life of the Lady Halkett* (1701): x *n.*, xi, 7, 193, 197–8, 199, 200–1, 202, 204, 205, 206
Cádiz, Spain: 154–7, 172; Lieutenant-Governor of (1664): 155; Mayor of

Cádiz, Spain—*contd.*
(1664): 156; English consul at (1664), *see* Westcombe, Martin
Caen, France: 96, 119
Calais, France: 97, 122, 132, 139, 140, 188; governor of castle at (1648): 122
Calderón de la Barca, Pedro (1600–81), Spanish dramatist: xviii, 215, 218
Callendar. *See* Livingston
Cambridge, Duke of. *See* James, 2nd Duke of Cambridge
Cambridge, University of: 98, 192; Jesus College, 95, 112, 129; Corpus Christi College: 194; Vice Chancellor of, *see* Ferne, Henry
Camden, William; mistakenly credited by Lady F with a published description of Ware Park gardens actually written by Sir Henry Wotton: 105, 208
Camoens, Luis de (1524?–80), Portuguese poet; his *Os Lusiadas*: xvii, 97, 136, 212, 213
Campbell, Lady Anne (1631?–60?); eldest daughter of Archibald Campbell, 1st Marquis of Argyll and 8th Earl, by Margaret (*née* Douglas): 51, 199
Campbell, Archibald (*c.* 1606–61), 1st Marquis of Argyll (1641) and 8th Earl (1638); supporter of the Covenant, of Charles I, of Charles II; executed for high treason: 199, 200, 203, 205
Campbell, Archibald (1629–85), created 9th Earl of Argyll (1663); styled Lord Lorne in his father's lifetime and for some period following his father's execution; supporter of Charles II, of Cromwell, of Monmouth's Rebellion; executed for high treason: 56, 200
Campbell, Lady Margaret (*née* Douglas; 1610–78), Marchioness and Countess of Argyll; second daughter of William Douglas, 8th Earl of Morton; married (1626) Archibald Campbell, 1st Marquis of Argyll and 8th Earl: 51
Campbell, Mary, Lady. *See* Fanshawe, Mary (1635–1701)
Campbell, Sir Thomas, Bt. (d. 1668); first husband of Mary, daughter of Sir Thomas Fanshawe, 1st Viscount Fanshawe of Dromore, by his second wife, Elizabeth (*née* Cockayne); nephew-in-law of Sir RF: 108
Canterbury, Archbishop of. *See* Sheldon, Gilbert
Canterbury, Dean of. *See* Turner, Thomas
Canterbury, Kent: 150
Capell, Arthur, 1st Baron Capell of Hadham, Herts. (1604–49); devoted Royalist; member of Parliament for Herts.; member of the Council of the Prince of Wales; captured at the fall of Colchester and executed: 113, 119
Capell, Elizabeth (*née* Morrison; 1610–61), Lady; wife (1630) of Arthur, 1st Lord Capell of Hadham; mother of Arthur Capell, 1st Earl of Essex: 114, 117
Capell, Mary (1630–1715); eldest daughter of Arthur, 1st Lord Capell of Hadham by Elizabeth (*née* Morrison); she married first (1648) Henry Seymour, styled Lord Beauchamp; she married second (1657) Henry Somerset, 3rd Marquis of Worcester, created Duke of Beaufort (1682): 117
Capuchins, an independent order of Franciscans: 12, 194
Caracena, Don Luis de Benavides Carillo y Toledo, Marquis of (d. 1668); commander of the Spanish army defeated by the Marquis of Marialva and Count Schönberg at Montes Claros, Portugal (1665): 175
Carew, Mr., accompanied body of Sir RF to Bilbao; probably same person as Mr. Carey below, 186
Carey, Mr., Under-General of the Horse in Fanshawe retinue to Spain (1664); probably the same person as Mr. Carew above: 153
Carey, Sir George; perhaps Sir George Carey of Bradford, Devon, son of Sir Edward Carey; knighted (1632); owner of house in Chancery Lane, London, leased by the Fanshawes (1655): 137
Carisbrooke Castle, Isle of Wight: 195, 210
Carlisle, Cumberland: 36, 45
Carmona, Spain, 161
Carnarvon. *See* Dormer
Carnero, Don Alonso de (d. 1721); secretary to the Spanish Duke of Medina de las Torres; probably the same person as Don Alonso: 169
Carpio, Don Luis de Haro, Marquis of (d. 1661); Prime Minister of Spain: 162, 216
Carpio, Spain: 162

Carteret [Cartright], Elizabeth (d. 1700); daughter of Sir Philip de Carteret by Ann (*née* Dowse); wife of Sir George Carteret, Lieutenant-Governor of Jersey; godmother to Lady F's eldest daughter Ann, who was born in Jersey: 118 (nn), 119

Carteret [Cartright], Sir George (1610?–80), Bt. (1645); Lieutenant-Governor of Isle of Jersey (1646); forced to surrender Jersey to Parliament (1651); on Restoration appointed Privy Councillor and Treasurer of the Navy; husband of Elizabeth (*née* de Carteret): 118, 119

Carteret [Cartright], Sir Philip de (1584–1643); knighted (1616); Lieutenant-Governor of the Isle of Jersey; uncle of Sir George Carteret whom his daughter Elizabeth married: 118

Castelmelhor, Dom Luis de Sousa Vasconcellas, Count of (1636–1720); Portuguese nobleman; *Secretario de la Puridad*; favourite of Alfonso VI; 148–9, 150, 179

Castile: Admiral of: 182; President of, *see* Castrillo, Conde de

Castleton. *See* Saunderson

Castrillo, Don Luis Mendez de Haro y Sotomayor, Count of; Spanish nobleman; President of Castile (1664); member of the Queen Regent's Council (1665): 170, 171, 176, 218

Catherine of Braganza (1638–1705), Queen Consort of England (1662–85); daughter of John IV, King of Portugal and Luisa Maria; married Charles II at Portsmouth (1662): 98, 142–3, 213–14, 219; not named: 146, 147, 149, 151, 188, 190

Cavendish, Lady Elizabeth (*née* Cecil; *c.* 1620–89), Countess of Devonshire; daughter of William Cecil, 2nd Earl of Salisbury; wife of the 4th Earl: 83, 84, 142 (nn), 206

Cavendish, Lady Mary. *See* Butler, Lady Mary

Cavendish William (1617–84), styled Lord Cavendish (1626–8), 4th Earl of Devonshire (1628); active Royalist: 142, 206

Cavendish, William (1641–1707), styled Lord Cavendish (1641–84), 5th Earl of Devonshire (1684), created 1st Duke of Devonshire (1694); eldest son of William Cavendish, 4th Earl, by Lady Elizabeth (*née* Cecil); married (1662) Lady Mary Butler; served with the Duke of York in defeat of the Dutch off Lowestoft (1665); supporter of the Prince of Orange; Lord Steward of the Household (1689–1707); one of the Lords Justices: 142

Cavers, home of Sir James Halkett's sisters in southern Roxburghshire: 79, 86, 205

Cecil, Robert (1563–1612), created Earl of Salisbury (1605); Secretary of State (1596–1612); Lord High Treasurer (1608–12); helped AH's father find a customs post under Sir John Wolstenholme, the elder: 110

Cecil, Thomas (1542–1622), created Earl of Exeter (1605); son of the statesman William Cecil, 1st Baron Burghley, by Mary (*née* Clark): 115

Chaillot [Shalliott], Convent of, on the outskirts of Paris: 187

Chamartín, Spain: 174

Charles I (1600–49), King of England, Ireland, and Scotland (1625–49)

— as Duke of York: 196

— as Prince of Wales: 5, 9, 10, 193, 196

— as King: 103, 109–21 *passim*, 133, 146, 193, 194, 201, 202, 208, 212, 214; and Col. Bampfield: xi, xii, 9, 23–4, 26–7, 27–8, 195; and the Civil Wars: xv, 16, 28, 96, 117–20, 195, 196, 197, 205, 209–10; Fanshawes' visit with (1647): xvi, 121; AM's father tutor to: 5, 9, 10, 196; AM's mother governess to children of: 10, 193, 196; and Sir RF: 114, 120

Charles II (1630–85), King of England, Ireland, and Scotland (1649–85)

— as Prince of Wales: xvi, 23, 112, 195, 196; and Col. Bampfield: 26, 197; and Sir RF: 96, 114, 116, 117, 121; his Council, 113, 116, 119, 209; at Scilly Isles (1646): 118; at Paris (1646): 119, 209

— as King: 85, 202, 205, 210; in Scotland (1650–1): x, 6, 49, 51–4, 56, 57, 58, 71, 200, 201, 204, 211–12; and AM: x, 6, 52–4, 200; and Lady F: xvi, 139–40, 143, 152, 188–91; and Will Murray: 5, 29–30, 200; intrigues for in Scotland: 66, 68, 203; and Col. Bampfield: 66,

Charles II as King—*contd.*
203–4; at the Hague (1649): 97, 125; marriage of: 98, 142, 213–14, 219; and Sir RF: 98–9, 103, 106, 122–43 *passim*, 149–64 *passim*, 170, 174–84 *passim*, 211, 212, 215, 216; and Sir John Harrison: 111; in Spain (1659): 138, 213; in France and Flanders (1659): 139; restoration of: 140–1, 192
Charles II (1661–1700), King of Spain (1665–1700)
— as Prince: 165, 169, 170, 173 (nn)
— as King: 176, 178, 179, 181, 183, 184, 187, 218
Charles V (1500–58), Holy Roman Emperor (1519–58), King of Spain 1516–56): 217
Charles (formerly the *Naseby*), the ship in which Charles II sailed from Holland (1660): 140 (nn)
Charles Emmanuel II (1634–75), Duke of Savoy; son of Victor Amadeus I by Christine de France, sister of Louis XIII: 176
Charlton, Kent, location of the estate of Sir Henry (Newton) Puckering: 5, 6, 11, 22, 81, 83, 84, 193, 194, 205
Chawmons, Joseph, Under-secretary to Lord Sandwich on mission to Spain (1666): 182
Church, Percy, Groom of the Privy Chamber to Queen Henrietta Maria (1635–41); later her agent in Paris: 187
Churchill, Mr., Page on Lord Sandwich's staff in Spain (1666): 181
Cinque Ports: 26, 197
Clancarty. *See* Maccarty
Clarendon. *See* Hyde
Clerck, Mr. (d. *c.* 1667), on Lord Sandwich's staff in Spain (1666); died in Spain and was buried in the garden of Siete Chimeneas: 181
Cobham, Kent: 30, 197
Cockayne, Elizabeth (1609–68), fourth daughter of Sir William Cockayne of Rushton, Northants; married (1629), as his second wife, Sir Thomas Fanshawe, later 1st Viscount Fanshawe of Dromore (eldest brother of Sir RF); Lady F is incorrect about the number of daughters surviving in 1676—there were actually only three: 106, 117 (nn), 191
Cockayne, Sir William (d. 1626), Knight, of Rushton, Northants; Sheriff of London (1609); Lord Mayor of London (1619); father of Elizabeth and thus father-in-law of Sir Thomas Fanshawe, 1st Viscount Fanshawe of Dromore: 106
Cole, Mrs., wife of Mr. Maitland; she had AM arrested for debt (1654, 1656): 81 (nn), 85, 206
Colepeper, Sir John (1600–60), created 1st Baron Colepeper of Thoresway (1644); ardent Royalist; Chancellor of the Exchequer (1642); Master of the Rolls (1643); member of the Council of the Prince of Wales; accompanied the Prince to Paris (1646): 113, 119, 121, 201
Colepeper. *See also* Culpeper
Colle, Mr., Lady F leased a house from him in Holborn Row (1667): 190
Colombes, France, residence of Dowager Queen Henrietta Maria, five (not two, as stated by Lady F) leagues from Paris, 139, 213
comets, visible in Spain (1664–5): 169, 175, 217, 218
Compton, Sir Francis (d. 1717): youngest son of Spencer Compton, 2nd Earl of Northampton by Mary (*née* Beaumont); married Elizabeth Bedell, niece of Sir RF: 190–1
Comyn, Nicholas, Mayor of Limerick, Ireland (1649): 124 (nn)
Consuegra [Corsuegra], Spain: 162
Cooper, Mr., Gentleman of the Horse to Sir RF; in Fanshawe retinue (1664): 153, 176, 180, 186, 188
Cooper, Anthony Ashley (1621–83), 1st Earl of Shaftesbury (1672); son of Sir John Cooper, 1st Bt., by his first wife Anne (*née* Ashley); succeeded his father as 2nd Bt.; Commonwealth man and member of the Lord Protector's Council; Lord of the Treasury (1667–72); Lord Chancellor (1672–3); fled to the Continent (1682) during Exclusion crisis: xvii, 189
Cooper, Richard, on Lord Sandwich's staff in Spain (1666): 182
Copley, Col. Christopher (d. 1664); son of Sir William Copley of Spotborough, near Doncaster; excluded from the Long Parliament by Pride's Purge; Colonel of the West Riding Regiment; devoted Republican; active member of Presbyterian Party: 119

Córdoba, Spain: 161–2
Cork. *See* Boyle
Cork, Ireland: 97, 123; revolt of: 123–4, 210–11; Red Abbey: 123, 124
Cornbury [Corneborow] Park, Oxfordshire; seat of the Earl of Clarendon (from which his eldest son took his title): 151
Corsuegra, Spain. *See* Consuegra
Coruña, La, Spain: 181
Cotainville, France: 119
Cotterell, Clement (*c.* 1650–72); son of Sir Charles Cotterell (Master of Ceremonies at Court, 1641–86), who was a friend of Lord Sandwich; the son served on Sandwich's embassy to Spain and died in the same action at Solebay in which Sandwich was killed: 181
Cottington, Francis (1579–1652), Baron Cottington of Hamworth (1631); Ambassador Extraordinary to Spain with Sir Edward Hyde and Sir RF (1649): 124, 129 (nn), 211
Covenanters. *See* Scottish Covenanters
Coventry, Sir William (1628?–86), politician; secretary to the Duke of York when he was Lord High Admiral; Commissioner of the Navy Board; member of the Privy Council (1665): 188
Cranfield, Anne (*née* Brett; d. 1670), Countess of Middlesex; married (1620), as his second wife, Lionel Cranfield (created Baron Cranfield of Cranfield, 1621; Earl of Middlesex, 1622; d. 1645): 188
Creghton [Creeton, Creyton, Creyghton], Mr., in Fanshawe retinue (1664): 153, 180, 187, 188
Crespi, Don Christoval, Spanish nobleman; Vice-Chancellor of Aragón; member of the Queen Regent's Council: 176 (nn)
Crew, AM's serving-woman: 33, 63, 66, 70, 81, 85; not named: 59, 62, 64, 69, 73
Crisp, Sir Nicholas (1599?–1666), Royalist privateer; expelled from the Long Parliament; knighted (1642); created Baronet (1665): 118
Cromwell, Oliver (1599–1658), the Protector [the Usurper]: xvii, 171, 196, 210; not named: 11, 61, 82, 129; in Scotland (1650): 49, 54, 58, 200; in Ireland (1649–50): 123, 124, 125, 126, 211; and Sir RF: 124, 135; death of, 137, 212; and Col. Bampfield: 195, 203, 206
Cropredy Bridge, over the Cherwell, five miles north of Banbury, Oxfordshire; cavalry engagement fought there 20 June 1644: 120
Crowne, Peter, Page on Lord Sandwich's staff in Spain (1666); train-bearer to the Earl of Manchester, the chief mourner at Lord Sandwich's funeral: 182
Cruz, Senhora, Sister Maria de la (Dona Maria Guzmán), Abbess of Alcantara; Catholic nun; daughter of the 8th Duke of Medina Sidonia and niece to the Queen Mother of Portugal: 145
Cueva, Doña Ana de la, Spanish noblewoman; wife of Don Melchor de la Cueva and daughter of his brother, the 8th Duke of Albuquerque, Don Francisco de la Cueva: 156–7 (nn)
Cueva, Doña Maria de la, Spanish noblewoman; a relative of the Duchess of Albuquerque: 182
Cueva, Don Melchor de la, brother of the 8th Duke of Albuquerque; husband of Doña Ana, daughter of the 8th Duke of Albuquerque: 155, 156, 157 (nn)
Cullcheth, Mrs., governess to Anne, Lady Howard before her marriage to Sir Charles Howard; wife of the steward at Naworth Castle: 33, 36, 45, 198
Cullcheth, Richard, steward at Naworth Castle: 36, 45, 198
Culpeper, Roberta Anna (d. 1661); daughter of Sir Thomas Culpeper, knight, of Place House, in St. Stephen's or Hackington, Kent; sister of Col. Thomas Culpeper; married (1659) Thomas Porter (d. 1680), younger son of Endymion Porter; apparently she was originally buried at the house of her brother: 150–1
Culpeper, Col. Thomas (1637–1708), only son of Sir Thomas Culpeper (of Place House, in St. Stephen's or Hackington, Kent; Lieutenant of Dover Castle) by Lady Barbara (*née* Sydney), widow of Sir Thomas Smythe, 1st Viscount Strangford: 150–1
Culpeper. *See also* Colepeper
Cummings, L. M., narrative biography of AM by, xxi

Cunningham, Dr. Robert (d. 1674); physician to Charles II in Scotland: 73, 78, 205
Cunningham, William (*c.* 1610–64), 8th Earl of Glencairn (1631); Royalist; Privy Councillor and Commissioner of the Treasury (Scotland, 1643); commander of Charles II's forces in Scotland (1653); Lord Chancellor of Scotland (1661): 201, 204
Cutler, Sir John (*c.* 1608–93), son of Thomas Cutler, citizen and grocer of London; knighted (1660); created Baronet (1660); Sheriff of Kent (1675–6): 151

Dalkeith. *See* Douglas
Dalkeith, Scotland: 62
Daniell, Andrew, Page on Lord Sandwich's staff in Spain (1666): 182
Darcy, Mary (*née* Kitson; d. 1644), Countess Rivers; wife of Thomas Darcy, Baron Darcy of Chiche (created Earl Rivers, 1626): 110
Darley Abbey, Derby, site of the estate of John Bullock, uncle-in-law of Lady F: 104
d'Aubigny. *See* Aubigny
d'Aubusson, Georges, Archbishop of Embrun; French Ambassador at the Court of Spain (1661–7); later Bishop of Metz; not named: 163, 164, 216
Davies (or Davy), Robert, of London; husband of Mary Smythe and brother-in-law of Thomas Fanshawe (great-grandfather of young RF) and of Sir Henry Fanshawe (grandfather of young RF); Lady F mistakenly calls him 'Sir John Daveis' and says that he comes from Kent: 104
Deal, Kent: 122, 150
Denbigh. *See* Feilding
Denham (or Dynham), Penelope (*née* Wenman), Lady: widow of Sir John Denham and owner of Boarstall House; she escaped the house during the siege in 1644, but apparently was residing there in 1651 when Sir RF was taken prisoner: 134
Denia, Spain: 183
Dennis, Mr., Footman on Lord Sandwich's staff in Spain (1666): 182
Desmond. *See* Preston
despensero, a daily allowance for food made to notables of the Spanish Court, including ambassadors: 169, 170, 217
Devereux, Frances (*née* Walsingham; 1569–1631) Sidney, Countess of Essex; daughter of Sir Francis Walsingham; widow of Sir Philip Sidney; married (1590) Robert Devereux, 2nd Earl of Essex: 208
Devereux, Robert (1566–1601), 2nd Earl of Essex (1576); favourite of Queen Elizabeth I; beheaded for high treason; married (1590) Frances (*née* Walsingham), widow of Sir Philip Sidney; father of the 3rd Earl: 208
Devereux, Robert (1591–1646), 3rd Earl of Essex (1607); Parliamentary general; son of the 2nd Earl by Frances (*née* Walsingham) Sidney: 109, 116, 117, 208, 209
Devonshire. *See* Cavendish
Dickson, David (1583–1663), Presbyterian clergyman: xiii–xiv, 65, 76–7, 84
Dieppe [Deepe], France: 17, 199
Digby, George (1612–77), 2nd Earl of Bristol (1653); Secretary of State (1642–9, 1657–9); Sir RF stood proxy for him at the first Feast of St. George (1661) and was installed (for him) K.G.: 141, 213
Digby, John (1586–1653), 1st Earl of Bristol (1622); Ambassador to Spain (1610–18, 1622–4); buried in Paris in the Protestant Churchyard: 107, 139
Digby, Sir Kenelm (1603–65), author, naval commander, and diplomatist; eldest son of Sir Everard Digby who was executed for participation in the Gunpowder Plot: 122
Dillon, James (1605–49), 3rd Earl of Roscommon (1642); earlier styled Lord Dillon; Treasurer and Keeper of the Great Seal of Ireland (1649): 124–5, 211
Dingwall. *See* Preston
Dongan (or Dungan), Euphemia Maria (*née* Chambers), Viscountess; daughter of Sir Richard Chambers; a lady of Spanish domicile who married William, Viscount Dongan: 159
Dongan (or Dungan), William (1630–98), created Viscount Dongan of Clane (1661); son of Sir John Dongan, Bt., by Mary (*née* Talbot); created Earl of Limerick (1686); an adherent of

Dongan (or Dungan), William—*contd.* James II; attainted (1691); died in exile: 159, 161
Dorchester, Dorset: 144
Dormer, Robert (1609–43), 1st Earl of Carnarvon (1628); in Madrid (1635); zealous Royalist and Cavalier leader; killed at the first Battle of Newbury: 113
Douglas, Ann (*née* Hay; d. 1700), Countess of Morton; daughter of Sir James Hay, 3rd Bt. of Smithfield; married (1649) Sir James Douglas of Smithfield, later (1681) 11th Earl of Morton: 51, 52
Douglas, Anne (*née* Villiers; d. 1654), 9th Countess of Morton; daughter of Sir Edward Villiers by Barbara (*née* St. John); married (1627) Robert Douglas, styled Lord Dalkeith, who became 9th Earl of Morton (1648) upon the death of his father; governess to Princess Henrietta Ann, she smuggled the child out of England in 1646: 65, 78, 121, 202, 205
Douglas, Sir Archibald (1600?–60?), 10th Laird of Mains: 51, 200
Douglas, Sir James, of Smithfield (d. 1686); became 11th Earl of Morton (1681); he succeeded his nephew William Douglas, the 10th Earl: 51, 52, 199, 200
Douglas, Robert (d. 1649), 9th Earl of Morton (1648); styled Lord Dalkeith until 1648; married (1627) Anne (*née* Villiers): 202
Douglas, William (*c.* 1584–1648), 8th Earl of Morton (1606); Royalist; Lord High Treasurer of Scotland (1630–6); father of Lady Mary Seton, Countess of Dunfermline, and of Lady Ann Hay, Countess of Kinnoull: 200, 202
Dover, Kent: 122, 138, 141
Downs, the, roadstead in the English Channel, 121, 210
Dronfield [Drawnfield], Derby., birthplace of Sir RF's grandfather, Thomas Fanshawe; the Fanshawe family held lands there: 103, 104
Drummond, Sir Patrick (d. before 1681); Conservator in Holland; cousin of AM's mother: 20, 194
Drummond. *See also* Ker
Dryden, John (1631–1700), English poet and dramatist; *An Evening's Love*: xviii *n.*
Dunbar, Battle of (13 Sept. 1650): x, 6, 54, 55, 200, 201; wounded soldiers from: 55–6
Dunfermline. *See* Seton
Dunfermline, Scotland, seat of the earls of Dunfermline; Charles II was entertained there by the 2nd Earl: 6, 7, 52–4, 55, 199
Dunnottar [Donotter], Scotland; Charles II entertained at the castle there (1650); later castle was besieged: 56
Dysart. *See* Murray, William

Earle, John, D.D. (1601?–65); Dean of Westminster (1660); Bishop of Worcester (1662); Bishop of Salisbury (1663): 143–4
East, Edward (d. *c.* 1693), of Pall Mall and Fleet Street, London; watchmaker to Charles I: 119
Écija, Spain: 161
Edgcumbe, Col. Piers, of Cothele (1609–66); Royalist M.P.; he married (1636) Mary (*née* Glanville); they had by 1663 two daughters and a younger son (aged nine), as well as the eldest son, Richard, all of whom were second cousins once removed of Sir RF: 144, 145
Edgcumbe, Sir Richard (1640–88), eldest son of Col. Piers Edgcumbe and his wife, Mary (*née* Glanville); second cousin once removed of Sir RF: 144
Edgehill, Battle of (23 Oct. 1642): 105, 208
Edinburgh, Scotland: 6, 50, 51, 63–5, 66, 70, 74, 199; Blackfriar Wind: 70, 72, 75, 204; Canongate: 50, 87, 199, 207; Castle: 87, 207; Netherbow: 63, 201, 202, 204
Elgin, Scotland: 60, 62
Elizabeth I (1533–1603), Queen of England (1558–1603): 104, 105
Elizabeth, Princess (1635–50), daughter of Charles I: 5, 10, 23, 195, 196; not named: 193, 196
Elizabeth, Queen of Bohemia (1596–1662); eldest daughter of James I of England; she married (1613) Frederick V, Elector Palatine; mother of Princes Rupert and Maurice: 140, 213
Elkonhead (Eltonhead?), Justice of the Peace at Woolwich, Kent: 84
Elphinstone, John (1623–1704), 3rd Lord Balmerino (1649); fined heavily by

Elphinstone, John—*contd.*
Parliament (1662) for his compliance with Cromwell's government: 71, 204
Elvas, Portugal, unsuccessfully besieged by the Spanish (1658–59): 174
Emperor's Ambassador's Lady: presumably the wife of the Ambassador to the Spanish Court from Emperor Leopold I (1664–5): 169, 174
Empress, the. *See* Margarita Teresa, Infanta of Spain
Erskine [Areskine], Anna (d. before 1682); second daughter of Alexander Erskine, styled Viscount of Fentoun, by Lady Anne (*née* Seton); niece of the 2nd Earl of Dunfermline: 52, 53 (nn), 56, 60, 62, 63, 200
Erskine, Sir Charles, of Cambo (*c.* 1620–77), 1st Bt.; son of Alexander Erskine, styled Viscount Fentoun, by Lady Anne (*née* Seton); Lord Lyon King of Arms (1663): 63, 201
Escorial [Escuriall], El, palace and monastery 31 miles north of Madrid, Spain: 167–9, 177–8, 217
Esquivias [Escivias], Spain: 166
Essex. *See* Capell; Devereux
Eton College, 5, 7, 9, 10: provost of, *see* Meredith, John; Murray, Thomas
Evelyn, Sir John (1601–85), of West Dean, Wilts.; father of Sarah (*née* Evelyn) Wray, second wife of Sir Thomas Fanshawe, 2nd Viscount Fanshawe of Dromore; first cousin once removed of John Evelyn, the diarist: 106, 175
Evelyn, John (1620–1706), the diarist; married (1647) Mary (*née* Browne), only daughter of Sir Richard Browne: 133
Evelyn, Mary (*née* Browne; *c.* 1635–1709); daughter of Sir Richard Browne and Elizabeth (*née* Pretyman); married (1647) John Evelyn, the diarist: 133
Evelyn, Sarah (d. 1717); daughter of Sir John Evelyn of West Dean, Wilts., by Elizabeth (*née* Coxe); she married first Sir John Wray, 3rd Bt. of Glentworth, Lincs.; second (1665) Sir Thomas Fanshawe, 2nd Viscount Fanshawe of Dromore (nephew of Sir RF); and third (1675) George Saunderson, 5th Viscount Castleton in the Peerage of Ireland; not named: 106, 175
Evora, Battle of (8 June 1663): 148
Exeter. *See* Cecil
Exeter, Devon, Cathedral Church in: 144. *See also* Ward, Seth
Eyre, Margaret (*c.* 1499–1573); daughter of Godfrey Eyre of Hassop, Derby., and widow of Hugh Wadd of Aston; she married, second, John Fanshawe of Fanshawe Gate (1504–78); great-grandmother of both Sir RF and Lady F, who mistakenly calls her her grandmother; actually Lady F's maternal grandmother was Dionis Barker: 104
Eyre, Godfrey, of Hassop, Derby.; father of Margaret Eyre (great-grandmother of Sir RF and of Lady F); Lady F calls him 'Rowland' and advances him one generation in error; he is the father of young RF's great-great-grandfather, not of his great-grandfather as Lady F states: 104
Eyre, Rowland. *See* Eyre, Godfrey

F., the Misses, at Naworth Castle: 38–40
Fallowfield, Father, Roman Catholic priest at Naworth Castle: 80
Fanshawe, Abigail (b. 1636), daughter of Sir Thomas Fanshawe, 1st Viscount Fanshawe of Dromore and his second wife, Elizabeth (*née* Cockayne); niece of Sir RF; not named: 106, 117
Fanshawe, Alice (1581–*c.* 1623), eldest daughter of Thomas Fanshawe and his second wife, Joan (*née* Smythe); half-sister of Sir Henry Fanshawe (young RF's grandfather); married (1602) Sir Christopher Hatton: 104
Fanshawe, Alice (d. 1662), daughter of Thomas Fanshawe of Jenkins and Susan (*née* Otten); she married (1659), as his second wife, John Fanshawe of Parsloes; thus she married a cousin of Sir RF and Lady F, and she herself is a first cousin once removed of them both: 107
Fanshawe, Alice [Sister Bedell] (*c.* 1602–66), eldest daughter of Sir Henry Fanshawe and Elizabeth (*née* Smythe); married (1619) Sir Capel Bedell, Bt., of Kirby, Northants; sister of Sir RF: 105 (nn), 108 (nn), 121, 135, 136, 190–1
Fanshawe, Alice (d. 1645), daughter of Sir Thomas Fanshawe, 1st Viscount Fanshawe of Dromore, and his second

Fanshawe, Alice (d. 1645)—*contd.* wife, Elizabeth (*née* Cockayne); niece of Sir RF: 106 (nn)

Fanshawe, Anna Maria (d. 1668), daughter of Sir Thomas Fanshawe, 2nd Viscount Fanshawe of Dromore, and his second wife, Sarah (*née* Evelyn) Wray; great-niece of Lady F and probably the one christened by her in 1667: 190 (nn)

Fanshawe, Anne (1609–25), youngest daughter of Sir Henry Fanshawe and Elizabeth (*née* Smythe); sister of Sir RF: 105 (nn)

Fanshawe, Anne (1628–1714), only child of Ann (*née* Alington) and Sir Thomas Fanshawe, later 1st Viscount Fanshawe of Dromore; her mother died at her birth; Anne herself never married; niece of Sir RF and cousin of young RF: 106, 108 (nn), 117 (nn)

Fanshawe, Ann (Nan) (1646–54), eldest daughter of Sir RF and Lady F; born on the Isle of Jersey: 96, 107, 119, 121, 122, 124, 133 (nn), 134, 135, 136

Fanshawe, Ann (Nan) (1655–?), sixth daughter (second of that name) of Sir RF and Lady F; she married a Mr. Ryder: 97, 107, 136, 141, 143, 169, 182; not named: 146, 153, 155, 157, 158, 160, 165, 174, 181, 185, 187, 188, 189, 190, 191, 217

Fanshawe, Catherine (1640–1726), daughter of Sir Thomas Fanshawe, 1st Viscount Fanshawe of Dromore, and his second wife, Elizabeth (*née* Cockayne); died unmarried; niece of Sir RF and cousin of young RF; not named: 106, 108, 117

Fanshawe, Charles (1643–1710), 4th Viscount Fanshawe of Dromore; 8th Remembrancer of the Exchequer; son of Sir Thomas Fanshawe, 1st Viscount Fanshawe of Dromore, and his second wife, Elizabeth (*née* Cockayne); nephew of Sir RF and cousin of young RF; not named: 106, 108, 117

Fanshawe, Elizabeth (*née* Smythe). *See* Smythe, Elizabeth

Fanshawe, Elizabeth (d. 1657), third daughter of Sir Henry Fanshawe and Elizabeth (*née* Smythe); died unmarried; sister of Sir RF; not named: 105, 108

Fanshawe, Elizabeth (d. 1641), daughter of Sir Thomas Fanshawe, 1st Viscount Fanshawe of Dromore, and his second wife, Elizabeth (*née* Cockayne); niece of Sir RF; not named: 106, 108

Fanshawe, Elizabeth (b. and d. 1649), second daughter of Sir RF and Lady F; born 13 June (not July) in Madrid, Spain; buried in the chapel of the French Hospital, Madrid: 97, 107, 129

Fanshawe, Elizabeth (1651–6), third daughter (second of that name) of Sir RF and Lady F: 97, 107, 133 (nn), 136, 137

Fanshawe, Elizabeth (Betty) (1662–?), eighth daughter (third of that name) of Sir RF and Lady F; she married (1684) Christopher Blount of the Middle Temple: 98, 107, 142, 151, 169, 175, 182; not named: 153, 155, 157, 158, 160, 162, 174, 178, 181, 185, 187, 188, 189, 190, 191

Fanshawe, Elizabeth (d. 1729), youngest daughter of Sir Thomas Fanshawe, 1st Viscount Fanshawe of Dromore, and his second wife, Elizabeth (*née* Cockayne); she married (between 1676 and 1685), as his second wife, Sir Thomas Fanshawe of Jenkins; niece of Sir RF and cousin of young RF: 107 (nn), 108 (nn)

Fanshawe, Evelyn (1669–87), 3rd Viscount Fanshawe of Dromore; only son of the 2nd Viscount and his second wife, Sarah (*née* Evelyn) Wray; Lady F calls him Thomas in error; great-nephew of Sir RF: 106, 210

Fanshawe, Harrison (b. and d. 1645), eldest son of Sir RF and Lady F: 96, 106, 107, 114

Fanshawe, Henry (*c.* 1506–68) of Jenkins, Essex; 1st Queen's Remembrancer of the Exchequer; brother of John Fanshawe of Fanshawe Gate; uncle of Thomas Fanshawe (Sir RF's grandfather) and therefore great-great-uncle of Sir RF; called 'Thomas' in error by Lady F; his daughters mentioned by Lady F were Anne (1562–84) and Susanna (b. 1567), who married Timothy Lucy, son of William Lucy of Charlecote: 104

Fanshawe, Sir Henry (1569–1616), of Fanshawe Gate, Derby, and Ware

Fanshawe, Sir Henry—*contd.*
Park, etc., Herts.; 3rd Remembrancer of the Exchequer; knighted 1603; eldest son of Thomas Fanshawe and his first wife Margaret (*née* Bourchier); married (after May 1593) Elizabeth, youngest daughter of Thomas (Customer) Smythe; father of Sir RF; grandfather of young RF; developer of Ware Park, which had been acquired by his father, Thomas Fanshawe: 95, 103, 104, 105, 108, 112, 113, 208

Fanshawe, Henry (1600–29), Captain in the Army; second son of Sir Henry Fanshawe and Elizabeth (*née* Smythe); brother of Sir RF and uncle of young RF: 106

Fanshawe, Henry (1634–85), of Dengey Hall, Essex; 7th Remembrancer of the Exchequer; son of Sir Thomas Fanshawe, 1st Viscount Fanshawe of Dromore, and his second wife, Elizabeth (*née* Cockayne); nephew of Sir RF and cousin of young RF; not named: 106, 108, 117

Fanshawe, Henry (1647–9), second son of Sir RF and Lady F: 96, 106, 120, 121, 123

Fanshawe, Henry (1657–8), fourth son (second of that name) of Sir RF and Lady F: 97, 107, 137

Fanshawe, Herbert Charles (HCF) (1852–1923), editor of the 1907 edition of Lady Fanshawe's Memoirs: v, xxi–xxii, 95

Fanshawe, Jane (d. 1639), daughter of Sir Thomas Fanshawe, 1st Viscount Fanshawe of Dromore, and his second wife, Elizabeth (*née* Cockayne); niece of Sir RF: 106 (nn)

Fanshawe, Joan [Sister Boteler] (1607–72), fourth daughter of Sir Henry Fanshawe and Elizabeth (*née* Smythe); she married first (1631) Sir William Boteler, Bt., of Teston, Kent; she married second (1647) Sir Philip Warwick of Frogpool, Kent; sister of Sir RF; godmother of Sir RF and Lady F's first son, Harrison, and of their daughter Ann (b. 1655): 96, 111, 119, 120, 137, 141; not named: 105, 108

Fanshawe, John (1504–78) of Fanshawe Gate, Derby; son of Henry (or Robert) Fanshawe (d. *c.* 1523); married second Margaret (*née* Eyre), widow of Hugh Wadd; great-grandfather of both Sir RF and Lady F; great-great-grandfather of young RF: 103–4 (nn)

Fanshawe, John (d. before 1666), third son of Sir Henry Fanshawe and Elizabeth (*née* Smythe); elder brother of Sir RF; died unmarried: 106

Fanshawe, John (1619–89) of Parsloes, Essex; eldest son of William Fanshawe of Parsloes and Katherine (*née* Wolstenholme); he married first (1639) Dorothea (*née* Kingsmill), by whom he had two sons: William (*c.* 1640–1708) and John (1644–*c.* 1662); he married second (1659) Alice, daughter of Thomas Fanshawe of Jenkins, by whom he had a son, John Fanshawe of Parsloes (1662–?); cousin of Sir RF and Lady F: 107

Fanshawe, John (d. 1693), son of Thomas Fanshawe of Jenkins and Susan (*née* Otten); brother of Sir Thomas Fanshawe of Jenkins; second cousin of young RF: 107 (nn)

Fanshawe, Katherine (b. *c.* 1590); second (not third, as stated by Lady F) daughter of Thomas Fanshawe and his second wife, Joan (*née* Smythe); half-sister of Sir Henry Fanshawe (grandfather of young RF); married (1608) John Bullock of Darley Abbey, Derby: 104

Fanshawe, Katherine (*née* Ferrers). *See* Ferrers, Katherine

Fanshawe, Katherine (b. 1652), fourth daughter of Sir RF and Lady F; died unmarried: 97, 107, 135, 143, 182; not named: 138, 139, 146, 153, 155, 157, 158, 160, 162, 165, 174, 178, 181, 185, 187, 188, 189, 190, 191, 217

Fanshawe, Katherine (d. 1684), third daughter of Sir Thomas Fanshawe, 2nd Viscount Fanshawe of Dromore, and his second wife, Sarah (*née* Evelyn) Wray; great-niece of Sir RF: 106, 107

Fanshawe, Lionel (1627–87), great-grandson of Robert Fanshawe of Fanshawe Gate; son of Lionel Fanshawe (1594–1653), Deputy-Lieutenant of Derbyshire, and his second wife, Anne (*née* Gill); the elder Lionel was a cousin of Sir RF; the younger Lionel served as secretary to Sir RF in both

Fanshawe, Lionel—*contd.*
Portugal and Spain: 145(nn), 153, 176, 180, 187, 188, 214
Fanshawe, Margaret (*c.* 1591–1640), youngest daughter of Robert Fanshawe of Dronfield by Dionis (*née* Baker); married (1616) Sir John Harrison of Balls Park, Herts.; mother of Lady F; grandmother of young RF: 95, 96, 104, 108–9, 110, 111
Fanshawe, Margaret (*c.* 1593–1658); third (not second, as stated by Lady F) daughter of Thomas Fanshawe and his second wife, Joan (*née* Smythe); half-sister of Sir Henry Fanshawe (grandfather of young RF); married (1616) Sir Benjamin Ayloffe: 104
Fanshawe, Margaret (b. 1653), fifth daughter of Sir RF and Lady F; she married (1675) Vincent Grantham of Goltho, Lincs.: 97, 107, 136, 143, 182; not named: 138, 139, 146, 153, 155, 157, 158, 160, 162, 165, 174, 178, 181, 185, 187, 188, 189, 190, 191, 217
Fanshawe, Mary (d. 1666), second daughter of Sir Henry Fanshawe and Elizabeth (*née* Smythe); married (1616) William Newce of Much Hadham, Herts.; sister of Sir RF: 105 (nn), 108
Fanshawe, Mary (1635–1701), daughter of Sir Thomas Fanshawe, 1st Viscount Fanshawe of Dromore, and his second wife, Elizabeth (*née* Cockayne); married first (1662) Sir Thomas Campbell, Bt., of Clay Hall, Barking, Essex (he d. 1668); married second (1668) her cousin Robert Sheffield; therefore she was no longer Lady Campbell when Lady F was writing the Memoirs; niece of Sir RF and cousin of young RF; not named: 106, 108, 117
Fanshawe, Mary (1656–60), seventh daughter of Sir RF and Lady F; in the text Lady F calls her the 'fourth daughter'—presumably the fourth daughter to die: 98, 107, 137, 141
Fanshawe, Sir Richard (1608–66); created Baronet (1650); knighted (1660); 5th Remembrancer of the Exchequer; Ambassador to Spain and Portugal; youngest son of Sir Henry Fanshawe of Fanshawe Gate and Ware Park by Elizabeth (*née* Smythe); married (1644) Ann, eldest daughter of Sir John Harrison of Balls Park; husband of Lady F and father of young RF: ix, x, xiv–xx *passim*, 95–186 *passim*, 208–21 *passim*; chronology of: 95–9; translation of Camoens's *Os Lusiadas*; xvii, 97; translation of *Pastor Fido*: 96; translation of Horace: 97, 184–5, 220; translation of *La Fida Pastora*: 98; translation of *Querer por solo querer*: 99; translation of *Fiestas de Aranjuez*: 99
Fanshawe, Richard (1648–59), third son of Sir RF and Lady F; buried in the Protestant churchyard in Paris: 96, 106, 121, 133 (nn), 136, 138, 139
Fanshawe, Richard (b. and d. 1663), fifth son (second of that name) of Sir RF and Lady F; died a few hours after his birth; buried in Lisbon in the Church of the Esperança: 98, 106, 148
Fanshawe, Sir Richard (1665–94), sixth son (third of that name) of Sir RF and Lady F; Lady F writes her Memoirs for him, her only surviving son: xvi, 98, 101–2, 107, 175–6; not named: 178, 181, 185, 187, 188, 189, 190
Fanshawe, Robert (1542–1613) of Fanshawe Gate, Dronfield, Derby.; married (1567) Dionis (*née* Barker); younger brother of Thomas Fanshawe, the great-uncle of Sir RF, and therefore great-great-uncle of young RF on his father's side, as Lady F states; however, he is also Lady F's grandfather, and thus great-grandfather of young RF on his mother's side: 95, 104
Fanshawe, Sir Simon (1604–80), Colonel of Horse; fourth son of Sir Henry Fanshawe and Elizabeth (*née* Smythe); elder brother of Sir RF; married Catherine (*née* Walter) Ferrers, widow of Knighton Ferrers of Bayfordbury, Herts., and became stepfather of Katherine Ferrers, who later married his nephew, Sir Thomas Fanshawe, 2nd Viscount Fanshawe of Dromore: 106
Fanshawe, Simon (1646–1716), 5th and last Viscount Fanshawe of Dromore; 9th Remembrancer of the Exchequer; son of Sir Thomas Fanshawe, 1st Viscount Fanshawe of Dromore, and his second wife, Elizabeth (*née* Cockayne); nephew of Sir RF and cousin of young RF; not named: 106, 108, 117

Fanshawe, Thomas (*c.* 1534–1601) of Jenkins and Dengey, Essex, and Ware Park, Herts.; 2nd Remembrancer of the Exchequer; son of John Fanshawe by Margaret (*née* Eyre); married first (*c.* 1568) Mary (*née* Bourchier); married second (*c.* 1579) Joan, daughter of Thomas (Customer) Smythe; grandfather of Sir RF; great-grandfather of young RF: 103–4, 105 (nn)

Fanshawe, Sir Thomas (1580–1631), of Jenkins, Essex, and Ware Park, Herts.; knighted (1624); Clerk of the Crown (1624); Surveyor General of the King's Lands (1625); notable member of Parliament for almost thirty years; eldest son of Thomas Fanshawe and his second wife, Joan (*née* Smythe); half-brother of Sir Henry Fanshawe (young RF's grandfather); he married (*c.* 1604) Ann (*née* Babington): 104

Fanshawe, Sir Thomas (1596–1665), of Fanshawe Gate, Derby, and Dengey, Essex, and Ware Park, Herts.; 4th Remembrancer of the Exchequer; dubbed Knight of the Bath upon the coronation of Charles I; created Viscount Fanshawe of Dromore in the Irish Peerage by Charles II (1661); expelled from the Long Parliament (1642), he suffered heavy financial losses in the Royalist cause; eldest son of Sir Henry Fanshawe by Elizabeth (*née* Smythe); eldest brother of Sir RF; married first (1627) Ann (*née* Alington); married second (1629) Elizabeth (*née* Cockayne): 96, 105–6, 107, 108, 113, 117 (nn), 119 (nn), 133, 135, 137, 151, 175, 190, 209, 218

Fanshawe, Thomas (1607–51), of Jenkins, Essex; son of Sir Thomas Fanshawe of Jenkins by Ann (*née* Babington); he married (1626) Susan (*née* Otten); they had three sons: Sir Thomas Fanshawe of Jenkins (below), William (d. unmarried 1683), and John (d. unmarried 1693); cousin of Sir RF and of Lady F: 107, 117, 153

Fanshawe, Sir Thomas (1628–1705), of Jenkins, Essex; son of Thomas Fanshawe of Jenkins by Susan (*née* Otten); knighted (1660); married first (1657) Margaret (*née* Heath) and had a daughter, Susanna (*c.* 1661–1714); married second Hon. Elizabeth Fanshawe, youngest daughter of Thomas, 1st Viscount Fanshawe of Dromore; second cousin of young RF: 107, 117, 137

Fanshawe, Sir Thomas (1632–74), 2nd Viscount Fanshawe of Dromore; 6th Remembrancer of the Exchequer; eldest son of Sir Thomas Fanshawe, 1st Viscount Fanshawe of Dromore, and his second wife, Elizabeth (*née* Cockayne); married first (1648) Katherine, daughter and heiress of Knighton Ferrers; married second (1665) Sarah, daughter and co-heiress of Sir John Evelyn and widow of Sir John Wray; nephew of Sir RF: 106, 117 (nn), 120, 175 (nn), 190, 191, 221

Fanshawe, Thomas, 3rd Viscount Fanshawe of Dromore. *See* Fanshawe, Evelyn

Fanshawe, William (1583–1634) of Parsloes, Essex; second son of Thomas Fanshawe and his second wife, Joan (*née* Smythe); half-uncle of Sir RF: 104

Fanshawe Gate, Derby, Fanshawe family estate in the parish of Dronfield: 95, 103, 104

Farnaby, Dr. Thomas (1575?–1647), schoolmaster and classical scholar; his school in Goldsmiths' Alley, Cripplegate, was attended by Sir RF: 112, 208

Feilding, Susan (*née* Villiers; d. 1655), Countess of Denbigh; married (1607) William Feilding, 1st Earl of Denbigh; she accompanied Queen Henrietta Maria to France as Lady of the Bedchamber: 121

Ferdinand II (1452–1516), King of Aragón (1479–1516); King of Castile and Léon (as Ferdinand V), 1474–1504; King of Sicily (1468–1516); King of Naples (1504–16): 129

Ferne, Henry, D.D. (1602–62), chaplain to Charles I; Vice-Chancellor of the University of Cambridge (1660, 1661); Master of Trinity College (1660–2); Dean of Ely (1661); Bishop of Chester (1662): 192 (nn)

Ferrer (or Ferrers), Captain Robert, on Lord Sandwich's staff in Spain (1666): 181

Ferrer, William, on Lord Sandwich's staff in Spain (1666): 182

Ferrers, Sir John (d. 1640), of Bayfordbury, Herts.; father of Knighton Ferrers by his second wife Anne (*née* Knighton): 106
Ferrers, Katherine (*c.* 1634–60), daughter of Knighton Ferrers of Bayfordbury, Herts., by Catherine (*née* Walter); step-daughter of Sir Simon Fanshawe; married (1648) Sir Thomas Fanshawe, later 2nd Viscount Fanshawe of Dromore, as his first wife, and died without heirs; it was through her that the Ferrers's property of Bayfordbury came into the Fanshawe family; niece-in-law of Sir RF and Lady F: 106, 121 (nn), 136, 141 (n)n
Ferrers, Knighton (1607–40), of Bayfordbury, Herts.; father of Katherine, who was the first wife of Sir Thomas Fanshawe (later 2nd Viscount Fanshawe of Dromore); married Catherine (*née* Walter); upon his death his widow married Sir Simon Fanshawe: 106, 121
fiesta de toros (feast of bulls): 174, 175
Fife, Scotland: 51, 200
Firth of Cromarty, Scotland: 200
Firth of Forth, Scotland: 200, 204
Fitch [Fitts], Col. Thomas, officer in Cromwell's Army: 60, 201
Fleming, Sir William (d. before 1672), Gentleman Usher to Charles I; Chamberlain of the Household of Charles II; sent in 1648 to invite Prince Charles to Scotland: 203
Fletcher, John (1579–1625), playwright; author of *The Humorous Lieutenant*: 54, 200
Floors, home of the Countess of Roxburghe near Kelso, Scotland: 66, 203
Foot's Cray [Fotts Cray], near Frogpool (now Frognal), Kent; burial place of the Warwick branch of the Fanshawes and also of Sir RF and Lady F's daughter Elizabeth (second of that name): 107, 137
Fordyce [Fordice], Banffshire, Scotland: 62
Forrest [Forett], David, minister of Kilconquhar, Scotland: 74, 205
Fossett, Mrs. Ursula, servant to the Fanshawe daughters on trip to Spain (1664): 154
France, Queen of. *See* Marie Thérèse
Frances, Laundress in Sir RF's retinue on trip from Madrid to Portugal (1666): 180
Francis, Groom in Sir RF's retinue (1666): 180, 186
Francis, Mrs., chambermaid in Fanshawe retinue (1664), 154
Fraser, Andrew (d. *c.* 1656), 2nd Lord Fraser of Muchalls (1636); Parliamentary Commissioner (1644, 1645, 1649): 63
Frederick V (1596–1632), Elector Palatine of the Rhine (1610–20); subsequently King of Bohemia (1619–20); married (1613) Elizabeth, eldest daughter of James I; father of Princes Rupert and Maurice: 213
Frederick Henry (1584–1647), Prince of Orange; father of William II, Prince of Orange; grandfather of William III, King of England: 193
Fregenal [Frexinal] de la Sierra, Spain: 180
French Ambassador to the Court of Spain. *See* d'Aubusson
Frescheville, John, Baron Frescheville of Staveley (1665); his daughter and co-heir, Elizabeth, married the son of Sir Philip Warwick by his first wife, Dorothy (*née* Hutton): 190
Frinton Hall, Essex, an estate held by Lady F: 191
Frogpool (now Frognal), Kent, site of the estate of Sir Philip Warwick, Sir RF's brother-in-law: 107, 136, 137, 190
Fuenterrabía, Spain: 213
Fuentes, Gaspar Perez Tello de Guzmán, Marquis of; Ambassador from Spain to the Court of Louis XIV: 161, 175
Fuentes, Spain: 161
Fyvie [Fivye], Aberdeenshire, Scotland: 6, 56–63, 200, 201

Gale [Gaile], Robert (1595–1659), chaplain to the Countess of Devonshire: 84
Galway, Ireland: 97, 126
Gardiner, Samuel Rawson (1829–1902), and 1875 edition of Halkett Memoirs: v, 3
Garmouth [Garmuth], Moray, Scotland: 62
Gaspar, El Negro, on Lord Sandwich's staff in Spain (1666): 182

Gately, Mr., Surgeon on Lord Sandwich's staff in Spain (1666): 182
Geffreys. *See* Jeffreys
Gentleman, Mr., Cook in Lord Sandwich's staff in Spain (1666): 182
German Ambassador to the Spanish Court (1664). *See* Poëtting, Graf Francis Eusebius von
Ghent, Flanders: 140
Gibbs, Mr., on Lord Sandwich's staff in Spain (1666): 182
Gibraltar, Straits of: 127
Gibson, Thomas, on Lord Sandwich's staff in Spain (1666): 182
Gifford (or Jefford), John (b. 1603), Colonel of Irish Foot: 123–4, 210, 211
Gilmour, Sir John, of Craigmiller, advocate; later (1661–70) Lord President of the Court of Session: 65
Glamis [Glames], Angus, Scotland: 56
Glanville, Mary (1616–92), daughter of Sir John Glanville of Broad Hinton (1568–1661) by Winifred (*née* Bourchier); married (1636) Col. Piers Edgcumbe; their children were second cousins once removed of Sir RF: 144 (nn)
Glencairn. *See* Cunningham
Gloucester. *See* Henry, Duke of
Glover, Mrs., AM's landlady in Edinburgh: 75
Goddard [Godhard], Thomas, English merchant in Madrid (1664): 166
Godolphin, Sir Francis, of Breage, Cornwall (d. 1666); father of Francis Godolphin, who accompanied Sir RF to Spain (1664), and of Sidney, later 1st Earl of Godolphin: 153
Godolphin, Francis (*c.* 1642–75), second son of Sir Francis Godolphin; went to Spain with the Fanshawes (1664) and again with the Earl of Sandwich (1666); died unmarried: 153, 164, 174
Godolphin, Sir William (1634–96); secretary to Lord Arlington and lent to Lord Sandwich to serve in Spain (1666); knighted (1668); became Envoy Extraordinary (1669) and then Ambassador in Spain (1671): 181
Góngora, Don Juan de; Master of the Mint and President of the Spanish Council of Finance until his dismissal in 1663: 174
Goodes, John, on Lord Sandwich's staff in Spain (1666): 182
Goring, George (1585–1663), created 1st Earl of Norwich (1644); son of George Goring of Hurstpierpoint by Anne (*née* Denny); Gentleman of the Privy Chamber of Henry, Prince of Wales; Master of the Horse to Queen Henrietta Maria (1628–39); created Lord Goring (1628); after the Restoration, Captain of the King's Guard: 130
Goring, George (1608–57), styled Lord Goring; son of the 1st Earl of Norwich by Mary (*née* Nevill); Royalist General; married (1629) Lady Lettice Boyle; he died in Spain and was buried in St. George's, a chapel of the English Jesuits in Madrid: 130, 211
Gower [Gore], Sir Thomas (*c.* 1605–72), of Sittenham, Yorks.; husband of Elizabeth (*née* Howard), daughter of Sir William Howard of Naworth and sister of Sir Charles Howard: 32, 198
Graham, James (1612–50), styled Lord Graham until 1626; 5th Earl of Montrose (1626); 1st Marquis of Montrose (1644); Royalist military leader; executed for treason in Scotland: 212
Granada, Spain: 128–9
Grandison. *See* Villiers
Grantham, Vincent, of Goltho, Lincs.; married (1675) Margaret, fifth daughter of Sir RF and Lady F: 107
Gravesend, Kent: 25, 138, 151, 196
Grenville [Grenvile], Sir Bevil (1596–1643), Royalist soldier; killed at the Battle of Lansdown; father of Sir John Grenville: 117 (nn)
Grenville [Grenvile], Sir John (1628–1701), created Earl of Bath (1661); son of Sir Bevil Grenville; Gentleman of the Bedchamber (1645); defender of the Scilly Isles; with Charles II in exile; aided in smoothing the way for the Restoration: 117
Grenville [Grenvile], Sir Richard (1600–58); Royalist; King's General in the West; uncle of Sir John Grenville; brother of Sir Bevil Grenville: 117
Guadiana River, Iberian Peninsula: 162
Guildford. *See* Boyle, Lady Elizabeth
Guildford, Surrey: 154
Guzmán, Dona Maria. *See* Cruz, Senhora

H., W., Advocate in AM's lawsuit concerning her inheritance: 64, 202
Hague, The, Netherlands: 97, 140
Halkett, Anna, daughter of Sir James Halkett by his first wife Margaret (*née* Montgomery); she married Sir Andrew Ker of Cavers: xiv, 6, 75, 79, 205, 206
Halkett, Sir Charles (d. 1697), son of Sir James Halkett by his first wife, Margaret (*née* Montgomery); created baronet (1671); married Janet (*née* Murray), daughter of Sir Patrick Murray of Pitdennis: xiv, 6, 7, 201, 205, 206–7
Halkett, Elizabeth (b. 1656), daughter of Lady H and Sir James Halkett: 6
Halkett, Grizell, sister of Sir James Halkett; married Sir Thomas Ker of Cavers: 79, 86
Halkett, Henry (b. 1658), son of Lady H and Sir James Halkett: 6
Halkett, Sir James (1610?–70), Scottish Royalist; son of Sir Robert Halkett of Pitfirrane; knighted (1633); colonel of a cavalry regiment in the army of Scotland; married first Margaret (*née* Montgomery); married second (1656) Anne Murray, ix, x, xii, xiii–xiv, 6, 7, 9, 65–87 *passim*, 201, 202, 204, 205, 206
Halkett, James, son of Sir James Halkett by his first wife, Margaret (*née* Montgomery): xiv, 6, 202, 205, 206
Halkett, Janet (*née* Murray), daughter of Sir Patrick Murray of Pitdennis; wife of Sir Charles Halkett: 206
Halkett, Jean (b. 1670), daughter of Lady H and Sir James Halkett: 7
Halkett, Margaret (*née* Montgomery), Lady, daughter of Sir Robert Montgomery of Skelmorlie; first wife of Sir James Halkett: 205
Halkett, Mary, daughter of Sir James Halkett by Margaret (*née* Montgomery); married Sir William Bruce of Kinross: xiv, 6, 75, 79, 86, 205, 206
Halkett, Robert (1661–92), son of Lady H and Sir James Halkett; commissioned a captain (1684); served under James II in Ireland (*c.* 1690); captured and imprisoned (1690–2): 6, 7, 201
Hambleton, Jane, woman in Edinburgh with the second sight: 69, 70
Hamerton, Hunts., location of the estate of Capel Bedell, Sir RF's brother-in-law: 97, 121, 136, 190
Hamilton, William (1606–51), styled Earl of Arran (1609–25); 3rd Marquis of Hamilton (1625–43); created 1st Duke of Hamilton (1643); Royalist; killed at the Battle of Worcester: 202
Hampton Court Palace, Middlesex: xvi, 96, 120, 142, 143, 195, 210
Harbord, Sir Charles (1640–72), son of Sir Charles Harbord (1595–1679), Surveyor-General to Charles II; the younger Sir Charles was knighted (1665), served with Lord Sandwich in Spain, and died in the same action at Solebay in which Sandwich was killed: 181
Hardin, Richard (d. 1658), Groom of the Bedchamber to Charles II: 53, 200
Haro, Don Luis de. *See* Carpio
Harrison, Abraham, son of Sir John Harrison by Margaret (*née* Fanshawe); elder brother of Lady F: 109
Harrison, Sir John (1589–1669), of Balls Park, Herts.; knighted (1640); M.P. for Lancaster from 1640 until he was disabled (1643); joined Charles I at Oxford (1643); active Royalist, heavily fined by Parliament; married first (1616) Margaret (*née* Fanshawe), youngest daughter of Robert Fanshawe of Fanshawe Gate, Dronfield, by Dionis (*née* Barker); married second Mary (*née* Shotbolt), daughter of Philip Shotbolt of Yardley, Herts., by Elizabeth (*née* Marsh); father of Lady F; grandfather of young RF: 111, 114, 115, 117, 119, 122, 133, 134, 141, 144, 175, 187, 188, 190, 191, 209, 221
Harrison, John, son of Sir John Harrison and his first wife, Margaret (*née* Fanshawe); eldest brother of Lady F; married (1645) Lettice (*née* Ludlow); he had at least three surviving daughters in 1669: Ann, Margaret, and Lettice: 109, 110 (nn), 111 (nn)
Harrison, John (b. 1670), eldest son of Richard Harrison (half-brother of Lady F) by Audrey (*née* Villiers); he was born 15 Sept. 1670, so Lady F is probably in error as to the date of his christening: 191

Harrison, Margaret (*née* Fanshawe). *See* Fanshawe, Margaret (*c.* 1591–1640)
Harrison, Margaret [Sister Turnor] (1627–79), daughter of Sir John Harrison by his first wife, Margaret (*née* Fanshawe); younger sister of Lady F; she married (1653) Edmund Turnor, who was knighted (1664): 109, 111, 122, 124, 136, 151, 191, 221; not named: 110, 114, 118, 119, 133
Harrison, Mary (d. 1685), daughter of Sir John Harrison by his second wife, Mary (*née* Shotbolt); half-sister of Lady F; she married, as his first wife, Sir William Lytton, son of Sir Rowland Lytton of Knebworth, Herts.: 109
Harrison, Richard (1646–1725), son of Sir John Harrison by his second wife, Mary (*née* Shotbolt); half-brother of Lady F; he married Audrey (*née* Villiers; d. 1715): 109, 120, 191
Harrison, sister; either Lady F's brother John's wife, Lettice; her half-brother Richard's wife, Audrey; or her half-sister, Mary: 191, 221
Harrison, William, of Beaumont, Lancs.; married Margaret (*née* Gardiner); father of Sir John Harrison; paternal grandfather of Lady F: 110
Harrison, William (d. 1643), son of Sir John Harrison by his first wife, Margaret (*née* Fanshawe); M.P. for Queensborough (1640); killed in a skirmish against the Earl of Essex near Oxford; brother of Lady F; she is in error concerning his place of burial, which was Oxford: 109, 110, 111, 201
Hartingfordbury [Hatonfortbery], Herts.; Fanshawe children left there to nurse (1648); Lady F leased an estate there (1668): 121, 190
Hatton, Mr., in Fanshawe retinue (1664): 153, 174
Hatton, Sir Christopher (1540–91), Lord Chancellor to Queen Elizabeth (1587); on his death his estates went to his cousin and heir, Sir Christopher Hatton (d. 1619), husband of Alice (*née* Fanshawe): 104
Hatton, Sir Christopher (d. 1619), of Kirby, Northants; married Alice (*née* Fanshawe), one of the half-sisters of Sir Henry Fanshawe (Sir RF's father); thus half-uncle of Sir RF: 104
Hay, Lady Ann (*née* Douglas) (d. 1667), Countess of Kinnoull; widow of George Hay, 2nd Earl of Kinnoull; mother of George Hay, 3rd Earl of Kinnoull: 56, 200
Hay, Archibald, cautioner to the Earl of Kinnoull on a bond due Jean Murray: 64, 202
Hay, George (*c.* 1596–1644), 2nd Earl of Kinnoull (1634); Royalist; involved in litigation with AM: 64, 199, 200, 202
Hay, George (*c.* 1623–49), 3rd Earl of Kinnoull (1644); son of the 2nd Earl by Lady Anne (*née* Douglas); Royalist; sent (1649) to the Orkneys to raise them for the King; involved in litigation with AM: 200, 202
Hay, Col. John (d. 1675), son of Sir John Hay of Baro, Haddington; Scotsman; Royalist soldier: 72
Hay, John (1596–1653), 8th Lord Hay of Yester (1609); 1st Earl of Tweeddale (1646); he married first (1624) Lady Jean (*née* Seton; d. 1625); he married second (*c.* 1642), Lady Margaret (*née* Montgomerie); active Scottish Royalist; he died either in May 1653 or as late as 1654; Lady H may be referring to him, or possibly to his son, the 2nd Earl and 1st Marquis: 64, 65, 202; the Tweeddale house in Edinburgh: 64, 66–7, 68, 70
Hay, John (1626–97), 2nd Earl (1653) and 1st Marquis of Tweeddale (1694); supporter of both Royalists and Covenanters; son of the 1st Earl and his first wife, Lady Jean (*née* Seton); it is not clear whether Lady H is referring to him or to his father, the 1st Earl, in her Memoirs: 202
Hay, Lady Margaret (1617–64), Countess of Tweeddale; daughter of Alexander Montgomerie, 6th Earl of Eglinton, by Lady Anna (*née* Livingstone); married (*c.* 1642), as his second wife, John Hay, 1st Earl of Tweeddale: 64
Haydon [Heyden], Mrs., owner of the Priory of Ware in Herts. which Sir RF leased for one year (1656): 137
Heath, Sir Edward, of Cottesmore, Rutland; father of Margaret, first wife

Heath, Sir Edward—*contd.*
of Sir Thomas Fanshawe of Jenkins: 107

Heath, Margaret (d. 1674), daughter and sole heir of Sir Edward Heath of Cottesmore, Rutland; first wife (1657) of Sir Thomas Fanshawe of Jenkins (second cousin of young RF): 107

Heath, Sir Robert (1575–1649), Attorney-General (1625); Lord Chief Justice of Common Pleas (1631): 133

Heaver, John, D.D. (d. 1670); fellow of Eton College (1661); Canon of Windsor (1662); chaplain to Sir RF: 143, 214

Hele [Heele], Sir Thomas, Bt., of Bradninch, near Modbury, Devon (d. 1670); Sheriff of Devon (1635–6); M.P. for Plympton (1626, 1628–9, 1640); attended the King at Oxford (1643); one of the chief commanders of the Royalist forces at the siege of Plymouth (1648); Lady F calls him 'Sir John' in error: 144

Helloe [Hellowe], Mr., Chief Butler in Fanshawe retinue (1664): 154, 180, 187

Henchman [Henshaman], Humphrey, D.D. (1592–1675); Bishop of Salisbury (1660); Bishop of London (1663): 106, 144, 191 (nn)

Henrietta Anne, Princess (1644–70); daughter of Charles I; wife of the Duke of Orléans; favourite sister of Charles II: 121, 122, 132, 202

Henrietta Maria (1609–69), Queen Consort of Charles I of England (1625–49); daughter of Henry IV of France; she was in England 28 July 1662–24 June 1665, residing at Somerset House: 9, 10, 29, 96, 114, 115, 116, 119, 120, 121, 122, 132, 139, 152, 187–8, 191, 193, 213, 220, 221

Henry, Duke of Gloucester (1640–60), third son of Charles I: 5, 10, 23, 140, 141, 193 (nn), 195, 196

Henry Frederick, Prince of Wales (1594–1612), elder brother of Charles I; Sir Henry Fanshawe (1569–1616) was one of his favourites: 105, 208

Herbert, Philip (1621–69), 5th Earl of Pembroke (1650); supporter of the Commonwealth, but Cupbearer and Bearer of the Golden Spurs at the coronation of Charles II; married first (1639) Penelope (*née* Naunton), widow of Paul Bayning, Viscount Bayning of Sudbury; married second (1649) Katherine (*née* Villiers); father of Lord William Herbert, later 6th Earl of Pembroke: 137, 212

Herbert, William (1640–74), styled Lord Herbert (1650–69); 6th Earl of Pembroke (1669); eldest son of the 5th Earl and his first wife, Penelope (*née* Naunton) Bayning; accompanied by Sir RF on a trip to France (1658): 137 (nn), 143–4

Hermiston, Midlothian: 64, 201–2

Hertford Church. *See* All Saints Church, Hertford

Heyden. *See* Haydon

Heysham [Hiessom], Joan, of Highfield, Lancs.; wife of Thomas Harrison of Beaumont, Lancs.; grandmother of Sir John Harrison (Lady F's father): 110

Highgate, Middlesex: 80

Hiliard, Mrs., a widow who had rented the manor at Burstall Garth, York, from Lady F: 191

Hind, probably Sir John Lawson's ketch; part of the fleet taking the Fanshawes to Spain (1664); commanded by Capt. John King: 154

Hinderskelfe (or Hinderskelle), York, Sir Charles Howard's house beyond York; site of the present Castle Howard: 32, 198

Hinojosa [Hinoesser], Doña Maria Ramirez d'Avellano Mendoza y Alvardo, Marchioness of; wife of the Count of Frigiliano; *camerera mayor* to Queen Maria Anna of Spain: 165; not named: 166, 176, 178, 181, 184

Hitch, Robert, D.D. (d. 1677); Dean of York (1665–77): 191

Hitchin, Herts., site of a manor held by Sir RF through a grant from Queen Henrietta Maria; Lady F was forced to give it up through lack of funds: 191, 221

Holdsworth [Howlsworth], Richard, D.D. (d. 1649); fellow of St. John's College, Cambridge; master of Emmanuel College, Cambridge, at the time of AH's mother's death; active in the Royalist cause; a notable preacher: 108, 109, 110

Holland. *See* Rich, Henry

Holles, Denzell (1599–1680), created Baron Holles of Ifield (1661); English Ambassador to Paris (1662–7): 216
Hollis, Dr. *See* Baylie, Richard, D.D.
Holmes, Sir Robert (1622–92), Captain of the *Reserve* (1663); knighted (1666); governor of the Isle of Wight (1672–92): 150
Honeywood, Sir Philip, Royalist agent (1656–9); Lieutenant-Governor of Portsmouth (1664); son of Robert Honeywood of Charing, Kent: 154
Hooton, Edward, Page on Lord Sandwich's staff in Spain (1666): 182
Hopton [Hopter], Sir Arthur (1588?–1650), diplomatist; accompanied, as his secretary, Lord Cottington, Ambassador Extraordinary to Spain (1629) and remained there as English agent; succeeded Lord Aston as Ambassador in Spain and remained there throughout the Civil Wars: 113
Hopton, Sir Ralph (1596–1652), created Baron Hopton of Stratton (1643); Royalist General; member of the Council of the Prince of Wales; died in exile: 113, 119
Howard, Anne, daughter of Edward, 1st Lord Howard of Escrick; wife of Sir Charles Howard of Naworth Castle, later (1661) 1st Earl of Carlisle; friend of AM; sister of Thomas Howard: xi, xiii, 5, 11, 12–13, 15, 19, 22, 31, 32, 33, 34, 35–50 *passim*, 51, 65, 193, 198. *See also* Walsingham, Lady Ann (*née* Howard)
Howard, Sir Charles (1629?–85) of Naworth Castle; created 1st Earl of Carlisle (1661); son of Sir William Howard of Naworth; husband of Anne Howard, daughter of Edward, 1st Lord Howard of Escrick; diplomatist: xi, 5, 32, 33, 34–50 *passim*, 51, 198
Howard, Edward (d. 1675), 1st Lord Howard of Escrick (1628); son of Thomas, 1st Earl of Suffolk; supporter of the Commonwealth; father of Anne and Thomas Howard: x, 5, 12–22 *passim*, 33, 194, 198, 206, 207
Howard, Edward (1646–92), son of Sir Charles Howard of Naworth Castle by Anne (*née* Howard); not named: 32, 37
Howard, Elizabeth, daughter of Sir William Howard of Naworth; one of the sisters of Sir Charles Howard residing at Hinderskelfe; wife of Sir Thomas Gower: 32, 198
Howard, George (1625?–91), 4th Earl of Suffolk (1689); son of Theophilus Howard, 2nd Earl of Suffolk; succeeded to the title upon the death of his brother James, the 3rd Earl: 24 (nn), 196
Howard, James (d. 1689), 3rd Earl of Suffolk (1640); son of the 2nd Earl by Lady Elizabeth (*née* Home); not named: 196
Howard, Mary (*née* Boteler; d. 1634), Lady, daughter of John, 1st Lord Boteler of Brantfield; wife of Edward, 1st Lord Howard of Escrick (married 1623); mother of Anne and Thomas Howard: 19
Howard, Theophilus (d. 1640), 2nd Earl of Suffolk (1626); brother of Edward, 1st Lord Howard of Escrick: 194, 207
Howard, Thomas (1561–1626), 1st Earl of Suffolk (1603); son of Thomas Howard, 4th Duke of Norfolk by Margaret (*née* Audley); father of Edward, 1st Lord Howard of Escrick, and of Theophilus Howard, 2nd Earl of Suffolk: 194
Howard, Thomas (1590?–1669), 2nd Earl of Berkshire (1626); 2nd son of Thomas Howard, 1st Earl of Suffolk, by his second wife, Catherine (*née* Knyvett); member of the Council of the Prince of Wales; Governor of the Prince of Wales, but did not go to France with him: 113, 119
Howard, Thomas (1625–78), 2nd Lord Howard of Escrick (1675); son of Edward, 1st Lord Howard of Escrick; was in love with AM; married (1646) Lady Elizabeth (*née* Mordaunt): x, xii, 5, 11–23 *passim*, 193, 194, 198
Howlsworth. *See* Holdsworth
Humber, River, Yorkshire: 191
Humorous Lieutenant, *The*, play by John Fletcher: 54, 200
Humphrey, Bishop of London. *See* Henchman, Humphrey
Hyde, Mr., godfather of AH: 108
Hyde, Anne (1638–71), Duchess of York; eldest daughter of Sir Edward Hyde, later 1st Earl of Clarendon, by his second wife, Frances (*née* Aylesbury); married (1659) James, Duke of York,

Hyde, Anne—*contd.*
and by him became mother of Mary II and Anne, Queens of England: 152 (nn), 188, 220.

Hyde, Sir Edward (1609–75), created 1st Earl of Clarendon (1661); Councillor to Prince of Wales (1644–9); Joint Ambassador to Spain (with Cottington) (1649–51); Secretary of State (1653–7); Lord High Chancellor (1658–67); married first (1629) Anne (*née* Ayliffe or Ayloff); married second (1634) Frances (*née* Aylesbury); godfather of Lady F's daughter Ann (born in Jersey): xvi–xvii, 112, 113, 119, 139 (nn), 130 (nn), 132, 137, 140, 141, 142, 148, 151, 171, 179, 195, 196, 197, 208, 209, 211, 212, 218, 219; Lady F's character of: 132–3

Hyde, Frances (*née* Aylesbury; 1617–67), Countess of Clarendon; daughter of Sir Thomas Aylesbury, Bt., by Anne (*née* Denman); second wife (married 1643) of Sir Edward Hyde: 141 (nn)

Ibarra [Iubara], Don Diego de (d. 1676), Governor of Cádiz, *pro tem.* (1664): 155, 156, 158; wife of: 155, 156, 158

Illescas, Spain: 163

Inchiquin. *See* O'Brien

Infanta of Spain. *See* Margarita Teresa; Maria Anna

Inquisitor General of Spain. *See* Aragón, Don Pascual de

Ireland, Lady F's comments on: 127

Irvia, Count of, Spanish nobleman; owner of the house the Fanshawes stayed in at Vallecas, Spain: 163, 169

Irving, Washington (1783–1859), American author; on the Alhambra: 211

Isabella I (1451–1504), Queen of Castile and León (1474–1504); wife of Ferdinand II: 129

Itonia, Marques of. *See* Aitona

Iubara. *See* Ibarra

James I (1566–1625), King of England (1603–25) and, as James VI, of Scotland (1567–1625): 10, 104

James II (1633–1701), King of England, Scotland, and Ireland (1685–8)

— as Duke of York: 215, 220; escape from St. James's Palace: x, xi, xix, 5, 6, 7, 23–6, 31, 41, 53–4, 195, 196; and insubordination against the Prince of Wales (1648): 29, 197; as Lord High Admiral: 141, 218; Lady F calls on: 152–3, 188

— as King: 7, 195, 196, 201

James, 2nd Duke of Cambridge (1663–7); second son of James, Duke of York by Ann (*née* Hyde); created Duke and Earl of Cambridge and Baron Dauntsey (1664): 188, 220

Jamett [Jemett], Mr., Page in Fanshawe retinue (1664): 153, 180, 186. *See also* Jarret

Jarrald, Richard, Under-secretary to Lord Sandwich on mission to Spain (1666): 182

Jarret, Master, accompanied Sir RF's body from Madrid to London; possibly the same as Mr. Jamett above: 188

Jeffreys, Colonel. *See* Gifford, John

Jeffreys [Geffreys], Mr., in Fanshawe retinue (1664): 153

Jeffrys, Mr., Page on Lord Sandwich's staff in Spain (1666): 181

Jenkins, Barking, Essex, estate of Thomas Fanshawe, the grandfather of Sir RF; inherited by Thomas Fanshawe of Jenkins, cousin of both Sir RF and Lady F: 103, 104, 136

Jerez, Spain, 159, 161

Jermyn, Henry (*c.* 1604–84), Baron Jermyn of St. Edmundsbury, Suffolk; created (1660) Earl of St. Albans; as Lord Jermyn was appointed Governor of Jersey in 1644; his father was Governor before him: 118

Jersey, Isle of: 96, 118–19, 121; Mont Orgueil Castle: 118 (nn); St. Elizabeth Castle (not St. Mary's Castle as stated by Lady F): 118 (nn)

John, Don, of Austria (1547–78), natural son of Emperor Charles V: 217

John [Juan], Don, of Austria (1629–79), natural son of Philip IV of Spain; general of the Spanish army invading Portugal (1661–4); after the death of Philip IV he gradually became head of the Spanish party against the Queen Regent and her Confessor, and wielded the real power of the kingdom after

John [Juan]—*contd.*
Charles II assumed authority as King of Spain in 1677: 148, 162, 183, 215
Juego [*Jogo*] *de Cañas*: 161, 169–70, 216, 217
Juego [*Jogo*] *de Toros*: 161, 216

Ker, Sir Andrew, of Cavers, Roxburghshire; husband of Anna (*née* Halkett); son-in-law of Sir James Halkett: 205
Ker, Lady Isabel (*née* Douglas; d. 1672), Countess of Roxburghe; daughter of William Douglas, 7th Earl of Morton; married (after 1643), as his third wife, Robert Ker, 1st Earl of Roxburghe; married second (1656) James Graham, 2nd Marquis of Montrose; AM visited her at Floors in Roxburghshire (1652): 66, 202–3, 204
Ker, Jean (*née* Drummond; d. 1643), Countess of Roxburghe; daughter of Patrick, 3rd Lord Drummond; married (1614), as his second wife, Robert Ker, 1st Earl of Roxburghe; governess to the children of Charles I: 10, 193
Ker, Robert (*c.* 1570–1650), created 1st Earl of Roxburghe (1616); took little part in the political and religious conflicts in Scotland during his lifetime: 193, 203, 204
Ker (originally Drummond), Sir William (d. 1675); succeeded his grandfather (1650) as 2nd Earl of Roxburghe; active Royalist and friend to AM: 71, 204
Kerke, Mr., Page on Lord Sandwich's staff in Spain (1666): 181
Kesten, Mrs. Elizabeth, Housekeeper in Fanshawe retinue to Spain (1664): 154
Kestian [Kesten], Mrs., Governess to the Fanshawe children on trip to Spain (1664): 154, 158, 176
Killegrew, William, on Lord Sandwich's staff in Spain (1666): 182
Kilmorey, Lady. *See* Needham, Bridget
King, Sir Andrew (d. 1678), London merchant; knighted (1660); accompanied Sir RF to Spain (1664); left Madrid (1665): 153, 164, 174
King, Capt. John, commander of the *Hind*, ketch on the Fanshawes' trip to Spain (1664): 154
Kingsmill [Kinsmall], Dorothea, daughter of Sir Richard Kingsmill of Malshanger, Hants; married (1639), as his first wife, John Fanshawe of Parsloes; cousin-in-law of Lady F and Sir RF: 107 (nn)
Kingsmill [Kinsmall], Sir Richard, of Malshanger, Hants; father of Dorothea, first wife of John Fanshawe of Parsloes; Lady F calls him in error 'Sir William Kinsmall': 107
Kinnoull [Kinowle]. *See* May
Kinross [Kinrose], Scotland; a seat of the Earls of Dunfermline: 6, 55, 58
Kinsale, Ireland; Lady F fled there to join Sir RF after the Cork uprising (Oct. 1649); Kinsale was surrendered to Cromwell's forces on 12 Nov. 1649: 123, 124
Knollys [Knowles], Joanna (*née* Wolstenholme), Lady, daughter of Sir John Wolstenholme, the elder, by Catherine (*née* Fanshawe); wife of Sir Robert Knollys of Grays, Oxon. (grandson of the famous Sir Francis Knollys); attended Margaret (*née* Fanshawe) Harrison, AH's mother, during an illness: 109
Knollys (heretofore Vaux), Nicholas (1631–74); son of Lady Elizabeth (*née* Howard) Knollys, Countess of Banbury; nephew of Edward, 1st Lord Howard of Escrick: 21 (nn)
Knollys, Lady Elizabeth (*née* Howard). *See* Vaux

L., M., a suitor proposed for AM by her mother: 18
Lancaster, Lancs., 111
Land's End, Cornwall, 117
Laud, William (1573–1645), Archbishop of Canterbury (1633–45); advisor to Charles I; executed for treason: 197
Launceston [Lanston], Cornwall: 117
Lawson, Sir John (d. 1665), of Ashford, Essex; Admiral; knighted (1660); commander-in-chief of the fleet taking Sir RF to Spain (1664); his ketch was probably the *Hind*: 154, 155, 157
Le Blanc, Mr., Page in Fanshawe's retinue (1664): 153
Le Blanc, Mrs., Waiting-woman in Fanshawe retinue (1664): 154
Lebrija [Lybria], Spain: 159
Lee, Sir Charles, of Billesley, Warwickshire; commander of a Company of Foot at Oxford (1645); Royalist; knighted (1645): 115

Legge, William (1609?–72), Royalist: helped Charles I to escape from Hampton Court and was with him during his flight to the Isle of Wight: 210
Leith, Scotland: 51, 71, 200, 204
Lemercier, Dona Mariana, wife of the Portuguese Secretary of State, Antonio de Sousa: 146 (nn)–147
Lenthall, William (1591–1622), Speaker of the House of Commons (1640–53): 26 (nn), 197
Leopold I (1640–1705), Holy Roman Emperor (1658–1705); second son of Emperor Ferdinand III and his first wife, Maria Anna, daughter of Philip III of Spain; married (1666) Margarita Teresa, the Infanta of Spain: 176, 183, 220
Lepanto, Battle of (7 Oct. 1571): 168, 217
Leventhorpe [Loventhorp], Sir Thomas (d. 1679), of Blakesware, Herts.; married (1654) Mary, daughter of Sir Capel Bedell by Alice (*née* Fanshawe; Sir RF's sister); nephew-in-law of Sir RF and cousin to young RF: 108
Levine [Lovin], Mr., in Fanshawe retinue (1664): 153, 164
Liche (or Lixe), Marchioness of, Spanish noblewoman; daughter of the Duke of Medina Celi and wife of Gaspar de Haro; probably the references to her husband are actually to her since he was in prison in 1665: 174, 175, 180, 182
Liche (or Lixe), Gaspar de Haro, Marquis of (d. 1687), Spanish nobleman; his other titles included Marquis of Carpio and Count-Duke of Olivarez; son of Don Luis de Haro; husband of the daughter of the Duke of Medina Celi; imprisoned after the Battle of Evora (1663) until 1668; HCF suggests that Lady F wrote 'Marques' in error for 'Marquesa': 174, 175, 180, 182
Lilburne, Col. Robert (1613–65), regicide; officer of the Parliamentary Army: 60, 201
Limerick. *See* Dongan
Limerick [Limbrick], Ireland: 97, 124; Mayor of, *see* Comyn, Nicholas; Recorder of, *see* Stackpool, Mr.
Linares, Spain: 162
Linch, Mr., on Lord Sandwich's staff in Spain (1666): 181
Lindsay, Alexander (1618–59); created 1st Earl of Balcarres (1651); supporter of the Covenanters and then of Charles II; capitulated to Cromwell after the Battle of Worcester, but rejoined Charles II on the Continent (1653); head of the Presbyterians and King's Secretary of State for Scotland; Governor of Edinburgh Castle; died in exile: 6, 63, 68, 71, 72, 73–4, 201, 203, 204, 205
Lindsay, Lady Anna (*née* Mackenzie), Countess of Balcarres; daughter of Colin Mackenzie, 1st Earl of Seaforth; married (1640) Alexander Lindsay, 1st Earl of Balcarres: 64, 73
Lindsay, Sir Robert (d. 1616); father of Helen, Lady Scott of Ardross: 205
Lindsay, Lady Sophia (*née* Seton; d. after 1641), daughter of Alexander Seton, 1st Earl of Dunfermline; married (1612) David Lindsay, 1st Lord Lindsay of Balcarres; mother of Sophia, Lady Moray, and of Alexander, 1st Earl of Balcarres: 69
Lindsey. *See* Bertie
Lisbon, Portugal: 98, 142, 145–50, 174
— Archbishop of (1662): 148
— Belém [Belline] district of: 145
— Church of the Esperança, burial place of Richard Fanshawe, second son of that name born to Sir RF and Lady F (1663): 107, 148 (nn), 150
— described: 150
— English consul at (1662), *see* Maynard, Thomas
— 1663 insurrection at: 148, 214
Lisola, François-Paul, Baron de (1613–75); French diplomatist; Spanish Ambassador to London (1643); Envoy Extraordinary from the Emperor to Spain (1666): 180, 182, 183
Litton. *See* Lytton
Livingston, James (d. 1674); created 1st Earl of Callendar (1641); supporter of the Covenanters and later of Charles I; Lieutenant-General of the Scottish Army raised to rescue the King (1648); after its defeat at Preston he fled to the Continent: 79 (nn), 81, 205
Lixe. *See* Liche

Logan, Mr., servant to Lord Balcarres: 73
Loire River, France: 132
London and Westminster
— Bishop of, *see* Henchman, Humphrey; Sheldon, Gilbert
— Boswell Court, near Temple Bar; Lady F leased a house there (1663): 151
— bowling green near Whitehall; Sir RF kept prisoner there in a little room (1651), 134–5
— Chancery Lane, residence of the Fanshawes' cousin Ann (*née* Osborne) Young located there, in which the Fanshawes stayed on several occasions; also location of a house leased by Sir RF (1656): 97, 134, 136–7
— Chapel Royal [King's Chapel], Whitehall: 152
— Charing Cross, Lady F took a room in one of the taverns there (1651) while awaiting opportunity to see Sir RF, then in prison: 134
— Dorset House, Salisbury Court, occupied by Sir Thomas Fanshawe of Jenkins when Sir RF and Lady F stayed there (1663): 151, 153
— Fire of: 187, 220
— Fleet Street, location of Mr. East's watchmaking establishment: 119
— Gatehouse, Westminster, Col. Bampfield imprisoned there (1649): 32, 34
— Goldsmiths' Hall: 209
— Goldsmiths' Alley, Cripplegate, site of Dr. Farnaby's school: 208
— Guild Hall, AM's lawsuit tried at (1654): 81
— Holborn Row, Lincoln's Inn Fields, site of a house Lady F leased from Mr. Colle for 21 years (1667): 190
— Hunsdon House in old Blackfriars, lodging of Lady F's (1650–1): 133
— Inner Temple: 95, 112
— Lord Mayor of (1663), *see* Robinson, Sir John
— the Mews, location of the residence of Mrs. Cole, who brought suit against AM: 81, 205–6
— Montague House, Bishopsgate Street, Sir John Harrison's town house (1642): 111
— Portugal Row, Lincoln's Inn Fields, a row of houses built on the south side of the fields and backed by Portugal Street; birthplace of Lady F's son Henry (b. 1647) and also Lady F's residence for a time after the Restoration: 98, 120, 141, 142, 188, 192
— Queen Street, location of Lady F's lodgings (1651): 133
— St. James's Palace: x, xi, 5, 23, 24–5, 152, 195, 196
— St. James's Park: 193
— St. Martin's Lane, location of the residence of the Murrays (AM's family): 23, 195
— St. Olave, Hart Street, parish in which AH was born (1625); Sir John Harrison had leased a house there from Lord Dingwall: 108, 111
— Savoy, the: 141; Queen's Chapel of, burial place of AM's father, mother, and brother William: 31, 197
— Somerset House, residence of Queen mother, Henrietta Maria (1662–5): 152
— Spring Garden: 11, 193
— Strand, the: 141
— Tower, the: 26
— Tower Hill, Sir John Harrison had a house there (1666): 188
— Tower Wharf: 188
— Wallingford House, on the site of the present Admiralty; during the latter years of the Commonwealth General Fleetwood lived in the house and Commonwealth business was conducted there: 138
— Whitefriars: 80
— Whitehall: 97, 141, 142, 152, 153; Sir RF prisoner at, 134–5; High Court of Justice at, 138; Duke of York's apartments at, 152–3; matted gallery of, 153
— Wood Street, Cheapside, 196
Londonderry, Bishop of. *See* Bramhall John
Long, Sir Robert (d. 1673), of the City of Westminster; Secretary to the Council of the Prince of Wales (1644); member of Charles II's Privy Council (1649–53, 1672–3); Chancellor of the Exchequer (1660–1); Auditor of the Exchequer (1662–73); created baronet (1662): 114, 116, 209
Lopez [Lopus] de Mendoza, Don, *Alguacil Mayor* of Seville and deputy of the Duke of Alcalá: 160, 161

Lorne, Lord. *See* Campbell, Archibald, 9th Earl of Argyll
Loud, Mr., on Lord Sandwich's staff in Spain (1666): 182
Louis XIV (1638–1715), King of France (1643–1715): 187 (nn), 220
Loventhorp. *See* Leventhorpe
Lovin, Mr., in Fanshawe retinue (1664): 153, 163
Low, a surgeon; Lady F charges him with attempting to betray the English fleet to Parliament (1648): 121
Lowe [Loe], Col. Hercules (d. 1677), Royalist officer; served as Col. Bampfield's second in his duel with Sir Henry Newton: 48–9, 199
Lucena, Spain: 157, 215
Ludlow, Henry (b. 1577), of Hill Deverill and (afterwards) Tadley, Hants; half-uncle of the famous Lieutenant-General Edmund Ludlow; married Lettice (*née* West); their eldest daughter, Lettice, married (1645) John Harrison (Lady F's eldest brother); the Ludlow family were staunch Parliamentarians, a fact ignored by Lady F: 109
Ludlow, Lettice, daughter of Henry Ludlow and Lettice (*née* West); she married (1645) John Harrison, Lady F's eldest brother: 109 (nn)
Luisa Maria de Guzmán (d. 1666), Queen Mother of Portugal; daughter of Juan Emmanuel Pérez de Guzmán, 8th Duke of Medina Sidonia; widow of King John IV of Portugal, who reigned 1640–56; mother of Alfonso VI of Portugal and of Catherine of Braganza, Queen Consort to Charles II of England: 145–6, 149, 152, 181, 214
Lybria, Spain. *See* Lebrija
Lyon King of Arms. *See* Erskine, Sir Charles, of Cambo
Lytton [Litton], Sir Rowland (d. 1674), of Knebworth, Herts.; father of Sir William Lytton: 109
Lytton [Litton], Sir William (d. 1705), son of Sir Rowland Lytton; married, as his first wife, Mary (*née* Harrison), Lady F's half-sister: 109 (nn)

Maccarty, Donough (1594–1665), 2nd Viscount Muskerry (1640); created 1st Earl of Clancarty (1658); Irish Royalist; married (before 1648) Eleanor (*née* Butler), sister of the 1st Marquis and Duke of Ormonde: 124
Macedo, Antonio de Sousa de; Portuguese Secretary of State (1662); formerly resident in London and at the Hague; he was married to Dona Mariana Lemercier: 145, 146 (nn), 149 (nn), 214
Mackenzie, Sir George (1630–1714), of Tarbat; later (1703) Earl of Cromartie; active Royalist intriguer in Scotland (1651); took part in the campaigns of Lords Balcarres and Glencairn, and in those of General Middleton; fled to the Continent (1654) and remained there until after the Restoration: 68, 69, 70, 203
Macky, Hary, Sir James Halkett's serving-man: 85, 86, 206
Macroom [Macrom], Ireland, 22 miles north-west of Kinsale; Sir RF and Lady F stayed at the castle there in 1649 on the eve of their departure from Ireland: 124
Madrid, Spain: 95, 97, 98, 99, 113, 129–30, 159, 160, 163–6, 169–86 *passim*, 193, 216
— the Basilica de Nuestra Señora de Atocha [Atocke]: 183, 220
— Buen Retiro, a palace in a park near the present site of the Prado: 165, 166–7, 217
— Casa del Campo, gardens of: 166
— Convent of the Descalzas Reales, built for the retreat of Queen Dowagers of Spain: 178, 183, 218, 220
— French Hospital, chapel of; the burial place of Elizabeth, second daughter of Sir RF and Lady F: 107, 129
— Gate of Guadalajara [Gadajara]: 178
— House of Siete Chimeneas: 166, 187, 217
— Palace of Philip IV: 176–7, 178
— Town Hall [House of the Town] (*Ayuntamiento*): 178
Mains, Laird of. *See* Douglas, Sir Archibald
Maitland, Mr., the husband of Mrs. Cole, the woman who had AM arrested for debt (1654, 1656): 81, 85
Málaga [Malegoe], Spain: 126, 128, 211; merchants of: 161, 216

Mallard, Mr., on Lord Sandwich's staff in Spain (1666): 182
Malpica [Melpique], 5th Marquis of, Spanish nobleman; head of the family of Ribera Barroso; one of the *mayor domos* of Philip IV of Spain; captain of the Royal Guard which accompanied Empress Margarita Teresa to Vienna (1666): 163, 164, 165, 183
Marchin [Marsin], Jean-Gaspard-Ferdinand, Comte de (d.1673); French soldier, formerly Commander and Marshal of the French armies; entered Spanish service (1653); General in the Low Countries for Spain; part of the Fanshawe family lived in his house in Madrid (1664): 163
Margarita Teresa (1651–73), Infanta of Spain; daughter of Philip IV; called the Empress after her betrothal to her uncle, Emperor Leopold I; she married him in 1666: 165–6, 169, 170, 173 (nn), 175, 176, 178, 179, 181, 183, 184, 220; her *aya*: 184
Maria Anna (1606–46), Infanta of Spain; daughter of Philip III; sister of Philip IV; proposed spouse of Charles I of England, she ultimately married Emperor Ferdinand III: 193
Maria Anna (1634–96), Queen of Spain (1649–65); daughter of Emperor Ferdinand III; second wife (married 1649) of Philip IV of Spain (her uncle); mother of the Infanta and of Prince Charles, later Charles II of Spain; Queen Regent of Spain from the death of Philip IV (1665) until her son assumed power (1677): 158, 162, 165, 166, 169–89 *passim*, 217, 218, 220
Marialva, Dom Antonio Luis de Ménésés, Marquis of, Portuguese general; also had the title of Count of Cantanhede: 148
Marie Thérèse (Maria Teresa of Austria) (1638–83), Queen Consort of Louis XIV of France (married 1660); daughter of Philip IV of Spain by his first wife, Elizabeth of France: 176
Marsden, Thomas (1637–1720), chaplain to the Fanshawes and to the English merchants at Lisbon (1663): 148
Marshall, Beatrice, editor of the 1905 edition of Lady Fanshawe's Memoirs: xxii
Marsin. *See* Marchin
Marston, Nathaniel (d. 1665), English Consul at Seville (1664): 160, 161
Mary I (Mary Tudor) (1516–58), Queen of England (1553–8): 166
Mary, Princess Royal (1631–60), eldest daughter of Charles I; married (1641) William II, Prince of Orange (1647); mother of William Henry, Prince of Orange, later William III of England: 10, 29, 132, 140, 193, 197, 208 (nn), 212 (nn)
Master of Ceremonies at the Court of Spain (1664). *See* Rojas
Maurice, Prince (1621–53), fourth son of Princess Elizabeth, eldest daughter of James I, and Frederick V, Elector Palatine of the Rhine; nephew of Charles I; lost at sea: 123, 210
Maynard, Thomas, English Consul at Lisbon (1662): 145
Mazarin, Jules, Cardinal (1602–61); French statesman; principal minister of the regent, Anne of Austria, after the death of Louis XIII: 206
Medina Celi, Don Antonio Luis de la Cerda, 7th Duke of (d. 1671); Spanish nobleman; Viceroy of Andalusia: 158, 159, 216
Medina de las Torres, Don Ramiro Nuñez de Guzmán, Duke of (d. 1669); Chief Minister of Spain and Lord Chamberlain (*Sumiller de Corps*): 98, 162–86 *passim*, 216, 217, 219, 220
Medina de las Torres, Doña Catalina Velez de Guevara, Duchess of; also 9th Countess of Oñate and Villamediana; Spanish noblewoman; third wife of the Duke: 163, 169, 170, 174–5, 180, 181, 182; her daughter: 169; her two sons: 183
Medina Sidonia, Gaspar Alonso Pérez, 9th Duke of; Portuguese nobleman; father of the Abbess of Alcantara and brother to the Queen Mother of Portugal: 145
Mein [Meene], John, shopkeeper in Edinburgh (1652): 63
Melham, Mr., on Lord Sandwich's staff in Spain (1666): 181
Mello, Dom Francisco de. *See* Sande, Marquis of
Melpique. *See* Malpica
Membrilla, Spain: 162

Meredith, John, D.D. (d. 1665); Provost of Eton (1662–5): 143 (nn)
Micklethwaite [Mickellthite], Paul, D.D. (1589–1639); Master of the Temple Church (1628); rector of Herstmonceux, Sussex (1637–9); and of Sandy, Beds. (1639); one of the group of ministers, graduates of Cambridge, who were friends of the Harrisons; HCF identifies as Thomas Micklethwaite, rector of Cherry Burton, near Beverley, Yorks. (1612–62), but Paul Micklethwaite seems more likely: 110
Middlesex. *See* Cranfield
Miriam, AM's maid: 16, 17, 18, 19, 22, 25, 26, 198 (nn)
Mitchell, Henry, on Lord Sandwich's staff in Spain (1666): 182
Mohun [Moone], Capt. Robert, commander of the *York*, one of the ships in the fleet taking the Fanshawes to Spain (1664): 154
Molina, Count of (d. 1664), Spanish nobleman; *Asistente* of Seville: 159, 160, 161
Monck, George (1608–70), created (1660) 1st Duke of Albemarle; famous Parliamentary general: 213, 219
Montagu, Col. Edward (1625–72), created (1660) 1st Earl of Sandwich; eldest son of Sir Sidney Montagu; Colonel of the Parliamentary forces; General of the Fleet (with Monck) and brought it over to Charles II (1660); Ambassador Extraordinary to Portugal (1661–2) to bring Catherine of Braganza to England; Ambassador Extraordinary to Spain (1666): 121, 179, 181–2, 184, 186, 187, 189, 210, 213–14, 219, 220
Montagu, Sidney (1650–1727), second son of Edward Montagu, 1st Earl of Sandwich, by Jemima (*née* Crew); went to Spain as part of his father's staff (1666): 181, 220
Montalto, Duke of, *Mayor Domo mayor* to the Queen of Spain (1664): 167
Monterey, Don Juan Domingo de Guzmán, Count of (1637–1716); Spanish nobleman; younger son of Don Luis de Haro; derived his title from his wife: 186
Montgomery, Sir Robert (d. 1684), of Skelmorlie; brother of Margaret (*née* Montgomery) Halkett, first wife of Sir James Halkett; his father and grandfather bore the same name: 75, 205
Montgomery, Robert, of Haslehead; nephew of Margaret (*née* Montgomery) Halkett, first wife of Sir James Halkett: 75, 205
Montrose. *See* Graham
Moone, Capt. *See* Mohun
Moore, Mr., Chaplain to Lord Sandwich's staff in Spain (1666): 181
Moors, and Granada, Spain: 128–9, 211
Mora, Spain: 162
Moray, Sir Robert (1608–73), Scottish Royalist and intriguer; cousin of Sir James Halkett; husband of Sophia (*née* Lindsay): 63, 65, 66, 67, 68, 69–70, 71, 201, 203
Moray, Sophia (*née* Lindsay), Lady (1624–53); daughter of Sir David Lindsay of Balcarres (created Lord Lindsay of Balcarres, 1612); sister to Alexander Lindsay, 1st Earl of Balcarres; she married (*c.* 1652) Sir Robert Moray: 63, 66–7, 69, 203
Moray. *See also* Stewart, Alexander
Moray [Murray], county of Scotland on Moray Firth (formerly called Elgin): 58, 62
Mordaunt, Lady Elizabeth (d. before 1677), daughter of John Mordaunt, 1st Earl of Peterborough; married (1646) Thomas Howard, later 2nd Lord Howard of Escrick: 5, 22–3, 194
Mordaunt, Henry (1623–97), 2nd Earl of Peterborough (1643); soldier, naval commander; governor of Tangier (1661–3); married Lady Penelope, daughter of Barnabas O'Brien, 5th Earl of Thomond, and first cousin of Lady Honora O'Brien: 148, 215
Mordaunt, John (1599–1643), created (1628) 1st Earl of Peterborough; Colonel of a Regiment of Foot, Captain of a Regiment of Horse, and General of the Ordnance in the Parliamentary Army (1642); father of Lady Elizabeth Mordaunt: 194
Mordaunt, John (1626–75), 1st Viscount Mordaunt of Avalon (1659); son of John Mordaunt, 1st Earl of Peterborough; played a leading part in effecting the Restoration; following it he was appointed Constable of Windsor

Mordaunt, John (1626–75)—*contd.*
Castle and Lord-Lieutenant of Surrey: 143
Morey, Henry. *See* Murray, William, 1st Earl of Dysart
Morice, Sir William (1602–76), theologian; Secretary of State (1660–8); appointed on the recommendation of General Monck: 140, 213
Morlaix, France: 117
Morley, George, D.D. (1597–1684); Bishop of Winchester (1662–84); Lady F is incorrect in stating that he was a member of the Privy Council: 151, 152
Morton (or Moreton), Thomas (1564–1659), Bishop of Durham (1632–59): 85
Morton. *See also* Douglas
Moses, family servant of the Murrays; later servant of Elizabeth (*née* Murray) Newton: 16, 17–18, 19
moss [mose] troopers: 44, 198
Mount Edgcumbe, Maker, Cornwall, 144
Muchalls [Mohall], Aberdeenshire castle (since called Castle Fraser), seat of the Frasers; suffered spoliation (1644) at the hands of Montrose: 63
Much Hadham, Herts., site of the estate of Lady F's brother-in-law, William Newce (husband of Sir RF's sister Mary): 136
Murray, Anne (*née* Bayning), daughter of Paul, 1st Viscount Bayning of Sudbury, by Anne (*née* Glemham); she married (1635) Henry Murray, AM's brother: 33–4, 193, 198; not named: 5, 83, 198, 206
Murray, Charles, Groom of the Bedchamber to Charles I; brother of AM: 52, 53, 193, 196; not named: 10, 11
Murray, Elizabeth. *See* Newton, Elizabeth
Murray, Henry (d. 1672), Groom of the Bedchamber to Charles I; married (1635) Anne Bayning; brother of AM: 5, 32, 193, 196, 197–8, 205, 206; not named: xiii, 10, 11, 25, 26, 31, 33, 41, 67, 81, 83
Murray, Jane (or Jean) (*née* Drummond; d. 1647), daughter of George Drummond of Blair; governess to the children of Charles I (1642–7); wife of Thomas Murray, Provost of Eton; mother of AM: 9–23 *passim*, 31, 50, 51, 64, 77, 82, 193, 194, 196, 197, 201, 202
Murray, Thomas (1564–1623); attached to the court of James VI in Scotland, he came to England with the King upon his accession to the English throne; appointed tutor to Charles I, then Duke of York; provost of Eton College (1622–3); husband of Jean (*née* Drummond) Murray; father of AM: 5, 7, 9, 10, 31, 196
Murray, William (Will) (1617–49), active Royalist; served Charles II until dismissed in 1649; brother of AM: 5, 23, 28, 29–31, 51, 52–3, 81, 194, 196, 197, 199, 205; not named: 10, 11
Murray, Sir William, of Hermiston, Scottish Royalist, 64, 201–2
Murray, William (d. 1653), created 1st Earl of Dysart (1643); Tutor and Secretary to Charles I as Prince of Wales; Gentleman of the Bedchamber to Charles I; son of Revd. William M. Murray of Dysart; nephew of Thomas Murray, Provost of Eton; carried instructions to the Scottish Commissioners at Breda (1650) for negotiating Charles II's return to Scotland; he is probably the 'Henry Morey' to whom Lady F refers: 133
Musgrove, Mr., tenant farmer of Sir Henry Newton's at Charlton, Kent: 17, 194
Musselburgh, Midlothian, Scotland; Cromwell's cavalry quartered there (1650): 71

Nantes [Nance], France: 97, 130, 131–2
Navas, Don Nicholas de la, Spaniard; Secretary to the Duke of Medina de las Torres (1666); subsequently Secretary to one of the Councils of State: 180
Naworth Castle, East Cumberland; seat of Sir Charles Howard, later (1661) 1st Earl of Carlisle: xi, xiii, 5, 32–50 *passim*, 60, 66, 79, 198, 199
Neale, Mr., a friend of AM's in London who arranged loans for her in connection with her lawsuit; the only non-family member to witness her wedding to Sir James Halkett: 83, 84, 85.
Needham, Bridget (*née* Drury; d. 1696), Viscountess Kilmorey; wife of Charles Needham, 4th Viscount Kilmorey (d. 1660); married second (1663), as his second wife, Sir John Shaw, Bt.;

Needham, Bridget—*contd.*
godmother of one of Lady F's nieces (a daughter of her sister Margaret Turnor): 191
Needham, Dr. Jasper (or Casper) (1622–79); one of the physicians of Charles II; physician to Lady F (1669–70): 191
Neville [Nevel] Henry (1620–94), political and miscellaneous writer; second son of Sir Henry Neville of Billingbear, Berks., by Elizabeth, younger daughter of Sir John Smythe of Ostenhanger (eldest son of Thomas Customer Smythe); Henry was therefore son of a first cousin of Sir RF; he was a Commonwealth man, later banished by Cromwell, but one of the Council of State of Richard Cromwell (1659); he was not (as Lady F says) a member of the High Court of Justice: 138
Newbyth. *See* Baird
Newcastle upon Tyne, Northumberland: 33, 86
Newce [News, Nues], Thomas (1616–52), son of William Newce by Mary (*née* Fanshawe), sister of Sir RF; nephew of Sir RF and cousin of young RF; the names of his brothers are not known; Lady F calls him 'William' in error: 108
Newce [News, Nues], William (1591–1652), of Much Hadham, Herts.; married (1616) Sir RF's second sister, Mary: 108, 136
Newport, Francis (1620–1708), 2nd Baron Newport of High Ercall (1651); created (1675) Viscount Newport of Bradford, and (1694) Earl of Bradford; married Lady Diana (*née* Russell); father of Francis Newport; Comptroller of the Household (1668–72); Treasurer of the Household (1672–87, 1689–1708): 153
Newport, Francis (b. *c.* 1656), third son of Francis Newport, 2nd Baron Newport of High Ercall; accompanied Sir RF to Spain (1664): 153, 164, 174
Newport, Monmouthshire, Sir RF taken prisoner at following the Battle of Worcester (1651): 212
Newton, Elizabeth (*née* Murray; d. 1689); only sister of AM; married (before 1644) Sir Henry Newton, afterwards Puckering: xiii, 6, 10–17 *passim*, 19, 22, 31, 32, 33, 41, 48, 67, 71, 78–85 *passim*, 193
Newton (afterwards Puckering), Sir Henry (1618–1701), of Charlton, Kent, and of the Priory, Warwick; wealthy Royalist; nephew of Sir Thomas Puckering, whose estate he inherited (1654); subsequently took the name Puckering; husband of Elizabeth (*née* Murray); AM's brother-in-law: 5, 16–17, 48–9, 57, 80, 83, 84, 193, 194, 198–9, 205; not named: 12, 31, 78, 81
Newton, Henry (living 1647), son of Sir Henry Newton by Elizabeth (*née* Murray); nephew of AM: 16 (nn)
Niça (or Niza), Dom Luiz Vasco da Gama, Marquis of (d. 1676); leading nobleman of Portugal; also held title of Count of Vidiguera: 148
Nichols, Sir Edward (1593–1669), Secretary of State to Charles I and to Charles II: 132, 141, 213
Nichols, John Gough (1806–73), editor of the 1875 edition of Lady Halkett's Autobiography: v, 3
Nicolas, Sir Nicholas Harris (1799–1848), editor of the 1829 and 1830 editions of Lady Fanshawe's Memoirs: v, xxii
Nicolls, Mr., Chaplain at Naworth Castle (1649–50): 32, 33, 35–47 *passim*, 49–50, 60, 198
Nieto, Nicholas, Page on Lord Sandwich's staff in Spain (1666): 182
Nieuport, Flanders: 140
Norfoulke, Serjeant, Mace-bearer to the Speaker of the House of Commons (1648): 26, 197
Northumberland. *See* Percy
North Water Bridge, Scotland: 63, 201
Norwich. *See* Goring
Nues. *See* Newce

O'Brien, Ellena [Elhena] (b. 1650), daughter of Murrough O'Brien, Lord Inchiquin; she died young: 123
O'Brien, Henry (1588–1639), 5th Earl of Thomond [Toumment] (1624); Governor of County Clare and of Thomond in succession to his father; Privy Councillor to Charles I; supporter of Strafford: 125
O'Brien, Lady Honora, fifth daughter of Henry O'Brien, 5th Earl of Thomond, by Mary (*née* Brereton); she married

O'Brien, Lady Honora—*contd.*
first (1656) Sir Francis Englefield; she married second (1665) Sir Robert Howard; probably the Fanshawes stayed with her at Castle Lemaneagh, near Lake Inchiquin, which was easily reached from Kilmallock: 125
O'Brien, Murrough, Baron Inchiquin (1614–74), created 1st Earl of Inchiquin (1654); married (1635) Elizabeth (*née* St. Leger); Vice President of Munster (1642); served Royalist and Parliamentarian causes alternately; High Steward to Queen Mother Henrietta Maria at the Restoration; went to Portugal (1662) in command of the troops lent by Charles II to his brother-in-law; Sir RF and Lady F stayed with him (1650) at Kilmalloch which he had seized and was occupying at that time: 123, 125, 126, 145, 214
Ocaña, Spain: 183
O'Duffy, Father Patrick [Patricio], an Irish Franciscan used as an agent by the Duke of Medina de las Torres (1664–6): 181
Ogilby, John (1600–76), fine printer and engraver; the Bible given to Sir RF was printed in 1660 in two volumes of royal folio and sold for £200: 143, 214
Oñate, Count-Duke of, Spanish nobleman (1666): 219
Orléans, France: 132
Ormonde. *See* Butler
Orrery. *See* Boyle, Roger
Overton, Col. Robert (*fl.* 1640–68), officer in Cromwell's Army: 60–1, 201
Oxford, city of, 96, 107, 111, 114, 209
Oxford University, St. John's College: 107, 115

Palma, Countess of, Portuguese noblewoman; daughter of Dom João Mascarenhas, Count of Palma; wife of Count of Obispo and Sabagal, who became also Count of Palma: 149
Palmer, Mr. (d. 1654), Mayor of Barnstaple (1643): 116
Palmer, Sir Geoffrey (1598–1670), of Carlton, Northants; Royalist; King's Attorney; created Baronet (1660); Attorney-General to Charles II (1660–70); attended Lady F's wedding: 112
Papal Nuncio in Madrid (1664–5): 167, 175
Pardo [Parda, Prada], El, location of a palace of the kings of Spain, eight miles north of Madrid: 166, 175
Parker, Mr., on Lord Sandwich's staff in Spain (1666): 181
Parkhurst [Parceust], Sir William (d. 1666), of East Lenham Manor, Kent; Royalist; knighted (1619); Master of the Mint after the Restoration: 114
Paris, 96, 97, 98, 119, 121, 132, 137, 138, 139–40, 187
— Faubourg Saint-Germain: 112
— Palais Royale: 121
— Protestant Churchyard, Lady F's son Richard (b. 1648) buried there: 139
Parry, Mr., in Sir RF's retinue on trip from Madrid to Portugal (1666): 180
Parsloes [Parsles], Dagenham, Essex; estate of William Fanshawe, uncle of Lady F: 104
Parton, Francis, Confectioner on Lord Sandwich's staff in Spain (1666): 182
Pastrana, Don Rodrigo de Silva y Mendoza, 5th Duke of (1614–75); Spanish nobleman; also the 8th Duke of Infantado and Lerma and the 5th Prince of Eboli; member of the Councils of State and War; one time *Mayor Domo mayor* to Queen Maria Anna; his wife was Doña Catalina de Mendoza y Sandoval: 183
Patrick [Patricio], Father. *See* O'Duffy, Father Patrick
Peacock, Mr., Footman on Lord Sandwich's staff in Spain (1666): 182
Pedro II (1648–1706), King of Portugal (1683–1706); styled Dom Pedro (1648–83); son of John IV by Luisa Maria de Guzmán; younger brother of King Alfonso VI, whom he deposed and imprisoned (1667); upon the death of Alfonso (1683) he became King Pedro II: 146, 149, 152 (nn)
Peirie, Alexander [Sainders Peeres], bailie of the Canongate, Edinburgh; AM lodged at his house (1650, 1652): 50, 63
Pembroke. *See* Herbert
Peñaranda, Don Gaspar de Bracamonte, Count of (d. 1676); Spanish nobleman; President of the Council of the Indies and Italy; member of the Queen Regent's Council: 176

Pendennis Castle, Falmouth, Cornwall: 117
Penzance, Cornwall: 117
Pepys, Samuel (1633–1703), diarist: 219
Percy, Algernon (1602–68), styled Lord Percy until 1632; 10th Earl of Northumberland (1632); Lord High Admiral (1638); General of the Army against the Scots (1640); Chief Commissioner from Parliament to treat with Charles I at Oxford; appointed by Parliament as guardian of Princess Elizabeth, the Duke of Gloucester, and the Duke of York at St. James's Palace (1648); supporter of the Restoration: 23, 24, 26, 195
Percy, Lady Elizabeth (*née* Howard; d. 1705), Countess of Northumberland; second wife (married 1642) of Algernon Percy, 10th Earl of Northumberland; responsible with him for the royal children at St. James's Palace (1648): 23 (nn)
Perin (or Perrin), Henry, Mayor of Portsmouth (1664): 154 (nn)
Perth, earldom of: 10, 193
Peterborough. *See* Mordaunt
Petersfield, Hants: 154
Philip II (1527–98), King of Spain (1556–98), King of Naples and Sicily (1554–98), and, as Philip I, King of Portugal (1580–98): 166, 216, 217
Philip III (1578–1621), King of Spain, Naples, and Sicily (1598–1621) and, as Philip II, King of Portugal (1598–1621): 166
Philip IV (1605–65), King of Spain, Naples, and Sicily (1621–65), and, as Philip III, King of Portugal (1621–40); married first (1615) Elizabeth of France (d. 1644); married second (1649) Maria Anna, daughter of Ferdinand III (d. 1696): 97 (nn), 124, 129, 130, 155–78 *passim*, 211, 215, 216, 217, 218
Phoenix, ship which took Charles I and retinue to the Scilly Islands (1646); part of the fleet taking the Fanshawes to Spain in 1664 (commanded by Capt. Richard Utber): 117, 154
Pimentel, Don Antonio de, Governor of Cádiz (1664); formerly Spanish Ambassador to Rome and to Sweden: 157–8
Pinkie [Pincky] House, near Musselburgh, Midlothian; a mansion of the Earl of Dunfermline: 79, 205
Piquett, Ann, Washmaid in Fanshawe retinue (1664): 154
Pitfirrane [Pitfirren], Fife, Scotland; family seat of the Halketts, two-and-a-quarter miles south-west of Dunfermline: 6, 9, 193, 206
Place, Mr., on Lord Sandwich's staff in Spain (1666): 182
Plymouth, Devon: 144
Poëtting, Graf Francis Eusebius von (d. 1678); Vice-Chancellor of Bohemia, Grand Marshall of the Court, and Governor of the Tyrol; German Ambassador at the Court of Spain (1664); not named: 183, 184; his lady: 163, 182, 186
Porter, Thomas (d. 1680), younger son of Endymion Porter; married (1659) Roberta Anna (*née* Culpeper): 150
Portman, Sir William (1644–90), 6th Baronet of Orchard Portman, Somerset; M.P. for Taunton and for Somerset: 144
Portsmouth, Hants: 120, 154; mayor of (1644), *see* Perin, Henry
Portsmouth, part of the fleet taking the Fanshawes to Spain (1644); commanded by Capt. Henry Terne: 154
Portugal, King of. *See* Alfonso VI
Poyns, Sir Robert, of Leicestershire; mistakenly listed by Lady F as one of the sons-in-law of Thomas (Customer) Smythe: 104
Preston, Richard (d. 1628); created Lord Dingwall (1609); created 1st Earl of Desmond (1619); favourite Gentleman of the Chamber of James I; father of Lady Elizabeth, Duchess of Ormonde; owner of the London house in which AH was born: 108
Preyer, Mr.; accompanied Sir RF's body from Madrid to Hertford; the name is probably written in error for John Price, below: 188
Price, John, Under-secretary to Sir RF; with the Fanshawe retinue (1664–6); probably the same person as Mr. Preyer above: 145 (nn), 146 (nn), 153, 174, 179, 180, 187, 188
Princess Royal. *See* Mary, Princess Royal

Priory, the, Warwick; estate of Sir Henry Newton which he inherited from Jane (*née* Puckering) Bale: 80, 205
Progers, Mr.; either Valentine or Henry Progers, both of whom were involved with the murder of Ascham: 129–30
Puckering, Sir Henry. *See* Newton (later Puckering), Sir Henry Puckering, Jane (d. 1652), daughter of Sir Thomas Puckering, Bt.; cousin of Sir Henry Newton; she was abducted and forcibly married by Joseph Walsh (1649); marriage set aside (1651); married (*c.* 1651) John Bale of Carlton Curlieu; she died in childbirth the following year; her cousin, Sir Henry Newton, inherited her property and took the name Puckering: 48 (nn), 198
Puckering, Sir Thomas (d. 1636), father of Jane (*née* Puckering) Bale; uncle of Sir Henry Newton: 198, 205
Puerto, El (El Puerto de Santa María), Spain: 158, 159
Pyman, Henry, Butler on Lord Sandwich's staff in Spain (1666): 182

Queen Mother of Portugal (1656–66). *See* Luisa Maria de Guzmán

Rana. *See* Araña
Rawdon [Royden], Sir Marmaduke, of Hoddesdon, Herts.; London merchant; M.P. for Aldborough; knighted (1643); Royalist soldier and commander of a troop of Horse (1645); Governor of Faringdon (1645–6): 115
Remembrancer of the Exchequer, patent of: 104, 113, 208, 209
Reserve, frigate which took Fanshawes from Lisbon to England (1663); commanded by Capt. Robert Holmes: 150
Resolution, flagship which took the Fanshawes to Spain (1664); commanded by Sir John Lawson: 154
Rice, Thomas, on Lord Sandwich's staff in Spain (1666): 182
Rich, Henry (1590–1649), created (1624) 1st Earl of Holland; held a number of household offices for Charles I; his loyalties vacillated between King and Parliament; joined the rising for the King in 1648, was captured at St. Neots, Hunts., and executed on the same day as the Duke of Hamilton and Lord Capell (9 Feb. 1649): 121
Rich, Robert (1587–1658), 2nd Earl of Warwick (1619); actively engaged in promoting colonization and colonial trade; commander of the Parliamentary fleet (1642–8): 210
Richmond. *See* Stuart
Ridgley, Dr. Thomas (1576–1656), Fellow of the Royal College of Physicians; physician to Sir RF: 137
Right. *See* Wright
Righton, Mr., Page on Lord Sandwich's staff in Spain (1666): 182
Rivers, Countess. *See* Darcy, Mary; Savage, Lady Elizabeth
Ro—, Ar—, helped AM treat wounded soldiers after the Battle of Dunbar (1650): 55
Robinson, Sir John, Bt. (*c.* 1625–80); knighted and created a Baronet (1660); Sheriff of London (1657–8); Lieutenant of the Tower (1660–80); M.P. for the City of London; Lord Mayor of London (1662–3): 152
Robinson, Capt. Robert (d. after 1680), distinguished naval commander; captured three Dutch men-of-war (1666); commander of the *Ruby*, frigate which took the Fanshawes to Portugal (1662); knighted (1673): 144
Roch, William, on Lord Sandwich's staff in Spain (1666): 182
Rojas, Don Pedro de, Master of Ceremonies at the Court of Spain (1664): 166; not named: 163, 180, 183, 186
Rookes, Mr., accompanied Sir RF's body to London (1666): 186, 188
Roscommon. *See* Dillon
Roxburghe. *See* Ker
Royden. *See* Rawdon
Ruby, frigate which took the Fanshawes to Portugal (1662); commanded by Capt. Robert Robinson: 144, 145 (nn)
Rupert, Prince (1619–82), created Earl of Holderness and Duke of Cumberland (1644); third son of Princess Elizabeth (eldest daughter of James I) and Frederick V, Elector Palatine of the Rhine; brother of Prince Maurice; Royalist military leader and commander of the Royalist Fleet: 122, 123, 210
Russell, Lady; possibly the wife of Sir William Russell (son of Sir Thomas

Russell, Lady—*contd.*
Russell of Strensham, Worcs.), who lived near the Harrisons in London; she attended Margaret Harrison (AH's mother) during an illness: 109
Russell, Richard, Page on Lord Sandwich's staff in Spain (1666): 182
Russell, William (1616–1700), 7th Earl of Bedford (1641); created 1st Duke (1694); went to Madrid (1635) to study the Spanish language; accepted command as General of the Horse in the Parliamentary service (1642), but the following year joined Charles I at Oxford; took an active part in effecting the Restoration: 113
Ruthven, Clara (*née* Berner), third wife of Patrick Ruthven, 1st Earl of Brentford (married 1633); godmother of Lady F's daughter Ann, born in Jersey (1646): 114
Ruthven, Patrick (1573?–1651), created Earl of Forth (1642) and of Brentford (1644); member of the Council of the Prince of Wales (1644); Marshal General and Commander-in-Chief of the royal army at the Battle of Edgehill; Lord Chamberlain to Charles II in exile: 113, 119
Rymer [Rimer], Henry (d. 1694), clergyman of Carnbee, Fife: 74, 205

S., Sir G., lent money to AM and helped her to obtain a purse from Charles II: 55, 56
S., Sir Ralph, uncle to Col. Bampfield's wife: 32
St. Albans. *See* Jermyn
St. Albans, Herts.: 151, 152
Saint-Denis, France: 139
St. Francis, order of: 194
St. Germain, Duke of, a Neapolitan previously known as Baron de Tutavilla; Governor of Badajoz and Estremadura; Viceroy of Sardinia (1668): 163
St. Johnstoun, Scotland; earlier name for the city of Perth: 56
St. Lawrence, Order of: 169
St. Michael's Mount; island off Cornwall in Mount's Bay: 117
St. Neots [Need], Hunts., battle at (1648): 121
Salinas de Rio Pisuerga, Marquis of, Spanish nobleman; Captain of the Royal Guard which accompanied Empress Margarita Teresa to Vienna (1666): 183
Salisbury. *See* Cecil
Salisbury, Wilts.: 143–4; Cathedral: 144
Salva Tierra, an estate in the neighbourhood of Madrid belonging to the Count of Salvatierra, son of the Duke of Alba: 184
Sanborne, Mr.; the Fanshawes stayed in his lodging-house in Caen (1646): 119
Sande, Dom Francisco de Mello, Count of Ponte, Marquis of (d. 1678); Portuguese nobleman; came to England with Catherine of Braganza and acted as her Chamberlain; had charge of the Portuguese embassy (1663–7); Ambassador to the United Provinces (1667); Ambassador to London (1671–8): 142 (nn)
Sanderson, Robert, D.D. (1587–1663); rector of Boothby Pagnell, Lincs. (1619–60); Chaplain to Charles I (1631); Bishop of Lincoln (1660); member of Lincoln College, Oxford, not Cambridge as Lady F states: 110
Sandoval, Cardinal, Archbishop of Toledo (d. 1665): 171, 176
Sandwich. *See* Montagu
San Esteban, Don Diego de Benavides y Bazán, 8th Count of (*c.* 1666); Spanish nobleman; Viceroy of Peru (1661–6): 162
San Esteban [St. Estevan] del Puerto, Spain: 162
San Lourenço, Count; Portuguese nobleman with a house on the Tagus River at Lisbon: 145
Sanlúcar [St. Lucar] de Barrameda, Spain: 172
San Sebastían, Spain, port from which the Fanshawes set sail for England (1650): 129, 130, 213
Santa Cruz, Dona Juliana de Lancastre, Countess of; Portuguese noblewoman; wife of the 4th Count of Santa Cruz; daughter of the Marquis of Govera: 149
Saunderson, George (1631–1714), 5th Viscount Castleton (1650); married first (1656) Grace (*née* Belasyse); married second (1675) Sarah (*née* Evelyn) Wray Fanshawe, widow of Sir John Wray and of Thomas Fanshawe,

Saunderson, George—*contd.*
2nd Viscount Fanshawe of Dromore: 106
Savage, Lady Elizabeth (*née* Darcy; 1581–1651), Viscountess Savage; daughter of Thomas Darcy, 1st Earl Rivers; widow of Thomas, Viscount Savage; created (1641) Countess Rivers for life: 115, 209
Savoy, Duke of. *See* Charles Emmanuel II
Scale's [Scalls] How Manor, South Lynn, Norfolk; a manor given by Sir John Harrison to one of Lady F's sisters or sisters-in-law (1668): 191, 221 (nn)
Schomberg, Frederick Herman von Schönberg (1615–90), 1st Duke of (1689); son of Hans Meinhard von Schönberg, Court Marshall of the Elector Palatine (Frederick V), by Anne, second daughter of Edward, 5th Lord Dudley; soldier; Marshal of France; served with most of the armies of Europe; accompanied William of Orange to England as his second-in-command: 145, 214
Scilly Isles; Lady F is in error when she states that the Prince of Wales's party left for Jersey after 'three weeks and odd days'; actually they were there one day short of six weeks: 118
— St. Mary's (or Star) Castle, residence of the Prince of Wales (1646); Lady F is in error when she places 'St. Marie's' castle on the island of Jersey: 118
Scot, Sir John, of Scot Hall (near Ashford, Kent); second husband of Katherine (*née* Smythe); brother-in-law of Thomas Fanshawe: 104
Scott, Col., Scotsman; Royalist soldier: 204
Scottish Covenanters (or Kirk Party): 132 (nn), 133, 200, 202, 212
Scott of Ardross, Helen (*née* Lindsay), Lady; wife of Sir William Scott (married 1634); aided AM during her illness at Balcarres: 74, 205
Scott of Ardross, Sir William, husband of Helen, Lady Scott: 205
Seale, Mr., of Plymouth; father-in-law of Mr. Tyler, a merchant in whose house the Fanshawes stayed (1662): 144
Seaton, Mr., servant of Lord Dunfermline (1652): 65
Seton, Alexander (1555–1622), created 1st Earl of Dunfermline (1605); Lord of the Session; Lord President of the Treasury; Lord Provost of Edinburgh (1598–1608); Lord Chancellor of Scotland (1605–22): 201
Seton, Charles (1615–72), 2nd Earl of Dunfermline (1622); husband of Lady Mary (*née* Douglas); leader (1639–40) of the Army of the Covenanters, but afterwards supported Charles I; fled to the Continent after the King's execution; returned to Scotland with Charles II (1650) and entertained him at Dunfermline; Extraordinary Lord of the Session (1669–72): 49, 52, 53, 56–68 *passim*, 70, 73, 199, 200–1, 203
Seton, Lady Henrietta (1652?–81), daughter of Charles Seton, 2nd Earl of Dunfermline, by Lady Mary (*née* Douglas): 61
Seton, Margaret (*née* Hay; d. 1659), Countess of Dunfermline; daughter of James, 7th Lord Hay of Yester; she married (1607), as his third wife, Alexander Seton, 1st Earl of Dunfermline; she married second (1633) James, Lord Livingston of Almond, later (1641) 1st Earl of Callendar; mother of Charles Seton, 2nd Earl of Dunfermline; sister of John Hay, 1st Earl of Tweeddale: 65–6, 79
Seton, Lady Mary (*née* Douglas; d. 1659), Countess of Dunfermline; daughter of William, 8th Earl of Morton; sister of Robert Douglas (later 9th Earl of Morton) and of James Douglas (later 11th Earl of Morton); wife of Charles Seton, 2nd Earl of Dunfermline: 6, 52–63 *passim*, 200
Seville, Spain: 159, 160–1, 162, 216; Alcázar: 160, 162; Corregidor of (1664): 161; English Consul at, *see* Marston, Nathaniel
Seymour, Henry (1612–86), Groom of the Bedchamber to Charles II (1650); a fellow servant with AM's brother Charles: 52, 56, 200
Shaftesbury. *See* Cooper, Anthony Ashley
Shalliott, France. *See* Chaillot
Sharpe, Elizabeth, wife of Revd. George Sharpe (married 1636): 63
Sharpe, Revd. George, minister of Fyvie: 63

Shatbolt. *See* Shotbolt
Sheeres [Shere], Sir Henry (d. 1710), mathematician and engineer; served with Lord Sandwich in Spain (1666); knighted (1685): 181
Sheldon, Gilbert, D.D. (1598–1677); Bishop of London (1660); performed the marriage ceremony of Charles II and Catherine of Braganza; Archbishop of Canterbury (1663): 142 (nn), 151 (nn), 152 (nn), 191
Sherwood, Friar (alias Capt. Taller); Roman Catholic who cheated Sir RF at cards when he was a young man travelling in France: 112–13
Shotbolt [Shatbolt] Mary (*c.* 1612–1705), daughter of Philip Shotbolt of Yardley, Herts., by Elizabeth (*née* Marsh); married (1645), as his second wife, Sir John Harrison; Lady F's stepmother; not named: 109, 117, 209
Shotbolt, Philip, of Yardley, Herts., father of Sir John Harrison's second wife, Mary: 109, 209
Sidney, Sir Philip (1554–86), soldier, statesman, poet; husband of Frances (*née* Walsingham): 208
Sierra Morena, mountain range in southern Spain: 162
Sierra Nevada, mountain range in southern Spain: 128, 211
Skelmorlie. *See* Montgomery of Skelmorlie
Skelton, Sir John (d. 1672), Royalist; Lieutenant-Governor of Plymouth (1665): 144
Slanning, Sir Nicholas (1606–43), of Maristow (near Tavistock, Devon), Royalist soldier; knighted (1632); Governor of Pendennis Castle (1635–43); lost his life in the Royalist cause in the attack on Bristol (26 July 1643): 117
Smith, Mr., in Fanshawe retinue (1664): 153, 174
Smithfield, near Aberdour, Scotland; seat of the Earls of Morton: 199
Smythe, Edward, said by Lady F to be a son of Thomas (Customer) Smythe: 104
Smythe, Elizabeth (1577–1631), youngest daughter of Thomas (Customer) Smythe; married (after May 1593) Sir Henry Fanshawe of Ware; mother of Sir RF; grandmother of young RF; according to HCF genealogical charts, there were five sons and five daughters of this marriage surviving at the time of Sir Henry's death in 1616: 95, 104, 105 (nn), 107–8 (nn), 112, 113
Smythe, Joan (d. 1622), third daughter of Thomas (Customer) Smythe; married (*c.* 1579), as his second wife, Thomas Fanshawe and bore two sons: Sir Thomas Fanshawe of Jenkins (1580–1631) and William Fanshawe of Parsloes (1583–1635); as the second wife of young RF's great-grandfather, she becomes what Lady F calls 'your great-grandmother-in-law': 104
Smythe, Sir John (d. 1608), son of Thomas (Customer) Smythe; knighted (1603); brother-in-law of Thomas Fanshawe (young RF's great-grandfather) and of Sir Henry Fanshawe (young RF's grandfather): 104
Smythe, Katherine, daughter of Thomas (Customer) Smythe and sister-in-law of Thomas and of Sir Henry Fanshawe; she married first Sir Rowland Hayward, Lord Mayor of London, and second Sir John Scot of Scot Hall, near Ashford, Kent: 104
Smythe, Mary, daughter of Thomas (Customer) Smythe; sister-in-law of Thomas and of Sir Henry Fanshawe; she married Robert Davies (or Davy) of London, whom Lady F calls in error Sir John Daveis of Kent: 104
Smythe, Philip (1634–1708), 2nd Viscount Strangford of Dromore; son of Sir Thomas Smythe, 1st Viscount, and grandson of Thomas (Customer) Smythe; two of his aunts married into the Fanshawe family: 104
Smythe, Sir Richard (d. 1628), of Leeds Castle, near Maidstone; knighted (1603); brother-in-law of Thomas and of Sir Henry Fanshawe: 104
Smythe, Robert, of Highgate; son of Thomas (Customer) Smythe; brother-in-law of Thomas and of Sir Henry Fanshawe; he was apparently not knighted, though Lady F calls him 'Sir': 104
Smythe, Thomas (d. 1591), of Ostenhanger, Kent; generally known as Customer Smythe because he served as Collector of Customs for the Port of London; his third daughter, Joan, was

Smythe, Thomas—*contd.*
the second wife of Thomas Fanshawe (young RF's great-grandfather); his youngest daughter, Elizabeth, the wife of Sir Henry Fanshawe, was Sir RF's mother and young RF's grandmother: 104

Smythe, Sir Thomas (d. 1625), son of Thomas (Customer) Smythe; knighted (1603); served as Ambassador to Russia (1604–5); brother-in-law of Thomas and of Sir Henry Fanshawe: 104

Smythe, Sir Thomas (1599–1635); knighted (1625); created Viscount Strangford of Dromore in Ireland (1628); son of Sir John Smythe of Ostenhanger, Kent; brother-in-law of Thomas and of Sir Henry Fanshawe; a companion of Sir RF on his early travels; married (1621) Lady Barbara (*née* Sydney); HCF, in error, calls him 'Sir John' and dates his death 1634: 104, 112, 150

Smythe, Ursula, daughter of Thomas (Customer) Smythe; sister-in-law of Thomas and of Sir Henry Fanshawe; she married first Simon Harding Salter of Radcliffe, and second William Boteler of Krytons, Beddenham, Beds.: 104

Smythe, William, said by Lady F to be a son of Thomas (Customer) Smythe: 104

Somerset, Edward (1603–67), styled Earl of Glamorgan (1644); 2nd Marquis of Worcester (1646); Royalist soldier; supplied the King with vast sums of money; sent to Ireland (1645) to raise troops for the Royalists; arrested there and imprisoned; later imprisoned in the Tower by Parliament (1652); released on bail (1655) by Cromwell and granted a pension: 126–7

Somerset, Henry (1629–1700), styled Lord Herbert; 3rd Marquis of Worcester (1667); son of Edward, the 2nd Marquis; created Duke of Beaufort (1682); married (1657) Mary (*née* Capell) Seymour, styled Lady Beauchamp: 117

Sousa, Antonio de. *See* Macedo

Sousa, Dom João de [Don Juan de], Portuguese nobleman; *Vedor* or Lord Steward of the Queen Mother of Portugal's household: 146, 147 (nn)

Southampton. *See* Wriothesley

Southampton, Hants: 119

Southwell, Sir Robert (1635–1702), diplomatist; son of Robert Southwell of Kinsale; knighted (1665): 181, 183, 219

Spain, Lady F's description of its people, customs, and foods: 171–4

Sparks, William, murderer of Antony Ascham (1650); later executed for this crime: 130, 171, 211

Speedwell, rechristened from the *Cheriton*; frigate on which Sir RF's family returned to England upon the Restoration of Charles II (1660): 98, 140

Spey River, Scotland: 62

Stackpool, Mr., Recorder of Limerick (1649): 124 (nn)

Stevenson, Isbell, a patient of AM's at Fyvie: 58

Steward [Stuard], Richard, D.C.L. (1593?–1651); Chaplain to Charles I; Provost of Eton (1639); Dean of St. Paul's (1641); Dean of the Chapel Royal (1643); Dean of Westminster (1645): 133, 139

Stewart, Mr., on staff of Lord Sandwich in Spain (1666): 181

Stewart, Alexander (1634–1701), 20th Earl of Moray (1653); house of in the Canongate, Edinburgh: 87

Stirling, Scotland: 57

Stafford. *See* Wentworth

Strangford, Viscounts of. *See* Smythe, Philip; Smythe, Sir Thomas

Stuard, Mr., on Lord Sandwich's staff in Spain (1666): 181

Stuart, James (1612–55), 4th Duke of Lennox (1624); created 1st Duke of Richmond (1641); devoted Royalist, contributing thousands of pounds to the cause; Lord Steward of the Household (1641); President of the Council of the Prince of Wales (1645); married (1637) Lady Mary (*née* Villiers) Herbert, daughter of the 1st Duke of Buckingham and widow of Charles Herbert, styled Lord Herbert of Shurland: 30, 197

Stuart, Lady Mary (*née* Villiers; 1623–85) Herbert, Duchess of Richmond; widow of Charles, Lord Herbert of Shurland; married second (1637) James Stuart, 1st Duke of Richmond: 30, 197

Stuart, William Johnston, presented manuscript of Lady Halkett's Memoirs to the British Museum: 3

Suffolk. *See* Howard

Sydney, Lady Barbara (1599–1643), daughter of Robert Sydney, 1st Earl of Leicester, by his first wife Barbara (*née* Gamage); married first (1621) Thomas Smythe, 1st Viscount Strangford; married second (1637) Sir Thomas Culpeper; mother of Col. Thomas Culpeper; not named: 150, 151

Tagus River, on the Iberian Peninsula: 166

Tankersley Park, York, estate of the 2nd Earl of Strafford; the Fanshawes stayed there (1653–4): 97, 136; church at Tankersley, burial place of Ann, eldest daughter of Lady F: 107, 212

Telegare, Countess of, Portuguese noblewoman: 148

Terne [Torne], Capt. Henry (d. 1665), commander of the *Portsmouth*, one of the ships taking the Fanshawes to Spain (1664): 154, 157

Thomond. *See* O'Brien

Thornhill, cousin of Lady F's; either a son of Sir John Thornhill of Bromley, or a son of Sir Timothy Thornhill of Wye, Kent; both Sir Timothy and Sir John were sons of Samuel Thornhill by Jane (*née* White); this cousin accompanied Sir RF to France on his early travels: 112

Thynne, Lady Isabella (*née* Rich), daughter of Henry Rich, Earl of Holland by Isabel (*née* Cope); married Sir James Thynne, master of Longleat, who, as son of the daughter of Sir Rowland Hayward and Katherine (*née* Smythe), was a first cousin of Sir RF: 115

Tillibardin. *See* Tullibardine

Tindall, John F. (d. 1674), Thomas Howard's tutor at Corpus Christi College, Cambridge: 16–19, 194

Tinojo (or Tinoco), Dom Diego, a Portuguese gentleman: 182

Titian (Tiziano Vecellio) (*c.* 1490–1576), Venetian painter, 168, 188, 217

Toledo, Spain: 162, 180, 219; King's Palace or Alcázar: 162; Cathedral of: 162; Governor of (1664): 162; Archbishop of, *see* Sandoval

Tompson, Albion, Trumpeter on Lord Sandwich's staff in Spain (1666): 182

Tor Bay [Tar Bay], inlet of the English Channel, South Devon: 154

Torne, Capt. *See* Terne

Torre de la Prada. *See* Pardo, El

Torre Juan Abad [La Tore de Juan Abad], Spain: 162

Torres Vedras, Countess of, Spanish noblewoman; wife of Don Francisco de Alarcón, Count of Torres Vedras: 182

Toumment. *See* O'Brien

Tring, Herts., site of a manor held by Sir RF from Queen Henrietta Maria; Lady F gave it up after Sir RF's death: 191, 221

Trucifal, Marquis of, a Portuguese nobleman to whom Philip of Spain gave the title; Maestro de Campo General in Sicily: 180, 182, 186

Truro, Cornwall, forty miles (not twenty as Lady F says) from Launceston: 117

Tullibardine [Tillibardin], earldom of: 10, 193

Turner, Thomas, D.D. (1591–1672), Dean of Canterbury (1644–72): 150

Turnor [Turner], Sir Edmund (1619–1707); knighted (1664); son of Christopher Turnor of Milton Erneys, Beds.; treasurer and paymaster at Bristol for the Prince of Wales; captured and imprisoned after the Battle of Worcester; after the Restoration was Commissioner in the Alienation Office and Surveyor-General of the Outposts; married (1653) Margaret (*née* Harrison), younger sister of Lady F, and acquired the estate of Stoke Rochford, Lincs., as a gift from Sir John Harrison to his daughter: 109, 136, 153, 191

Turnor, Sir Edward (1617–76), of Haverhill, Suffolk; knighted (1660); Speaker of the House of Commons (1661–70); Solicitor General (1670); Serjeant-at-Law and Lord Chief Baron of the Exchequer (1671); godfather to the daughter of Sir Edmund Turnor: 153, 191

Turnor, Sir Edward (1643–1721), son of Speaker Sir Edward Turnor by his first wife, Sarah (*née* Gore); knighted (1664);

Turnor, Sir Edward (1643–1721)—*contd.* accompanied the Fanshawes to Spain (1664): 153, 163
Turnor, Elisabeth (1666–1713), daughter of Sir Edmund Turnor and Margaret (*née* Harrison); Lady F's niece: 191 (nn)
Tweeddale. *See* Hay
Tyler, Mr., a merchant of Plymouth (1662): 144
Tyndall. *See* Tindall

Utber [Utbert], Capt. Richard (d. 1669); commander of the *Bristol*, ship in the fleet taking the Fanshawes to Spain (1664); a native of Lowestoft, he became Vice-Admiral: 154, 157
Utrera, Spain: 159–60

Valdemoro, Spain: 162
Valevin [Veleam], John, Secretary on Lord Sandwich's staff in Spain (1666); was also present at Sandwich's funeral (1672): 182
Vallecas, Spain, on the outskirts of Madrid; location of the Fanshawe's first house in the area (1644): 160, 163, 217
Vane, Sir Henry (1613–62), the younger; Parliamentary statesman and author; son of Sir Henry Vane, the elder (1589–1655), Secretary of State; executed: 135, 212
Vaux, Lady Elizabeth (*née* Howard) Knollys, Countess of Banbury (1586–1658); daughter of Thomas Howard, 1st Earl of Suffolk; sister of Edward, 1st Lord Howard of Escrick; aunt of young Thomas Howard; married (1605), as his second wife, William Knollys, 1st Earl of Banbury; married second (before July 1632) Edward, 4th Lord Vaux of Harrowden: 21, 23, 194
Veleam. *See* Valevin
Velez (or Veler), Doña Maria de Cordova, Segorbe y Aragón, Marchioness of; Spanish noblewoman; *governante* (*aya*) to Charles II of Spain; her husband, the Marquis, was the King's Governor: 178, 181 (nn)
Vélez-Málaga, Spain: 128
Venetian Ambassador to the Court of Spain (1664): 166, 217
Verney, Sir Ralph (1613–96), of Middle Clayton, Bucks., 1st Baronet (1661); knighted (1641); politician; friend of AM's brother-in-law, Sir Henry Newton: 198
Vicálvaro, Spain: 174
Victory, frigate; one of two ships of that name in the English Navy (1667); either a smaller ship captured from the French in 1665 or a second-rate of over 1,000 tons: 188
Vienna, residence of the Holy Roman Emperors: 183
Villa Franca, Dona Maria Countinho, Countess of; Portuguese noblewoman, daughter of Count of Vidiguera; wife of Don Roderigo da Camora: 148
Villarta [Villa Harta] de San Juan, Spain: 162
Villiers, Audrey (1652–1715), eldest daughter of George Villiers, 4th Viscount Grandison of Limerick; she married (1668–9) Lady F's half-brother Richard; not named: 109, 191
Villiers, Lord Francis (1629–48), third son of George Villiers, 1st Duke of Buckingham; killed at a skirmish near Kingston, Surrey, 7 July 1648: 121
Villiers, George (1592–1628), 1st Duke of Buckingham (1623); patron of Edward, 1st Lord Howard of Escrick: 194
Villiers, George (1628–87), 2nd Duke of Buckingham; Gentleman of the Bedchamber to Charles II; Colonel of a Regiment of Horse at the Battle of Worcester (1651); Ambassador to Paris (1670, 1671) and Joint Ambassador (1672): 141
Villiers, George (d. 1699), 4th Viscount Grandison of Limerick (1659); knighted (1644); his eldest daughter, Audrey (d. 1715), married Richard Harrison, Lady F's half-brother: 109, 191

Wallace [Walace], Hugh [Hew], AM's landlord at Edinburgh (1653): 70
Waller, Edmund (1606–87), poet; Royalist plotter; married second (1644) Mary (*née* Bracey; d. 1677); Lady F was godmother of their daughter, who d. 1651: 122, 133, 210
Wallis [Walley], John, D.D. (1616–1703); mathematician of Emmanuel College, Cambridge; afterwards Professor of

Wallis [Walley], John—*contd.* Geometry at Oxford; Chaplain to Charles II after the Restoration; his father was the Revd. John Wallis (1567–1622), minister at Ashford, Kent (1602–22): 110

Walsh, Joseph, abductor of Sir Henry Newton's cousin, Jane Puckering: 48 (nn), 198

Walsingham, Lady Ann (*née* Howard), 4th daughter of Theophilus Howard, 2nd Earl of Suffolk; niece of Edward, Lord Howard of Escrick; wife of Thomas Walsingham of Little Chesterford, Essex; served as messenger between her cousin, Thomas Howard, and AM: 12, 21, 193, 194

Walsingham, Thomas, of Little Chesterford, Essex; husband of Lady Ann Howard, daughter of Theophilus Howard, 2nd Earl of Suffolk: 194

Walter, Catherine (d. 1642), second daughter and co-heiress of Sir William Walter of Wimbledon; she married first Knighton Ferrers of Bayfordbury, Herts., by whom she had a daughter, Katherine (later the first wife of Sir Thomas Fanshawe, 2nd Viscount Fanshawe of Dromore); she married second Sir Simon Fanshawe, elder brother of Sir RF: 106, 121 (nn)

Ward, Seth, D.D. (1617–89); Bishop of Exeter (1662); Bishop of Salisbury (1667): 144 (nn)

Ware, Parish Church of, Herts.: 99, 105, 106, 191–2; St. Mary's Chapel of: 99, 106, 191

Ware, Priory of, Herts.; originally a Franciscan house located on the banks of the Lea; owned (1656) by Mrs. Haydon and leased by the Fanshawes: 137

Ware Park, Herts., Fanshawe family seat; the manor was purchased by Thomas Fanshawe in 1576 from Katherine, Dowager Countess of Huntingdon: 95, 98, 103, 105, 133, 191, 208, 221

Warrington, Francis, on Lord Sandwich's staff in Spain (1666): 182

Warwick, Elizabeth (*née* Frescheville; 1635–90); daughter-in-law of Sir Philip Warwick; she married Philip, a son of Sir Philip's first wife, Dorothy (*née* Hutton), and was not directly related to the Fanshawes; she married second (1685) Congress Darcy, Earl of Holdernesse: 190 (nn)

Warwick, Sir Philip (1609–83), of Frogpool, Kent; Secretary to Charles I at Hampton Court and on the Isle of Wight; after the Restoration he was Secretary to the Earl of Southampton, Lord High Treasurer; married first (*c.* 1638) Dorothy (*née* Hutton) by whom he had his only son, Philip; married second (1647), as her second husband, Joan (*née* Fanshawe) Boteler, Sir RF's sister; he was godfather of Lady F's second son by the name of Henry: 107, 120, 136, 187 (nn), 190, 221

Warwick, Philip (d. 1683), son of Sir Philip Warwick by his first wife, Dorothy (*née* Hutton); married (1661) Elizabeth, second daughter of John Frescheville of Staveley; Envoy Extraordinary to Sweden (1680): 190 (nn)

Warwick. *See also* Rich

Washington, Elizabeth, wife of Col. Henry Washington; aided in the escape of James, Duke of York, from St. James's Palace (1648): 25, 196

Washington, Col. Henry (1615–64), Royalist officer; husband of Elizabeth: 25, 196

Washington, Col. John (1632–77); emigrant to Virginia; son of Revd. Lawrence Washington by Amphilis (*née* Twigden); cousin of Col. Henry Washington: 196

Washington, Capt. Lawrence (1635–77); emigrant to Virginia (1658); brother of Col. John Washington; cousin of Col. Henry Washington: 196

Watts, Sir John (d. *c.* 1680); knighted (1645) for his defence of Chirk Castle; he was residing at Tewin, three miles north-west of Hertford, in 1663 when the Fanshawes visited him; he and Sir RF were contemporaries at Jesus College, Cambridge: 151

Weeden [Weedin, Weedon], Mr., Page in Fanshawe retinue (1664): 153, 180 186

Wentworth, Thomas (1593–1641), created 1st Earl of Stafford (1640); executed for high treason: 210

Wentworth, William (1626–95), 2nd Earl of Strafford (1641 and 1662); Royalist

Wentworth, William—*cont.*
and active supporter of William of Orange; only surviving son of the executed 1st Earl by his second wife, Lady Arabella (*née* Holles): 122, 136, 210, 212
Werden (or Worden), Sir John (1640–1716); politician; eldest son of Robert Werden of Cholmeaton, Chester, by his first wife, Jane (*née* Buckham); Secretary to the embassy in Spain and Portugal under Lord Sandwich (1666–9); created Baronet (1672); Envoy to Sweden and Holland (1672): 181
Westcombe, Martin (d. between 1708 and 1736), English agent and consul at Cadiz (1689) who for a long time resided in Spain; created Baronet (1700): 154, 157
White, Mr., member of Lady F's retinue on her departure from Madrid (1666): 187
Wier, Jonathan, purchaser from Lady F of a lease on the estate of Frinton Hall in Essex: 191
Wight, Isle of: 210
Wilde (or Wild), George, D.C.L. (1610–65); Anglican minister; Bishop of Derry (1660–5): 30, 197
Wilkins, John, author of *Mercury*; *or*, *The Secret and Swift Messenger*: 203
William, Cook for Fanshawe retinue (1666): 180, 187
William II, Prince of Orange (1626–50); son of Frederick Henry, Prince of Orange; married (1641) Mary, Princess Royal of England; father of William Henry, Prince of Orange, later William III of England: 193, 197, 209 (nn), 210 (nn)
William III (1650–1702), King of England, Scotland, and Ireland (1689–1702): 197, 201; as William Henry, Prince of Orange (1650–1702): 122, 210, 212
Williams, Thomas, on Lord Sandwich's staff in Spain (1666): 182
Wilton, Wilts., actually four miles (not two as Lady F says) from Salisbury: 143
Winchester, Bishop of. *See* Morley, George
Windebank [Window Banke], Sir Francis (1582–1646), Secretary of State and principal adviser to Charles I; attacked by Parliament for alleged preferential treatment of Catholics; fled to France (1640); two of his daughters became nuns of a Catholic order in France: 113, 114, 132, 209
Windsor, Berks., Castle and King's Chapel at: 143
Winston, Dr. Thomas (1575–1655), Professor of Physic at Gresham College (1615–42); a noted physician: 108
Winter, Sir John (1600?–73?), Secretary to Queen Henrietta Maria (1638–69): 188
Witcherly. *See* Wycherley
Witherington, Sir [ ], coach passenger with AM (1654): 79–80
Wolstenholme, Catherine (*née* Fanshawe), Lady; wife of Sir John Wolstenholme, the elder (knighted 1616); probably the daughter of Colyn Fanshawe of Brimington (the brother of Henry Fanshawe, first Queen's Remembrancher); godmother of AH: 108
Wolstenholme, Sir John (1562–1639), the elder; merchant-adventurer; Farmer of Customs of London; incorporator of the East India Company; husband of Catherine (*née* Fanshawe); employer of AH's father, Sir John Harrison: 110
Wolvercote, Oxford, St. Peter's Church; marriage place of Sir RF and AH (18 May 1644): 111
Woodcock, Sir Thomas (d. 1679); knighted (1660); captain of a company in the Holland Regiment; active minor agent in connection with the Restoration; second-in-command at Windsor Castle (1662): 143
Woolwich, Kent, the parish next to Charlton; site of the civil marriage ceremony of AM and Sir James Halkett (1 Mar. 1656): 84
Worcester. *See* Somerset
Worcester, Battle of (3 Sept. 1651): xvii, 97, 134, 200, 205, 212
Worden. *See* Werden
Wotton, Sir Henry (1568–1639), author of *The Elements of Architecture*; his remarks on Ware Park gardens are mistakenly attributed by Lady F to William Camden: 208
Wray, Sir John (d. 1664), 3rd Bt., of Glentworth, Lincs.; first husband of Sarah (*née* Evelyn); after his death she married, as his second wife, Sir Thomas

Fanshawe, 2nd Viscount Fanshawe of Dromore: 106, 175
Wright [Right], Sir Benjamin, son of Revd. Robert Wright, B.D., of Dennington, Suffolk; English merchant in Madrid where he resided for about twenty years; served as interpreter for Lady F: 153, 164, 165
Wriothesley, Thomas (1608–67), 2nd Earl of Southampton (1624); faithful Royalist, he was reappointed Privy Councillor and Lord High Treasurer at the Restoration: 188–9, 220, 221
Wycherley [Witcherly, Wicherly], William (?), probably the English dramatist (1640?–1716); in Fanshawe retinue (1664): xviii, 153, 164, 174, 215, 216, 218
York, Duchess of. *See* Hyde, Anne
York, Yorkshire, 79, 85, 86
York, ship of the fleet that took Fanshawes to Spain (1664); commanded by Capt. Robert Mohun, according to Lady F: 154
Youghal [Yachall], Cork, Ireland, Lady F's port of entry when she joined Sir RF in Ireland (1648): 122
Young, Anne (*née* Osborne); her grandmother, Ursula Smythe, was the sister of Elizabeth (Sir RF's mother) and also the sister of Joan (the second wife of Sir RF's grandfather); thus Anne, who married Ellis Young, was a near relation; she was godmother to Lady F's daughter Elizabeth (b. 1651): 134, 135, 136